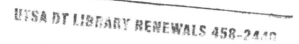

Conversation and Cognition

Written by some of the leading figures in the fields of conversation analysis, discursive psychology and ethnomethodology, this book looks at the challenging implications of new discourse-based approaches to the topic of cognition. Up to now, cognition has primarily been studied in experimental settings. This volume shows how cognition can be reworked using analyses of engaging examples of real life interaction such as conversations between friends, relationship counselling sessions and legal hearings. It includes an extended introduction that overviews the history and context of cognitive research and its basic assumptions to provide a frame for understanding the specific examples discussed, as well as surveying cutting edge debates about discourse and cognition. This comprehensive and accessible book opens up important new ways of understanding the relation between language and cognition.

HEDWIG TE MOLDER is a senior lecturer in Discourse Analysis in the Communication Science Section at Wageningen University, The Netherlands. She has published on a number of topics including government communicators' talk, online interaction and discourse on food choice.

JONATHAN POTTER is Professor of Discourse Analysis in the Social Sciences Department at Loughborough University, UK. He has published eight books, including *Discourse and Social Psychology* (with Margaret Wetherell, 1987), more than forty book chapters and sixty journal articles.

Conversation and Cognition

Edited by

Hedwig te Molder
Jonathan Potter

CAMBRIDGE
UNIVERSITY PRESS

PUBLISHED BY THE PRESS SYNDICATE OF THE UNIVERSITY OF CAMBRIDGE
The Pitt Building, Trumpington Street, Cambridge, United Kingdom

CAMBRIDGE UNIVERSITY PRESS
The Edinburgh Building, Cambridge, CB2 2RU, UK
40 West 20th Street, New York, NY 10011–4211, USA
477 Williamstown Road, Port Melbourne, VIC 3207, Australia
Ruiz de Alarcón 13, 28014 Madrid, Spain
Dock House, The Waterfront, Cape Town 8001, South Africa

http://www.cambridge.org

First published 2005

Printed in the United Kingdom at the University Press, Cambridge

Typeface Plantin 10/12 pt.   *System* LATEX 2$_\varepsilon$ [TB]

A catalogue record for this book is available from the British Library

Library of Congress Cataloging-in-Publication Data
Conversation and cognition / edited by Hedwig, te Molder, Jonathan Potter.
    p.   cm.
Includes bibliographical references and index.
ISBN 0 521 79020 4 – ISBN 0 521 79369 6 (pb)
1. Discourse analysis – Psychological aspects.   2. Cognition.
I. Molder, Hedwig te.   II. Potter, Jonathan, 1956-
P302.8.C66   2004
401′.41 – dc22

ISBN 0 521 79020 4 hardback
ISBN 0 521 79369 6 paperback

To the memory and inspiration of Robert Hopper

Contents

Contributors

PROFESSOR DAVID BOGEN Executive Director, Institute for Liberal Arts & Interdisciplinary Studies, Emerson College, Boston, USA.

PROFESSOR JEFF COULTER Department of Sociology, Boston University, USA.

PROFESSOR PAUL DREW Department of Sociology, University of York, UK.

PROFESSOR DEREK EDWARDS Discourse and Rhetoric Group, Department of Social Sciences, Loughborough University, UK.

PROFESSOR JOHN HERITAGE Department of Sociology, University of California, Los Angeles, USA.

PROFESSOR ROBERT HOPPER Late of the Department of Speech Communication, The University of Texas, Austin, USA.

PROFESSOR MICHAEL LYNCH Department of Science & Technology Studies, Cornell University, Clark Hall, USA.

PROFESSOR DOUGLAS MAYNARD Department of Sociology, University of Wisconsin, Madison, USA.

PROFESSOR ANITA POMERANTZ Department of Communication, State University of New York (SUNY), Albany, USA.

PROFESSOR JONATHAN POTTER Discourse and Rhetoric Group, Department of Social Sciences, Loughborough University, UK.

PROFESSOR NORA CATE SCHAEFFER Department of Sociology, University of Wisconsin, Madison, USA.

PROFESSOR ROBERT SANDERS Department of Communication, State University of New York (SUNY), Albany, USA.

DR HEDWIG TE MOLDER Communication Science, Wageningen University, The Netherlands.

DR ROBIN WOOFFITT Department of Sociology, University of York, UK.

Acknowledgements

This collection brings together a unique group of leading scholars from the fields of conversation analysis, discursive psychology and ethnomethodology. It features cutting edge debates about discourse and cognition along with illustrative and engaging examples of real life interaction. Some contributors argue that the notion of cognition in interaction analysis can and should be abandoned, others that it should be reworked and others again that it must be preserved but clarified. We hope that this volume provides a thought-provoking overview and reappraisal of the role of mental concepts in the empirical study of text and talk.

When we started it, too many years ago, we could not have imagined the journey that would follow. In many ways, the major issue on which it is focused turns out to be different from what we suspected: more heterogeneous, less definitive in its boundaries and place, and, overall, very much alive. During the process of writing and editing, we never got bored with any of the contributions, and we are grateful that the contributors never got (really) bored with waiting. Their past work has defined the contours of the debate and they show themselves to be ideally placed to move it forward.

Several people have been a continuous source of inspiration and helpful criticism to us. We wish to thank Derek Edwards, Alexa Hepburn and Liz Stokoe as well as the stimulating intellectual context of Loughborough's Discourse and Rhetoric Group. Communication Science at Wageningen University has provided a supportive and challenging environment for discourse work. Frank de Groot has given valuable technical support in preparing the chapters for publication. We gratefully acknowledge the continuing support, patience and good humour of Catherine Max and Sarah Caro at Cambridge University Press.

The book is dedicated to Professor Robert Hopper, who died in December 1998, and was the first to complete his contribution for this volume. After being invited to a pre-conference on discourse and cognition, his enthusiasm for the topic was contagious and he felt no hesitation in writing about it. We hope the spirit with which he explored the convolutions inside these complicated questions will shine throughout the book.

Transcription conventions

The following conventions were developed by Gail Jefferson.

[]	Square brackets mark the start and end of overlapping speech. Position them in alignment where the overlap occurs.
↑↓	Vertical arrows precede marked pitch movement, over and above normal rhythms of speech. They are for marked, hearably significant shifts – and even then, the other symbols (full stops, commas, question marks) mop up most of that. Like with all these symbols, the aim is to capture interactionally significant features, hearable as such to an ordinary listener – especially deviations from a common sense notion of 'neutral', which admittedly has not been well defined.
→	Side arrows are not transcription features, but draw analytic attention to particular lines of text. Usually positioned to the left of the line.
Underlining	Underlining signals vocal emphasis; the extent of underlining within individual words locates emphasis, but also indicates how heavy it is.
CAPITALS	Capitals mark speech that is obviously louder than surrounding speech (often occurs when speakers are hearably competing for the floor, raised volume rather than doing contrastive emphasis).
°↑I know it,°	'Degree' signs enclose obviously quieter speech (i.e., hearably produced as quieter, not just someone distant).
that's r*ight.	Asterisks precede a 'squeaky' vocal delivery.

(0.4)	Numbers in round brackets measure pauses in seconds (in this case, 4 tenths of a second). Place on new line if not assigned to a speaker.
(.)	A micropause, hearable but too short to measure.
((text))	Additional comments from the transcriber, e.g. context or intonation.
she wa::nted	Colons show degrees of elongation of the prior sound; the more colons, the more elongation.
hhh	Aspiration (out-breaths); proportionally as for colons.
.hhh	Inspiration (in-breaths); proportionally as for colons.
Yeh,	'Continuation' marker, speaker has not finished; marked by fall-rise or weak rising intonation, as when enunciating lists.
y'know?	Question marks signal stronger, 'questioning' intonation, irrespective of grammar.
Yeh.	Periods (full stops) mark falling, stopping intonation ('final contour'), irrespective of grammar and not necessarily followed by a pause.
bu-u-	Hyphens mark a cut-off of the preceding sound.
>he said<	'Greater than' and 'lesser than' signs enclose speeded-up talk. Sometimes used the other way round for slower talk.
solid.= =We had	'Equals' signs mark the immediate 'latching' of successive talk, whether of one or more speakers, with no interval. Also used as below (lines 3–5), where an unbroken turn has been split between two lines to accommodate another speaker on the transcript page.
heh heh	Voiced laughter. Can have other symbols added, such as underlinings, pitch movement, extra aspiration, etc.
sto(h)p i(h)t	Laughter within speech is signalled by 'h's in round brackets.

For further details see Hepburn (in press), Hutchby and Wooffitt (1998), Jefferson (1985), Psathas and Anderson (1990) and ten Have (1999).

1 Talking cognition: mapping and making the terrain

Jonathan Potter and Hedwig te Molder

Overview

This book addresses issues of conversation and cognition. For the first time some of the world's experts on interaction analysis have been brought together to consider the nature and role of cognition. They address the question of what part, if any, cognitive entities should play in the analysis of interaction. They develop different answers. Some are consistent with current thinking in cognitive psychology and cognitive science; others are more critical, questioning the idea that cognition is the obvious and necessary start point for the study of human action.

The question of the relation of language and thought has been a central one in cognitive and developmental psychology for more than thirty years. For the contributors here the focus is not on language as it is traditionally understood but rather on talk or, even more specifically, on talk-in-interaction. That is, not on language as an abstract set of words, meanings, or a system of contrasts as it has usually been conceived, but talk as a practical, social activity, located in settings, occurring between people, used in practices. This approach has significant implications for the way traditional issues of cognition are treated. Talk and cognition have been brought together only rarely in the past and often for particular purposes local to one discipline. However, there are some important precursors to the current enterprise, and we will describe them in detail below.

It is worth noting at the outset that because of its interdisciplinary focus this book is likely to have audiences with different levels of knowledge, understanding and expectation. In particular, we hope it will be of interest to at least three groups of researchers. First, it will be of interest to those people whose primary topic is the study of interaction. The issue of how (if at all), or in what way, cognition figures in interaction is a live and complex one with important implications for how analysis can be done and what might be possible. Second, it will be of interest to discursive psychologists and the wider community of social psychologists who have attempted to develop an alternative to traditional social cognitive perspectives. For them, it will refine several of the issues and highlight the value of considering them in terms of natural interaction. Third, we hope the book will be interesting to the very broad community of cognitive scientists. Cognition has been understood in a wide range of ways in this community (some of which we will describe below) but only rarely has the start point been research on natural interaction.

The contributors to this book are some of the foremost analysts of natural interaction in the world. Although each has his or her individual take on things, they mostly draw on one or more of the connected approaches of ethnomethodology, conversation analysis and discursive psychology. We will have more to say about these approaches later. For the moment we will use thumbnails.

Ethnomethodology is an approach to the methods that people use for making sense of, and accomplishing the order of, their social worlds. It highlights the use of ad hoc, situation specific procedures to generate order. Most recently its emphasis has been on the way action must be understood in terms of the full, embodied, practical specifics of its setting. The key figure in the development of ethnomethodology is the sociologist Harold Garfinkel (Garfinkel, 1967, 2002). In this collection Michael Lynch, David Bogen and Jeff Coulter have been most associated with this perspective.

Conversation analysis (CA) is the study of natural talk as a medium for action and interaction. A very large body of studies from a conversation analytic perspective have been done on both everyday and institutional talk. Conversation analysis has its origins in the lectures of the sociologist Harvey Sacks (now published as Sacks, 1992), and the work of his colleagues Gail Jefferson and Emanuel Schegloff (e.g. Sacks, Schegloff and Jefferson, 1974). Many of the contributors to this collection have a broadly conversation analytic perspective, including Bob Sanders, Anita Pomerantz, Douglas Maynard, Nora Schaeffer, Robert Hopper, John Heritage, Paul Drew and Robin Wooffitt. This predominance reflects the way conversation analysis has become one of the most powerful and empirically cumulative fields in the study of interaction.

Discursive psychology (DP) is an approach that considers psychology as an object *in* and *for* interaction. That is, it focuses on how psychological categories and constructions are used by people in everyday and institutional settings. While ethnomethodologists and conversation analysts have mainly worked within sociology and have often found issues of cognition rather peripheral, discursive psychologists have mainly worked within psychology and consequentially have a longer history of addressing these issues. Key figures in the development of discursive psychology are

Derek Edwards and Jonathan Potter (Edwards, 1997; Edwards and Potter, 1992). In this collection Derek Edwards, Hedwig te Molder, Jonathan Potter and Robin Wooffitt (again) are most associated with this approach.

There is considerably more theoretical and analytic homogeneity here than even this listing of just three approaches suggests. Both conversation analysis and discursive psychology pick up from and develop themes from ethnomethodology. Moreover, for the most part all three approaches emphasise that:

a) Talk is a medium of action.
b) Talk is locally and situationally organized.
c) The point of view of the interactant is basic to understanding talk-in-interaction.
d) The primary analytic approach is empirical study of natural interaction.

These features have led researchers in this area in a very different methodological direction to most cognitive scientists. In particular, the emphasis on action, context and natural talk leads away from working with either experimental manipulations or invented and decontextualized examples. It is worth emphasising, however, that although this body of work has provided a basis for doubt about those methods it was not, on the whole, this that led researchers in the direction they took. The tradition of work in conversation analysis evolved out of a combination of novel theorizing about interaction stimulated by Garfinkel and Sacks, and the development of tape recording technology that allowed conversation to be studied in a way previously impossible. Having developed a powerful analytic approach for working directly with records of interaction, experimental simulations of interaction seemed to be of limited value and potentially misleading.

The broad sweep of the arguments here means that we will inevitably not be able to cover all potentially relevant literature. For example, we will not cover the writing of critics of cognitive approaches such as Gergen, Harré and Shotter (e.g. Gergen, 1994, 1999; Harré, 2002; Shotter, 1993) who work largely with theoretical and conceptual analysis. Examples of such work are collected together in Still and Costall (1991), and include a number of arguments inspired by the work of Gibson (1986). This work has some significant virtues, yet it does not provide for the focused investigation of questions about cognition in interaction that is developed in the chapters collected here.

In the rest of this introductory chapter we will try to accomplish a series of things. First, we will describe some of the questions that the book is intended to illuminate. Second, we will consider some of the historical, conceptual and philosophical features of the notion of cognition, including its relation to language. Third, we will characterize some of the key features of the set of perspectives that has been developed in the broad field of cognitive science and cognitive psychology more specifically. This will introduce a set of issues that will help to explicate the relevance of work in interaction described later in this chapter, and in the chapters that follow. It is also intended to highlight the variety and complexity of what cognitive researchers have achieved and what points of entry into this work there might be for interaction researchers. Fourth, we will describe the way issues of cognition have been dealt with in existing work on interaction, concentrating particularly on ethnomethodology, conversation analysis and discursive psychology. Fifth, and finally, we will provide a synoptic overview of the contributions to this book ending with some comments on future progress.

1.   Questions of cognition and interaction

The questions addressed in this collection are derived from empirical studies of interaction. The book is intended to extend and clarify issues to do with the nature and role of cognitive entities in interaction analysis. However, it is precisely that focus that makes for some interesting and potentially novel implications for more traditional cognitive psychologists and cognitive scientists.

The papers in this collection are relevant to a range of questions. Some of the most important are:

- How does cognition figure in the *analysis* of interaction? Alternatively, can (and should) such analysis be done without recourse to cognitive notions?
- If speakers draw on cognitive notions, what is their status? That is, what *kind* of thing is cognition for participants in interaction? How is it invoked, described and oriented to by speakers in the course of interaction?
- In the strongest case, is interaction only explicable in terms of a set of cognitive precursors (cognitivism)? How far can these precursors reflect lay notions and orientations of conversational participants and how far must they be derived from technical analyses?
- How does interaction research throw light on continuing questions about the possible relations between mental terms and cognitive entities?
- What implications does the exploration of these questions have for experimental work in cognitive science?

These are complicated questions that raise fundamental issues about method, theory and the nature of psychology. The aim is to clarify them, underscore their significance, and show the way towards their answers.

Some papers consider a cognitive level of analysis indispensable (e.g. Sanders). Some papers suggest that interaction analysis can reveal the role of particular kinds of cognitive entities (e.g. Schaeffer and Maynard, Drew and Pomerantz). Some suggest that analysis should respecify cognitive notions in interactional terms (Lynch and Bogen, Wooffitt). Some develop an agnostic approach (Hopper) or wish to consider cognitive notions in terms of topics or orientations in participants' talk (Edwards and Potter). One paper (Coulter) provides a trenchant (and conceptually based) critique of the whole enterprise of cognitive science.

2.   Cognition as an object in language and philosophy

Characterizing contemporary cognition and its development is not an easy task. Cognitive science is now a broad and heterogeneous intellectual field cutting across the disciplines of psychology, computer studies, anthropology, linguistics, neuroscience and philosophy. It mixes highly technical conceptual and metaphysical analyses with issues that arise out of programming and domain-specific applied work on computer systems and human factors. There is no single notion of cognition cutting across this field. Histories in textbooks and encyclopaedias show a wide range of philosophers cited as key figures (including Plato and Aristotle, of course) as well as a varied selection of nineteenth and twentieth century psychologists and figures from other disciplines. Let us start with the dictionary.

The term cognition

The *Oxford English Dictionary* (2002) helpfully distinguishes an everyday sense of cognition from a more philosophical notion:

1. a. The action or faculty of knowing; knowledge, consciousness; acquaintance with a subject. (Obs.)
   1447 O. Bokenham Seyntys (1835) 154 Illumynyd she is wyth clere cognycyoun In hyr soule.
   1528 Lyndesay Dream 577 Filicitie they had Inuariabyll, And of his Godhed cleir cognitioun.
   1604 T. Wright Passions v. 237 With conscience and perfit cognition of innocencie.
   1606 Shakes. Tr. and Cr. v. ii. 63, I will not be my selfe, nor haue cognition Of what I feele.
   1682 Sir T. Browne Chr. Mor. (1756) 106 A retrograde cognition of times past.
   1796 Burney Mem. Metastasio II. 389 Tasting the first aliments of scientific cognition.
   b. Apprehension, perception. (nonce-use.)
   1822 Lamb Elia Ser. i. iii. (1865) 34 In thy cognition of some poignant jest.

2. Philos. a. The action or faculty of knowing taken in its widest sense, including sensation, perception, conception, etc., as distinguished from feeling and volition; also, more specifically, the action of cognizing an object in perception proper.

1651 Stanley *Poems* 231 This Divines call intellectual intuitive cognition.

1690 Locke *Hum. Und.* iv. iii. §6 Finding not Cognition within the natural Powers of Matter.

1847 Lewes *Hist. Philos.* (1867) I. Introd. 113 A faculty of cognition a priori.

1879 Adamson Philos. Kant 45 The several elements which, according to Kant, make up the organic unity of Perception or real Cognition.

b. A product of such an action: a sensation, perception, notion, or higher intuition.

1819 Shelley Peter *Bell III, 473 note*, Peter's progenitor . . . seems to have possessed a 'pure anticipated cognition' of the nature and modesty of this ornament of his posterity.

1856 Meiklejohn tr. *Kant's Krit. P.R.* 79 The fact that we do possess scientific a priori cognitions, namely, those of pure mathematics and general physics.

1873 H. Spencer *Princ. Psychol.* I. iii. viii. 369 With purely intellectual cognitions . . . also with . . . moral cognitions.

1881 J. H. Stirling *Text-bk. Kant* 468 Let a cognition be intellectually what it may, it is no cognition proper, it is not properly Knowledge, unless and until it have an actual perceptive application.

A few things are worth noting about these definitions and the examples quoted. First, an idea of cognition residing *inside* the person (e.g. 'in hyr soule' from 1447) goes back several hundred years. Second, both the everyday and philosophical senses of the term have an epistemic element. Cognition is related to knowledge; it is cognition *of* something. This reflects the Latin root of cognition as getting to know, acquaintance, knowledge. The move from Latin to English, then, can be understood as a move from an objective to a subjective view of knowledge. Third, cognition can be of something which is itself 'psychological' (obviously the idea of psychology must be used with caution here or we will end in vicious circularity). Thus there is 'perfit cognition of innocencie' or 'cognition Of what I feele'. Alternatively, it can be something 'outside' the person, such as 'times past'. Fourth, note that the philosophical senses of cognition reflect the argument between empiricists and rationalists, with cognition requiring 'actual perceptive application' versus the idea of 'a priori cognitions' of 'mathematics and general physics'. Finally, we can see the linking of cognition to 'perception' that is at the heart of much modern cognitive psychology.

Philosophical precursors to cognitive science: Descartes and Locke

The modern philosophical account of cognition is crucially dependent on the work of two seventeenth-century philosophers: Rene Descartes and

John Locke. Descartes is, of course, the philosopher who most famously helped shape modern thinking about the nature and role of cognition. He addressed epistemic issues about truth and knowledge through considering what could be fallible in the quest for what could be indubitable. For him, the world of objects might not exist because, after all, they might be the vivid illusions of dreams. Yet there has to be an 'I' doing that thinking, whether true or illusory and that could be the foundation for knowledge. As he put it:

> It was absolutely essential that the 'I' who thought this should be somewhat, and remarking that this truth '*I think therefore I am*' was so certain and so assured that all the most extravagant suppositions brought forward by the sceptics were incapable of shaking it. (Descartes, 1970: 101)

We might not be able to see how things are in the outer world, but we do know their appearance in our inner world. Nothing, in the end, is better known to the mind than itself. By inventing a superior class of inner perceptions, Descartes ingeniously attempted to surmount the agonizing problem of the outer world's deceitfulness.

As Rorty (1979) argues in his critical analysis of the history of Western philosophy, the notion of mind does not emerge in philosophical debates until Descartes. For the Greeks, the essential matter was how to obtain an unmediated picture of reality, that is, how to see reality directly without being distracted by any of its mere appearances. After Descartes, knowledge was still understood in terms of perception, but now the eye as the central metaphor for acquiring knowledge had been exchanged for another powerful image: the mirror. Knowledge of the world was no longer directly available, but only through a mirror in which nature is being reflected indirectly. As Rorty puts it: 'The question "How can I escape from the realm of appearance?" was replaced by the question "How can I escape from behind the veil of ideas?"' (1979: 160).

Part of Descartes' legacy to cognitive science is a basic mind/body dualism. In his writing it is possible to see this as required to manage a problem of his own making. Having established the special nature of the mind, how can it make contact with anything else? Descartes' rather ad hoc pineal gland solution was an early attempt to solve a problem that is still very much alive in different ways in contemporary cognitive science.

Descartes set the scene for a treatment of perception as the mind's mirror on the world, with mind as the solid foundation for knowledge to be built on. Departing from earlier Greek and medieval conceptions, he developed the notion of an *idea* that would apply exclusively to the content of the human mind (Kenny, 1967). Some fifty years later Locke drew on this same notion of an idea in his account of the nature of knowledge and what has become a classic picture of the working of language.

Locke viewed ideas as a basic currency of thinking and therefore philosophy. These ideas came from 'sensation and reflection'. This is the way the famous white paper (*tabula rasa*) comes to be filled in its 'almost endless variety'. Knowledge in turn comes either directly from experience or, in a move echoed in modern cognitivism, 'the internal operations of our minds perceived and reflected on by ourselves, is that which supplies our understandings with all the materials of thinking' (Locke, Bk I, Ch. I, pt. 2). Simple ideas come through sensation to a passive mind. Then activities of mind turn these into complex ideas through basic processes of combination, comparison or separation. As he put it:

> The acts of the mind, wherein it exerts its power over its simple ideas, are chiefly these three: (1) Combining several simple ideas into one compound one; and thus all complex ideas are made. (2) The second is bringing two ideas, whether simple or complex, together, and setting them by one another, so as to take a view of them at once, without uniting them into one; by which way it gets all its ideas of relations. (3) The third is separating them from all other ideas that accompany them in their real existence: this is called abstraction: and thus all its general ideas are made. (Locke, Bk. II, Ch. XII, pt. 1)

Mind here is an agent processing information much as, in more refined and technical forms, it appears in contemporary cognitive psychology.

Locke's reasoning about mind is bound up with his account of language. He developed what Roy Harris (1988) has described as a *telementation* account of language. In this account language is understood as a conduit for communicating ideas from one mind to another.

> *Words are sensible signs, necessary for communication of ideas.* Man, though he have great variety of thoughts, and such from which others as well as himself might receive profit and delight; yet they are all within his own breast, invisible and hidden from others, nor can of themselves be made to appear. The comfort and advantage of society not being to be had without communication of thoughts, it was necessary that man should find out some external sensible signs, whereof those invisible ideas, which his thoughts are made up of, might be made known to others. (Locke, Bk. III, Ch. II, pt. 1, italics in original)

Note here the emphasis on ideas hidden invisibly inside the person and the role of language being to make them visible (Coulter develops Harris's argument about telementation in his contribution to this volume).

Words are secondary to ideas for Locke. Indeed, the first use of words is for *recording* thoughts, rather like a Dictaphone might be used to record a letter. The second use is for *communicating* thoughts. Because of their conventional and arbitrary nature (Locke prefigures Saussure here) he sees words as an imperfect way of transmitting ideas. The recipient may well find them doubtful and uncertain as cues to the precise ideas of the speaker. In contrast, if you are recording your thoughts for yourself using words your record can be perfect:

Any words will serve for recording. As to the first of these, for the recording our own thoughts for the help of our own memories, whereby, as it were, we talk to ourselves, any words will serve the turn. For since sounds are voluntary and indifferent signs of any ideas, a man may use what words he pleases to signify his own ideas to himself: and there will be no imperfection in them, if he constantly use the same sign for the same idea: for then he cannot fail of having his meaning understood, wherein consists the right use and perfection of language. (Locke, Bk. III, Ch. IX, pt. 2, italics in original)

Language, then, becomes an aid to thinking and can enable our own memories and ideas to be captured, yet can only capture those of others in an indistinct manner.

Rorty (1980) has argued that Descartes and Locke virtually invented the modern idea of the human mind. In Greek philosophy there had been no easy way to distinguish what might later be called 'states of consciousness' from objects and events in the world. Descartes extended the notion of thought so that it would cover many of what we would come to think of as cognitive psychological terms: doubting, understanding, imagining and so on. Locke extended these ideas into a quasi-scientific programme of considering the generation and composition of ideas and the processes this involved. Words were left as imperfect traces of those inner ideas.

We do not want to suggest that Descartes and Locke are the only important philosophical contributors to ideas about cognition. However, they lay out many of the features that stayed in place until the sorts of critique of this picture of mind came from linguistic philosophers such as Ryle and Wittgenstein in the twentieth century. They still have a central role in modern cognitive science. Some of these issues are explored below, particularly in Coulter's chapter. For the moment we will move away from philosophy to consider the development of modern cognitive science.

3.   Modern cognitive science

Histories of contemporary cognitive science identify the key dates as just following the Second World War. For example, Gardner's (1985) excellent overview suggests the so called 'Hixon symposium' of 1948 as the setting where a number of key figures who had developed their thinking in different fields of war work came together. Many features of modern cognitive science have their origin in work on missile guidance systems, problems of people using complex apparatus such as cockpit displays, and the new science of computing. Technical advances here went in concert with the major social upheavals of the war and challenges to old orthodoxies. The most important orthodoxy to be challenged was that of the behaviourist tradition that had dominated for the three decades up to the war, particularly in North America. Its role as the position to be countered can be seen in the title of McCulloch's contribution to the symposium: 'Why the Mind Is in the Head'. The capitalization of 'Is' here went against the general behaviourist caution about the attribution of inner entities. Gardner describes this title as provocative in 1948 – yet within thirty years the success of cognitive science would make it as orthodox as what came before.

The five decades that have followed have been a period of furious development for cognitive science that has grown up with the evolution of integrated circuits, computing and the Internet. For us the interest is in the nature of the cognitive in cognitive science. What *kinds of things* are described as cognitive processes and cognitive states? What styles of explanation are characteristic in cognitive science? Our overview of cognitive science is not intended to be comprehensive. Instead we will highlight some central moments and features of the area.

Information theory and artificial intelligence: Shannon, Turing and Marr

Theoretical and technological advances in the mid twentieth century led to the development of information theory. Shannon's crucial insight was that the states of an electronic switch (on/off) could be treated as equivalent to logical propositions (true/false). This was refined into the notion of a *bit* of information, that is, the information required to reduce future uncertainty by choosing one of two equal options. This was crucial in the development of programming languages that would run on computers, where the transistors (on/off switches) in integrated circuits would allow large, and (with time) enormous, amounts of information to be 'processed' (Gardner, 1985).

Information here is an abstraction. It has been separated from *both* particular languages such as English or French, and also from particular processing or communication systems. It can be transmitted via wire or radio, and processed by different kinds of computers. Crucially it was possible to start thinking of human brains as processors of information. This, in turn, could allow the old behaviourist concepts of stimulus and response to be transformed into new information processing concepts of input and output.

If human brains could be treated as processors of information like computers, could the reverse be true? Could computers be treated like brains, or, more pertinently, can they think? Alan Turing's (1950) famous and influential answer to this question is to turn it into a practical rather than an abstract or philosophical question. The Turing test involves an imaginary interrogator who asks questions of an agent in another room via a teleprinter. The job for the interrogator is to find out whether she is talking to a man or a machine. The job for the machine is to answer questions *as if* they were a man. They can be evasive, playful, or whatever. Here Turing imagines A as a machine pretending to be a person:

Q: Please write me a sonnet on the subject of the Forth Bridge.
A: Count me out on this one. I could never write poetry.   (Turing, 1950: 234)

The key point about this test is that if the computer passed, if it were programmed in a way that convincingly imitated a person, then there were no good grounds for saying it was not thinking (Turing dismissed a lot of what he took to be poor grounds, such as that it did not have a soul, machines can't be creative). We can note at this point that issues of personhood are foregrounded, but issues of what interaction is, and how language operates in activities such as imitation are taken for granted.

Whether or not cognitive scientists accepted the full implications of the Turing test, they increasingly used metaphors from computing and information processing for understanding human cognition – input and output, hardware and software, storage, programming and so on are commonplace.

As Gardner (1985) notes this has led to continued disputes on how strongly to treat the hypothesis of artificial intelligence. On the one hand, the weak view of artificial intelligence treated programming as a way of exploring potential ways in which humans could solve problems or process information. On the other hand, the strong view suggested that programs are intelligent in themselves, or even that they have their own cognitive states. Searle's (1980) so-called Chinese room argument was designed to criticize such an idea (in a playful inversion of the Turing test).

More directly interesting for our current purposes is not the question whether machines can be programmed to think, but whether a programmed machine that can duplicate human skills is operating *in the same way* as the human. That is, should we expect to find some underlying psychological correlate of the programming? This kind of question became most refined in the influential work of the neuroscientist David Marr. For us Marr is important not just because he is one of the most important figures in cognitive science, but because his work highlights some of the very different ways in which notions of cognitive processes and entities are understood.

Marr worked on visual perception, but his arguments are taken to have more general implications for cognitive science. In his research he argued that to understand the visual system it is necessary to work with different levels of analysis (Marr, 1982 is the central reference here). The first level is that of *computational theory*. This specified the goals and functions of the system. For example, one of the things that the visual system will need to do is translate two-dimensional images from each eye into a single three-dimensional image. This might involve a range of more complex functions. The second level is that of *representation and algorithm*. What kinds of procedures might operate on the images to render them into three-dimensions? What kind of programs and representations would be required? The third level is that of *hardware implementation*. Experimental work will attempt to discover organizations of axons and visual neurons that might be the systems for processing such information about stereoscopic vision.

The success of work such as Hubel and Wiesel (1977) on the early processing of visual information in the eye and Lettvin *et al.* (1959) on specialized receptors in the neurophysiology suggested that more sophisticated processing structures might exist. For Marr research is a two-way process, where computational theory and its representations might guide studies of physiology, but studies of physiology might suggest alternative algorithms and, ultimately, computational theories.

Marr's theory shows how early ideas about information processing and metaphors of the mind and brain as sophisticated computers have been developed since Turing and Shannon's time. In particular, he suggests that particular organizations of brain physiology might be designed to do specific jobs. Note also that Marr's work is giving a central place to the operation of computer programs on representations. The centrality of modularity and representations is something well established in much of recent cognitive science.

Marr's division into three levels is only one way of breaking things up. For example, it is conventional in cognitive psychology to distinguish three rather different levels of information processing: mental, cognitive and neural (e.g. Best, 1999). The mental level of processing is focused on things that people are conscious or aware of such as how people manipulate images or ponder problems in maths. The cognitive level of analysis is focused on processes of analysis that may not be part of people's consciousness. The neural level is the actual operations of neurons, ganglions and so on that perform the tasks that are involved in the cognitive and mental processes.

Linguistics as a vision of competence: Chomsky and Skinner

In Gardner's (1985) history of cognitive science he traces the significance of the linguist Noam Chomsky's work for cognitive science back to the MIT symposium on information theory of 1956. Chomsky impressed others with the formal precision of his work. He was not just offering a new theory of language, but changing the whole way in which language should be understood and studied. His review of Skinner's (1957) behaviourist account of language was widely treated as devastating and providing an important impetus to the establishment of a cognitive science as the successor to behaviourism.

Chomsky's (1959) review argued that behaviourist stimulus-response models of language learning could not account for the creativity of language. People can and do produce unique but also grammatical utterances for which there is no plausible reinforcement history. Moreover, he noted that it is particularly unclear what stimulus might be relevantly eliciting any particular linguistic response. The stimulus-response account starts to become empirically empty. Chomsky encouraged a move away from the strongly empirically based work of Skinner toward an approach much more guided by theory. Indeed, he emphasised the power of people's intuitions about language, and particularly its grammatical form, suggesting that in many cases empirical work was not necessary to check claims. At the epistemological level, this was backed up by a move to a more nativist concept of language to counter Skinner's relentlessly empiricist image of language being learned through behavioural conditioning. He suggested that all of us have an innate Language Acquisition Device (LAD). This enables a child to learn a particular language for the first time through hypothesis testing backed by knowledge of human universals. In this way the child could arrive at the specific grammar appropriate for the particular language in her culture (Chomsky, 1965).

Let us stand back and tease out some features of Chomsky's approach that have implications here. The first is that Chomsky's critique of Skinner's and others' approaches to language emphasised the importance of grammar and grammatical universals. In criticizing both behavioural approaches and then current linguistic orthodoxy he redefined what is essential about language. This is seen most powerfully in his well-known distinction between competence and performance (Chomsky, 1965). Competence is a person's knowledge of the set of underlying rules of grammar that enable the generation of well-formed grammatical sentences. Performance is the actual sentences that speakers produce and that may be a-grammatical or ill formed in a variety of ways. The important research enterprise would be to focus on competence which, while it may not be observable, is what is crucial about language. Performance may be hard to eliminate from research, as there is no direct empirical route to the study of competence (Chomsky emphasised the value, but also the fallibility of the researcher's grammatical intuitions). Nevertheless, the task of this form of research was to get beyond the flawed world of performance to the rather more fundamental world of competence.

A second, and closely related, implication of this is that active, practical, situated and interactional features of language are secondary. Indeed, the focus is very much on *language* rather than, for example, *talk* (something that happens between people in settings), *conversation* (with its interactional nature), or *discourse* (with its performative emphasis). Skinner's behaviourist approach was taken to have shown the futility of a more empiricist approach to language. With the benefit of hindsight, particularly hindsight illuminated by thirty years of conversation analysis, there is something a little absurd about the way Chomsky confidently and successfully framed Skinner as the arch empiricist. His *Verbal Behaviour* is full of imaginary examples and speculations, and all of these are tightly built using the theoretical language of behaviourism: operants, stimulus and response, rewards and punishments, mands and tacts (the specific terms for utterances with different kinds of reinforcing roles). It is very far away from an observational science of language in use.

A third implication of Chomsky's approach was that cognition was essentially modular. This went strongly against the behaviourist approach to language learning that treated it as the consequence of the sum of different stimuli and reinforcements. For Skinner there was no essential difference between general laws of learning and the laws that operate when learning language. Chomsky's postulation of the LAD was the basis for a vision of mental specialization grounded in neurological systems. This modular vision extended to a swathe of mental phenomena became a central part of contemporary cognitive science.

Modules and representations: Miller and Fodor

A key paper in the establishment of the cognitive perspective in psychology was George Miller's '*The magical number seven plus or minus two*' (1956). The simple thesis (that, for example, people tend to be limited in the number of discrete items they can recall) belied the challenge to behaviourist orthodoxy that emphasised plasticity rather than limitations.

Miller went on with Galanter and Pribram (1960) to develop an alternative model of action that was based on TOTE units (Test Operate Test Exit). They used hammering in a nail as a simple example. You *test* to see that the nail is sticking up. You *operate* the hammer to bang it in. You *test* to see if it is still sticking up and so on as many times as it takes. When you *test* and find the nail is flush then you *exit*. These simple feedback units could be combined together to generate more complex actions. The empirical success of TOTE analysis was limited, but its vision of the organization of action was important in cognitive science. In particular, it offered the basis of a modular account, with large numbers of TOTE units being yoked together to perform complex tasks.

A key figure in the development of modular accounts of cognition was the philosopher (and close colleague of Chomsky) Jerry Fodor (1983). His work provides the most thoroughgoing philosophical embrace of cognitive science and cognitivism: the programme of explaining action by way of the contents and organization of individual human minds. Rather than see mind built up through the combination of simple ideas into more complex (as in the classic picture at the heart of Locke's philosophy) he argues for specialized modules for different kinds of processing. These may have their basis in brain systems. For example, Fodor breaks down human 'input systems' into a series of modules. For vision, say, there might be 'mechanisms for color perception, for the analysis of shape and for the analysis of three-dimensional spatial relations. They might also include quite narrowly task-specific 'higher level' systems concerned with the visual guidance of bodily motions or the recognition of faces of conspecifics' (1983: 47).

Fodor has developed a classic cognitive science information processing approach that puts representations at the heart of mind. For him, to understand what cognitive processes do it is vital to understand how representations are manipulated. Such an approach is at the heart of cognitive science:

> The central hypothesis of cognitive science is that thinking can best be understood in terms of representational structures in the mind and computational procedures that operate on those structures. (Thagard, 2002)

Fodor (1975) argues that as thinking requires the manipulation of representations, then there must be a language of thought. Representations must be symbolically encoded in some way, and there must be rules for the manipulation of those symbols. And Fodor develops Chomsky's nativist approach by suggesting that humans have considerable innate knowledge that will be triggered by features of the environment.

Internal critiques and developments: Connectionism and situated cognition

The overview over the past few pages has picked out only a very few features of what is the huge and heterogeneous field of cognitive science. We have tried to give a flavour for interaction researchers for whom the main ideas in cognitive science may be less familiar. Two sorts of developments are worth noting, because of their potentially radical implications for cognitive science and their interest for the arguments of this book. They are connectionism and situated cognition.

Connectionism emerged within cognitive science in the 1980s. It was inspired by observations of the operation of networks of computer processors with low capacity joined together. Such networks could be 'trained' to do tasks, such as discriminate between different perceptual arrays. Information processing would be achieved through the 'interactions of large numbers of simple processing elements called units, each sending excitatory and inhibitory signals to other units' (Rumelhart et al., 1986: 10). These were seen to mimic the organization of neurons in the brain and therefore be better simulations of how actual cognitive processes might be performed. Thus 'words, objects, simple concepts (e.g., DOG), etc. are assumed to be coded as a pattern of activation across many processing units, with each unit contributing to many different representations' (Bowers, 2002, p. 414).

Although a range of attempts have been made to reconcile connectionist approaches with mainstream cognitive approaches, there are important tensions between them (see Garson, 2002). Here are three examples. First, the emphasis on distribution of the representation of information across networks goes against the modular and hierarchical view in much cognitive science. Memory and knowledge would not be stored symbolically and locally, but would reside in the nature and connection of units. Second, connectionist approaches typically model processing as something happening in parallel across the system rather than sequentially in modules. Indeed, connectionist researchers have argued that the speed of processing of neurons means that important cognitive operations must be done in parallel because they would be impossible to complete within observed reaction times if done sequentially. Third, classic cognitive science builds on concepts from (a particular version of) folk psychology. For instance, Fodor (1988) argues that the folk psychology of desires, goals, plans and beliefs is too good to be false. It is not just a way of speaking, but also a representation of elements of cognitive processing. Many connectionists argue that although folk psychology provides intelligibly for human affairs, that fact alone does not make it an accurate picture of the organization of cognitive processing.

Connectionism is very much a development within cognitive science. Connectionists accept most of the same meta-theoretical and methodological premises as other cognitive scientists. They tend to work with computer programming and experimental simulations in laboratories. However, there are critics from the broad cognitive science tradition who have become concerned that some of the taken for granted elements of cognitive research are less a product of empirical study than an artefact of particular theoretical assumptions and methodological decisions. For example, Ulric Neisser authored the hugely influential first textbook in cognitive psychology (Neisser, 1967). Yet within ten years he was arguing that the study of cognition had focused too much on cognition and behaviour abstract from its natural settings of use (Neisser, 1976). The rationalist emphasis of figures such as Chomsky and Fodor treated many features of cognition as wired in at birth, removing much interest in considering them in natural settings. Moreover, the formulation of many cognitive science problems in programming terms (of either a modular or connection nature) treated their solution as something to be achieved, at least in the first instance, in the abstract.

Critiques of traditional cognitive work evolved into a broad programme variously described as ecological cognition, everyday cognition or distributed cognition (not to be confused with *social* cognition, that has largely focused on the explanation of social processes through the properties of individual cognition – see Fiske and Taylor, 1991). Researchers in this tradition have often been influenced by Russian psychologists such as Lev Vygotsky. Their general argument is that cognition is not well understood as a product of isolated individual maturation but that features of peoples' cognitive competence are formed through interaction in situations where culture, language and features of social settings themselves provide the scaffolding of individual thought (see Rogoff and Lave, 1984). The individual is apprenticed into sophisticated forms of problem solving rather than developing into them naturally. For example, Jean Lave's (1988) studies of everyday mathematical abilities showed that women were able to make subtle proportional calculations about special offers on packets of supermarket food that they could not work out when presented in the abstract. The setting and the embodiment of mathematical concepts in familiar practices provided the scaffolding for sophisticated computation.

One feature of this tradition of research is that it breaks down the customary boundary in cognitive science between mental operations and features of the environment. For example, Ed Hutchins argues that a largely conventional cognitive science perspective can be applied to whole systems rather than just the human agents with them. He suggests this is compatible with the broad project of cognitive science:

Cognitive science . . . concerns itself with the nature of knowledge structures and the processes that operate on them. The properties of these representations inside the system and the processes that operate on representations are assumed to cause or explain the observed performance of the cognitive system as a whole. (1995: 266)

Although this approach has traditionally been concerned with individual agents, Hutchins suggests that the unit of analysis can be extended with very little modification to cover a larger socio-technical system; this is a unit of *distributed cognition* (Hutchins and Klausen, 1996).

Hutchins applied this perspective to the cockpit of a commercial airliner and, particularly, the issue of how pilots land planes at a speed appropriate for the weight of the plane and the configuration of wing flaps. He makes a range of observations about the cognitive properties of this system for representing and 'remembering' speed through dials and displays, and specific configurations and additions to the dials.

Both connectionism and the various strands of work on everyday or shared or distributed cognition raise profound questions for more conventional cognitive approaches. They offer challenges and suggest extensions. However, for the most part researchers within these traditions have accepted cognitivism as the primary form of explanation in psychology. That is, to understand actions we need to make reference to some kinds of internal representations (whether distributed or hierarchical and localized, whether largely innate or built through the internalization of cultural categories and norms). Cognition is not just the substrate or accompaniment to action, but the most immediate thing that explains action.

One of the characteristics of the contributions to this collection is that they are not working with the assumption that the explanation of action requires an understanding of cognitive states or processes of some kind. Mostly they argue for analysis of interaction that is sufficient in its own terms. However, such an analysis has potential implications for the study of, and conception of, cognition; and these are a central focus for this book.

4.   Interactional research and cognition

For the most part, conversation analytic research in particular, and interaction research in general, has developed in the context of sociology and communication departments where the key issues are to do with social structure, influence, order and so on (for overviews see Hutchby and Wooffitt, 1998; ten Have, 1999). Conversely, questions of psychology have rarely been explicitly addressed and even more rarely have the questions that are fundamental to the discipline of cognitive psychology and the broader field of cognitive science been considered. That is not to say that the connections are not there to be made – just that there has been no need to make them. However, this has resulted in a situation where conversation analytic work has developed with varied and often inexplicit assumptions about the nature and role of cognition. And the converse is broadly true of cognitive science; it has developed with a model of interaction that is largely stipulative or intuitive rather than based on detailed empirical work.

Elsewhere there is a tradition of 'discourse processes' that has a direct focus on psychological issues, but this has tended to use traditional cognitive science methods such as experimental studies with vignettes and has paid less attention to natural interaction (for a review, see Graesser, et al., 1997). We will discuss some of this work below. Discursive psychology is the perspective that has addressed cognition in the context of interaction most systematically in a psychological context (e.g. Edwards, 1997; Edwards and Potter, 1992, 1993; Potter and Edwards, 2001). We will overview these traditions in turn, starting with conversation analysis. First, however, we will highlight some of the general features that are likely to be at issue in interaction research of this kind and cognitive science.

Seven points of potential contrast between cognitive science and interaction studies

As we have noted above, cognitive science is a broad and heterogeneous field encompassing different disciplines and styles of research. Any generalization is likely to come up against a range of exceptions. Nevertheless, it is useful to highlight some differences between the style of research that makes up the core of cognitive science and interaction research of the types discussed here. We will take themes from the cognitive work we have just surveyed to make the point most clearly.

(a) Abstraction   Cognitive science, as we have seen, has drawn heavily on an abstract notion of information. The attempt was to develop an approach to information that was independent of content and could allow processing through on/off switches in their electronic or neurological form. As we noted above, this abstraction has been a fundamental feature of the development of cognitive science. In many ways it has been a strength. However, ethnomethodology and conversation analysis have both worked against abstraction of this kind. Garfinkel has stressed the need to understand action in terms of all the specific, local and idiosyncratic details of settings and procedures (Garfinkel, 2002). Sacks has stressed that no feature of conversation can be excluded a priori from relevance to interaction. Lexical selection is finely and relevantly tuned to requirements of interaction; and elements of talk such as laughter particles, or even sniffs, may be coordinated and have interactional significance (Sacks, 1992).

(b) Competence and performance   Cognitive science has overwhelmingly adopted some form of this distinction and seen the explication of competence as a central research goal. This has often been combined with a view of performance as chaotic, ad hoc, and intractable,

a product of multiple uncontrolled variables. In contrast, both CA and DP have avoided this dichotomy. This is seen, most profoundly, in the preference for dealing with naturally occurring interaction captured in audio and video, and transcribed in a way that captures details of delivery. This is not simply a movement from studying competence to studying performance. On the one hand, as Chomsky noted, researching competence almost invariably involves some kind of study of performance. On the other, CA and DP analyses are often focused on the organization of performance.

The subtlety of the move here can be highlighted by considering the different way rules are understood. The rules of Chomsky's transformational grammar are intended to produce all and only well formed sentences in a language (1957). In contrast, the rules of Sacks et al. (1974) classic work on conversation are intended to explicate the organization of speaker transition in talk. Three things are worth noting about rules in this CA work. First, the rules do not only account for smooth speaker transitions, they also account for various kinds of trouble (such as overlap and delay). These are characteristic of the sorts of (apparent) conversational disorder that encouraged cognitive scientists to move away from tackling such material. Second, note that these phenomena are largely invisible to cognitive science work that has used standard orthographic representations of talk. Third, the generation of these rules from performance data is strongly focused on what cognitive scientists would call their 'psychological reality', which is our third point of contrast.

(c) Psychological reality   Much work in cognitive science has been devoted to generating a system that could produce output that is equivalent to, or similar to, that of competent individuals. The task of showing that this system has a cognitive reality in terms of inner psychological representations and processes is a distinct one, as is the further task of considering what kind of brain organization of neurones and axons could sustain that task. Psychological reality is thus important, interesting, but not necessarily the start point for much work in cognitive science. Again, conversation analysis and discursive psychology do not make the same basic assumptions about output, competence and cognition. Nevertheless there is a strong emphasis on what cognitive researchers would gloss as psychological reality as they *start with* the perspective of speakers. Using the classic linguistic distinction of Kenneth Pike (1954), they are emic rather than etic perspectives. Thus, the rules for turn taking do not just generate orderly speaker transition in a mechanical manner; rather their normative status means that departures can be highly inferential. Speakers can be shown to *orient* to these rules as they interact. This is a

special kind of psychological reality – not one defined by in-the-head mental processes, but by the participants orienting practically in the course of ongoing interaction to the relevant features of the interaction. What this means in practice is illustrated in a number of the chapters below.

(d) Ecological naturalism   We have already noted that from within cognitive science researchers such as Neisser and Hutchins have argued for a greater degree of ecological naturalism in research. Nevertheless, only a tiny proportion of such research currently studies cognitive processes in natural settings. It is notable that cognitive sciences have developed only the most primitive representational practices for capturing and managing natural interaction in the way that conversation analysts have.

This can be shown in a number of ways. However, as an illustration take the following typical example from the methods section of a research article:

The experimenter began by drawing their attention to the bags of toys and saying, 'These toys are special. Do you know why they are special? These toys are special because each one has a different little thing inside.' The experimenter then opened one of the toys and said, 'See this toy? Look, it has a sheep inside.' Gesturing to all of the other toys she said, 'Each one of these toys has a different little thing inside. That's what makes them special. Each one has something different inside.' (Birch and Bloom, 2003: 282)

This is an idealization of the interaction in a number of ways. It does not include interactional details about, for example, the coordination of the experimenter's talk with contributions from the child or their displays of recipiency. Do they display attention? Do they ask questions? It renders the talk into well-formed sentences with conventional orthographic punctuation. It is not possible to recover information about emphasis, intonation, delays and repairs and so on. The interaction is, in effect, cleaned up and abstracted. Indeed, it is not clear if this is what actually happened in any case or what *should have* happened. From within the logic of cognitive science this is a quality of the paper. However, interaction researchers are likely to be interested in the many features of what is going on but which are simply obscured in such a representational practice. The issue here is the implication that of these features has for the way cognition is understood.

Even work such as that of Neisser and Hutchins that has a more ecological focus has been based on cognitive presuppositions, and has often been done without the degree of attention to interactional detail that we will see treated as essential in the studies below.

(e) Experimental manipulation   Cognitive science has typically been developed through experimental work using some kind of hypothetico-deductive approach to test models couched in terms of variables and abstract processes. CA and DP have overwhelmingly been developed through inductive studies of natural interaction. The cumulative success of conversation analysis has shown the value of an analytic strategy that has not found mainstream favour in psychology. The logic of these research strategies is entirely different on a number of levels. However, the contrast is slightly more complex than this bald difference suggests. Although CA studies are typically attempting to explicate the workings of a particular phenomenon in a corpus of conversational data, there is considerable attention paid to deviant and counter cases. The process of analysis involves its own finely developed form of hypothesis testing. In particular, the analysis focuses on evidence that participants are actually orienting to the claimed phenomenon – CA's own form of psychological reality is wired into its method.

(f) Representation   Arguably the notion of representation is at the very heart of modern cognitive science. CA and DP both also emphasise the importance of representation (Potter, 1996; Schegloff, 1972). However, the cognitive and interactional notions of representations are crucially different. In cognitive science representations are mental entities, perhaps represented symbolically or in the form of some kind of program. In CA and DP, in contrast, the focus is on actual descriptions in actual talk or actual texts, and the involvement of those descriptions in actions. For example, how are particular lexical items selected from an indefinite range of possibility to support a particular action (an invitation, say, or a criticism)? How are descriptions constructed to be adequate or literal, and how can such constructions be unpicked or undermined in interaction (Goodwin and Goodwin, 1997)? This work on representations as interactional objects, involved in practices, has a range of potential implications for cognitive science notions of representations as a mental currency, not least because the nature of cognitive representations is often methodologically dependent on discursive representations in the form of vignettes or answers to researchers' questions.

(g) Modularity   A central aspect of much (non-connectionist) cognitive science is its emphasis on the modular basis of cognitive processes. A range of different modules of different degrees of complexity and proposed psychological reality has been proposed. CA and DP have a very different decompositional logic. Their focus is on turns of talk and actions accomplished in talk. Although they may identify distinct

elements of turns and actions, they are not attempting to decompose interaction processes into mental modules within individual cognitive systems.

These points of contrast are intended to highlight some initial differences between the two broad approaches. For the most part interaction research has not addressed issues of cognition directly – and that is what makes this collection so significant. However, there are some important exceptions to this. In the next section of this chapter we will briefly review some of these exceptions.

5.   Conversation analysis, ethnomethodology and cognition

We will divide earlier interaction work into conversation analysis, ethnomethodology and discursive psychology. This is a slightly arbitrary division, and risks exaggerating differences, but it is designed to make the work accessible particularly to those unfamiliar with it. We will start with the foundational work of Harvey Sacks.

Sacks, talk and cognition

Sacks' working career through the 1960s to his untimely death in the mid 1970s parallels an important part of the development and huge expansion of cognitive science. And his work (mostly captured in transcribed and edited records of his lectures from 1964–72, now published as Sacks, 1992) at times exhibits some of the abstract formalism of cognitive science as well as some of its language. Nevertheless, the approach to language is fundamentally different. He did not start with the John Locke picture of language as a set of signs for transporting thoughts from one mind to another. Instead, he focused on the practicality of talking. In particular, he considered the fundamental issue of how language can be something learnable and understandable. This led very early on to a caution against researchers using intuitions about cognition to constrain analysis. The very first published lecture (delivered in the spring of 1964) ends:

When people start to analyze social phenomena, if it looks like things occur with the sort of immediacy we find in some of these exchanges, then, if you have to make an elaborate analysis of it – that is to say, show that they did something as involved as some of the things I have proposed – then you figure that they couldn't have thought that fast. I want to suggest that you have to forget that completely. Don't worry about how fast they're thinking. First of all, don't worry about whether they're 'thinking.' Just try to come to terms with how it is that the thing comes off. Because you'll find that they can do these things. Just take any other area of natural science and see, for example, how fast molecules do things.

And they don't have very good brains. So just let the materials fall as they may. Look to see how it is that persons go about producing what they do produce. (Sacks, 1992a: 11)

Conversation analysis has largely followed through this injunction in its practice, and this has had the effect of disengaging it from cognitivist thinking. Instead of attempting to work out what entities and processes may 'underlie' talk as a prerequisite for analysis, the conversation analytic programme has developed through considering the organization of actual talk. Its development within sociology meant that it could flourish without attending to cognition, nor receive the attention of cognitive scientists.

Part of the logic of this disengagement for Sacks is his positive focus on what is visible/hearable in interaction. He started from the point of view of conversationalists making sense of one another via what is said (in all its rich detail of intonation, stress, timing and so on). From this point of view cognition – mind, thoughts, intentions and so on – are relevant to, and involved in, interaction in terms of their current hearability in the interaction itself. Sacks quoted approvingly Freud's observation that 'the problem is not how is it that people come to think that others know their thoughts, but how is it that people come to think so deeply that others don't know their thoughts (Sacks, 1992, vol. 1: 114)?

As an example, he considers a group therapy session where three boys jointly produce a single utterance.

Joe: (cough) We were in an automobile discussion,
Henry: discussing the psychological motives for
Mel: drag racing in the streets.
          (1992a: 144–5)

Sacks tracks this material in a number of analytic directions. One of his observations is about the way this collaborative utterance *displays* a particular shared understanding. It is a powerful method for these boys to show that they concur on the topic of the talk; more powerful, he suggests, than one of the boys claiming that the topic is one thing, and the others agreeing with him. As Sacks puts it, the way they fit their talk together allows the hearer to see 'that they "*know what's on each other's minds*," (1992a: 147, emphasis added). We will return to this basic topic when discussing Schegloff's work and work in discursive psychology.

Sacks developed the issue of shared understanding in a number of ways. It is not surprising, given his sociological background, that this was such a major topic for him. Another phenomenon he focused on in relation to this topic was second stories. He noted that a regular feature of the organization of talk is that when one person tells a story of some kind the recipient of that story will tell his or her own story, a second story.

This second story displays an equivalent experience. Its important feature is that the speaker does not *claim* they have the same experience; they *show* they have that experience through the telling. Again we see Sacks approaching the issue of shared experience from the point of view of the speaker and listener, and considering the question of shared experience as a practical question to be solved interactionally – in this case the answer being to provide a second story.

One of Sacks' basic ideas is that talk is *recipient-designed* in all kinds of non-accidental ways. It is a medium for doing interaction and designed in its rich detail to work in that way. He illustrates this in a manner particularly pertinent to our discussion when considering the writing of Virginia Woolf. He speculates about how her writing contributes to a sense of the exploration of inner states. He notes, for example, that descriptions such as 'Mr Jones came into the room' are informative and communicative for a reader. However, when Woolf uses a description such as 'he walked into the room' the *lack* of this kind of recipient-design generates a sense of someone living in their inner world:

The idea then is that things like non-complete, non-objective, non-nominalized references do perhaps reproduce in some way, how a person having feelings that they're not in the first instance having by reference to their communicatability, has them. (Sacks, 1992b: 405)

Again, we see how Sacks starts with the interactional and communicative role of language. He highlights the special literary work that Woolf engages in to give a sense of an inner life in the face of the pervasive emphasis on interaction and recipiency.

Sacks built many of the foundational ideas in modern conversation analysis through the lecture courses available as published volumes. These ideas were refined and developed in larger scale empirical studies by colleagues such as Gail Jefferson and Emanuel Schegloff.

Schegloff and socially shared cognition

Schegloff (1991) has explicitly addressed the implications of conversation analysis for the way the notion of shared knowledge is understood in the context of a collection of papers on 'socially shared cognition' (Resnick *et al.*, 1991). He comes at the issue of shared knowledge starting with Garfinkel's (1967) ethnomethodological discussion of that topic. This raised problems for the (still common) cognitive science picture of shared knowledge as equivalent to two computer memories having the same contents:

When even the sense of ordinary words and very simple sentences could be shown not to engender identical explications when presented to different persons, when those explications themselves had to be reconciled to provide them a 'sense of equivalence,' and when *those* reconciliations in turn required such reconciliation, the notion of 'common culture' or 'shared knowledge' as composed of same substantive components – whether norms or propositions – held by different persons became increasingly difficult to defend. (Schegloff, 1991a: 152)

In line with the basic ethnomethodological programme, Garfinkel developed a *procedural* sense of shared knowledge. That is, the issue ceased to be a *cognitive* question of underlying mental equivalence, but became a *practical* one of the way particular methods could be used to confirm (or deny) that knowledge is 'held in common'.

Again, the start point of conversation analysis is different from most cognitive science. Rather than beginning with the isolated individual and adding 'the social aspect for supplementary consideration' Schegloff argues that 'the fundamental or primordial scene of social life is that of direct interaction between members of a social species' (1991: 154). This points to the centrality of studying how agreed knowledge, understanding and so on are managed and coordinated in interaction. One of the central features about conversation highlighted by Sacks is the way that the turn taking system of talk is fundamental to coordinating understanding. Take this simple example.

A speaker makes an invitation of some kind in a turn of talk. The recipient's very next turn of talk is the place where they can accept (or reject, or put off, or query) the invitation. Moreover, and relevantly here, *in so doing*, that speaker *shows* that they have understood that they have been invited (and what kind of invitation it is, to what kind of event, and so on). The *display* of understanding is crucial, because it is the idea of understanding as an *interactional* phenomenon that is live here. Shortcoming in this display may occasion *repair* in the very next turn – the displayed 'misunderstandings', 'confusions' and so on can be picked out, commented on, fixed.

In Schegloff's conception there are consequentially different structurally provided places where shared understanding (socially shared knowledge or, in a more sociological language, intersubjectivity) can be defended in conversation (Schegloff, 1992b). One crucial place is in the turn that follows the invitation (generically, the second turn). All kinds of issues and confusions can be attended to in this place. The third turn is also crucial. If speakers can reveal their understandings in the second turn then, it can happen, 'that they can also reveal understandings that the speakers of that prior talk take to be problematic – in other words, what they take to be misunderstandings' (1992b: 1300). The third turn, then, is the place where the repair of such misunderstandings can be initiated. Indeed, Schegloff suggests that third turns are the last *structurally provided for* place for the defence of shared understanding.

Take the following example of repair in the second turn.

Marcia: ...Becuz the to:p was ripped off'v iz car which
             iz tihsay someb'dy helped th'mselfs.
Tony: Stolen.
             (0.4)
Marcia: Stolen. Right out in front of my house.
             (Schegloff, 1992b:1302)

The first thing to note about this is that in Marcia's *first* turn we can already see her attending to prospective problems of understanding her utterance (she reworks what she is saying to 'helped th'mselfs', perhaps because of the possible ambiguity of 'ripped off'). This is just a more explicit element of what Sacks notes as the generic feature of talk: that it is recipient designed. Nevertheless, Marcia has not completely sorted out the understanding problem, as we can see from Tony's turn in the second position. He offers a candidate understanding of Marcia's turn, which she confirms.

Schegloff (1992b) suggests that the vast majority of understanding problems get sorted out through speakers designing their talk appropriately for recipients and the context, through speakers modifying and self repairing in the course of that talk, and through recipients in the second turn picking up problems that, despite this, have appeared in the talk. Nevertheless, problems can still arise. Through a careful analysis of a large corpus of examples Schegloff shows how repair can work in the third turn. Here is a simple example.

Dan: Well that's a little different from last week.
Louise: heh heh heh Yeah. We were in hysterics last week.
Dan: No, I mean Al.
Louise: Oh. He...
             (Schegloff, 1992b:1203)

Note the way in this group therapy data that Dan, the therapist, repairs the understanding of what he has said was offered by Louise. Schegloff highlights the sorts of dangers – for relationships, for individuals – that can arise from letting failures of understanding slip past:

When a source of misunderstanding escapes the multiple repair space, a whole institutional superstructure that is sustained through talk-in-interaction can be compromised. And since virtually anything in the talk can be such a source of misunderstanding, the potential for trouble for that institutional superstructure can be vast. It is against those systematic potentials for subversion of social order that repair after next turn is the last structurally provided defence. (1992b: 1337)

The broader point to note is the way common understanding is treated here as a procedural problem by Schegloff, on an analytic level, and by the participants at a practical level. There are different places for checking and modifying understanding, with different possibilities and constraints on them. These procedures are there for producing and constituting common understanding (or 'socially shared cognition', or 'intersubjectivity'). There is no way for participants to check such understanding independently of those procedures. This raises major questions for further work on, for example, common knowledge that attempts to consider it as an issue best studied through the examination of individual performance.

While Sacks' and Schegloff's work has focused on the implications for understanding cognition from conversational organization, other workers within this tradition have developed different issues. In the work of Lucy Suchman we find a reworking of the central cognitive notion of plans.

Suchman and situated actions

Suchman opens her influential work on plans by contrasting two pictures of how navigation works taken from anthropology. In one picture (from studies of European navigation) the navigators use universal principals to develop a plan that is then drawn on at each stage of the voyage to reach the goal. In another picture (from studies of Trukese navigators of the Pacific) the navigators start with an objective and head off toward it using a wide range of information about wind, tide, clouds and so on in an ad hoc manner. Suchman goes on to make the suggestion that studies of European navigation have not looked at it carefully enough, for if they had they would have found that it is much closer to the Trukese than had been imagined. Indeed, she suggests that all planned actions are more or less like the actions of the Trukese. As she put it:

Planned, purposeful actions are inevitably situated actions. By situated actions I mean simply actions taken in the context of particular, concrete circumstances. In this sense, one could argue that we all act like the Trukese, however much some of us may talk like Europeans. We must act like the Trukese because the circumstances of our actions are never fully anticipated and are continually changing around us. (Suchman, 1987: ix)

She suggests that plans can only be a weak resource for activities. Indeed, their apparent central role in action may be as much a consequence of the emphasis on rationality in Western cultures as their actual constraining role.

Suchman develops this argument on the basis of general ethnomethod-ological thinking. Ethnomethodology has criticized conventional theories of action for underestimating the extent to which actions are dependent on features of local and idiosyncratic settings and ad hoc procedures (see Garfinkel, 1967 in particular). For a plan to operate in practice it needs to have specified connections to all of the available details of settings and the various contingencies within them. The risk is that a plan that can guide activity through a sequence of actions will need to become huge, perhaps impossibly huge, as it attempts the impossible task of encoding all those details and contingencies in symbols.

Suchman develops a subtly, but importantly different view, which uses plans as resources for *projecting* and *reconstructing* courses of action in terms of prior intentions. Crucially the consequence of this view is that 'the prescriptive significance of intentions for situated actions is inher-ently vague' (Suchman, 1987: 27; see also, Suchman 1988, 2000). This vagueness is not a flaw when compared with full specification; rather the vagueness is precisely what makes plans useful for their projective and reconstructive tasks – they can be applied to an indefinite number of situations in deft and locally specific ways.

These theoretical ideas are illustrated and extended through a study of people operating photocopiers. This beautifully shows up the highly complex local and ad hoc interpretations that users make of the sequences of instructions that are intended to guide them through to the comple-tion of tasks such as producing a two-sided bound document. Suchman recorded dialogue between users, the various actions they performed on the machines (selecting options from lists, pressing buttons, and so on), the information presented by the machine (such as numbers on dis-plays), and, finally, the 'official' rationale for the information based on the designer's specification of the user's goals.

The analysis shows up the continual reconstruction of what is going on by the users. The point of the analysis is to highlight the tension between a planful model of action embodied in the machine's menu system and the local practices of users, seen from their dialogue as they jointly attempt to achieve tasks. For example, participant F selects the change option on the display, adjusting what is displayed from 2 to 0. The dialogue goes like this:

F: ((reading)) "Describe the document to be copied-" Oh, we
      already did: No, we don't want to do that.
E: Maybe we have to do it to copy that [i.e. the next page].
F: (Looks around machine)
      (laugh) I don't know.
      (Suchman, 1987:151)

Suchman uses this prosaic and familiar interaction around the photo-copier to highlight the basic tension between the orderly plans and out-comes that are specified in the manual, and to provide the rationale for the menu system that the operators work with, and the more messy, trial and error, considerations that appear in the talk. The operators seem to nav-igate the controls of the photocopier like the Trukese across the Pacific – they (often) get there in the end, producing their bound and double-sided documents, but their actions on the way are ad hoc. They use the menus, but they provide *local* interpretations of their sense. They refer to a range of background considerations and reconstruct the orderliness of what they do as they go along, often in terms of goals and plans.

The implications of Suchman's work, along with a range of similar stud-ies, comes from the questions it raises for the assumptions that action is based on plans. Insofar as cognitive scientists have assumed that human actions work in this kind of planful way, and attempt to model the psycho-logical requirements for such planful behaviour, the models may be flawed by the failed assumptions. In particular, it raises problems for approaches such as Fodor's that posit a language of thought in which plans, etc. are developed. At its strongest it suggests that the whole enterprise of cogni-tive science may be limited by its failure to provide an adequate account of human action in its natural habitat.

6.   Discursive psychology and cognition

Unlike conversation analysis and ethnomethodology, discursive psychol-ogy has developed largely within (social) psychology and has addressed psychological issues from the start. The general theoretical and ana-lytic framework shares many features with conversation analysis and eth-nomethodology. For general overviews see Edwards (1997), Edwards and Potter (1992a, 1993, 2001, this volume), Potter and Edwards (2001). What makes it discursive psychology is that psychological topics are con-sidered through the way talk and texts are used in action. Psychology is here a topic *in* people's talk, and a resource *for* that talk. This involves studying the way psychology is formulated (described, named, invoked or more indirectly oriented to) in interaction, as well as studying psycho-logical categories and notions (such as mentalistic terms and metaphors) as tools for performing actions.

One of the features of DP has been its reformulation of a range of cen-tral topics in cognitive science in discursive terms. For example, studies have focused on the notions of memory (Goodwin, 1987; Edwards and Potter, 1992a, b; see also Lynch and Bogen, 1996, this volume; Woof-fitt, 1991), attitudes (Potter, 1998a; Puchta and Potter, 2002; Wiggins and Potter, 2003; te Molder, 1999); categories and identity (Edwards, 1991, 1997; Lamerichs and te Molder, 2003), emotion (Edwards, 1997, 1999a; Locke and Edwards, 2003) and scripts (Edwards, 1994, 1997). To this list can be added some researchers with a more anthropological and interactional focus. Charles and Marjorie Goodwin have researched *seeing* (Goodwin, 1995a, 1997, 2000a, b, c; Goodwin and Goodwin, 1996, 1997). They have considered the way in which seeing is practically accomplished in the work of air traffic control, geochemistry and oceanography. For example, the category jet black has a technical sense in particular chemical processes. Diverse and locally managed practices are used to establish that a particular filament can be counted as jet black, and new members have to be apprenticed to be able to see this colour (Goodwin, 1997). Let us consider examples of DP work focusing on the topics of 'script formulations' and 'shared knowledge'.

1.   Script formulations

Derek Edwards' (1994, 1995, 1997) work on script formulations illustrates what is distinctive about DP compared with the majority of work in cognitive science. Edwards notes the way that in cognitive science scripts have been treated as abstractions from experienced reality which instruct people what to do in familiar situations (Nelson, 1986; Schank and Abelson, 1977). They are mental representations that help people know what to expect and do in restaurants, cinemas and other familiar settings, as well as allowing exceptional or unusual events to be identified through their deviation from the script. This way of understanding scripts exemplifies how representations are understood in cognitive science as fundamental to human conduct.

Edwards (1994) distinguishes three possible references of the term script. They are:

Script-W	Refers to ordered and orderly features of the world itself.
Script-PC	Refers to features of an individual's perception and cognition.
Script -D	Refers to the way events are described as orderly, or to departures from the standard order.

Take the classic example of a restaurant. *Script-W* would be the sequence of events that happen when going into a restaurant. *Script-PC* would be the set of propositional representations of actions in sequence tied to the restaurant setting, derived from perception of many restaurants. *Script-D* would be a description of what went on in the restaurant as orderly, or perhaps a description that showed how what went on departed from what was expected.

Classic script theory typically has the order of development of these scripts as:

$$Script\text{-}W \rightarrow Script\text{-}PC \rightarrow Script\text{-}D$$

The objective nature and order of events (*Script-W*) is perceptually apprehended by the individual. This perceptual information is then the basis for building up cognitive scripts (*Script-PC*). These scripts, in turn, provide the semantics for people talking about, describing and recalling routine places and events (*Script-D*). In contrast, DP proposes that this order can be inverted. Initially this is a methodological by-product of starting with a focus on discourse. However, Edwards notes that once the focus is on *Script-D* formulations it becomes hard to see them as a mere by-product of perceptually refined mental scripts derived from regular experiences.

Edwards shows that *script formulations* are analyzable as interactionally occasioned phenomena. That is, they are not produced haphazardly as conversational non-sequiturs, rather they construct events in particular ways as parts of particular actions at particular moments in interaction. In particular, they present actions as orderly and following from standard routines (as anyone would follow) or as deflected from such routines by idiosyncratic personal dispositions. DP and cognitive science agree in seeing scripting as central in human affairs, but DP starts with the practical role of *Script-Ds* in actions, and providing accountability to those actions. Their place is more central than in cognitive science where they have been treated as a reflection of perceptually derived cognitive *script-PCs*.

An example can illustrate the role of scripts in actions and accountability and some of the issues it raises. This extract comes from a phone call between two elderly Californian women and describes some features of a restaurant that one of the women went to. As such it provides an empirical example to consider the nature of scripts against.

```
1   Lottie:   (…) we went in: to the ((Name)) place on the way
2             back an: uh e-had (.) uh: they ah an a:fter dinner
3             dri:nk 'n God there wasn' a sou:l ih We were the only
4             ones at the bar an' there was about two parties in
5             th[e dining] room ·p·hhhhh
6   Emma:       [°Ye:h.° ]
7   Lottie:   An' I didn' wanna say-eh: A:deline said she a'ways
8             wanted uh see it so .hnhh I never said anything
9             but- uh: Claude said today he says wasn' that the
10            dirtiest place?=
11  Emma:     =[ Ye:s ]
```

```
12  Lottie:   =['n I  s]ai:d you know? (.) I: felt the same thing
13            but I didn't wanna say anything to you but I jus'
14            fe[: lt ]
15  Emma:     [Ya:]h
16  Lottie:   dirty when I walked on the ca:r↓p*et.h ·hh
17  Emma:     Well you know we were there in ↑Ju:ne
18            youknow Bud played go:lf inna (.) when the air
19            conditioner went o::ff? ·hhh An' we're about (.)
20            the only ones that ha:d an air conditioned room
21            the ↑rest of 'em were bro:ken. ·hhhAn' we went down
22            to breakfast 'n there was only about ↑two people to
23            help for breakfast with all these guys goin' to pla:y
24            go:lf. They were a:ll teed o:ff:.
25  Lottie:   Ye[:ah?
26  Emma:       [·hhhhh Because (.) °*uy°
27            ↑Bud u-couldn' e:ven eat his breakfast. He o:rdered
28            he waited forty five minutes 'n he had to be out
29            there to tee off so I gave it to uh: (.) Karen's:
30            little bo:y.
31            (0.7)
32  Emma:     ((swallow)) I mean that's how bad the service ↓w*as
33            .hh (.) °It's gone to pot.°
34  Lottie:   u-Oh*::: (.) e-[Y e:: a h.      Ye<]
35  Emma:                   [°But it's a° beauti]ful ↓go:lf
36            ↓°course.°
            (NB:IV:10: R:35 – from Edwards, 1997:147–8)
```

We do not have any trouble recognizing this string of negative assessments of the restaurant as a complaint. On the basis of cognitive science we would expect the complainable matters to be identified by reference to scripts of what should and should not go on at restaurants. However, when we start to consider this practically it becomes difficult to sort out what is included in the 'restaurant script' (*script-pc*) and what is not. While this script might well pick out Bud not getting his food as a problem (line 27), would it pick up the insufficiency of people at the bar (lines 3–4) or the sticky carpet (line 16), or even the need to get on the golf course (lines 27–9)? These are produced in the description (*script-d*) as noticeable failures of what is to be expected. Yet if all considerations such as these were to be included as parts of the standard restaurant script it would become enormously cumbersome.

The DP approach is not to consider how such scripted descriptions (*script-d*) could be a product of noticeable departures from mentally represented scripts (*script-pc*), but to consider the way they are constructed from an indefinite range of possibilities to bring off the act of complaining. The script formulation (*script-d*) warrants the complaint. Edwards notes that the empirical details are finely tuned to the performance of complaining, and potentially problematic as features of a cognitive script (*script-pc*). For example, some of the elements here that are built as negative, might elsewhere be built 'as characteristics of a desirably folksy, laid-back, informal sort of restaurant that contrasts favourably with places that are antiseptic, regimented and characterless' (1997: 148–9). This suggests that having decontextualized, mental templates of good restaurants and how they operate might not be the most useful prerequisite for dealing with and talking about restaurants. It might be more useful to have 'descriptive details as inventively produced and made relevant as part of the production of situated accounts' (1997: 149).

DP shifts the analytic focus from cognition to description, from *script-pc* to *scripts-d*. In part this reflects a different but complementary focus of study. However, the tension is potentially sharper. Edwards observes that in practice cognitive psychological work on scripts does not, and cannot, access *scripts-pc* directly, but typically works from *script-d* to *script-pc*. This is true of theoretical treatments, researchers' accounts of scripts, experimental and simulation procedures and studies of narrative completions. Thus research on script formulations and their role in situated actions is likely to be fundamental to appreciating what any possibly reformulated script theory in cognitive science is required to explain. Just as with Suchman's (1987) work on plans, the general implication is that simplified ideas about the 'language of thought' and the relation between scripts and actions are likely to be flawed. As Edwards puts it, script formulations provide:

a basis for accountability, rather than a program for generating the activity itself. We should add that they may also be invoked reflexively *within* action sequences as formulations of the kind of activity it is, as a criterion for what to do next, or for what has gone wrong. But each time they occur in these ways they feature as actions in their own right, in the form of situated descriptions. (1997: 166)

2.   *Shared knowledge*

We have already discussed Schegloff's approach to the notion of shared knowledge. Let us develop this discussion by considering both Edwards' (1997, 1999b) work on shared knowledge and Herbert Clark's (1996) discussion of the topic. Clark's work is worth considering because he is a rare example of a cognitive psychologist who has drawn on interaction research. It highlights important tensions between cognitive and interactional approaches.

For Clark, when two people share knowledge, or 'common ground', this is 'the sum of their mutual, common, or joint knowledge, beliefs, and suppositions' (1996: 93). Clark asks: given that two mental spaces contain the same knowledge, how can they be coordinated through talk? For

Edwards there are basic problems of this way of formulating the question of shared knowledge (Edwards, 1999b). For him it closes off two issues that are at the centre of interaction. First of all, concerns with knowledge in interaction are inseparable from concerns about description. Second, agreement is something that is established through conversational means. The first of these has been particularly emphasised in DP, the second picks up from the tradition running through Schegloff and Garfinkel of treating shared knowledge as a procedural issue that we have already discussed.

Let us illustrate these points with an example. The following is the start of a call to a child protection helpline:

```
1              ((phone rings))
2    CPO:      .hh Hello you are through to the NSPCC?
3    Caller:   Hello em .hh I'm actually phoning (0.2)
4              f-for some advice regarding an incident that I
5              witnessed today.
     (CPO = Child Protection Officer, from Potter & Hepburn, 2003)
```

At this point the Caller has some knowledge that the Child Protection Officer does not. For Clark common knowledge will be established when both share that knowledge. However, the DP perspective highlights the role of specific descriptions and the inseparability of knowledge and description. Note that in using the term 'incident' here the caller does not evaluate, or assign responsibility. It is the most limited of characterizations. As such, it orients to the expertise of the Child Protection Officer by allowing the status of the incident to be established interactionally (Potter and Hepburn, 2003; cf. Zimmerman, 1992). From a DP perspective, there is no easy way of separating the 'knowledge' or 'belief' from its linguistic construction. Moreover, for the participants the linguistic construction must be paramount – it is what they are starting with.

Edwards' second point is that 'agreement' in interaction is something accomplished actively and practically rather than being simply a consequence of the overlap of putative underlying 'knowledge' or 'belief states'. Again, this is not just a DP point, but follows from basic thinking in ethnomethodology and CA. Take our example again. After the Child Protection Officer has checked for ethical permission and described the role of the helpline, she continues with the following:

```
1    CPO:      [·hh] °tch° okay so y- you (0.2) something
2              you've witnessed today has worried you:.
3              (.)
4    CPO:      .h[h h ] u:m (.) can you just tell me a little bit
5    Caller:   [Yeah]
6    CPO:      about that.
```

Note here the way the CPO ascribes a mental state to the Caller ('worried' – line 2) as well as describing what has worried her as 'something' (line 1). Again, for discursive psychologists the first issue is what the talk is doing in public and practical terms (again, reflecting the necessary primacy of talk for the interactants). Rather than reflecting a shared understanding of underlying mental contents, the ascription 'worried' can be an element in constructing an appropriate stance for the caller from which to be making the call. Moreover, the word 'something' (like the caller's own word 'incident' earlier in the call) allows the precise nature of the phenomenon to be established over the course of the call, supported by the CPO's skills in child protection. For DP, then, terms for mental states such as 'worried' and descriptions of events such as 'an incident' or 'something' are explicable as delicately interactionally designed specifics. In this case, they are moves in the business of doing orderly reporting of child abuse, occasioned by that business, rather than traces of actual mental states and perceptions.

As with the example of scripts and script formulations, the approach developed in DP is not necessarily in opposition to more traditional cognitive science notions. It presents a different focus on mental or psychological phenomena, starting with how those things are constructed, managed, and oriented to in natural interaction. Goodwin's studies of seeing, for example, start from vernacular understandings of seeing situated in interaction where seeing is important, such as the work of archaeologists (Goodwin, 2000a). Yet one of the consequences of such research is often to show up possibly unwarranted assumptions about the nature of descriptions and formulations that are embedded in the methods of cognitive science and psychology more generally (e.g. Antaki et al., 2000; Edwards and Potter, 1992a; Maynard et al., 2002; Puchta and Potter, 2002; Schegloff, 1999).

This way of approaching cognition is strikingly different from that common in cognitive science where psychological objects such as perception and memory are well-established technical domains, fenced in by the standard theories and methods of psychology and related sciences. Often it is not just specific claims that are at stake here, but broader approaches to empirical work through which claims could be tested, and the broader theoretical perspective in which the claim is embedded. These obstacles have made dialogue complicated – yet the potential is there. The payoff is the possibility of developing some genuinely new ways of considering questions of cognition. This is one of the goals of the current book. For the rest of this introductory chapter we will overview the contributions and set them in context.

7. Contributions to this book

We have tried to set the scene for the chapters that follow with a necessarily synoptic mapping of the terrain of cognitive science and interaction research. This highlighted some of the subtle considerations about the nature of cognition that are at stake. As a broad-brush distinction between the two areas we might characterize the cognitive science question as what kind of competence is required to produce particular actions? In contrast, the interaction question can be characterized as how (if at all) does cognition figure as something in and for interaction? This raises further questions of whether the answer to the former question has implications for the latter, and vice versa. Does the competence concept in cognitive science map onto the interactional objects of interaction research? These challenging questions are not going to be answered in a simple way in what follows, but they do offer the most elaborate consideration of them that has so far been produced.

The chapters are organized into two halves. The first set address basic issues of the interface between cognition and action, and the implications of such research for method. Whereas Robert Sanders argues for the findings of cognitive science as a limit on the claims of interaction research, Jeff Coulter offers the most thoroughgoing rejection of both cognitivism as an explanatory principle and cognition as a coherent research topic. These two chapters mark out two boundary cases. Anita Pomerantz follows up the implications of treating cognition as something relevant to interaction analysis by commenting on, and refining, an analytic approach. This couples direct analysis of interaction with the use of video stimulated comments from participants who were part of the original interaction. Nora Cate Schaeffer and Douglas Maynard argue the other way, highlighting how basic features of interaction have consequences for the responses in standardized surveys. They consider cases that are typically treated as deviations from standard scripts produced by 'cognitive processing' and suggest that they should be understood as something interactive and collaborative. Finally in this section Robert Hopper's chapter marks a transition point. He analyses a corpus of phone calls made during the first days of President Lyndon Johnson's presidency, a data set perfectly suited to addressing the notion of strategic thinking. He asks what interactional evidence is there that the president's talk in those calls was strategically planned.

The second half of the book addresses the issue of cognition through a series of studies of how particular 'mental phenomena' figure in interaction. Paul Drew analyses 'confusion' and tries to show how analysis might identify it as a 'mental state', independently of participants' orientations to that state. John Heritage focuses largely on the particle 'oh' and its potential relation to changes of mental state. Robin Wooffitt, Michael Lynch and David Bogen address questions to do with the mental and interactional status of memory, in both cases arguing for a noncognitive approach. Wooffitt considers the phenomenon of flashbulb memories through a discussion of the organization of descriptions of unusual or surprising events. Lynch and Bogen discuss the status of memory in discussion of Oliver North's testimony to the Iran-Contra affair. Finally, Derek Edwards and Jonathan Potter illustrate a non-cognitive approach to claims to knowledge and description, liking and thinking.

We will spend a bit of time describing the argument of each chapter and then draw out some of the broader issues they address. We will take the contributions in turn.

1.   Sanders: testing 'observations'

Sanders argues that discourse researchers should pay serious attention to the findings of cognitive science. Indeed, he contrasts his own stance with what he sees as the neo-behaviourism of discursive psychologists. He notes that although much of the time discourse researchers can safely ignore the findings of cognitive research there are times that it is important to take such findings into account. He develops this argument by considering examples from CA (Schegloff, 1996) and DP (Potter, 1998b). In each case he suggests that the analysis involves a hidden attribution of motive to speakers, and that there is evidence in the material that alternative motivations might be available, or that the material might simply reflect their cognition or, as he puts it, the utterances could be 'actually expressions' of how speakers 'in fact did experience' something, and that what [they] said could have been 'dictated by [their] inner state'. The challenge for interaction researchers is to show how an analysis can be developed that does not depend on an inner, psychological notion of motive and to demonstrate the insufficiency of the idea of inner states dictating what is said (for more on these arguments see, for example, Potter, 1996; Schegloff, 1972; Wittgenstein, 1958).

Sanders considers examples from both child and adult interaction to illustrate the way in which interpretations made by researchers should be disciplined by the cognitive science findings about processing limitations. For example, he returns to an extract analysed by Schegloff (1996) and suggests that the analysis requires that the speaker is performing a particular cognitive task that involves a word search. The issue is the relation of this task to experimental work. If Schegloff is right his 'analysis makes a contribution to cognitive science for revealing the power of the cognitive resources we bring to bear in producing discourse objects; but if cognitive scientists should find that it is not cognitively possible, then Schegloff "observed" something that did not actually take place' (Sanders, this volume, p. 75).

Sanders' chapters raises fundamental issues about the relation between cognition and interaction, and highlights just how difficult they are to answer. In the case of the Schegloff example, if there was a strong tension between his finding and that of experimental work in cognitive science, one place to start might be to ask questions about the 'operationalization' of the task in the experiment. Maybe the research approach itself would become the analytic focus. The service that Sanders has done is to offer specific and detailed interpretations of materials and to highlight their relationships to particular studies in cognitive science. More generally, his challenge is to see how far talk must be understood as psychologically motivated and dictated by inner states. One of the features of the chapters in the second half of the book is the novel and rigorous way in which they pick up and develop these issues.

2.   Coulter: language without mind

While Sanders makes the case for interaction researchers taking the findings of cognitive science more seriously than they have up to now, Coulter makes a trenchant case for the incoherence of the whole cognitive science project. In a series of publications (particularly Coulter, 1979, 1983, 1990; see also Button et al., 1995) he has drawn on linguistic philosophy (notably Ryle and Wittgenstein) and ethnomethodology to argue for a position that is anti-mentalist, anti-Cartesian and anti-'telementational'. Instead he argues, following Norman Hunter (1971), that linguistic expressions convey intelligibility without the need to supplement them by something like thinking, deliberation, disambiguation or similar operations as commonly claimed by linguistic theory.

Coulter is dismissive of the common cognitive science approach to discourse comprehension involving cognitive representations. He argues that such an approach confuses understanding discourse with interpreting it, and compounds the problem by developing empirical tests that presuppose the existence of the very thing they are supposed to be testing. He restates the linguistic philosophical critique against mentalism in a strong form that provides a way into this important and relevant body of work.

Coulter also devotes considerable space to highlighting what he sees as a cognitivist strand in the work of conversation analysis, although much more in the work of Schegloff than Sacks. He suggests that Schegloff has drifted into a form of cognitive science that treats parties involved in an interaction as if they were performing analysis or cognitive operations such as problem solving as they interpret talk. That is, it turns talking into a talking and thinking combination. Whatever the merits of this particular critique of Schegloff, whose view of cognition we have illustrated above, Coulter has highlighted a potential ambivalence over the status of cognitive terms and cognitive states in conversation analytic work. We will see this ambivalence explored in different ways in the papers in the second part of this book. It is clear that most of them concede more to a cognitive perspective than Coulter is willing to. The value of Coulter's chapter in this collection is that it offers the most fully non-cognitive, indeed *anti*-cognitive position, thus requiring those who wish to include a cognitive level of analysis of cognitive findings, to make the case for that inclusion.

Whereas Sanders and Coulter mark out different poles on basic issues of the status of cognition, Pomerantz and Schaeffer and Maynard are more concerned with how issues of cognition become live in analysis.

3.   *Pomerantz: using video stimulated comments*

Up to now Pomerantz has addressed the role of cognition in interaction research in different ways. On the one hand, she has developed analyses that show how concepts that are traditionally seen as falling under the purview of cognitive science (attitudes, knowledge) can be understood as interactionally embedded (Pomerantz, 1980, 1984a, b). Her hugely influential work on assessments, for example, shows the way in which assessments can be studied as a conversational practice without starting with the speaker's attitudes (Pomerantz, 1984a). On the other hand, she has attempted to address explicitly the way cognition should be understood, and inserted into, interaction analysis (Mandelbaum and Pomerantz, 1990; Pomerantz, 1990/1991). In her chapter for this volume she addresses issues of cognition from a methodological direction, attempting to marry the two strands of her work.

Many psychological methods take a cognitivist approach to the actor. When a person is interviewed, for example, about why they did something the assumption is that people can access again the very same cognitive resources that led to the action in the first place – their opinions, say, or desires. At the very least the assumption is that they can access reliable memories of the event. As we have seen above, conversation analysts in particular have been sceptical of this way of working, and have overwhelmingly opted to analyze records of actual interaction occurring in natural situations. The advantage is that it captures organizations of interaction, and features of actions and events, that are often hard to formulate, let alone remember. For example, the closing stages of telephone calls have an exceedingly regular pattern to them (see Hopper, 1992; Schegloff and Sacks, 1973), but it is doubtful that people could precisely recall that pattern.

Pomerantz is well aware of the reasons that conversation analysts in particular have avoided interviews and questionnaires. However, she takes the position that there may be cognitive phenomena such as understanding, or aims, that are relevant to peoples' practices. She argues that there are times when reports of such phenomena are a pathway to the phenomena themselves, and that the evidential basis of such reports can be strengthened by stimulating people to comment on video showing their own interaction. Pomerantz develops her argument through a rigorous consideration of particular cases. To end with she considers some basic conversation analytic notions – such as *display* and *orientation* – and suggests that it would be valuable for analysts to go beyond the agnostic stance on cognition implied by these terms, and accept – both in principal and for some analytic practices – that it may be possible to distinguish *real* understandings from *displays* of understanding, and *perceptions* from *orientations*. The challenge here, then, is the suggestion that CA is already more cognitivist than is usually recognized.

4.   *Schaeffer and Maynard: interaction and 'cognitive processing' in
      survey interviews*

In this chapter Schaeffer and Maynard focus on the question of how 'cognitive processing' contributes to the conduct of standardized surveys. It is similar to the Pomerantz chapter in its focus on methodology. However, it argues in the opposite direction. Whereas Pomerantz is arguing for the introduction of some cognitive notions, and some methods underpinned by cognitive thinking, into interaction analysis, Schaeffer and Maynard attempt to show that a range of phenomena in the administering of standardized surveys are more interactional than psychological. The chapter builds on a series of powerful and influential studies of survey research interaction (Maynard and Schaeffer, 1997, 2000; Maynard et al., 2002; see also Houtkoop-Steenstra, 2000).

Schaeffer and Maynard review traditional psychological work on standardized interviews that typically treats both smooth answering and troubled answering as the consequence of the individual cognitive processing of the interviewee. However, they suggest that a close examination of sequences where there is trouble shows that the interviewee's actions are closely coordinated with the actions of the interviewer. For example, they note that silences like the one on line 250 of the following are typically treated as markers of cognitive processing by psychologists.

```
248   IV:    Ohhkay (uh:) would this be considered (.) retail trade
249          whole (.) tale (.) trade or something else.
250          (3.5)
251   FR:    Well (.) Like I say it's just a janitoral service that
252          cleans (.) businesses
253          (0.5)
254   FR:    [when they]'re closed
255   IV:    [Uh  Okay]
256          (3.0)
257   IV:    O::::kay::
258          (1.2)
259   IV:    And let's see what kinda work does he usually do at his
260          job .uh:: [(ju-)]
```

Schaeffer and Maynard, however, suggest that the delay may be a *display* of uncertainty. It may be an interactional resource, indicating that the answer is perhaps not an expected one in that it is a repeat of earlier information (Well (.) Like I say). And the interaction proceeds with the interviewer displaying that they have constructed a codable answer from the respondent's talk. In terms of what is displayed by the interviewee, the interviewer shows that they have picked it up.

Using a series of examples Schaeffer and Maynard argue that 'in many cases the interviewer performs work that the individualistic psychological model of cognitive processing locates in the respondent' (this volume, p. 129). They claim an agnostic stance on the matter of individual cognitions, preferring to focus on what can be observed in the interaction, and how the actions of the interviewer contribute to what had traditionally been seen as cognitive.

5.   *Hopper: a cognitive agnostic in conversation analysis*

This chapter is one of the last pieces of work written by Robert Hopper before his death. His writing has been highly influential within conversation analysis, as has the influence of his numerous PhD students across the fields of sociology, communication and social psychology (see Glenn *et al.*, 2003). This book is dedicated to Robert Hopper – and it is appropriate that he has produced something both subtle on the issue of cognition and fascinating in its insight into the early days of the LBJ presidency.

Hopper's discussion of the status of cognition in conversation leads off from John Heritage's (1990/1991) important paper on the nature of strategy. Heritage tried to distinguish two kinds of strategy. On the one hand, there is strategy where the actor thinks out a goal beforehand and has a conscious, maybe surreptitious plan of how to achieve it. Hopper calls this a pre-strategy – a mentally represented strategy existing and guiding the subsequent interaction. On the other, there is strategic action that is the result of simply following particular conversational routines (which might have some internal complexity) in a non-conscious or planful manner. Hopper calls this an emergent-strategy as the strategic action emerges with the interaction. As he puts it:

no participant anticipates or plans this pattern. Rather, the speakers generate the sequence out of the normal turn-by-turn course of interaction. The pattern turns out to be a kind of found art for analysts, and to some degree for actors. (this volume, p. 140)

Heritage considers this distinction (differently glossed) in terms of two phone calls that are part of a corpus used in many conversation analytic studies. In each call a personal narrative about the recent assassination of Robert Kennedy and the movement of the body is 'touched off' by the organization of the call. Heritage suggests that the two calls together provide evidence for the operation of a pre-strategy. The surprise displayed in the second call seems disingenuous following so soon after the same pattern in the first call. Hopper is more doubtful, and considers the potential workings of these two kinds of strategy in a corpus of calls made from and to President Johnson's office soon after he became president. This series of calls, often doing rather similar things (thanking supporters, accepting congratulations and so on) allows for a more extended examination of the interactional criteria that might be developed for identifying pre-strategies.

Hopper teases away at these calls, trying to identify what evidence would be strong enough. For example, he notes that LBJ receipted a series of compliments in calls in much the same way, but suggests that as a competent conversationalist such receipts are a standard resource, and not something that needs to be consciously planned. However, he notes that the pattern of compliment responses evolves through standard forms to something close to boasting and fishing for compliments, then back to more standard compliment receipts. He focuses on another feature of the calls, which is the introduction of the term 'thrift' into compliment responses. Here is an example (C is compliment, CR is compliment receipt, T is the 'thrift' mention):

C→   DC: ... congratulations on what I thought was a magnificent performance this morning.
CR→   LBJ: Well, I did the best I could.
C→   OC: Well, I thought it was just exceptional (.) really
CR→   LBJ: Bob Anderson and General Eisenhower did say (.) they're
T→   glad we were talking about economy and prudence and watching the dollar ((LBJ continues))

Again, Hopper explores the possibility that these mentions are pre-strategy, a way of LBJ subtly developing the cost cutting agenda that was part of his presidency while deftly doing compliment receipts. Yet even with these latter examples it is hard to show it was planned beforehand, particularly with the fluid insertion in the conversational flow. Even as a pre-strategy it would be more Trukese than European! Hopper concludes cautiously that there are some cases where pre-strategies may be operating but they are both a-typical and hard to pin down. Hopper's chapter is, in many ways, the centre of the book setting up issues that are picked up in a series of studies in the second half of the book.

6.   *Drew: is confusion a state of mind*

Like Hopper, Drew introduces his chapter with a series of cautions against the reading of 'states of mind' from what people say. He notes that the standard conversational patterns for turning down invitations, for example, suggest a state of mind on behalf of the speaker (wanting to accept, but constrained by circumstances). Yet such declinations 'can enable speakers to disguise their actual states of mind (what their actual intentions are, how they really feel etc.)' (this volume, p. 162). Nevertheless, Drew argues that careful analysis of examples can reveal a connection between talk-in-interaction and cognition (see also Drew, 1995).

Drew considers examples of invitation refusals where early and inexplicit signs of refusal are picked up and acted on. He suggests these are 'cognitive moments'. That is, they are moments where a speaker can, in a profound sense, read the other's mind; they can identify intentions and act on those intentions. He develops this way of thinking with the example of 'confusion'. He starts by considering examples where participants use the category 'confusion' attributionally. However, he attempts to go beyond such participants' uses.

His more ambitious aim is to identify 'confusion' as a participant's mental state that has been generated through interaction. Confusion is explored in detail with a series of examples. Drew identifies a number of features that support the use of the analytic category 'confusion' (including repair initiations, styles of acknowledgement, and characteristics of

intonation). Drew notes that this mental confusion is interactionally generated through the confounding of expectations derived from conversational norms. It is the interaction that generates the mental state rather
than the other way around. Nevertheless, this confusion as a cognitive
object need not be salient to participants – for example, participants
do not remark on it. It is not being used as a resource in the interaction, to request clarification say, rather it is evidenced through its conversational symptoms. The general point is to use information about
interaction and its normative organizations to be able to identify, as an
analyst, a particular mental state of confusion. Drew is trying to show
how cognitive psychological topics can be informed by careful analysis of
conversation.

7.   Heritage: cognition in discourse

Heritage's important earlier contribution to theorizing issues of cognition
and interaction has been described above, and is discussed in detail in
Hopper's chapter. In his chapter for the current volume Heritage starts
by noting examples where descriptions of events (in a doctor's surgery, in
a call to the police) are marshalled in a way that displays something about
the position of the caller as 'innocent' or 'unmotivated', thereby under-
pinning the reasonableness or credibility of the reports. This is linked
to a tradition of work that includes studies in ethnomethodology, conversation analysis and discursive psychology (Edwards, 1997; Heritage,
1984a; Pollner, 1987) and picks up themes that will be explored further in the chapters by Wooffitt, Lynch and Bogen, and Edwards and
Potter.

The focus of this chapter, however, is not the relation of cognition
to description, but the way cognition may be embodied in talk-in-
interaction. Heritage has done a series of studies of the use of the particle
'oh' in interaction to indicate a 'change of state' (Heritage, 1984b, 1998,
2002). In his chapter he teases out cognitive themes in this work. For
example, he considers the way 'oh' can 'embody the experience of a recollection' and display that experience for interactionally relevant purposes,
such as when receiving good or bad news, or how it can be used to show
that something relevant has been remembered. In the context of questions it can show that the questioner has not expected the answer. More
generally, he notes the way 'oh-receipts' are linked to the interactional-
sequential logic of questions where the questioner proposes her or himself
as uninformed on some matter and simultaneously projects the answerer
as informed. The questioner's 'oh-receipt' marks the change of state and
ratifies the answer as news. Where such a logic is absent (in classroom

teaching, say, or news interviews) so are 'oh-receipts'. Oh-receipts, then, are closely bound up with epistemic issues of who knows and who does not.

Heritage develops this line of thinking with an exploration of relation between the use of oh-receipts and knowledge entitlement. Oh-receipts can be used to show epistemic supremacy in interaction such as the following:

```
Eve:    No I haven't seen it Jo saw it 'n she said
        she f- depressed her ter[ribly
Jon:                          [Oh it's [terribly depressing.
Lyn:                                   [Oh it's depressing.
```

Heritage highlights the way in sequence Jon and Lyn, who have seen a film, agree with Eve, but oh-preface that agreement. In doing so they index the independence of their access to the film 'and in this context that, relative to Eve, they have epistemic priority: direct rather than indirect, access to the movie' (this volume, p. 199).

Analyses of cases of this kind highlight the way certain elements of talk can be used to display changes of knowledge state, or authority compared to other speakers. Heritage returns repeatedly to the fundamental question for this collection; what is the relation of 'oh' to a change in mental state? His answer is that there *may* be a relationship: 'it might be possible to think of *oh* as directly tied to the experience (and the neuropsychology) of undergoing a 'change of cognitive state', such that the utterance of 'oh' indexes the arrival of such a state as its outward marker' (this volume, p. 216). Nevertheless he offers a number of cautions: cognitive states may change gradually while *oh* utterances are point events; *oh* may be withheld despite the cognitive event; or produced without such an event; and its production is subject to interactional and turn organizational considerations. He argues instead that we treat *oh* first and foremost as a live matter of participants' social concern and accountability, rather than an abstract topic of psychological investigation.

8.   *Wooffitt: from process to practice*

Heritage, Hopper and Drew focus on particular conversational practices and consider their possible involvement with both everyday issues of practical psychological importance and their possible status vis-à-vis cognitive states and processes. They do not tackle the literature on cognitive science, or consider the way it has dealt with the relevant phenomena. In contrast, Wooffitt starts off by considering a particular phenomenon in the psychological literature, that of 'flashbulb memories'. The classic account of flashbulb memories has the receipt of dramatic or shocking news (of the death of President Kennedy, say) leading to a special kind of vivid and enduring memory encoding such that people can not only remember the event, but the routine circumstances in which they received news of it. Recent work has painted a considerably more complex picture. However, Wooffitt's aim is to show that some of the features associated with flashbulb memories are features of the pragmatics of describing certain kinds of events; that is, how they are a conversational rather than a cognitive phenomenon.

Wooffitt draws on his own earlier work (Wooffitt, 1992) in which he studied the organization of reports of 'anomalous events' (poltergeists, UFOs, and such). In particular, it analyzed some of the ways in which speakers constructed reports of such events in ways that attend to a likely sceptical audience. It drew in turn on Sacks' (1984) classic work on the way people may 'do being ordinary' for particular purposes and on Jefferson's (forthcoming) development of this line of thinking. Wooffitt notes that when participants describe anomalous events they are (from a psychological perspective) recollecting those events; the descriptions can be studied as memories.

Wooffitt picks out a number of features of these descriptions that might be relevant to cognitive research. For example, they commonly contain X-Y constructions where the X is a description of the speaker's actions and Y is the report of the first awareness of the phenomenon:

> an' I went in there (.) er:m w- with my mother in
> law and uhm: (.4) friends that were with me
> (1.3)
> **X**   hhh (.) and I was just looking at the coffin
> **Y**   and there was David standing there (.3)
> he was in Blues

Wooffitt argues that the X part of these formulations works as a device designed to establish and display the mundane environment of the experience and the mundane orientation to it by the speaker. As the first part of a contrast it sets up, and highlights, the special or unusual nature of the Y component. It also displays what the speaker was not doing, that is hoping or waiting for something anomalous to happen, and thus perhaps displaying out of the ordinary beliefs. For Wooffitt the point about this pragmatic organization of reports is that if we fail to grasp its practical and rhetorical orientation we may start to see it simply as the consequence of cognitive coding. So the idea that flashbulb memories encode mundane particulars in the brain, through some cognitive and neurological process, fails to consider that such particulars may be an artefact of reporting anomalous or dramatic events. More generally, Wooffitt argues for an enriched approach to human memory, less focused on its cognitive or neurological basis and more attentive to its pragmatics.

9.   Lynch and Bogen: my memory has been shredded

Like Wooffitt, Lynch and Bogen focus on a phenomenon that cognitive psychologists would subsume under the category memory. While Wooffitt draws more directly on conversation analysis and the work of Sacks and Jefferson, Lynch and Bogen draw on ethnomethodology, and the work of Garfinkel as well as the broader tradition of linguistic philosophy. Like Coulter, they are less concerned to develop a dialogue or rapprochement with cognitive psychologists, than to rework everything. They argue that they are not aiming to provide an alternative geography of cognition 'because the concept of "cognition" itself is likely to be dissolved in the course of the displacement from an abstract space of mental representation to a contexture of communicative practices' (this volume, p. 227).

Lynch and Bogen's approach to 'cognitive' topics works with three intertwined strategies. First, select a cognitive science topic such as memory or perception, but located within a particular social setting. Second, consider how this topic becomes intelligible through actions and expressions that are bound to, and understandable within, interactional, pragmatic and political contexts. Third, provide an understanding of the available descriptions of cognitive events or processes in terms of their role in interaction.

Building on their influential study of national scandals, and Iran-Contra in particular (Lynch and Bogen, 1996), they illustrate these basic strategies using the kinds of materials (senate hearings, recordings, documents) that those scandals have incidentally made available. For example, they examine the use of 'memory lapses' in Oliver North's contributions to the Iran-Contra investigation, and the way practices of shredding documents were developed to provide for 'plausible deniability' of key claims. North used 'I don't remember' in testimony so many times that it came to be called the Contra-mantra. They show how his 'don't remember' responses had the virtue of defeating what McHoul (1987) calls the binary logic of yes-no questions. The problem with such questions is that either option can lead to further trouble. On the one hand, a 'yes' can implicate guilt. On the other, a denial is vulnerable to suggesting strategic dissembling if further contradictory evidence is produced.

Lynch and Bogen focus in particular on the interactional logic that distinguishes 'I forgot' from 'I don't remember', noting that the former

potentially concedes much more. They also discuss the role of the counterfactual conditional form of many memory claims in the testimony.
These are claims of the form:

North: I was probably told that in eighty-five or I would've
           asked more questions that I did about it.

In this case, for example, North is able to present a failure to remember
something as indicative that his was acting in an appropriate manner; that
is, a manner that would be unremarkable and therefore unmemorable.
They conclude:

The possibilities of remembering and forgetting are thus logically bound to assessments of particular persons and agent-categories, and are associated with judg-
ments about plausibility and credibility and defences against accusation. (this
volume, p. 239)

They are particularly pessimistic about any integration of this research
with the domain of 'cognitive science', arguing instead that they are
addressing topics in their home environment in a way that cognitive
scientists have failed to do.

10.   *Edwards and Potter: discursive psychology,*
        mental states and descriptions

As we have noted above, Edwards and Potter have been developing a distinctive discursive psychological approach for over a decade, applied to
'psychological' topics such as memory, attribution, categories, scripts and
so on (see Edwards, 1997; Edwards and Potter, 1992a, b, 1993). This
chapter picks out some of the themes in this work as well as summariz-
ing its general programmatic features. It summarizes three basic strands
of DP work: (a) it has respecified and criticized mainstream cognitive
research; (b) it has produced analytic studies of the psychological thesaurus, exploring the situated and rhetorical uses of psychological terms
in peoples' talk; (c) it studies the way psychological themes and orientations are managed, whether psychological terms are used or not.

   This chapter picks out strand b in particular, but simultaneously
addresses the central DP issue of how descriptions of actions and events
provide for psychological inferences. It deals variously with knowing and
not knowing, telling, wanting, hoping, liking and not liking, and thinking.
In each case, the aim is to show how the delicate situated rhetorical use
of those psychological terms is bound up with the performance of practical actions. A particular theme of these analyses is to show that such
terms cannot be understood as simply the expressions of mental states

in the manner of telementation. They can thus be contrasted with cognitive science approaches that might look to treat such words as cognitive tokens.

DP can also be contrasted with a linguistic philosophical approach of the kind developed by Ryle and Wittgenstein and illustrated in this collection by Coulter. Part of this contrast is that DP does not attempt to show cognitivist understandings are incoherent or wrong, but rather to study their use as a practice within public forms of discourse (see Potter and Edwards, 2003). People may talk on the '*proposed and oriented to basis,* that their words are expressing inner thoughts and feelings' (this volume, p. 256) in clinical psychology, for example, or everyday settings. This becomes the analytic topic of DP. This special kind of 'indifference' is similar to that pressed by Lynch and Bogen, and by Wooffitt, although Wooffitt is more optimistic about the potential for fruitful dialogue with cognitive scientists, as are Edwards and Potter.

8.   Issues and implications

This collection includes a range of mature analyses of interaction. Although they take various positions on the status of cognition, and the different kinds of things cognition might be (if anything at all!) they offer very different kinds of analyses to those common in cognitive science. Even Sanders – who in terms of this collection is most directly sympathetic to the application of cognitive science ideas to interaction research – works with a style of analysis unusual in, maybe even antithetical to, the overwhelmingly experimental and conceptual modelling tradition of cognitive work. We will end this introduction and overview by highlighting a few of the issues and implications that will be addressed in different ways in the collection. Without attempting to be comprehensive we will address three themes raised by the chapters and ask more questions than we answer. We hope that readers can usefully hold these in mind while reading the chapters and perhaps return to them at the end.

Plans, strategies and the language of mind

We have already noted a tension between the model of cognitive processes as operating through a language of mind which is closely related to the folk psychology of desires, goals, plans and so on and the ethnomethodological approach to goals and plans that emphasises their complex and often post hoc relation to practice. As we indicated in our discussion of Suchman's (1987) work, in the ethnomethodological picture plans are as much to do with accountability as they are causal templates driving action.

Hopper's paper attempts to address the issue of planning through a focus on process. Can we capture the working of planning in interaction through considering the procedures for receiving compliments? He searches for evidence that pre-strategies have been in operation in a series of such receipts. He asks if there is evidence that the speaker has strategically (in a consciously prepared way) thought out a modification of a compliment receipt to achieve a secondary purpose (e.g. to emphasise the theme of 'thrift' to key figures that will be politically important)? He shows that it is particularly difficult to analytically pin down the operation of such pre-strategies. Part of the difficulty is that any strategy will have to be played out through the contingencies of interaction and work with socially established conversational procedures. Therefore, if there is a strategy at work it has to be fluid and responsive.

This study raises as many deep questions as it answers. If it can be established that there *may* be pre-strategy at work, as Hopper asserts, this leaves the question of what the *status* of such a strategy is. The sort of evidence that is provided is of modifications to standard forms, or standard forms being organized to allow them to piggyback further actions. The implication is that the standard forms are automatic and strategy allows a further level of orchestration of the automatic forms, e.g. to build references to thrift into complement receipts. However, that does not *demonstrate* that such a 'higher order' plan was 'represented' in 'consciousness', perhaps in a propositional form, although it implies a picture of that kind. It *clarifies* the deep cognitive science question, because it directs research attention to particular phenomena, but it does not *answer* that question. For example, could we conceive the sorts of 'higher order' strategic 'thinking' suggested in Hopper's chapter to be itself standardized, more off-the-shelf than bespoke, not requiring a unique propositional solution but dependent on the kind of rich conversational learning history that a human would have who used talk as their major means of getting things done, day in day out, throughout their lives?

Pomerantz has a more developed cognitive ontology in her chapter, suggesting that *understanding*, *aims* and *concerns* can all, on occasion, be treated as cognitive phenomena that influence how a person selects and employs a specific practice. Although she argues effectively for the value of methods of stimulated recall in accessing such things and thereby contributing to improvements in practices, this does not *in itself*, show that such things are cognitive phenomena in the way that a cognitive psychologist might understand the term. To show that a concern can be usefully 'accessed' does not *in itself* show that the concern is a cognitive *object*, a combination of propositions and emotional colour perhaps, existing in a mental space (for a contrasting analysis of 'concern' see, Potter and

Hepburn, 2003). Concerns, aims and understandings are vital parts of lay accounting and they may appear as such in the stimulated recall setting. That does not make their use in that methodological setting a merely descriptive one. Pomerantz argues that we should distinguish between a *display* of understanding, for example, and *actual* understanding. But even if this distinction can be sustained, it does not *in itself* show that understanding must be understood as a cognitive state (Coulter, 1979).

Moments of mind reading

Both Drew and, to a lesser extent, Heritage operate with a distinction between 'verbal conduct' and the speaker's 'cognitive state'. Plainly this distinction is fundamental for exploring the potential connection between this interactional research and research in cognitive science. However, is this distinction discovered in their material, or is it assumed? Is what Drew calls a 'cognitive state' the same thing as a cognitive scientist would mean by that term? We have described some of the variety of assumptions about cognitive states in section 3 above. Drew suggests, in a move similar to that of Pomerantz, that the CA use of the term 'orient to' for characterizing certain features of conduct may be an (inexplicit) cognitive usage. That is, it may simply *stand for* a cognitive state. From this perspective when Emma *orients to* a delay in accepting an invitation as indicating that her invitation is going to be turned down, she is (mentally, internally) *recognizing* that the declination is coming (Drew, this volume, p. 170). The key point, though, is the status of such a *recognition*. Is it a word that is practically useful to explicate Emma's conduct (for example, the upgrading of the invitation with the provision of beer), or is it a conscious (or even unconscious) cognitive state? Does Drew analytically confirm the latter, or is the latter a plausible everyday characterization of what is going on in a culture that tends to offer cognitive characterizations of conduct?

Take the example of 'confusion', which is Drew's main topic. He brilliantly marshals the procedures and findings of CA to identify confusion in conduct. Most relevantly, his analysis attempts to identify confusion that is neither oriented to as such nor used as a resource. However, assuming that he has been successful in this task, does this success show that there is an associated *cognitive state* of confusion? Does everything that people do or show have an associated mental state? Is Drew *discovering* the presence and consequence of cognition or *presupposing* it?

Similar questions can be posed with respect to Heritage's analysis of oh-receipts and changes of state. His analysis skilfully delineates the various pieces of interactional work that 'oh' particles can perform. And he highlights various lines of interactional evidence that suggest that although 'oh' signals a change of state it does not necessarily accompany, on a momentary basis, a change in experience, or cognitive state, or neuropsychology.

The question that remains is whether some inner, psychologically represented change (in consciousness, or cognition, or neural states) takes place, whether yoked immediately to 'oh' or somewhat temporally disengaged. Does the existence of such a change require any specific cognitive analysis? Could 'change of state' be an interactionally inspired gloss on something that we can both access analytically, and recognize as language users, but not require that there is a difference in propositional representations embodied somewhere in neuroanatomy? Could it be equally compatible with some kind of yet to be fully developed connectionist account of competent conduct that requires no realized propositional representations? Indeed, could 'oh-receipts' and the 'changes of states' they signal be useful accounting devices primarily oriented to action, providing a neat, simplified practical way of displaying position change in interaction as an easily understood either/or?

However challenging these questions are for interaction analysis they are at least as challenging for cognitive science insofar as they incorporate either implicit or explicit theories of conduct. The beautifully realized analysis of Drew and Heritage identify phenomena of interaction that a comprehensive cognitive theory of action would need to account for and so far the image of conduct in cognitive science has tended to be abstract and simplified.

The study of mind in action

The possibility of creative debate between cognitive scientists and interaction researchers is an exciting one, and one we hope this collection encourages. As we have indicated, although potentially fruitful the dialogue will be a complex one. The differences are not just of theory and findings; they are about metatheoretical assumptions and methodological practices. For cognitive science researchers used to testing claims through experimental simulations or abstract programming exercises, the sorts of detailed, inductively based descriptive studies typical of conversation analysis and discursive psychology are likely to be hard to accommodate. Hopefully, this volume will highlight the value of taking this research seriously.

Nevertheless, it is likely that some of the interactional research will generate more critical tension with cognitive science work. At the level of theory, interactional research underscores difficulties with the idea of an actor as a socially isolated problem solver. Even the researchers in this collection who most fully embrace at least the *principle* of cognitive states and representations as a topic of study (Sanders, Pomerantz, Drew and, perhaps more cautiously, Heritage, Hopper and Schaeffer and Maynard) highlight just how far any potential cognitive analysis must take into account socially shared and conventionalized procedures of interaction. At the level of method, different strands of interaction research in both CA and DP have highlighted the failures of cognitive science research to encompass the action orientation of talk in research settings. Schaeffer and Maynard provide an excellent example of this in their chapter. It may be that at least some of the inferences from cognitive research studies are artefacts of the failure to appreciate this action orientation (see Edwards, 1997).

Beyond these different kinds of engagement there is another possibility here developed most explicitly in Wooffitt, Lynch and Bogen, and Edwards and Potter, and underscored by Coulter's critique of the very enterprise of cognitive science. This would involve the development of a field of study that would consider phenomena that had been subsumed into cognitive science from a practical and interactional perspective. It would consider both the (ostensibly) mental lexicon and its role in various mundane and institutional practices, and the way (purportedly) psychological issues (knowledge, accountability, attitude, stake and interest) figure within particular practices. This approach would be non-cognitivist in that it would not attempt to *explain* conduct by reference to cognitive entities (such as knowledge, motive, attitudes and so on); those things would figure as topics of study. Whatever else they are, all of the contributions to this volume could be understood as contributions to such an enterprise. Whether it is called the sociology of mind, praxiology, discursive psychology or even social psychology (psychology in and for social practices – why not?) such an interdiscipline has exciting prospects.

Acknowledgement

We would like to thank Derek Edwards, Alexa Hepburn and Liz Stokoe for commenting on an earlier version of this chapter.

Part I

The interface between cognition and action

2 Validating 'observations' in discourse studies: A methodological reason for attention to cognition

Robert E. Sanders

A prominent conversation analyst once questioned my interest in the cognitive foundations of social interaction, saying things like, 'What's the point?' 'Can it help me do my work?' 'What discursive practices can it reveal?' I did not find the scepticism surprising. While the matter is debatable – as publication of this volume demonstrates – interest in, tolerance for, or direct references to, cognition are actively eschewed by a sizable number of researchers within 'discourse studies' (in which I include, alphabetically, applied linguistics and sociolinguistics, argumentation studies, conversation analysis, discourse analysis, discursive psychology, ethnography of communication, language pragmatics, rhetorical communication and semiotics). This chapter addresses those researchers and shows at least one way in which attention to cognition can make a valuable contribution to our work – in fact, analysts all along have been attending to cognition in one of the ways I discuss here, while denying that attention to cognition is relevant.

Of course, I need to be more specific and narrower about what I mean by 'cognition'. The term can refer to speakers'[1] underlying inner states at the moment of producing discourse objects (perceptions, emotions, wants, intentions, etc.), and also applies to more enduring cognitive content (beliefs, concepts, knowledge structures, values, memories) and response biases (e.g., personality traits, habits, attitudes), as well as to processing algorithms that are of interest in cognitive science. In this essay I will be mainly concerned with the value for discourse studies of (1) attention to speakers' underlying inner states in the moment of speaking, specifically whether they were motivated just then to produce the action in question, and (2) attention to cognitive processing.

There are a number of interlocking reasons why there is an animus towards attention to cognition within discourse studies. Most basically, the problem is that attention to cognition runs counter to an anti-cognitivist, neo-behaviourist approach to which many researchers in discourse studies subscribe. It is an approach that mirrors Goffman's (1967) project of accounting for public conduct with as little reference as possible

57

to actors' inner lives, referring instead to the situational and institutional (to which we have added discursive) environment and its constraints on actions in the moment. I refer to this as a *neo*-behaviourist stance because, as Edwards and Potter point out in an exposition of discursive psychology, it is not strict behaviourism in the positivist, *etic*, sense of examining behaviours as uninterpreted, physical occurrences. It is an interpretivist, *emic*, examination of behaviours as social/institutional occurrences, actions, that foregrounds 'participants' own concepts and understandings as these are deployed in practices of interaction' (Edwards and Potter, 1992, p. 100). Edwards and Potter say that 'Such a focus [on social practices conducted primarily through language] does not exclude a concern with the mental or cognitive, but this [the mental or cognitive] . . . is primarily understood in terms of the part it plays in interaction'. But they also note that this approach is sometimes avowedly anti-cognitivist, and 'considers mentalistic concepts such as memory in terms of publicly available social practices' (1992, p. 100).

Thus, like strict behaviourists, many in discourse studies confine their enquiries to persons' observed behaviour and environment, doing so partly to gain stronger ground empirically, and greater parsimony. And again like strict behaviourists, they also confine their enquiries in that way because they contend that the orderliness of the phenomena – in our case, discourse objects regarded as social rather than psychological phenomena – is to be found in their observable composition and positioning rather than underlying mental processes.

But there are more specific, more telling reasons for an animus towards attention to cognition in discourse studies, most of them implicit, many of them sound. They boil down to the following series of ontological, and following that, practical, concerns. Ontologically, (1) cognition is arguably irrelevant: the properties and regularities of interactions and texts may not be reliably an externalization of inner states (cognitions), but instead may result from discourse practices and activities with their own organizing logic, an organizing logic that may even constrain or interfere with the expression, and perhaps even the occurrence, of inner states. (1a) There has been a notable lack of success in attitude-change research in establishing a systematic relationship between persons' inner states (especially beliefs and attitudes) and their public actions (Deutscher, 1973, 1993). (2) Attention to cognition is associated with an emphasis on *individual agency* and *individuals' behaviour*, including linguistic behaviour, whereas discourse studies predominantly emphasise *collective* or *co-constructed discursive practices*.

Then there are practical considerations. (1) Regardless of whether it is for the sake of making visible the intentions, attitudes, or even cognitive processing from which the content and positioning of discourse objects presumably spring, attention to cognition does not contribute to, and potentially may distract from, what is to be learned about the orderliness of discourse from a close analysis of naturally occurring interactions and texts. (2) A close analysis of persons' discourse practices is more likely to provide useful data for researchers of cognition than vice versa. (3) Even if a discourse object were an externalization of an inner state, analysts do not have a reliable basis for knowing that it is, or what the inner state is, in any instance (see Heritage, 1990/91). (4) Attention to cognition in discourse can promote the 'intentional fallacy' (as literary critics used to call it) – the view that a discourse object's meaning or function is based on the speaker's intention in producing it (Searle, 1969), or at least on what intention the speaker intended to be recognized as having (Grice, 1957). This invites analysts to rely on ascriptions of speaker intention to support claims about discourse meanings, instead of relying on analysis of a discourse object's composition and positioning in a larger whole. It also poses the danger of overlooking meaningful variations in objects' composition and positioning whenever ascribed intentions are regarded as being constant.

I do not take issue with the neo-behaviourist stance above nor do I contest the more specific concerns I enumerated, in fact I endorse them. Yet I contend that the animus towards attention to cognition they foster needs to be tempered. The primary reason for this, which I develop in the body of this chapter, is that attention to underlying cognition, i.e., persons' inner states and processing algorithms, respectively, gives us a warrant for many of our 'observations' and a check on their soundness. In the following sections, I will elaborate on the reasoning for this, and after that discuss some relevant empirical instances.

Attention to cognition

The need for attention to cognition, despite the arguments against it, arises from the fact that the phenomena we analyze are not physically objective behaviours (motions) but *meaningful* behaviours (actions, through speech and other expressive resources). As a result, our 'observations' of what has occurred actually are *interpretations* of the discourse objects in question, as well as interpretations of relevant specifics in their environment (including the specification of what makes such specifics 'relevant'). The problem is to ensure that our observations/interpretations are valid, and not just in the 'eye of the beholder'. There are two reasons for wanting that. One is to capture an essential fact about discourse: for the producers and consumers of particular discourse objects, their meaning and function is relatively stable and reliably knowable, not inter-pretively open-ended in the way literary texts are. Unless that were so, the phenomena we examine – meaningful expression, communication, inter-action – could not occur. The other reason to concern ourselves with the validity of our observations/ interpretations is so that we can carry on as social scientists (to advance knowledge about the systemics of texts and interactions) rather than as literary critics (to enrich understandings of particular discourse objects).

The problem more specifically is that many of our claims are about 'what people do with words', and the specific components, compositions and sequential positioning of discourse objects which accomplish that. Evidence for these claims depends on its being descriptively accurate that the objects we examine *are doing* what we say they are. We currently rely on one safeguard to ensure this, a potent one, but only one. This safeguard is a variation on linguists' reliance on their own intuitions as native speakers as a valid source of descriptive claims about specific syntactic objects such as whether they are well- or ill-formed, same or different, compound or complex, Type X or Type Y, etc. (cf. Searle, 1969). The version of this implicit in discourse studies is:

As long as we are all speakers of the same language (analysts and their colleagues, and the producers and consumers of the discourse objects in question) and equiv-alently acculturated, the native social and discursive knowledge with which ana-lysts' colleagues are equipped allows our colleagues themselves to serve as a check on the soundness of specific observational claims insofar as research reports give them access to the 'raw data' on which analysts' claims are based.

This methodological safety net applies, but in a more complicated way, when it comes to ethnographic research, and more generally, to the increasing linguistic and cultural diversity of our scholarly community and our data. Ethnographers have to be sure that their observations and claims are submitted to natives for confirmation (see Philipsen, 1977). And in a linguistically and culturally diverse scholarly community, those of us who are not native to the discourse phenomena under consider-ation have to rely on those of our colleagues who are to spot analysts' 'observational' and descriptive idiosyncrasies. It is consistent with this that cross-cultural comparisons have been used to both uphold and ques-tion descriptive/interpretive claims (e.g., Moerman's, 1988, support of some conversation analysts' generalizations; or Rosaldo's, 1982, critique of Searle's, 1976, claims about directives).

Still, such safeguards are not always enough. Theoretical linguists, who also rely on their intuitions as a validity check, do not rely on them solely. They also rely on the internal consistency and completeness of formalisms that are founded on those intuitions and should be sustainable across the intuitions of diverse analysts. We lack formalisms in discourse studies (so far) that could provide such checks on our intuitions. For the most part we seem to have done well without them – claims seem grounded robustly enough in the raw data adduced for them that there are few debates about analysts' descriptions. Yet we need some kind of additional check on our observations/interpretations, at least sometimes. There are specific instances when it is debatable how to describe/interpret a discourse object (even with reference to the way producers and consumers of the object treated it), and yet a claim the analyst is making depends on only one of the object's descriptions/interpretations being valid and not others that are discursively possible.

Of course, it is sometimes equivocal how to describe/interpret discourse objects because of their composition and positioning, not because of our limitations as analysts, and when that is the case, their equivocality is a fact about them that needs to be captured. But there are instances when discourse objects may seem descriptively/interpretively equivocal to analysts that are not so to their producer (and possibly consumers to whom they were addressed), but the analyst does not know enough to resolve it. Analysts then have the following choices. (1) Abandon any such discourse object as evidence, and/or supplement it with additional, less equivocal, instances. This is the most scientifically prudent option, but it is not always feasible. There are times when analytic interest is in the specific object(s) in question, or when less equivocal instances are unlikely to exist (as in the case of children's discourse). (2) Undertake to find out (e.g., through interviewing informants) what the producer and perhaps consumers of that object know (situationally, culturally) that would resolve its equivocality. This can enrich and ground our work when practicable, but for much of our data, consumers and producers are either anonymous, inaccessible, or ill-equipped to provide answers (as in the case of impaired speakers or, again, children). Failing the first and second options, we end up at the third. (3) Undertake to establish whether or not it is at least *cognitively possible* – with reference to the person's inner states in the moment and/or processing capabilities – for the producer of the discourse object to have formed it as he or she did so it would have the description/interpretation in question.

My interest here is in the third recourse, when attention to cognition is needed for the purpose of validating descriptions/interpretations. Specifically, in order to establish whether it is cognitively possible for the producer to have made that use of those words, we have to consider whether the producer *would have* done so (given his or her inner states at the time) and whether the producer *could have* done so (given the complexity of the processing involved). Despite the animus towards attention to cognition in discourse studies, the concern with 'would have' is relatively common already and, as I will elaborate, unavoidable. My purpose in bringing it up is not to recommend something we already do, but to show that it is commonly done, and that it can be done with sufficient rigour that we need not try to disguise it. The concern with 'could have' introduces a new reason for attention to cognition, and a new source of corroborating evidence.

Before proceeding, I should address two concerns. First, it might seem undesirable that validating our observational claims in terms of what people cognitively would and could do positions work in discourse studies as being accountable to work in cognitive studies. But it could not be otherwise, unless we are prepared to contend that people are unfettered by limits on what is cognitively possible when they produce or comprehend discourse objects. Moreover, the relationship between studies of discourse and of cognition runs in the other direction too. It is just as possible for our observations about what people do with words (and other modes of expression) to provide a check and corrective on what studies of cognition deem is possible (see Schegloff, 1991b; Goodwin, 1995b).

Second, it might seem unavoidable that if we attend to cognition, we will be unable to sustain our emphasis on the co-construction of discourse objects and discursive practices. It is true that much work on cognitive processes (reasoning, problem-solving, etc.) has had an individualistic focus. In addition, this work has been normative about how people *should* reason, more than descriptive of what people actually do, and thus at odds with the focus in discourse studies on the well-formedness of situated, observed practices. However, Lave (1988) has helped counter the latter tendency (towards citing norms rather than describing practices) by addressing cognitive processes that are utilized in situated activities and are adapted to everyday practicalities, bringing cognitive studies out of the laboratory and into the field. And my own work (Sanders, 1987, 1997) counters the former tendency (towards an individualist perspective) by giving attention to cognitive processes by which individuals participate with others in co-constructing interactions, specifically, interactively produced discourse objects.

Observational claims and issues of 'would'

Motivation to produce the action in question

Aside from its seeming inconsistency with an animus towards attention to cognition, it is not at all remarkable that consideration of speakers' motives is already commonplace in discourse studies, as I will illustrate. This is because it is important within discourse studies to account for the situated meaningfulness of a discourse object, which usually includes identifying what action it counts as. Because actions presuppose intention, they therefore cannot be identified or described without reference to the speaker's motive in producing the discourse object in question.

Edwards and Potter (1992a) contend that for the purposes of discourse studies, our interest is in the *social* or *discursive reality* of inner states, which is what Grice (1957, 1975) and perhaps also Searle (1969) attended to – a 'concern with the mental or cognitive . . . understood in terms of the part it plays in interaction' (Edwards and Potter, 1992a, p. 100). But this should not be taken to mean that we do not end up considering what the speaker's actual inner state was. If we are to make claims about the situated meaningfulness of a discourse object based in part on what intentions we ascribe to the person who produced it, it would be circular to cite the intentions we can infer from that object alone, on that interpretation. Analysts' practice typically includes ascribing a motive that *any reasonable person* could be expected to have under the circumstances, given the discursive choices the person evidently made in producing the discourse object(s) in question. But that is still a flimsy reed.

I have proposed that inferences of motive are bolstered by the degree to which they are internally consistent across a larger, encompassing discursive whole to which the person contributed (Sanders, 1987). Inferring a consistent motive across discourse objects that a person produces in a given instance provides us with grounds for ascribing motives that are independent of what can be inferred just from the discourse object of interest. Moreover, insofar as we concern ourselves with the *consistency* of motives inferred from the composition, positioning and production of discourse objects within a larger whole, we end up taking into account something whose basis is not purely discursive – that consistency. It is difficult to identify a source of such consistency other than the person's actual inner states. Granted that this only gives us access to inner states through the person's discourse, and indirect access at that, it is as much access as anyone typically has to a person's inner states, whether one is an analyst, or someone to whom the discourse was addressed, or the person who produced it.

I have posited elsewhere (Sanders, 1997) that an inferential procedure that applies to both speech and physical actions within conventional tasks and activities, is to first posit the simplest, most direct – the optimal – way to meet the current demand to continue the task or activity in progress. One can then infer what the speaker's motivation would have been (beliefs, emotions, wants, etc.) to add to or alter that optimal response so it becomes less direct and more complicated in that specific way.[2] This provides a basis for ascribing the motive that any reasonable person would have under the circumstances, as well as inferring that specific person's motive from the composition, positioning and production of particular discourse objects. This is what we find analysts having done, or having a basis for doing, in the following cases.

Illustrative cases

In the following two cases, an observational/interpretive claim is made that depends critically on the inner states the analysts ascribe to the speaker. In the first analysis, the motive is ascribed entirely on the basis of what any reasonable person would have wanted in that circumstance when the discourse object in question was produced. I will show that that analysis can be bolstered, but also it has to be amended, when one recognizes that there is a consistent motive for *both* the utterance in question and the utterance that follows. The second case below is also about an observational/interpretive claim that relies on inferring a motivation that any reasonable person would have, but the analysis in this case is bolstered with evidence that the ascribed motivation is consistent across turns by the same speaker.

'Motivation' attributable to the speaker as a reasonable person

Schegloff's (1996) analysis of the action, *confirming an allusion*, began with the observation that persons sometimes directly echo what the prior speaker just said. In some cases this happens in the following environment. Person A speaks in such a manner as to allude to his or her state of mind or physical state, a perception, a feeling, an assessment, etc. Person B produces a formulation of what was alluded to. Person A repeats Person B's formulation of the allusion, using the same words, often in the course of going on to say something more. Schegloff characterizes the functionality of exact repetitions that occur after an allusion and a formulation as confirming both that there had been an allusion and confirming the correctness of Person B's formulation of what Person A had alluded to. Among his examples is the following, where a radio interviewer (Edwards) is interviewing a writer (Shreve):

Edwards:		D'you:: (.) don' write fer- (.) English professors.=
Shreve:	→	=·mhh No=I don' write fer English professors.. ·hh
		I don' think I have an enormous following amongst
		English professors? nhhh
Edwards:		.hhh You write fer readers.
Shreve:	→	.hh I really write fer readers. 'n I think . . .

Following his explication of the action *confirming an allusion* Schegloff introduces and discusses 'less transparent instances'. One of these is the following, where a speaker markedly does a word search whose result is to *avoid* producing an exact repetition. Schegloff takes this as an active effort by the speaker to avoid confirming an allusion, and thus as evidence of the speaker's awareness of what an exact repeat would count as at that sequential point. This happened during Shane's and Michael's telling of an incident, where in their tellings there is some repartee about who is at fault. Schegloff explains that the story is first told by Michael as an illustration of ways in which Shane is 'less than generous'. Michael's story is that he had been riding a bike for half an hour and was very thirsty, that Shane offered to get Michael a glass of water, and that Michael was disappointed that instead of the 'big mo:njo drink' he was expecting, Shane presented him with a 'Fuckin dixie cup'. At that point, Shane, positioned as being to blame for this, provides an account in which, despite Shane's remonstrations, it was Vic the server who refused to dispense a larger portion (referred to in line 31 as '[h]ee' –' 'At's w'd'ee put (it in)'):

```
31    Shane:                ...'At's w'd'ee put (it in) I(h) said wait a minute. Vi:c.
32                          {nh ·hh (·)/(0.6)} I said (ziss is) f'r d'two
33                          peo:ple.
34                          (1.7)
35    Shane:                An (.) he s'd (we:y) muh man at's w'tche ge: t,
36    Nancy:                mm hm hm
37                          (0.8)
38    Michael:    →         Eez gitt'n li'l cheap there. ha:[h.
39    Shane:                                               [Y: ah. I think
40                →         he's gett'n a li'l bit uh ti:ght. wid is eh::p
41                          (1.4)
42    Shane:                B't I had the big glass . . .
```

Schegloff's interest in this datum is that when Michael makes an assessment about Vic (line 38: 'Eez gitt'n li'l cheap there'.), Shane almost but not quite echoes it. After starting to echo Michael's assessment of Vic (lines 39–40), Shane vocally hesitates ('uh'), and then instead of using the same adjective as Michael had ('cheap') he replaces it with the synonym 'ti:ght'. The question is, was Shane actively seeking to avoid echoing Michael perfectly, and thus avoid the action of confirming an allusion, as Schegloff posits? Or was it just a coincidence that Shane markedly searched for a word that could have but did not duplicate Michael's? If we regard it as the former, then we end up having to conclude something that Schegloff has been arguing for some time – that utterances are designed fundamentally as actions, including actions for which we do not even have a name in our vocabulary of action-verbs (contrast the action *to confirm an allusion*, with such actions as *to promise*, *to advise*, *to warn*, *to threaten*, etc.).

In order to describe Shane's word search as an (anti-)action – the *dis*confirmation of an allusion – Schegloff would at minimum have to show that Shane was *motivated* to do that (anti-)action. Schegloff does so by adducing a motive that any reasonable person in Shane's position would have, to avoid undercutting himself. He considers that because Shane told the story in such a way as to shift blame from himself to Vic, he set the stage for Michael to be the one to then explicitly blame Vic. It would have thus been self-defeating for Shane to confirm his allusion by echoing Michael, thus making it official that it was he who was blaming Vic.

This redirection of blame away from Shane . . . would be subverted if Shane were understood to have himself planted this sense of Vic having been at fault for the episode, with Michael merely making it explicit. (Schegloff, 1996: 104)

Sometimes ascribing motives on the basis of what reasonable persons in general would want in that circumstance is all that we can do, and so the matter would have to end there. Given the happenstance that Shane undertakes a word search at the last juncture for ending up echoing Michael or not, it does at least provide grounding for Schegloff's observation/interpretation.

However, the motive Schegloff ascribes to Shane is not consistent with the motive that can be inferred from what Shane goes on to say after a silence. At line 42, Shane adds 'B't I had the big glass'. He thus discloses that Vic had given him *two* glasses of water, one larger than the other, and that he (Shane) had taken or been given the large one for himself. This reveals that either Shane is to blame after all for the small portion that Michael had been given and complained about, or that Vic had provided Shane with a bigger glass than he did Michael because he favoured Shane or was being 'ti:ght' towards Michael personally. There is no evident reason for Shane to have added this disclosure other than wanting to reveal his 'guilt' or favoured status or Michael's victimage. This is at odds with the motive Schegloff ascribes to him for his previous word search – that he had sought to shift blame away from himself and wanted to avoid being on record as doing so – and thus jeopardizes Schegloff's 'observation' that Shane's word search was the (anti-)action of *dis*confirming his prior allusion to Vic as the one to blame.

However, it happens that in this case there is a different motive one can ascribe to Shane that supports making the same observational claim that Schegloff did (that Shane was avoiding the confirmation of an allusion), a motive moreover that applies both to the word search in question and to Shane's subsequent disclosure. This consistency of motive across utterances strengthens the observational claim.

Consider that Shane's disclosure in line 42 represents him as having had his own interests met while Michael's were not, and that he had thus got the better of Michael in the process. Shane's having then recounted the event so as to shift blame away from himself, leading Michael to then blame Vic, is a parallel case – Shane saw to his own interests (by shifting blame) and got the better of Michael (who did not see through this and was taken in so as to shift blame from Shane to Vic). Shane's disclosure in line 42 exposes both of his misdeeds at once, and in doing so his own chicanery (and wit), and Michael's ingenuousness. Let us ascribe to Shane the motive of wanting to play this double trick on Michael and get credit for it. Doing so required that he lure Michael into being his unwitting victim (perhaps for the second time), and only then disclose what he had done. Had he confirmed his allusion, then he would have given Michael grounds for having blamed Vic, and thus would not have positioned Michael as his victim 'again'. In addition, if he had gone on to disclose that Michael had been his victim previously, after having sought to make Vic the one to blame and acknowledging it, Shane would have seemed mean-spirited and not playful or clever.

One cannot claim that Shane disconfirmed an allusion without being able to attribute relevant motivations to him. The question for analysts is how can one know what a speaker's motivations were. One option is to posit the motives that any reasonable person would have given the situational exigency of the moment, with that exigency being inferred from what the participants say, how they respond to each other, and what else one knows about the situation. It is this approach that Schegloff took in assessing the situation as one in which Shane was faced with undercutting himself if he confirmed the allusion, something reasonable persons would want to avoid. The alternative, or perhaps an additional, method is to examine two or more utterances by the same person to find out whether they can be interpreted as acts that have a common motivational (or intentional) basis. I applied this latter method in reanalyzing Shane's motivation, and we see it being applied as well in the following case.

'Motivation' attributable to the speaker consistently across turns
Potter (1998b) examines multiple utterances produced by Leslie in which she describes to her husband a passer-by she had seen walking in their neighbourhood, about whom she had informed the police. Potter's focus is that Leslie's utterances are composed in such a way as to render this passer-by as having been a suspicious or sinister character: 'this very shifty

looking character'; 'e ↑looked ih (0.2) u- ↑right in ↓our dining room'; 'An' a ↑very sorta sidelong cra:fty look'; 'hhe wz carrying a ↑suit↓case you see:, . . . An a Bee:jam ba:g [((a supermarket bag))]'.

The thesis Potter pursues is that it would miss something important to regard these utterances as simply externalizing and foregrounding Leslie's actual inner perceptual experience of observing this passer-by. They have a strategic aspect. They portray her inner experience of the man in a way that justifies Leslie's having reported the man to the police. If this observation/interpretation of Leslie's utterances were descriptively accurate, then Potter has empirical support for a contention he has often made (also see Sanders, 1989), that inner experience does not dictate what we say, but that it provides us with raw material, a generic resource, to draw on as needed for the discursive purposes at hand.

But is it descriptively accurate to regard Leslie's utterances as having that strategic aspect? The alternative possibility is that these utterances are actually expressions of (her memory of) the way she in fact did experience the man and his conduct, that they were dictated by her actual inner state at the time (e.g., fear or suspicion). To observe/interpret Leslie's descriptions as being the actions he contends they are, Potter would have to adduce a motivation – other than what her inner states dictated – for Leslie to produce the descriptions in just that way. And Potter does just that. He first adduces a motivation that could be attributed to any reasonable person in Leslie's culture in the same position. Potter stipulates that in Leslie's culture, 'reporting someone who has not committed a crime to the police is potentially a delicate matter. It may make you vulnerable to be treated as a snitch, a busybody, or even as paranoid'. (Potter, 1998b, p. 37). Hence, for one to make a report simply about a suspicious person, any reasonable person in this culture is faced with the exigency of having to make such reporting seem justifiable. This ascribed motivation (wanting to seem justified in reporting the man, not a busybody or paranoid) is consistent – applies equally well – across Leslie's' several utterances in which she describes/vilifies the passer-by. But, of course, those are precisely the utterances whose description/interpretation are in question, and so if the matter ended there, the analysis would be circular. However, it is also consistent with this ascription of motivation that, as Potter shows, when Leslie reaches the point in her narrative where she reports that she informed the police about this man, she represents herself as having been uncertain and hesitant ('So I thought ↑well I dunno I'll tell the police about him'), a state that presupposes that she orients to calling the police as a delicate matter.

The strength of Potter's claim that Leslie's descriptions had a strategic aspect is that he specifies a motivational basis for this that is grounded in two independent ways. The motivation is grounded first in ascribing an exigency that Leslie faced: given a cultural premise that making reports to the police about a suspicion is a delicate matter, the exigency for reasonable members of the culture is that in disclosing such actions they have to show that they were justified. Second, Potter could ascribe the same motive to different descriptions – to the way Leslie described the passer-by and the way she described her decision to make the report.

Observational claims and issues of 'could'

Consider what is required of someone to produce an action – a specific, desired action. It puts a notably greater cognitive burden on the speaker than just expressing a particular thought or feeling. To reliably state a proposition that expresses a particular thought or feeling, one only needs a mastery of a language shared with one's hearers. To reliably effect a particular action, however, one is faced with projecting what details of form and content a discourse object must have, in the moment, to achieve a particular functionality,[3] i.e., to effect a specific change in the social/discursive or psychological status quo. It is logically possible, however, that to achieve a particular functionality, one would have to express something one does not want to – or that in expressing what one wants to, the resulting utterance would have an undesired functionality. The safest and simplest solution that circumvents having to expend much cognitive effort would be to adopt a conventional formula whose functionality is relatively certain and whose content is relatively unimportant by virtue of being recognizably a conventional formula.

But when one has no conventional formula to draw on, shaping what one says to have *the* desired (or *a* desired) functionality, and also to express what one wants to, poses a compositional task that roughly corresponds to the logic of Brown and Levinson's (1987) politeness strategies. Prior to speaking a person would have to be able mentally to compare alternative ways of phrasing what he or she wants to express in order to identify a phrasing that has the/a desired functionality, or alternative phrasings with the desired functionality whose content one is willing to express. If no phrasing options are found that have the/a desired functionality and also directly express what one wants to, one can either devise indirect or mitigated forms of expression, or opt to express something else that has the desired functionality, or refrain from speaking altogether.

We have good informal evidence that people do engage in such processing (mainly the occurrence of self-corrections and word searches, as well as a variety of efforts to improve a person's interaction skills; cf. Greene and Burleson, 2003). It is another matter whether such processing is typically exhaustive or involves shortcuts like conventionalized solutions and satisficing; whether it is ever done consciously, and to what extent and under what circumstances; whether there are individual differences in such processing, for example in speed or complexity, etc. Whatever the details, the complexity of the computations one would have to engage in, and/or chances of error, would probably increase in proportion to how ill-defined the context is, and/or how little background knowledge the hearer can be counted on to have to make the needed connections between what was said and the local context.

While much research on language processing has been done, we know relatively little about discourse processing, especially the cognitive (com-putational) resources speakers typically rely on to produce actions (but see Greene, 1984, 1995; and O'Keefe and Lambert 1995). We do not know enough to be immune to the following conundrum. When a speaker (of a certain kind) is 'observed' to produce an action, but it seems compli-cated to have produced the action in that way in that context, it is equally possible that (a) the observation is open to question because persons (of that kind) may not be capable of the processing that the speaker would have had to do in the present case, or (b) the observational claim is sound, and the production of that action in that way in that context is revealing, as noted above, about the power of the computational resources speakers (of that kind) have at their disposal.

Of course, we will not be able to resolve the soundness of an obser-vational claim in that way if it is the case that we do not know enough about the relevant cognitive processes to decide the matter. Corroborat-ing observational evidence would be needed that this is something people do. Barring that, it would be prudent to be tentative about the observa-tional claim, pending a check of existing research on cognitive processes to ascertain whether people have been found capable of such processing by decomposing the action in question so as to specify (at least some of) the computations and discriminations that the speaker would have had to make. Failing that, it would become a matter for future research on cognitive processes to find evidence as to whether persons have computa-tional resources that would make it possible for them to produce actions with the complexity of the one in question.

Illustrative cases

In this section, I will first discuss two instances in which it is equivocal whether the speaker in question is producing actions or not, depending on what cognitive resources we credit that person with having. The first involves a toddler, the second a normal (non-impaired) adult.

A toddler's interaction

The following interaction was between 19-month-old Allison and her mother (Bloom, 1973, pp. 106–07). Although her mother clearly treats Allison's utterances as actions, this could be over-interpretation if one adopts a conservative position about the linguistic/expressive competence of toddlers, let alone their pragmatic, and especially their neo-rhetorical (Sanders and Freeman, 1997), competence.[4] Instead of achieving functionality as responses to her mother, Allison's utterances could just as easily be regarded as purely expressive noticings/namings of the various objects around her as they came to her rapidly shifting attention (cookie, juice, cup). It is easy to analyze the first part of the interaction in that conservative way:

1 A: Mommy *((offers cookie to M))*
2 M: Oh, thank you.
3 A: Cookie.
4 M: Thank you. *((taking cookie))*
5 A: Juice. *((looking at empty cups))*
6 M: Juice? Shall we have some juice? *((shaking juice can))*
7 A: Cup. *((pointing inside cup))*
8 M: In the cup?

From a conservative perspective, discounting Allison's mother's attributions, Allison did not offer a cookie in line 1 but held it up for display, perhaps to call Mother's attention to it. Her utterance 'Cookie' in line 3 merely named it. In the same way, her utterance 'Juice' in line 5 was not a request (as her mother evidently understood it) but a naming in response to seeing a can of juice. Her utterance 'Cup' in line 7 would likewise have been a naming response to seeing the cup. But of course, like the liberal reading below, this conservative reading does not rest on empirical observables. It is predicated on denying that it is cognitively possible for Allison to do much more than call attention to objects, states and behaviours by naming them (whether naming objects just to do so or because the referent has become salient to the child for any of several dispositional reasons, e.g., liking it, wanting it, frightened of it, etc.).

However, we have some basis in work on cognitive and linguistic development to reject the conservative view, and to regard Allison's mother as correct in having understood her to have initiated a request to have juice. Wootton (1997) gives considerable attention to children's requesting, both in terms of direct observation of their discourse, and in terms of research on cognitive development. He cites Bruner, Roy and Ratner (1982) to support the claim that children do start requesting (rather than seeking to take) objects at around twelve months. Moreover,

Allison's syntactic forms, and her use of physical displays and gestures as supplementary, are typical of requesting practices among children of her age. Wootton goes on to survey existing ideas about the cognitive basis children have for doing this, the most relevant one here being scripts: 'Nelson (Nelson and Gruendel 1981) first explored the possibility that through participation and observation children build up event representations, scripts concerning canonical ways in which familiar events proceed' (Wootton, 1997, p. 37). This seems potentially applicable not just to the basics of requesting in which I will propose that Allison engaged – to achieve transfer of the possession of an object – but in Allison's case to the several steps canonically involved in serving a drink of juice about each of which she could and did make a request (whether to serve juice at all, then in what kind of vessel to serve it).

Allison's request sequence about juice continues beyond the extract above, and the larger sequence makes visible two aspects not captured by Wootton's data, nor by work on children's cognition that he cites. The question is whether it is cognitively possible for Allison to do what she seems to be doing. The following is a fuller extract:

5   A: Juice. *((looking at empty cups))*
6   M: Juice? Shall we have some juice? *((shaking juice can))*
7   A: Cup. *((pointing inside cup))*
8   M: In the cup?
9   A: *((Picks up one cup; picking up second cup; holding it*
10   *up to M))* Mommy juice
11 M: Mommy juice?
12 A: No. *((putting cup down))* Baby. *((shaking own cup))*

The first aspect of interest here is that if we consider this series of requests as interconnected, then each of Allison's successive requests build on the (presumptive) success of the prior request. Note that Allison did not directly answer Mother's question-formulation in line 6 ('Juice? Shall we have some juice?') of her request in line 5. Instead of directly answering Mommy's question-formulation with 'Yes,' she said 'Cup' in line 7. Nor did she answer 'yes' in lines 9–10 to her mother's question-formulation in line 8 ('In the cup?') of Allison's putative request in line 7 for the juice to be served in a cup. Instead she said 'Mommy juice' (holding up the second of two cups) in line 10. If she was in fact being responsive in lines 7 and 9–10, then Allison must have relied on the Gricean Cooperative Principle to implicate 'Yes' while, and by making an additional request: line 7 could implicate '[Yes I do want juice but I want it to be served in a] cup'; and lines 9–10 could implicate '[Yes I do want it served in a cup, but I want this particular cup used for] mommy juice'. Answering her mother in those ways requires that Allison be cognitively able to project what could be said in that moment to achieve a specific functionality (a request, an implicature), and to solve that problem with notable efficiency (in that her utterance of a single word in lines 7, and a word pair plus gestures in lines 9–10, each achieve both an affirmative response and a further request).

In short, if we observe/interpret that Allison was being responsive in each subsequent request to what was said before, Allison had to be capable of producing and apprehending indirectly expressed propositions. She had to interpret her mother's formulation-questions as indirectly assenting to her prior request ('Juice? Shall we have some juice?'; 'In the cup?'; 'Mommy juice?'). Allison also had to expect Mommy to interpret each of her subsequent requests as indirectly affirming that the answer to her mother's prior formulation-question was *yes*. To my knowledge there is little basis in work on children's discourse processing for concluding one way or another whether children of Allison's age could orient consistently to what their own and an interlocutor's utterances express indirectly.

It is clearly a question that would be useful to us for cognitive scientists to pursue (as well as a question that our data suggests cognitive scientists would find it useful to pursue). If children younger than, say, 24 months, are not found to be capable of comprehending indirectness, then we have to regard Allison as producing a disconnected series of requests (to have juice, to use a cup, etc.). If they are capable of apprehending and producing utterances on that basis, however, then we would have support for observing/interpreting Allison as having produced a single, complex, request incrementally (to have juice served in a cup, and moreover in a specific cup and/or served to mommy as well).

The second aspect of this request sequence that Wootton's (1997) study does not capture occurs in line 12. Allison's utterance seems responsive (it directly answers a *yes-no* question with 'No'). Yet it says 'No' to a question that simply echoes in interrogative form what Allison had just said.

9   A: *((Picks up one cup; picking up second cup; holding it up to M))*
10   Mommy juice
11   M: Mommy juice?
12   A: No. *((putting cup down))* Baby. *((shaking own cup))*

Allison's response in line 12 seems unequivocally to be a rejection and correction of what her mother's prior question-formulation implicated. Admittedly it is unclear what is specifically at issue for Allison. Her request in lines 9–10 is equivocal, and this may be why her mother simply echoes it rather than providing a formulation as in her prior turns: in holding up a cup and saying 'Mommy juice', Allison might have been asking Mommy to have juice *also*, or she might have been asking mommy to serve her juice in a particular cup, either the cup for mommy's juice or *not* that cup. Allison's correction in line 12 can apply to either reading. For Allison to say 'no', while switching which cup she held up, and offer the correction 'Baby' could have been in response to understanding her mother as asking in line 11 whether she wanted Mommy to have juice *instead* of Allison, rather than *also*. Or it could have been in response to understanding her mother as asking whether Allison was inviting Mommy to have juice, whereas Allison had asked that her juice be served in a particular cup (either not Mommy's cup, or in Mommy's cup). Either way, Allison had to have been capable of detecting ambiguity, a difference in the meaning of 'Mommy juice' as she meant it, and 'Mommy juice?' as her mother meant it, and perhaps even the ambiguity in her own prior utterance and the resulting potential for her mother to have misunderstood. But while it seems indisputable from what we see in this instance that Allison detected ambiguity in one or more prior utterances, this is not something of which children of that age have been found capable.

Swinney and Prather (1989) studied the ability of children between 4,0 and 5,6 to comprehend *lexical* ambiguity (which I will posit is a cognitively simpler, more basic matter than the discourse ambiguity Allison seems to have comprehended). They found that the younger children do not comprehend lexical ambiguity. Their method was to give children sentences that included an ambiguous word, with half the sentences favouring the most common meaning of the word, and half the less common. In conjunction with being given those sentences, the children were shown a picture which illustrated either the common meaning of the ambiguous word or the uncommon meaning. They were asked to respond to a question about the picture, such that one meaning or another of the ambiguous word they had been given would make salient the qualities of the picture about which they were asked, and prime their response to the question. If they had access to both meanings of the word, regardless of sentence context, they were expected to answer the question with the same latency regardless of what sentence they had been given. If the sentence context led the child to have one meaning or the other for the word, the sentence was expected to affect latency in answering the question, and to indicate that the child did not apprehend both meanings (the ambiguity) of the word. Swinney and Prather (1989) report that the younger children (4,0 to 4,7) differed markedly from the older ones (4,8 to 5,6):

The older group provides data that look remarkably similar to data for adults; picture decisions for pictures related to both interpretations of the ambiguity are primed, regardless of the contextual bias of the sentence. (p. 236)

The younger children's performance . . . looks as though there is activation of
only the most frequent meaning of an ambiguous word . . . independent of the
contextual bias of the sentence. . . . (p. 236)

Faced with such findings, it would be unreasonable to insist that Allison
must certainly have detected the discursive ambiguity of the utterance
'Mommy juice', even though it then becomes an imponderable what she
was responding to in line 12 by saying 'No. . . . Baby'. At the same time,
an instance as suggestive as Allison's response, especially if others like it
were found, should behove developmental cognitive scientists to pursue
the matter further.

An adult's interaction

The issue of whether it is cognitively possible for speakers to do what an
analyst 'observes' is not restricted to such special cases as toddlers whose
cognitive resources have not been certified. It also arises in the analysis of
what (normal) adults are 'observed' to do. I will illustrate this by returning
to a datum discussed above, Shane's word search that Schegloff (1996)
analyzed in his exposition of the action, *confirming an allusion*.

Even though it seems that Shane *would* have avoided confirming an
allusion, and so he can be described as engaging in a word search for that
purpose, Schegloff's analysis also depends on its being something a person
could do to engage in such a word search, for the purpose of *dis*confirming
an allusion. For that, persons in interaction would have to be capable of,
in effect, monitoring their lexical options at each selection place and
adjusting for possible interactional consequences of confirming or not
confirming an allusion within 1 or 2 seconds.[5] If he is right, Schegloff's
analysis makes a contribution to cognitive science for revealing the power
of the cognitive resources we bring to bear in producing discourse objects;
but if cognitive scientists should find that it is not cognitively possible,
then Schegloff 'observed' something that did not actually take place.

The cognitive task Shane had to have engaged in has two parts. The
first is to monitor his utterance for the act it would count as, and the
other to do a word search to self-correct it. The first task is likely to
be the more complicated, in that Shane would have had to (a) monitor the form and content of his utterance in the moment of producing
it for what act it would count as, such that he could detect on the way
to fully echoing Michael's prior utterance that in doing so it would confirm an allusion, and (b) assess that this act was undesirable because
it would work against him at that point. To my knowledge there has
not been research on whether speakers monitor their utterances as they

Table 2.1 *A portion of Table 1, from Green (1975) Latencies in Making 'Match' Decision in Milliseconds*

	word match	word rhyme	phrase-related
memorize sentence	1230	1487	1345
continue sentence	1323	1542	1828

produce them for their functionality, and assess and possibly self-correct them on that basis. Obviously it would bear on the validity of Schegloff's observational/interpretive claim whether people are found capable of such monitoring.

However, there is experimental work on word and sentence processing that bears on the second part of Shane's cognitive task, which was to engage in a word search where he compared the word 'cheap' in Michael's sentence with alternative words Shane could use as a synonym. For example, Green (1975) conducted an experiment in which participants were asked to determine whether a word was or was not in a sentence they just read, with their choices being a word that had been in the sentence, a word that rhymed with that one, and a word that was a synonym of that one. For example, given the sentence 'A heavy rock destroyed the shed', participants were asked to determine if either 'rock', 'frock', or 'boulder' were in the sentence. Green manipulated the extent to which participants would apprehend the content of the sentence they read by asking participants in one condition to simply recall the sentence after attending to a series of numbers (as distracters), and participants in the other condition to prepare to write a next sentence continuing the one they read (requiring them to process the content). Table 2.1 gives the processing times Green reported in each experimental condition, in milliseconds.

Note that they range from a low of 1.2 seconds to a high of 1.8 seconds. The response time was longest when the experimental participants had been made to process the sentence's meaning, and then were asked on the word recognition task whether a synonym for a word in the sentence had actually been in the sentence.

There is a rough correspondence between the task in Green's (1975) experiment and what was involved in 'Shane's' word search. It relates to prior findings on which Green (1975) based his experiment that 'the time required to decide that two words are different increases with their phonological or semantic similarity' (p. 276). Shane would have had to assess one or more alternative possible words to fill the adjective slot in the sentence he was producing, so as to end up with the same semantics as Michael's word 'cheap' but by virtue of its being an alternative word, avoiding the act of confirming an allusion. There is also a rough correspondence between the processing times Green reported and the apparent duration of Shane's word search (mostly the duration of his vocalization of 'uh'). Of course, the first part of Shane's cognitive task – to monitor the functionality of his utterance, detect a problem, and set about to avoid it – would almost certainly increase the overall processing time, but perhaps this occurred prior to the onset of the word search, while he was speaking the first few words of the utterance.

Accordingly, while I do not know of research on cognitive processing that fully supports a claim that persons can do what Shane appears to have done – must have done if Schegloff's observation/interpretation is sound – there is some research that indicates that it is possible and none that counters it.

Conclusion

It is certainly the case that doing cognitive science can distract from rather than help in analyzing discourse objects, interactions and texts. And it is also the case that attention to cognition can take on an individualistic approach to the production of discourse objects that is insensitive to its co-constructed, essentially social, foundation. But these are perils that can be avoided in discourse studies without trying to deny that it is relevant or helpful to attend to cognition. Discourse studies inescapably rest on assumptions about what persons cognitively *would* and *could* do with their words in any given instance. Such assumptions are built into every observational claim we make. While we can go about our business most of the time as if this weren't so, sometimes the only way to ground and justify, or challenge, observational claims in discourse studies is to attend to the assumptions about cognition on which they rest.

NOTES

1. I intend my argument to apply to written as well as spoken discourse. Accordingly, I have tried to use terms that are neutral as to speaking or writing, but this sometimes seemed more likely to confuse than enlighten. Hence, it seemed best to retain such terms as 'speaker' and 'hearer', especially since all the data I examine involves spoken interaction, even though statements using those terms often apply just as well to 'writer' and 'reader'. At the same time, instead of the term 'utterance', I use the term 'discourse object' to refer to any situated, produced, linguistic object, written as well as spoken. And 'social/symbolic practices' here refers not just to forms and genres of social interaction, but forms and genres of text as well, both written and spoken (letters of recommendation, public speeches, legal briefs, newspaper articles, short stories, sermons, etc.).

2. It is possible that hearers will infer a state of mind from the speaker's utterance that does not correspond to the speaker's actual state of mind. Sometimes speakers actively try to induce this (when being deceptive), and sometimes it happens because speaker or hearer or both made a mistake, and sometimes it happens because the speaker's state of mind is unsettled and perhaps not knowable even to him or herself. But for all practical purposes it only matters whether the inference corresponds with what the speaker intended the hearer to infer.

3. This is not necessarily a conscious process, any more than the grammatical parsing is conscious that persons necessarily do in producing and interpreting sentences. A key indicator that it occurs is speakers' self-corrections, often during the very utterance of the discourse object.

4. While Bruner's (1975) position is generally accepted that pre-linguistic children are communicative, and behave so as to achieve specific functionalities, there is much less consensus about when very young children (between ages 1 and 4) become capable of doing this with words. There has been relatively little close analysis of children's participation in interactions before the age of 3,0, and it is difficult to administer tests of grammatical 'knowledge', let alone pragmatic and neo-rhetorical reasoning, to very young children.

5. This time estimate is based on assuming that Shane's word search began just as he was speaking the word prior to 'uh', and ended just prior to vocalizing the (substituted) next word, 'tight'.

3   Language without mind

Jeff Coulter

Introduction

'Language is dependent on mind' – so says John Searle (1983: 161), and he certainly speaks with the contemporary philosophical consensus in the United States and elsewhere. Indeed, such a conception of the human capacity for language extends back at least to Aristotle's *De Interpretatione*, to Descartes, and can be found also in Locke, de Saussure, Chomsky, Fodor and many others. Animal cognition studies, whilst ostensibly mounting a challenge to such a conception, have nonetheless frequently been framed within the terms of just this conception, the key issue being formulated as: to what extent can creatures without minds successfully and productively manipulate and employ linguistic signs between themselves? Or, does work such as that of Sue Savage-Rumbaugh (1994, 1998) with her bonobo apes, Kanzi and Panbanisha, rather show that such creatures possess at least the rudiments of mind or mentality? It is instructive to note that many of Savage-Rumbaugh's commentators have generally lined up on one side or the other of the following proposition: she has demonstrated that apes have minds (even though of a rudimentary sort) or she has shown that symbol manipulations of relatively elaborate kinds do not require minds (because apes don't have them). I believe that issues such as these can best be addressed conceptually, and that we do not require to look to the behaviour of primates to resolve the issue of the relationship of language to mind.

In what follows, I shall be offering some arguments designed to undermine the very initial assumption that the explanation of the capacity to speak or to manipulate linguistic signs successfully and productively by any creature, human or animal, requires reference to mind or mentality. In Wittgenstein's words: 'Language did not emerge from reasoning' (1969: para. 457). Elaborating upon this theme in Wittgenstein's later writings, Malcolm (1991) argued systematically against what he saw as an excessively 'intellectualist' or 'ratiocinative' picture of the exercise of human linguistic capacities, claiming instead that such capacities are akin to instinctive ones. Naturally, in the prevailing climate of thought, Malcolm at once opened himself up to the charge of a regression to elementary and outmoded behaviouristic notions. However, we shall see that matters are more complex than this, and that various themes in Malcolm's Wittgensteinian argument can be linked to Harris's (1981) well-known rejection of what he termed a 'telementational' view of human linguistic communication. (I shall define this concept shortly). What emerges is a far different view of the nature of language from the one which has prevailed in linguistics and psycholinguistics – and, to a lesser extent, in discourse studies and sociolinguistics – in recent years. Rejecting all residues of a neo-Cartesian kind, embodied in the telementational conception and its kin, requires being able to see how it is that language use and comprehension in our daily lives are neither 'psychological phenomena' nor is their elucidation to be dependent upon appeals to 'mentalistic' notions. Further, and perhaps more radically, it will be argued here that commonplace ideas about speakers' and hearers' thoughts, intentions, strategies and their cognates are not properly to be understood as 'mental' phenomena nor assimilated to *any* 'theory of mind', lay or professional. If the arguments are right, then a good deal of theorizing in current studies of human linguistic communication is misplaced and, above all, otiose.

The 'telementational' myth

In his book, *The Language Myth*, Roy Harris undertakes a systematic debunking of a variety of what he argues are errors in modern linguistic theory. Among these, and prominently, is what he calls the 'telementational' myth of linguistic communication. According to this fallacy, 'linguistic knowledge is essentially a matter of knowing which words stand for which ideas' (Harris, 1981: 9). A language is construed as a system for the conveyance of 'thoughts', and a language community is a group of persons who have come to use the 'same words' to express the 'same thoughts' and to combine these words into sentences for discursive purposes.

Suppose A has a thought that he wishes to communicate to B, for example, that gold is valuable. His task is to search among the sentences of a language known to both himself and to B, and select that sentence which has a meaning appropriate to the thought to be conveyed; for example, in English, the sentence Gold is valuable. He then encodes this sentence in its appropriate oral or written form, from which B is able to decode it, and in virtue of knowing what it means, grasp the thought which A, intended to convey to him, namely that gold is valuable. (ibid.: 10)

Although this version of 'telementationalism' omits the current dogma about the compositionality or 'generativity' of language use and comprehension, Fodor's generative-grammatical version is essentially the same but with the added recognition of this feature. For him,

> A speaker is a mapping from messages onto wave forms, and a hearer is a mapping from wave forms onto messages . . . The speaker, in short, has a value of M (message, thought – JC) in mind and the hearer can tell which value of M it is . . . The mapping from messages to wave forms and vice versa is indirect: Wave forms are paired with messages via the computation of a number of intervening representations . . . (Fodor, 1975: 108–09)

In the fourth chapter of his book on the myths of language (entitled: 'Form and Meaning'), Harris (1981: 86–111) documents the consequences of such a theoretical position from Locke, the Port Royal grammarians, to Saussure, to Katz and transformational grammar. John Searle, in a Grice-inspired discussion of 'speakers' meanings' in his recent book, *Mind, Language and Society* (1998: 140–6), has expanded upon this 'telementational' conception in the following way:

> . . . what the speaker <u>means by the utterance</u> of the sentence is, within certain limits, entirely a matter of his or her intentions. I have to say 'within certain limits' because you can't just say anything and mean anything. You can't say, 'Two plus two equals four' and mean that Shakespeare was a pretty good poet as well as a playwright. At least you can't mean that without a lot of extra stage setting. . . . But sentences are tools to talk with. So even though language constrains speaker meaning, speaker meaning is still the primary form of linguistic meaning, because the linguistic meaning of sentences functions to enable speakers of the language to use sentences to mean something in utterances . . . The key to understanding meaning is this: meaning is a form of derived intentionality. <u>The original or intrinsic intentionality of a speaker's thought is transferred to words, sentences, marks, symbols, and so on</u>. They have not just conventional linguistic meaning but intended speaker meaning as well. (Searle, 1998: 140–1, emphases added)

Intentionalist conceptions of meaning and comprehension are clearly derived from the 'telementational' conception insofar as they are based upon the notion that what gives an utterance its intelligibility is the linking together of the conventional (rule-bound) meaning of the sentence uttered to the thought the speaker intended to convey by uttering it. In what follows, these theses will be criticized systematically. That some of them still inform the work of many (if not all) contemporary analysts of linguistic discourse and communication is beyond dispute (e.g., Graesser *et al.*, 1997): that they continue to comprise obstacles to actual analytical work as well as to an adequate theoretical appreciation of the nature of language use and comprehension in communication between people is the central focus of this chapter.

Malcolm's 'non-ratiocinative' account of language

Drawing upon Wittgenstein's remarks about our human capacity to follow rules 'blindly' (i.e., non-reflectively, without deliberation), one of his
most lucid and able interpreters, Norman Malcolm, presents us with a
view of language as having a close relationship to instinctive behaviour
(Malcolm, 1991: 27–47). He begins by noting that Wittgenstein drew a
distinction between those uses of language which were learned, immediate, unreflective, linguistic expressions of pain, fear, surprise, desire,
delight, etc. (*Ausserungen*) – viz., verbal extensions of prelinguistic reactions and instinctive conduct – and those uses which are built upon these,
ramify from them. In *Zettel* (1967), para. 540, Wittgenstein noted that it
is not only a primitive reaction to tend or to treat the part that hurts when
one is oneself in pain, but also that the same is true in cases *when someone
else is*. Thus, Malcolm (1991: 27) proposes to treat the expression 'He is
in pain' as a learned linguistic replacement for an unlearned reaction just
as much as is 'I am in pain'. Wittgenstein explained what he meant by the
term 'primitive' in the following: '. . . this way of behaving is *prelinguistic*:
that a language-game is based *on it*, that it is . . . not the result of thinking' (*Zettel*, para. 541). One of Wittgenstein's favourite aphorisms was
Goethe's 'Im Anfang war die Tat' – 'In the Beginning was the Deed' –
not the Word. Peter Winch elaborates upon the significance of this:

Goethe was drawing attention to the <u>creative</u> role of 'the deed', and in Wittgenstein this is expressed in the importance ascribed to certain primitive human
actions and reactions for <u>concept-formation</u> . . . (e.g.) he draws attention to the
fact that when I see someone point with his finger, I characteristically don't look
<u>at</u> his finger, but <u>away</u> from it in what I call 'the direction in which he is pointing' –
and I <u>have</u> this latter concept only by virtue of the fact that I <u>do</u> naturally, along
with everyone else, react to his outstretched arm and finger in that way. (Winch,
1983: 176)

Winch goes on to note that our concept of a 'cause' is closely connected
to our typical reactions as human beings towards states of affairs we
want to be rid of, citing Wittgenstein's remarks: '<u>We react to the cause</u>'
(Wittgenstein, 1976: 410 – emphasis in the original). Further, in the same
essay by Wittgenstein, we find the following comment:

– We also speak of 'tracing' the cause; a simple case would be, say, following
a string to see who is pulling it. If I then find him – how do I know that he,
his pulling, is the cause of the string's moving? Do I establish this by a series of
experiments? (ibid.: 416)

Here, Wittgenstein's foil is the intellectualist conception of the idea
of a 'cause' favoured by Hume-inspired philosophical reflection. For

Wittgenstein, our basic concepts of 'cause' and 'effect' are grounded in our immediate responses, our conduct toward states of affairs which puzzle us, trouble us, etc. There is no inferring, guessing, concluding, and the like. In other words, no *ratiocination* is involved. Linguistic expressions are, in Malcolm's felicitous term, 'grafted' onto our actions, reactions and responses. Notice as well that there is a fundamental *lack of uncertainty* in these actions and reactions. Language learning is predicated upon not doubting – the possibility of doubt comes *later*. It is also in the exceptional situation, not in what we call the 'ordinary' one, in which doubting can arise.

In *On Certainty*, Wittgenstein (1969: para. 477) asks: 'Why should the language-game rest on knowledge?' It would be absurd to ask of the infant drinking its milk: does he know that milk exists? Just as absurd as asking: 'Does a cat know that a mouse exists?' (ibid.: para. 478). Knowing, thinking, conjecturing, believing, are simply not facets of the conduct here, although in the human case such conduct naturally displayed is the prerequisite for further *linguistic* 'graftings'. Such linguistic graftings enable articulations and distinctions in conduct to be displayed and observed, but these do not themselves necessarily, in all cases, require the ascription of propositional, discursive or deliberative thought. A dog may think that its master is about to strike it: it displays this non-discursive thought in its recoiling, yelping, running away, etc. from its master's angry expression and raised hand toward it; in the *human* case, there is, however, now room in the prelinguistic reaction for the later acquisition of linguistic articulations of such reactions: 'Daddy intended to hit me', 'I thought he was going to hit me', etc. Malcolm goes on to stress the ways in which language games are acquired as *capacities* to 'play' them, and not as a matter of having learned, through processes of hypothesis formation and testing, informational items with their combinatorial rules. This distinction is crucial, because it enables us to see how misguided and misleading is the 'telementational' conception. In Malcolm's words (1991: 35, emphasis added):

A normal child gradually masters these differences (between expressions, different activities, different circumstances – JC), not in the sense of being able to describe them, but in the sense of conforming with them in its use of words. When this happens the child is said to 'understand the meaning' of those words.

More critically for the current discussion is Malcolm's assertion that his (Wittgensteinian) arguments about the grafting of much of a child's first language onto instinctive behaviour (richly depicted) apply *not only* to its most elementary forms. He goes on to note that 'the whole of the developed, complex, employment of language by adult speakers embodies something resembling instinct.' (ibid.: 35). *This* is a bold thesis indeed, flying in the face of so much current thinking about the nature of language use and comprehension in everyday life. Before exploring it in more detail, let us enter some crucial *caveats* here. Neither Wittgenstein nor Malcolm are arguing that we *never* 'think before we speak', 'form intentions prior to uttering something', 'reflect upon the best way of putting something', 'pursue a strategy in choosing what to say and/or how to say it', and so on. What *is* being proposed is that such *practices* are *not* essential to, nor constitutive of, most of our communicative conduct using linguistic resources. Our use of techniques and devices for expressing ourselves linguistically, our following the rules we follow, does not (normally) require nor involve prior spates of reflective action at all. How can such an anti-mentalist, anti-Cartesian, anti-'telementational' position be defended for the complexities of mature, adult, competent linguistic communication?

A great deal of unlearned and unthinking (but *not* therefore 'thought-less'!) conduct informs our use and understanding of linguistic expressions. Natural 'agreement in reactions' and in actions, not prior propositional knowledge or thought, undergirds so much of our linguistic exchanges that we tend to over-intellectualize such cases when we use terms like: 'assumes', 'has the idea that . . .', 'believes that . . .' and their ilk to characterize them. Our relationships to each other in and through the use of language are not primarily, nor in most subsequent instances, relationships best expressed in terms of 'knowing' but, rather, of behaving. Not of 'thinking', but of acting. Of course, this is *far* from being any sort of resurrection of Skinnerian behaviouristic theses about 'verbal behaviour' as conditioned linguistic 'responses' to 'stimuli'. However, it is also far from being any sort of (re)affirmation of a Chomskian telementational alternative.

One especially cogent summary formulation of the thesis of linguistic self sufficiency is that of J. F. M. Hunter. He writes:

Whether in saying things meaningfully, or in understanding what other people say, or what we read, we do not need, and do not generally use, any logical or psychological paraphernalia of any kind: the words themselves are quite sufficient. We do not need to imagine a room to understand a description of a room; we do not need a sample of pain or yellowness to understand what 'pain' and 'yellow' means; we do not need to translate an expression into another expression, and we do not need to guess, or interpret, or apply rules: we understand language just as it stands. (Hunter, 1971: 283)

Language use and comprehension does not normally require thought or thinking. Discursive thinking is (roughly) thinking *of* or *about* something or someone: a 'thought' is (as Searle notes) an intentional concept inasmuch as a thought is that which it is *of* or *about*. However, Searle's concept of linguistic expressions as cases of 'derived' intentionality over-looks the crucial point that what for him have 'intrinsic intentionality', namely, thoughts, are *themselves* (usually) constituted by linguistic (or other symbolic) *expressions*. Granted, a thought is not *identical* to its expression (since the same thought can be expressed in different expres-sions, and the same expression in different contexts can express the same thought), but, nonetheless: no means of expression, no thought. Why, then, privilege 'thought' over 'language' in respect of 'intentionality'? (Brentano's notion, not the ordinary concept, is involved here). Hunter is indicating something simple, yet also deeply hard to grasp for those of us in the grip of a certain philosophical picture of how language works: he is saying that linguistic expressions are themselves self-sufficient for the conveyance of intelligibility, and are not (normally) *in any need of supplementation by* thinking, deliberation, analysis, contextualization, disambiguation or other intellectual operations such as are routinely postulated in much linguistic theory.

'Interpretation' and linguistic comprehension

Let us consider at some length a major contender for mentalistic concep-tions of language use and comprehension: the widespread assumption (or thesis) that understanding someone's utterance is *essentially* (and not just occasionally, exceptionally) a matter of 'interpreting' it, of 'interpret-ing its meaning', or of 'having an interpretation of what it means'. This assumption unites thinkers as otherwise diverse as Alfred Schutz, John Searle and Donald Davidson. It is a very widespread doctrine indeed. Take Schutz for example. He writes:

> There exists between the sign and that which is signified the relation of representa-tion . . . (That) signitive relation is . . . a particular relation between the interpretive schemes which are applied to those external objects here called 'signs'. When we understand a sign, we do not interpret the latter through the scheme adequate to it as an external sign but through the schemes adequate to whatever it signifies. (Schutz, 1967: 118–19)

By contrast, as Meredith Williams notes in her discussion of this issue, Wittgenstein argued that: 'Interpretations by themselves do not deter-mine meaning' (Wittgenstein, 1958: para. 198, in Williams, 1999: 42). There is nothing in Schutz's discussion to rule out exactly what Wittgenstein warned against – the prospect of an idle regress in which one can adduce further (and possibly conflicting) interpretations of interpretations . . . (After all, any interpretation can itself be variously interpreted.) For some, equally diverse, thinkers (such as Kripke on the one hand and Derrida on the other) the prospect of this regress is not only embraced – it is positively celebrated as a deep form of 'meaning scepticism'. For Wittgenstein, in sharp contrast, it is the sign of a profound confusion.

Take the case of 'understanding a rule'. Must this require an act of 'interpreting' it? To many, the answer is an unequivocal 'Yes'. What fixes the sense of a rule is the interpretation accorded to it by rule-followers. But as James Edwards remarks:

> Unless one imagines an interpretation as a kind of magical mental act whose 'meaning' is absolutely and intrinsically transparent from the first, one must realize that merely adding an interpretation to a rule gets one no further in answering the question of how rules actually do their work. (Edwards, 1990: 167)

He goes on to remind us of the point of Wittgenstein's discussion of the sign-post. Someone may add chalk marks on the ground to aid a traveller in using a cross-roads signpost. Edwards comments:

> Are such marks any less in need of interpretation than the signpost itself? Sometimes they may be clearer in meaning, of course, as when the signpost has sunk over to hang at a crazy angle; but this illustrates just the point that needs to be appreciated: only in certain circumstances is an 'interpretive' chalk mark clearer in meaning than the signpost it is intended to interpret. (In some cases the interpretation may even muddy the waters more, not clarify them.) (Edwards, 1990: 167)

This is not to deny that, in some cases, we may find the meaning of an utterance, the point of an action, the sense of a rule, obscure to us such that we may need an interpretation. However, as Edwards points out, 'successful interpretations (of a rule) are in effect nothing more than illuminating restatements of the original rule itself . . . As with the rule itself, the power of an interpretation appropriately to guide one's behavior does not reside in the interpretive formula per se, but in the particular circumstances in which the formula is learned and used' (ibid.: 168–9). Even 'private' interpretations make sense only against a public, institutional background of customary responses.

'Understanding' an utterance or activity is akin to an achievement, whilst 'interpreting' them is an activity. Although on occasion we may use the terms interchangeably (as in, e.g., 'my understanding of it was as follows . . .' = 'my interpretation of it was as follows . . .'), note that the grammars of these words diverge in many of their uses. To interpret something is to come up with, to make, to have, an interpretation; to understand is very often simply to be correct about something, or to be able to do and/or say appropriate things *in response to*, in relation to, what has been done and/or said. Wittgenstein (1958: para. 506) gives us the following scenario:

The absent-minded man who at the order 'Right turn!' turns left, and then, clutching his forehead, says 'Oh! right turn' and does a right turn. – What has struck him? An interpretation?

To have actually understood something is very often simply a matter of now knowing how to proceed, what to do – it is in many respects a capacity. This may be *contrasted*, in a wide range of instances, to what it is to have *interpreted* something. Most of our routine understandings of what others do and say are not accompanied by *text* of any kind, whilst our interpretations are (in most instances) embedded in text of *some* kind. On these grounds, we can see how thoroughly muddled are views such as the following (Graesser *et al.*, 1997: 292):

When people comprehend discourse, the speech or printed messages are not merely copied into their minds. Instead, the human mind actively constructs various types of cognitive representations (that is, codes, features, meanings, structured sets of elements) that interpret the linguistic input . . . Each type of cognitive representation is functionally important during the process of comprehending and producing text and talk.

These writers confuse understanding with interpreting, and also treat 'understanding' as if it were a process-verb when, in fact, it is akin to an achievement-verb (as Ryle noted more than fifty years ago). To make matters worse, they seem to believe that their postulated 'cognitive representations' in the 'minds' of speakers and hearers can be given empirical substantiation by various tests. However, when one examines such proposed empirical tests, it turns out that they *presuppose* rather than demonstrate the existence of such 'representations'. For example, we are told (ibid.: 293): 'A group of readers might recall a text after they finish comprehending it. The content that is recalled should to some extent resemble the cognitive representations. If a theory predicts that text statement A is more central to the cognitive representation than statement B, then the likelihood that readers later recall A should be higher than that of B'. Such quasi-experimental scenarios can, of course, be bases for utterly mundane inferences (e.g., as to distinguishable aspects of interestingness, memorability, and the rest): *nothing* in them entails or even licences theoretical talk of the kind which is used to embellish them.

Discursive practices and 'cognitive processes'

There is a great temptation to treat studies of practical, communicative activities and interactions as opportunities for cognitivistic speculation.

Ethnomethodological talk of 'practical reasoning' appears to lend itself to such speculation, and such a direction has been explicitly embraced by Aaron Cicourel in his 'cognitive sociology' (Cicourel, 1974). On the whole, however, most practitioners of ethnomethodological inquiry do not conceive of themselves as contributing to cognitive theorizing, following instead Garfinkel's famous dictum:

. . . there is no reason to look under the skull since nothing of interest is to be found there but brains . . . Indeed questions will be confined to the operations that can be performed upon events that are 'scenic' to the person. (Garfinkel, 1990: 6)

Nonetheless, in his 'Introduction' to Volume One of Harvey Sacks' *Lectures on Conversation* (1992), Emanuel Schegloff offers some remarks which propose that some of Sacks' problems and observations pertain to 'the cognitive operations of persons' (ibid.: xxxvii) such that their 'relevance to cognitive science seems transparent'. (ibid.)

Although Schegloff documents the early influence of Chomsky on Sacks, I do not believe that what Sacks accomplished can be construed in terms of revealing persons' 'cognitive operations'. Indeed, the tenor of much of his work is hard to reconcile with any extant program of work in cognitive science, being resolutely focused upon the exploration and analysis of observable social practices, interactional and social 'objects' (a term which Sacks often used to characterize his materials). Nonetheless, since Schegloff was a close collaborator with Sacks, and a distinguished analyst within the tradition which Sacks inaugurated, the matter bears further discussion.

First of all, Schegloff is far from treating all or even most of Sacks' work as cognitivist. He differentiates between the varieties of analytical themes and strategies used by Sacks throughout his very wide-ranging lectures and publications. Nonetheless, he claims to have identified certain types of problems and solutions to them coeval with cognitivist interests. He writes:

There is a form of problem which Sacks takes up a number of times in the early lectures, each time on a distinct target, which can best be characterised as an 'analysis of the ordering of cognitive operations' (or the ordering of interpretive procedures). (Schegloff, 1992c: xxxvii)

(Note that in this passage Schegloff uses an expression never to be found in Sacks' work, but one frequently deployed by Aaron Cicourel in implementing his explicitly 'cognitivist' sociological program: 'interpretive procedures'). Treating the phenomenon of 'intentional misidentification' of persons in conversational exchanges, Sacks is claimed to have proposed that persons orient to it as a sort of cognitive problem – how can speaker-hearers identify someone correctly when an address term employed does not 'apply' to anyone present? Schegloff comments:

He [Sacks] argues that, if they were finding 'who is being addressed' by finding to whom the address term referred, then they would find no solution. Rather, he argues, they first use sequencing rules to find whom the current speaker would properly be addressing, and they use the product of that analysis in deciding how the address term is properly to be interpreted. He is thus able to sort out the order in which these analyses are conducted – first, addressee, then address term – and it turns out to be just the opposite from what one might have thought. (ibid.)

In the passage above, Schegloff attributes several 'shadow actions' (I owe this term to Wes Sharrock, who is not responsible for the argument being developed here). That is, Schegloff attributes to speaker-hearers: (1) the production of an 'analysis', (2) 'deciding', (3) 'interpreting' and (4) 'sorting out the order in which these analyses are conducted'. *None* of these describe anything that the speaker-hearers in question could be said to have actually done: they are without criterial satisfaction in the instances being inspected. This does not inhibit Schegloff from ascribing them, however. On what grounds? The only 'warrant' (the scarequotes are very deliberate here) could be forthcoming from the tacit (in Schegloff's case, explicit) adherence to cognitivist assumptions – the analyzing, deciding, interpreting and sorting of analyses are 'cognitive operations'. They are mental processes (or mental practices) accompanying their 'scenic' activities in the setting. I shall return to consider Sacks' analysis further on.

Schegloff goes on to consider another analysis of Sacks': the use of the 'possessive pronoun'. He comments:

Sacks argues that a hearer/receiver must first determine that what 'my' is attached to is a 'possessable' – the sort of thing which in that culture can be possessed (rather than a category from a membership categorization device, for example), in order to decide that 'my' is being used to claim possession. Once again, an ordering of analyses – of cognitive operations – seems clearly involved. (Schegloff, 1992c: xxxviii – emphasis added)

But once again, the inference to the presence of 'cognitive operations' is itself only a function of the illicit introduction of 'shadow actions' into the characterization of the issue. What evidence is there *within the actions* of the speaker-hearers that they go through iterative 'operations' of 'determining' and 'deciding' things about the use of 'my'? Since there is none, then their 'determinings' and 'decidings' are postulated as mental or cognitive processes. Of course, in the anodyne sense of the term 'cognition' (as meaning, simply, 'knowledge'), speaker-hearers can usually be credited with knowing (i.e., being able to distinguish) the various ways in which 'my' is used – sometimes possessively, sometimes in other ways – and such knowledge is elegantly described by Sacks' distinction between 'possessables' and 'possessitives' (Sacks, 1992a: 383–7, 605–09), but Schegloff's reading of the issue clearly commits him to much more than this. Further on, we are told:

> Before analyzing a [use of] 'that' for the sequential tying connection it makes to some other (ordinarily prior) utterance, a hearer has to do a syntactic analysis to determine that the 'that' is the sort which can tie back to some earlier component of the talk. (Schegloff, 1992c: xxxviii)

Here, speaker-hearers are not only claimed to be engaged in 'sequential analysis' – they are also involved in 'syntactic analysis' in order to figure out which use of 'that' is the one they confront whenever the term is used. In this way, Schegloff argues, they (we) distinguish between the various uses of 'that', as in, e.g., 'I decided that years ago', 'That's a challenge' and 'I still say though that . . .'. This grossly over-intellectualizing construal of what is involved treats ordinary speakers and hearers as proto-linguists – even as proto-conversation analysts themselves! Concluding, he observes:

> Whatever the particulars. . . . the problem-type addressed to the ordering of cognitive or psycholinguistic or interpretive operations are theoretically central to the responsibilities of a sociological, or more generally interactional, sector of what now are called the cognitive sciences. (ibid.: xxxix)

Insofar as the stock-in-trade of the cognitive sciences consists in the postulation of 'underlying', unobservable, 'unconscious', mental processes (described as 'computations' or in some other way), Schegloff's linkage here is quite explicit – some of Sacks' work can be found to contribute to the postulation of exactly the same sorts of phenomena, whether he (Sacks) actually thought in such terms or not. But do the actual cases and Sacks' analyses of them point in this direction? I do not believe that any of them do, and that Sacks' own way of reasoning was very far removed from any cognitivist – or more broadly 'mentalistic' – concerns. Rather, Sacks' procedure (in the cases under discussion, as often elsewhere) consisted in formulating a logic or a logical apparatus to account for the unproblematic (to actual speakers and hearers) *orderliness* in the actions he analyzed. He nowhere attributes features of his own analytical apparatus to speakers and hearers as constituents of their minds (and in this sense, as in others, departs radically from Chomsky). The logic (grammar, or rules) for identifying persons intentionally misidentified can be described without its being made to appear as a description of a series of steps *consciously (or 'unconsciously') worked through by speaker-hearers in all instances*. Sacks's analyses often lay out *procedural possibilities* as ways to explicate what for practical lay speakers of a language are simply taken-for-granted, utterly mundane and ordinarily unproblematic facets of their speaking and hearing. They know (can tell) who has been intentionally misidentified: they know (can tell) in what respect 'my teacher' differs from 'my automobile': they know (can tell) what 'that' is being used to talk about when they hear it uttered. Sacks is not in the business of attributing to them any sort of underlying 'mental apparatus' at all, but of explicating some rules or procedures with which their conduct is in accord. To begin to work out such rules, Sacks may well occasionally treat members' activities *as if* they were wholly explicit matters of solving problems, but nowhere does he argue that *members themselves* treat these massively recurrent uses, interactional events, etc. as solutions to problems they themselves explicitly confront (and must explicitly solve) in their discursive practices. The logic is *implicit in the practices*, not a mental addendum to them. The entire cognitivist idiom is quite alien to Sacks's own analytical concern.

Conclusion

In our everyday lives, we are used to hearing admonitions to 'say what's on your mind', 'express your thoughts more succinctly', 'think before you speak', and the like. We sometimes have occasion to complain that an utterance did not adequately express what we intended it to, or that we couldn't tell what someone else intended when he said something. These cases form a natural background for the over-extrapolating propensities of theorizing and nurturing as they do a readiness to embrace mentalistic conceptions about the use and comprehension of language. Theories of mind (even of animal mind) become either the assumed foundation for, or the goal of, the analysis of language in use. However, as I have tried to show, such theoretical speculations are not only misleading, they are actually idle. Only if one surrenders the sense of variegated concepts like 'reaction' or 'instinctive' to the behaviourists (and they have absolutely no monopoly in respect of their use) might one harbour misgivings about giving up the entire neo-Cartesian picture.

Although the thrust of a good deal of recent work in the formal analysis of communicative practices and interactions is away from cognitivistic concerns, such concerns frequently crop up even here. Part of the problem is the tendency to treat hearers as 'analysts' *in general* (rather than on specific occasions when 'analyzing' is a proper characterization of their *practice*, of what they are *doing*). Similarly, the propensity is evident again in the treatment of speakers as 'designers' of what they say. This is sometimes correct, but as a generic characterization it can be very misleading. Ascriptions of 'intentions' to speakers and hearers can be notoriously problematic on those occasions of discourse when no clear criteria for such an attribution is evident, or when the satisfaction of some such criteria is only equivocally manifested in the scene. The point, however, is that intention-ascriptions are not *in general* problematic by virtue of an intention being somehow a 'mental', interior phenomenon available only and ever on inferential grounds. Often, someone's intentions are wholly evident in what they do and say in the circumstances of their doings and sayings. When they are not, this is because their conduct cannot be found to satisfy the criteria in the setting for the ascription of some intention, or because the contextual information relevant to the discernment of criterial satisfaction is not (or not fully) available. And 'intentions' are far from being omnirelevant in our commonplace communicative exchanges.

Finally, note that all of the problematic concepts under review here – thought, intention, interpretation, etc. – are only to be construed as having something to do with people's 'minds' if one buys into the whole Cartesian bag of tricks from the outset. 'Mind' is either a vernacular notion with commonplace uses, or a philosophical reification. There is nothing intrinsically 'mental' about thinking, intending or interpreting. It is we *as agents* (not as 'minds') who do these things when we do them. We do have vernacular expressions such as: 'I had you in mind when I said that', or: 'In his mind, it made perfect sense'; nonetheless, such locutions do not commit their users to Cartesian theory. They succumb to perfectly 'theory-innocent' paraphrases without residue (e.g., 'What I said pertained to you', or: 'It made sense to him'). Mentalism, telementationalism and cognitivism are not only theoretical fictions: they actually can impede our understanding of how we speak and hear, how we say and do things, in our everyday lives. The best way of avoiding such confused commitments is to ground our analytical work on human conduct in the logical grammar of our language rather than in operational definitions and theoretical assertions.

4 Using participants' video stimulated comments to complement analyses of interactional practices

Anita Pomerantz

As conversation analysts, we analyze the sense-making practices that participants use to accomplish conversational actions, identities and roles. We study these practices by closely observing the details of the conduct of people in interaction as captured or rendered on videotape and/or audiotape recordings. For a number of reasons, many conversation analysts have been strongly reluctant to turn to the participants of an interaction as informants about aspects of the interaction. The reluctance is based on scepticism about a model of social action in which aspects of cognition are used to explain social action, the methods of eliciting self-reports of subjects' perceptions, the validity of such reports, and the temptation to privilege informants' accounts over, or even substitute them for, investigators' analyses of practices.

Through much of my professional career, the sole data I used for my analyses were audiotapes and videotapes of interaction. In some more recent studies, my collaborators and I used ethnographic data along with tape-recordings of interaction. We collected video stimulated comments as data, obtained by asking each of the participants of the interaction under investigation to view a videotape of the interaction and offer comments while viewing it.[1] I will refer to the initial videotaped interaction as Event$_1$ and the subsequent interaction in which an Event$_1$ participant offered comments while viewing the videotape as Event$_2$.

The position that I am advocating is the following: the conversation analytic program of research is built on close analysis of interactional data, for example, audio and videotapes of interaction. However, in some circumstances, using participants' comments in conjunction with recordings of interactions provides the potential for enhancing one's analytic claims and/or for opening up avenues for investigation that otherwise might go unnoticed. In this chapter, I hope to show that investigators can use video stimulated comments to infer *interpretations*, *aims* and *concerns* to which the participants may have oriented as they interacted, and that investigators can use the inferred *interpretations*, *aims* and *concerns* to clarify or illuminate aspects of practices that otherwise may have been described more tentatively or conjecturally.

The position I advocate here grew out of my experiences on a multi-discipinary research team in which we studied medical interaction. For that project, we videotaped medical interactions (Event$_1$) and audiotaped video stimulated comments (Event$_2$).[2] As we worked with the comments, we were concerned with two interrelated issues: the status of the comments and the analytic use they might have. These two issues are discussed in subsequent sections of this chapter. In that project, the comments enabled us to see things in the interaction that we otherwise might have missed and were used to enrich our analyses.

This chapter has the following organization: the first section introduces some of the assumptions about cognition that are consistent with using video stimulated comments as data, the second discusses the purpose of using participants' comments as data, the third explores the kinds of matters that researchers infer from participants' comments, the fourth provides examples of how conversation analysts might use comments to enhance their analyses, and the final section discusses some implications of the position I advocate in this chapter.

Assumptions about cognition

Social scientists who use questionnaires to ascertain the participants' thoughts, perspectives, views, beliefs, values, attitudes, etc. generally assume that the cognitive elements of interest are relatively stable and that they influence the conduct of persons. In contrast to an interest in stable cognitive elements, researchers collecting video stimulated comments generally are interested in the ever-changing thoughts, perceptions, reactions, concerns, etc. that the participants experience as they engage in interaction. In previous work (Pomerantz, 1995), I briefly described the contrasting assumptions or models associated with employing questionnaires versus video stimulated comments:

In the first model of social action, researchers assume that individuals have abstract and generalized beliefs that are relatively stable and stand apart from concrete situations. Individuals select communication practices and courses of action that are consistent with these beliefs. . . . [In the second model], individuals decide how to communicate based on the characteristics of the current interaction. This model moves in closer to the perspective of the participant and travels with them in time as they interact. In responding to what a patient just said or did, for example, a physician attempts to satisfy institutional demands, deal with numerous concerns, and honor multiple beliefs and commitments. (p. 411)

Collecting comments is consistent with an interest in the participants'
moment to moment understandings as both reflecting and shaping their
interactional conduct.

For investigators who want to make claims about the thoughts, reactions, interpretations, concerns, aims, etc. that were experienced and/or
relevant to the participants during $Event_1$, using video stimulated comments as data is less than ideal. Closer to the ideal would be if participants
could report their thoughts, feelings, reactions, observations, interpretations, etc. while interacting.[3] Because concurrent verbalizations cannot
be done in normal face-to-face interaction, investigators have used other
methods aimed at yielding data that they claim can represent the ongoing
thoughts, feelings, reactions, etc. during an interaction.[4] An alternative
to concurrent verbalization is to have participants report the thoughts,
interpretations, explanations, concerns, etc. that they experienced in an
interaction when the interaction is finished. The obvious disadvantage
to retrospective reporting is that many of the thoughts, reactions, interpretations, etc. that occurred during an interaction are unavailable for
reporting when the interaction is over. With the aim of retrieving more of
the stream of thoughts, reactions, interpretations, etc. that occur during
an interaction, investigators simulate the experience of participating in an
interaction with the experience of viewing the interaction on videotape.

> . . . we need a means of simulating the *in vivo* stream of thought that occurs
> during interaction. The most descriptively rich and realistic simulation yet devised
> involves the use of video-assisted recall, in which individuals first interact, then
> reconstruct their earlier thoughts and feelings while viewing a videotape of the
> discussion. (Sillars, Roberts, Leonard, and Dun, 2000: 479)

In the above passage, Sillars et al. refer to individuals' 'reconstructing'
their earlier thoughts and feelings, a term that leaves the process of accessing earlier thoughts rather opaque. Researchers invoke two explanations
for how watching a videotape of an interaction gives participants access
to the thoughts and feelings they had while engaged in the interaction:
recollecting and re-experiencing. For researchers who see recollection
as a mechanism for retrieval, watching the interaction on videotape is
thought to provide cues to prompt the participant to recollect his or her
previous thoughts and feelings. For those who see re-experiencing as the
mechanism, watching the interaction on videotape is thought to allow
the participant to become involved and react in ways that resonate with
his or her previous reactions. The strongest support for the latter explanation are Gottman and Levenson's findings (Gottman and Levenson,
1985) that physiological data obtained during $Event_2$ were significantly
related to physiological data obtained during $Event_1$: '. . . these subjects

appear to sweat, change their heart rate, and change their pulse transmission times at nearly the same time points when viewing the videotape of the interaction as they did when they were in the original interaction'. (p. 157) Regardless of the choice of explanation, the primary purpose in collecting video stimulated comments is to gain access to the thoughts, feelings, concerns, interpretations, reactions, etc. that were oriented to by the participants during Event₁.

Let me be clear about my own position on cognitive phenomena. I make use of two distinctly different approaches to cognitive phenomena. One approach is to treat 'intentions', 'concerns', 'motives', and other cognitive concepts as Members' concepts. While performing conversational activities such as praising, blaming, complaining, disagreeing, challenging, etc., Members attribute 'motives' to their own and each other's conduct, they read each other's 'intentions', they state their 'concerns'. This approach is consistent with a research program aimed at analyzing Members' shared sense making practices.

The second approach is to assume that cognitive phenomena such as *understandings*, *aims* and *concerns* exist and, at times, even influence the selection and employment of specific practices. This approach is consistent with a research program aimed both at analyzing how practices function and at understanding how actors come to employ particular practices over other practices. It is with this second approach to cognitive phenomena that I pursue an interest in supplementing analyses of interaction with video stimulated comments.

Purpose of using comments as data

Researchers who collect video stimulated comments do so because they regard such data as helpful or essential to satisfy the aims of their studies. For example in a study on conflict processes, Sillars et al. (Sillars et al., 2000) tape recorded interaction and collected video stimulated comments because they regarded both kinds of data as essential for understanding the direction of conflict interaction:

In the broadest terms, our argument is that the developmental course of conflict turns on the intersection of subjective thought and overt talk. . . . Thus, to appreciate the subtlety and complexity of communication in conflict, it is helpful to consider what people are thinking as they interact and how their interpretive frameworks might vary.

For Sillars et al. (Sillars et al., 2000), video stimulated comments provide access to the participants' thoughts and interpretive frameworks during the conflict interaction and are required to understand the complexity of communication.

As indicated earlier, my primary aim as a conversation analyst is to analyze the practices that participants use as they interact. An analysis of a practice may include describing the methods the interactants use in producing and understanding it, the circumstances in which it is relevant to employ it, the interactional options made relevant by its use, the types of relationships constituted and reflected in its use, and the orientations that participants can be seen to be displaying when using it. Let me emphasize this last point. Some analyses of practices include a discussion of specific concerns and constraints to which the actors may be seen to be oriented when employing the practice.

I will illustrate this point by drawing on my analysis of the practice of 'telling my side' as a fishing device (Pomerantz, 1980). As described in that text, two uses of this practice are to elicit information and to beget an invitation. I argued that using this practice to elicit information involves displaying particular relational orientations and/or normative constraints. In not directly requesting the information yet still structuring the inter-action so as to provide an opportunity for the recipient to proffer the information, a speaker positions himself or herself as displaying an ori-entation to respecting the recipient's right to privacy while simultane-ously working around it. Likewise, in using 'telling my side' to beget an invitation, a participant displays an orientation to the propriety of the party-giver alone having the right to invite guests. 'In simultaneously not inviting oneself and providing multiple opportunities for the host to prof-fer an invitation, the caller is displaying an orientation to the matter of who properly invites while nevertheless "working around" that propriety' (pp. 197–8). In other words, to accomplish the conversational action via a specific practice may entail displaying, and being seen to display, orien-tations to specific constraints and concerns associated with performing that conversational action.

In the previous illustration, I talked about actors 'displaying orienta-tions' and their possibly 'being seen to be oriented' to specific concerns and constraints. These are different kinds of claims than those that assert that the actors possibly or probably 'were orienting' to specific concerns and constraints. This chapter raises the question of whether participants' actual orientations are relevant for analysts of interaction. Assuming that participants actually orient to *interpretations*, *aims* and *concerns* while they interact, and assuming that we could make reasonable guesses about some of the orientations of participants while interacting, would there be any payoff in doing so?

One possible payoff would be to deal more explicitly with the thorny issue of how participants select the particular practices that they do. Some conversation analytic researchers have made claims about the fit between the features of a practice employed by actors and proposed *interests* or *concerns* of those actors. As an illustration, Pomerantz, Fehr and Ende (Pomerantz, Fehr and Ende, 1997) analyzed a practice employed by preceptors (supervising physicians) in introducing themselves to the patients of the interns whom they were supervising. The preceptors described their relationship to the intern in ways that minimized the hierarchical differences between them:

```
4/12/94
Intern:         (          ) Dr Davis, he's one of the attending doctors.
Preceptor:      Hi ma'am, my name's Dr Davis, I work with Dr Moore.

8/22/95
Preceptor:      I'm Dr Brice.
Patient:        Brice?
Preceptor:      Yes. Dr Rossberg and I work together...
```

In each of the above introductions, the preceptor characterized the relationship he or she had with the intern as 'working with' or 'working together'. We argued that the selection/employment of these characterizations may have been responsive to multiple *interests* or *concerns* of the preceptors, one of which was to preserve the intern's role as the patient's physician and as a competent professional in front of the patient.

If an analyst has an interest in making claims about the *understandings*, *aims* and *concerns* to which the participants possibly or probably oriented in the course of interacting, the question that arises is how to get at such matters. Investigators may infer the participants' *understandings*, *aims* and *concerns* from the participants' conduct and/or from their reports. Neither source is foolproof nor guarantees access to the matters to which a participant oriented during an interaction. In an earlier text, Mandelbaum and I (Mandelbaum and Pomerantz, 1991) discussed how analysts may infer participants' *concerns* from their conduct. In this chapter, I discuss how analysts may infer participants' *understandings*, *aims* and *concerns* from video stimulated comments.

What is inferred from the participants' comments: issues of validity

Researchers who collect video stimulated comments are not of one mind as to what they are, and should be, eliciting from the participants. Some researchers attempt to have the participants report only the thoughts and feelings that they experienced during Event$_1$. For example Sillars et al. (Sillars et al., 2000) attempted to determine as much as possible the participants' streams of thought and feelings during Event$_1$:

The goal of the recall session was to simulate what spouses actually thought and felt as they interacted. . . . The simulation appeared to provide a successful approximation to in vivo thought. The reconstructed thoughts we collected had a realistic quality and were remarkably candid. (p. 486)

When researchers attempt to ascertain the thoughts and feelings that the participants experienced during $Event_1$, they design their instructions accordingly, e.g. by telling them to stop the videotape anytime they recall having had a specific thought during the conversation (Waldron and Cegala, 1992).

Other researchers attempt to have participants serve as informants in whatever ways they can. This more open ethnographic approach recognizes that participants make different kinds of comments: they report on previous thoughts and reactions that they experienced during $Event_1$, they make observations derived from viewing the videotape, they explain practices they assume are unfamiliar to outsiders, and/or they offer explanations of conduct designed specifically for the investigator. Ethnographically oriented investigators design their instructions so as to encourage a range of comments. Such instructions direct participants to address both the investigators' interests and 'anything else of interest'. For example in the following excerpt the investigator directs the participant to comment on matters relevant to teaching and whatever else he sees as possibly relevant:

[11/22/95] (VS with Preceptor)

Researcher:	We have been looking at the interaction, the discourse, the actual strategies used. At this point we are more concerned with complementing that with your perceptions, your understandings of relevant moments.
Preceptor:	Oh.
Researcher:	Now, what our interests are really include teaching,
Preceptor:	Right.
Researcher:	and teaching is generally done when you see the intern off-base in some way. Where you see that there's some guidance and direction necessary.
Preceptor:	I see.
Researcher:	So we'd like your perceptions on when you see something particularly that the intern is doing, maybe in presenting the patient, where you think there is some kind of re-direction that's called for, and then if you have any comments on how you did that kind of thing,
Preceptor:	Mm mhm
Researcher:	We'd like to hear that too.
Preceptor:	Okay.
Researcher:	So anything that you see as particularly relevant to your work as a preceptor on this occasion.

Given instructions such as these, it is not surprising that the participants' comments would include their observations, interpretations, recollections, etc. One implication of eliciting a variety of kinds of comments is that on a case by case basis the investigator needs to assess the plausibility of whether the reported-on matter was likely to have been oriented to during $Event_1$.

While I think some matters to which the participants possibly or probably oriented during $Event_1$ can be inferred from some of the participants' comments, there is good reason to conclude that the participants' comments should not be read as representing or approximating the participants' streams of thought during $Event_1$. A distinction that Ericsson and Simon (Ericsson and Simon, 1993) make between *verbalizations of thoughts* and *social verbalizations* is pertinent to this discussion. They claim that when subjects verbalize their thoughts they do not describe or explain what they are doing – they simply verbalize the information they attend to while generating the answer. Social verbalizations, on the other hand, are not verbalizations of the thoughts associated with doing a task but rather are verbalizations which attend to the social situation.

Explanations, descriptions, justifications, and rationalizations are socially motivated verbalizations generated to communicate to one or more listeners. Successful communication with listeners requires additional processes to attain coherence and take account of differences in background knowledge. Hence social verbalizations may be quite different from the sequences of thoughts generated by subjects themselves while solving problems, performing actions, and making evaluations and decisions. (p. xiv)

Ericsson and Simon discuss the issue of distinguishing between verbalizations of thought and social verbalizations.

Concurrent verbalizations, unlike social verbalizations, often lack coherence and contain frequent disjointed sequences without explicit relations between the thoughts. Think-aloud protocols leave unanswered how the solution was generated in detail and why a given method was adopted among many possible methods. In contrast, a verbal account that explains and describes each step will satisfy the social demands for coherence and reasonable completeness. (p. xv)

The video stimulated comments reported in published studies often consist of well-formed, coherent talk. It seems likely that whatever fleeting thoughts occur to participants as they interact, they are distinctly different from the thoughts and feelings as indicated in the comments. In the best case scenario, a comment would modify or transform an original thought yet still indicate something of it. Needless to say, there is no formula to determine what parts of the comment reflect $Event_1$ versus $Event_2$ thinking, and I doubt that such a formula could be worked out.

Some matters are systematically omitted or excluded from being commented on. One basis for matters being absent from comments is that they did not receive sufficient attention for subsequent mentioning. Ericsson et al. (1993) report that subjects proffer more verbalizations when reading problematic texts than when reading well-formed texts. In a similar vein, Langer (Langer, 1989) argues that people tend to be 'mindless' when activities are effortless and routine and 'mindful' when encountering a novel situation, when behaviour becomes effortful, when behaviour is interrupted by external factors that do not allow for its completion, when experiencing a negative or positive consequence that is sufficiently discrepant with the consequences of prior enactments of the same behaviour, and when the situation does not allow for sufficient involvement. Benoit and Benoit (Benoit and Benoit, 1986) critique Langer's dichotomy of 'mindless' or 'mindful' states as an oversimplification, suggesting that it is more accurate to view attentiveness as existing on a continuum with various and varying degrees of attentiveness or concentration. In addition to lack of sufficient attention, there are many other bases for omitting or excluding matters oriented to during $Event_1$ from a participant's comments, for example, privacy concerns, sensitivity about the matter, issues of self-presentation, and so on. It should be clear by now that there is no simple correspondence between the matters to which the participants oriented while interacting and the matters on which the participants report in their comments.

Another complication confounding attempts to infer the matters to which the participants oriented during $Event_1$ is that some comments may be artifacts of watching the videotape. Schwartz and Garamoni (Schwartz and Garamoni, 1986) suggest that viewing oneself on the videotape leads to a heightened self-awareness and more attention focused on oneself. They propose that two problems occur when the camera is positioned to record behavior from the observer's viewpoint rather than the participant's viewpoint. 'First it fails to provide the most appropriate memory prompt because it does not recreate the performance as experienced by the subject. Second, and most importantly, videotaping and playing back an audience's perspective heighten self-awareness and make salient aspects of the public self...' (p. 193) They recommend positioning the cameras over the head of each of the participants while they interact to capture the subjects' perspectives. While multiple cameras so positioned attempt to minimize the differences between the physical scene encountered while watching the videotape and the physical scene available while interacting, stationary cameras do not do what our eyes do.

A further complication is a difference in the knowledge of the interaction's outcome when participants engage in interaction as compared with when they watch a videotape of the interaction. When making comments while watching Event$_1$ on videotape, the participants know what is going to happen next. It is unclear how knowing the ending affects the matters on which the participants comment and the ways in which they shape what they report.

To summarize, in using the participants' comments to make inferences about matters to which the participants oriented during Event$_1$, investigators need to be aware of a number of challenges to the validity of their claims. First, participants may not be able to, or may elect not to, talk about the matters to which they oriented during an interaction. Second, the matters about which the participants report, as well as how they shape the reports, may be 'recipient designed', that is, shaped for the investigators with whom they interacted during the video session. Third, participants may make comments while watching the video that have no bearing on matters experienced during Event$_1$.

These challenges should encourage investigators to treat participants' comments as complex products that may point to matters from Event$_1$ and/or may be shaped for the investigator co-present in Event$_2$ and/or may be an artifact of viewing the videotape. When attempting to draw inferences about matters to which a participant possibly or probably oriented, an investigator should consider at the very least how and possibly why the reported matter became a reportable matter during Event$_2$.

How can comments be useful in conversation analytic studies?

In a study which used both recordings of interaction and video stimulated comments as data, Pomerantz et al. (1997) described three benefits of using the two data sources:

1) Participants reported the relevance of issues at certain places in the interaction that the investigators overlooked in their observations. The investigators were able to use the comments as suggestions for sites of close observation.

2) By closely observing interactional details, the investigators analyzed strategies or practices that seemed to be solutions to certain sets of participants' concerns. When the participants articulated those concerns in their comments, it provided some confirmatory evidence that the participants probably had oriented to those concerns.

3) Some actions, reactions and/or concerns were reported as withheld or not displayed. Considering the reportedly withheld actions, reactions and concerns in conjunction with examining the conduct that was enacted at those points added a dimension to the analyses.

In the remainder of this section, I illustrate how conversation analysts have used both recorded interaction and a participant's comment as data. My first illustration is drawn from materials that my collaborators and I collected in a medical setting. For this illustration, I selected a comment from the video session with the preceptor and the segment of interaction which prompted the preceptor to comment. Transcripts of the interactional segment (Event$_1$) and of the preceptor's comment (Event$_2$) are given below with the parties designated as 'Doctor' and 'Patient'.

Event$_1$ (segment of interaction) [2-16-93[2]:38]

```
 1   Doc:   .hhhhhh Have you ever (.) t-uh tried to (.) take any medicine
 2          for: the night sweats?
 3          (0.5)
 4   Doc:   M-[m ((negative))
 5   Pat:      [I have uh never had anythin::g .hh As a matter of fa:ct
 6          uh(.)when they did this uh lungectomy it [was at (        ).
 7   Doc:                                            [Mhm,
 8   Doc:   [Yah,
 9   Pat:   [.hmhhh .t At that ti:me where I was livin', (.) they took me
10          (0.2) to the closest hospita[l.
11   Doc:                               [Right.
12   Pat:   .hmhh.hh A:nd so but they did get my records.
13   Doc:   Mhm,
14   Pat:   from there and transfer it, and no one has even questioned me
15          about it and I even had to request a chest X-ray. Nobody
16          (.)
17   Doc:   mYeah
18   Pat:   I was never followed up
19   Doc:   Yeah.
20   Pat:   over all of these years.
21   Doc:   Oka[y,
22   Pat:      [And that's what BOTH(h)ERS me. because I say if: I we:re (.)
23          had been followed up
24          (0.2)
25   Pat:   I don't think (.) maybe. (0.8) it could have ha:ppened.
26   Doc:   We[ll
27   Pat:     ['cause it's possible, (      ) it wouldn't have gotten to this
28          point.
29   Doc:   Yah.
30          (1.0)
31   Doc:   I don't kno: w I it's u-hard to know what p[eople could have
32          do:ne.                                     [
33   Pat:                                              [That's what I
34          seh-I t-
35   Doc:   [Yeh
36   Pat:   [I can't sa:y.=
```

```
37   Doc:    =Yeah, [I can't either.
38   Pat:          [But that is my feeling.
39   Doc:    Yah,
40   Pat:    that you do:n't (0.7) just walk awa(h)y fr(h)om
41               [a  si[tuation l i k e  th[a : t  w i t h o u t  a n y
42   Doc:          [Mh  [No it shouldn't.  [It should 've been followed up.
43           (0.3)
44   Doc:    But I but I'm (.) I ['m not su:re.,
45   Pat:                       [Any follow up.
46           (0.4)
47   Doc:    how much difference it would make, .hh Diz lemme ask a couple
48           more questions about the night sweats though...
             ((preceptor continues questioning patient about her symptoms))
```

Around line 44, the participant stopped the tape and said:

Event$_2$ (video stimulated comment)

```
1   Doc:    She just said that my previous doctor's committed
2           malpractice, and I'm now answering that question.
```

In his comment, the doctor provided a commentary on the talk that he was viewing on the videotape. With the comment 'she just said that my previous doctor's committed malpractice', the doctor gave an interpretation of what the patient was really saying that was different from what she apparently was saying. In interpreting the meaning of the patient's talk, the doctor used the terminology of a legally punishable offence ('committed malpractice'). While the doctor did not explicitly tell the researcher in his comment his version of the patient's motive, a motive that is implicated in his comment is that the patient was telling him about the previous medical incident to see if he would confirm her view that the previous doctor committed malpractice which would strengthen her conviction that she has a legal case. In other words, in his comment on this segment of talk, the doctor implied that the patient's intentions were possibly litigious.

How plausible is it that the doctor, while interacting with the patient, interpreted the patient's intention as possibly litigious? There are obvious alternatives: he may have replayed the conversation in his mind when the interaction was over and retrospectively interpreted the patient's intention as such or he may have interpreted the patient's intention as such only upon watching the videotape of the interaction. My claim that the doctor probably interpreted the patient's intention as possibly litigious during the interaction is supported by the doctor's conduct during the interaction. In other words, the support for the claim that the doctor had probably oriented to the patient's intention as possibly litigious rests on the compatibility between the proposed orientation and the practices that the doctor employed during the interaction.

The aspects of the doctor's conduct that are compatible with his having interpreted the patient's intention as possibly litigious are his attempts to undermine what would be the grounds for a legal suit, his use of cautious claims to undermine the patient's grounds for a suit, and his use of a reference term that seemed to distance specific doctors, and doctors in general, from being referred to as the potentially culpable parties.

As the patient described a previous experience with health providers, she portrayed the event as one in which she received less than proper medical attention ('no one has even questioned me about it', 'I even had to request a chest X-ray', 'I was never followed up', 'over all of these years' on lines 14–15, 18, 20).

```
5    Pat:   [I have uh never had anythin::g .hh As a matter of fa:ct
6           uh(.)when they did this uh lungectomy it [was at (        ).
7    Doc:                                             ⌊Mhm,
8    Doc:   [Yah,
9    Pat:   [.hmhhh .t At that ti: me where I was livin', (.) they took me
10          (0.2) to the closest hospita[l.
11   Doc:                               [Right.
12   Pat:   .hmhh.hh A:nd so but they did get my records.
13   Doc:   Mhm,
14   Pat:   from there and transfer it, and no one has even questioned me
15          about it and I even had to request a chest X-ray. Nobody
16          (.)
17   Doc:   mYeah
18   Pat:   I was never followed up
19   Doc:   Yeah.
20   Pat:   over all of these years.
21   Doc:   Oka[y,
22   Pat:      [And that's what BOTH(h)ERS me. because I say if: I we:re (.)
23          had been followed up
24          (0.2)
25   Pat:   I don't think (.) maybe. (0.8) it could have ha:ppened.
26   Doc:   We[ll
```

In response to the patient's portrayal of not having received proper medical attention, the doctor offered acknowledgments which did not display any affiliation or alignment with the patient's position ('mYeah', 'Yeah', 'Okay' on lines 17, 19, 21). As the interaction proceeded, the patient shifted from detailing medical neglect to the consequences of the alleged neglect. On lines 22–25, she named a specific injury (i.e., her current medical condition) as a possible consequence of the medical neglect she had just detailed. When she suggested that the lack of follow-up care was possibly responsible for her current medical condition, in other words, that she had suffered damages or injury for which medical practitioners could be held responsible, the doctor started to take issue. In his initial response ('But' in line 26), the doctor displayed a lack of alignment to, and indicated possible upcoming disagreement with, the patient's suggestion that medical providers could be held responsible for the patient's current medical condition. In his turns that follow, he attempted to undermine the grounds for her possible suit.

In two of his responses, the doctor's assertions can be seen as attempts to undermine the patient's grounds for filing a suit (lines 31–2 and 42–4, 47). In both of these attempts, the doctor incorporated *cautious claims*.

```
22   Pat:    [And that's what BOTH(h)ERS me. because I say if: I we:re (.)
23           had been followed up
24           (0.2)
25   Pat:    I don't think (.) maybe. (0.8) it could have ha:ppened.
26   Doc:    We[ll
27   Pat:      ['cause it's possible, (        ) it wouldn't have gotten to this
28           point.
29   Doc:    Yah.
30           (1.0)
31   Doc:    I don't kno: w I it's u-hard to know what p[eople could have
32           do:ne.                                    [
33   Pat:                                              [That's what I
34           seh-I t-
35   Doc:    [Yeh
36   Pat:    [I can't sa: y.=
37   Doc:    =Yeah,[I can't either.
38   Pat:          [But that is my feeling.
39   Doc:    Yah,
40   Pat:    that you do:n't (0.7) just walk awa(h)y fr(h)om
41             [a si[tuation l i k e  th[a : t  w i t h o u t   a n y
42   Doc:       [Mh [No it shouldn't.   [It should 've been followed up.
43           (0.3)
44   Doc:    But I but I'm (.) I ['m not su:re.,
45   Pat:                        [Any follow up.
46           (0.4)
47   Doc:    how much difference it would make,
```

In saying 'I don't kno:w I it's u-hard to know what people could have do:ne.' (lines 31–2), the doctor was strictly accountable for the limited claim of not knowing, or having difficulty knowing, any medical treatment that would have been efficacious in preventing the patient's medical condition from developing. While his on-the-record assertion contained a claim of his not knowing any efficacious preventative treatments, it could be heard to imply that there were no effective preventative treatments currently known in medicine. If the implication were true, it would undermine the patient's proposal that her current condition may not have developed had she been followed up.

The use of such *cautious claims* is prevalent in disputes, both in and out of court (Pomerantz, 1984). In this case, the doctor's use of *cautious claims* while attempting to undermine the patient's grounds for a suit is compatible with his possibly having interpreted the patient's intention as possibly litigious.

The doctor's limited claim of his not knowing, or having difficulty knowing, of an efficacious preventative treatment for the patient's condition has the power to undermine the patient's proposal inasmuch as the doctor is seen to be someone who would/should know the available preventative treatments. That is, his limited claim gains its power to undermine the patient's proposal by virtue of who the doctor is seen to be. Inasmuch as a medical expert claims not knowing any efficacious preventative treatment, it is likely that any such treatments are not part of current medical knowledge. Thus the ability of the doctor's assertion to undermine the patient's proposal plays off the identities of the participants as 'doctor' and 'patient'. If medical science does not have any efficacious preventative treatments, a lay person's proposal that her current condition could have been prevented had she been followed up is implausible.

Additionally, the doctor's use of 'people' in 'I don't kno:w I i̱t's u-ha̱rd to know wha̱t pe̱ople co̱uld have do̱:ne' seems consistent with his having interpreted the patient's intention as possibly litigious. The patient referred to the agents responsible for neglecting her with a plural pronoun (i.e., 'they') and used the passive voice without referring to responsible agents when talking about the lack of follow up care (lines 14 and 18–19). In employing the reference 'people' instead of 'they' or 'the doctors' in his assertion, the doctor seemed to somewhat deflect the focus away from both doctors as a category and those particular care-givers involved in the case.

In his second challenge to the patient's proposal, the doctor again incorporated *cautious claims*: 'No it shouldn't. It should've been followed up. (0.3) But I but I'm (.) I'm not sure, how much difference it would make' (lines 42–4, 47). While the on-the-record claim the doctor made was one of uncertainty as to whether the lack of having been followed up was consequential for the patient's current condition having developed, the implication of his assertion was that not having been followed up almost certainly made no difference. In both the earlier assertion and this one, the doctor used a limited or cautious claim to imply a state of affairs that would undermine the patient's proposal.

While we can not know for sure whether the doctor oriented to the patient's intention as possibly litigious while he was interacting with the patient, an examination of the doctor's conduct during the interaction suggests that it is at least plausible. There are several aspects of the doctor's conduct that seem compatible with his having interpreted the patient's intention as possibly litigious. First, the doctor worked to undermine the very grounds upon which a suit could be brought – that a designated party is responsible for specific damages or injuries. Second, the doctor's use of *cautious claims* is compatible with an orientation to being held strictly accountable for one's claims, such as in legal proceedings. Third, in selecting the reference term 'people', the doctor seemed to have avoided invoking both the category of doctors as well as the health care providers responsible for the lack of follow up care.

The remainder of the illustrations of using ethnographic data to supplement analyses of interaction are drawn from the work of Douglas Maynard. In his book, *Bad News, Good News: Conversational Order in Everyday Talk and Clinical Settings*, Maynard (Maynard, 2003) discusses the 'limited affinity' between conversation analysis and ethnography. The use of ethnography, he says, 'neither replaces nor is necessary to the capturing of talk's sequential organization. It simply may help explain the existence of interactional practices, particularly when sequential analysis reveals curious-seeming patterns'. (Chapter 3, p. 35)

Maynard suggests that participants' narratives may serve to complement sequential analysis of talk. While he does not discuss the types of matters that are revealed by examining participants' narratives, the three examples that he offers suggest that he treats participants' narratives as capable of clarifying on some occasions the aims to which the participants oriented and the strategies that they employed as they interacted.

In a study of HIV and AIDS counselling practices, Kinnel and Maynard (Kinnell and Maynard, 1996) observed what they considered a puzzling, somewhat inexplicable pattern: despite official recommendations about tailoring teachings to the needs of individual clients, counsellors often gave information to clients that was not relevant to them personally. The ethnographic account that helped to explain this puzzling conduct was that the counsellors were attempting to satisfy multiple aims: to assist the clients with their needs as well as relay information to the community by way of their clients.

In a study of interaction in an oncology clinic, Lutfey and Maynard (Lutfey and Maynard, 1998) observed that when the oncologist cautiously asked the patient if he had discussed 'a program called Hospice' with the hospital social worker, the patient and his partner collaboratively shifted the topic from Hospice to a nursing home where the patient could go upon discharge. Maynard suggests that based solely on the interaction, the investigators might have concluded that the oncologist was somewhat unsuccessful in the attempt to have the patient and his partner consider Hospice as an option. However, the oncologist's narrative suggested that he or she had a somewhat different aim in talking about Hospice. In commenting on the encounter, the oncologist said: 'Sometimes I use the discussion of Hospice not so much because it's important to me that the patient accept a home Hospice program, but . . . to get the conversation really directed where you want it to go, which is on death and dying issues' (Lutfey and Maynard 1998:325). In his or her narrative, the oncologist claimed to be operating with an aim that was different from the one the investigators had inferred from the discourse and claimed to be using the topic of Hospice strategically. Inasmuch as the reported aim was different from the one the investigators had initially inferred, it was useful in supplementing the analysis of interaction.

In a study on delivering news in HIV/AIDS counselling sessions, Maynard noticed that the ways in which the counsellors delivered bad news were in unmarked forms, for example by telling the client to read the test results without providing any foreshadowing or hinting what the news might be. Given that bad news so often is delivered in a marked form, Maynard was initially puzzled by the occurrences of this news delivery pattern. The participants' narratives provided a way to understand the pattern. When asked about their strategies for delivering bad news, the counsellors reported that one of the primary aims was to elicit an emotional response from the client. (The view generally held in that clinic was that counselling work could not get started without it.) Maynard found the participants' narrative accounts helpful in pinpointing a function of using marked or unmarked news delivery formats. Based on the narrative account, Maynard had stronger grounds for proposing that a marked form in delivering bad news provides the recipient opportunity for greater control or management of the expression of the emotions associated with the bad news whereas an exposed form denies the recipient those opportunities.

Discussion

Throughout this chapter, I have argued that there are some analytic uses to having access to the participants' comments as well as to the interaction itself. The argument rested on the assumption that at times participants have *aims* when they interact, make *interpretations* of each other's talk, and have *concerns* that bear on their interactional conduct. Furthermore, these aims, interpretations and concerns may be different from the aims, interpretations and concerns that other participants and researchers infer based on the participants' conduct and/or their narratives.

The assumptions I make regarding cognitive phenomena colour my perspective on the range of analytic questions that are interesting to ask and the choices we have for our analytic terminology. I will clarify my perspective by explicating several distinctions I make while analyzing interaction. The first distinction is between a participant's *understanding* and his or her *display of understanding*.

Recall the earlier discussion of the comment in which the doctor reported an interpretation of the intention behind the patient's talk, an interpretation that he purportedly made while interacting with the patient. In understanding what the patient was really saying and in analyzing her intention, the doctor was doing the sorts of analysis that interactants routinely do on each other's talk, the sort of analysis which professional analysts of discourse and interaction treat as objects of their enquiries.

The primary way in which conversation analysts deal with the issue of participants' understandings is as Members' work. In the course of interacting, Members have ways of displaying their understanding of co-participants' talk, of determining whether or not they understand their co-participants' talk, and of determining whether or not they have been understood by their co-participants. Schegloff (1991a) described how the organization of interaction provides for participants to display an understanding of that to which their talk is addressed.

Built into the very organization by which opportunities to talk are allocated to participants in ordinary conversation is a related 'understanding-display' device (Sacks, Schegloff, and Jefferson, 1974). The consequence is that speakers almost necessarily reveal their understanding of that to which their talk is addressed, whether that is prior talk, other conduct, or events and occurrences 'scenic' to the interaction. (p. 167)

Heritage (1986) called our attention to the fact that Members' understanding of prior talk involves their analyses of that prior talk.

. . . each 'next' turn at talk will, in dealing with the previous turn, display its producer's analysis or understanding of the previous turn's content, import and relevancies. (p. 5)

While understanding as a Members' accomplishment has been widely studied, an issue that has been pretty much neglected is whether there are understandings that the participants have, or analyses that they make, which they do not display. In the quotations above, Schegloff wrote '. . . speakers almost necessarily reveal their understanding of that to which their talk is addressed . . .' and Heritage wrote '. . . each "next" turn at talk will . . . display its producer's analysis or understanding . . .'. If I were to rewrite their texts to fit with the point I am making, I would change Schegloff's excerpt to read '. . . speakers almost necessarily reveal an understanding of that to which their talk is addressed' and Heritage's to read '. . . each "next" turn at talk will . . . display an analysis or understanding of its producer . . .' (emphasis added).

I think my colleagues would not seriously dispute the phenomenon of persons at times not displaying their understandings and analyses. With just a little thought, we can conjure up the sorts of understandings that are likely to be withheld. For example, certain motives or intentions attributed to co-participants may be detrimental or counterproductive to put on the table and criticisms of certain categories of persons may be routinely withheld.

One source or basis upon which to claim that a person understood a remark differently than he or she displayed is an informant's comment. In advocating the use of informants' comments in this chapter, I am opening up the question as to whether analysts can and should take into account the possibility of non-displayed understandings and interpretations at particular identifiable places in the interaction. If reports of specific with-holds are credible, a researcher might be able to make stronger claims about conduct that is performed in the place of conduct not performed.

To reiterate, I am claiming that we should distinguish between participants' understandings and participants' displays of understanding. In distinguishing between those two concepts, we make room to study the occasions on which these two matters are discrepant.

Another concept that could stand being clarified is participants' *orientations*. In conversation analytic culture, claims about the participants' orientations are commonly made. For example, in illustrating the concept of conditional relevance, one might say that upon a participant's making a request, the recipient orients to the relevance of granting or refusing the request. Evidence to show that participants orient to the relevance of granting/refusing might include both the routine enactment of grantings and refusals as well as the participants' treating absences of a granting or refusal as noticeable and remarkable occurrences. In this discussion, I am drawing a distinction between the participants' orientations and the inter-actional evidence that supports the claim of the participants' orientations.

Claims about participants' *displaying an orientation* to a rule, a propriety, a violation, an impropriety, etc. also are commonly made. For example, in discussing the phenomenon of interactants not explicitly praising them-selves or doing so with only very modest terms, analysts might say that the formulations display the participants' orientation to the impropriety of self-praise. Here, too, I am making a distinction between displays of an orientation and the orientation itself.

In both examples that I have just given, the concept of *orientation* is distinguished from displays or evidence of the orientation. It might be useful to further clarify what we mean by *orientation*. If participants *orient* to the relevance of granting/refusing the request, are we saying that they *perceive* that relevance or are we saying something else? To me it seems that we are comfortable using the term 'orientation' but feel as if we are committing to a psychological perspective if we use any alternative terms.

I close this chapter with a brief discussion on the benefits and dangers of using ethnographic data to supplement analyses of interaction. As I have been discussing the benefits of using participants' comments to supplement interactional data throughout the chapter, a list of the benefits should suffice. Participants' comments may serve as suggestions of places in the interaction for close investigation; they may help us to understand the bases of puzzling patterns of interactive conduct; they may serve as correctives of inferences we may be making about the apparent aims, concerns, or understandings of the participants; they may serve as confirmatory evidence for claims about the functions of features of discourse; and they may lead us to investigate possible instances of conduct standing in place of possibly withheld actions.

Some of the dangers of using participants' comments have been discussed in the section on threats to validity. In line with that discussion, I would emphasize that there is an inclination to take a participant's report on face value and not see how the comment came to be produced on the occasion in which it was offered and what the speaker might have been doing with it. Moreover, there is a temptation to treat the inferred interpretation, aim, or concern as stable and explanatory rather than as shifting, amorphous, or however else it may be manifest.

A danger that I have not discussed earlier is having one's attention drawn to the apparent informativeness of the comment and hence pulled away from the details of the interaction. Maynard (2003) aptly described this danger:

The impulse to grasp wider contexts surrounding an utterance points toward obtaining more ethnographic information and data. Without proper *analytic control* of contextual information, however, investigators paradoxically may *lose* data in which the produced orderliness or important facets of social organization actually reside. (p. 70)

. . . ethnographic insistence on the relevance of larger and wider institutional structures can mean a loss of data in and as the interaction, for attention shifts from actual utterances in the fullness of their detail and as embedded within a local interactional context to embrace narrative or other general accounts concerning social surroundings. (p. 72)

As conversation analysts know, analytic observations come from very close attention to the details of interactional conduct. Without that close attention to detail, we do not happen upon the puzzles and surprises that are so much a part of our work. If using participants' comments leads an investigator to attend to the comments over the interaction, far more is lost than can possibly be gained.

One last note. This chapter should not be read as an argument aimed at convincing conversation analysts to use a combination of ethnographic and interactional data. Rather, it is an attempt to raise issues about the status and import of the mental lives of participants in interaction and to promote reflection on our analytic questions and language choices.

Acknowledgements

My thanks to Jonathan Potter and Hedwig te Molder for pushing me to state more clearly my assumptions about cognition and to Doug Maynard for helpful comments on an earlier draft of this chapter.

NOTES

1. This method of gathering data is variously referred to as *stimulated recall, post-performance videotape reconstruction, video reconstruction, video-assisted recall protocol,* or *video-recall*. In order to avoid incorporating the assumption that the participants are 'recalling' or 'reconstructing' their earlier thoughts into the name, I will refer to this type of data as *video stimulated comments* or simply *comments*.
2. We collected five kinds of data for the project: we videotaped medical interactions, audiotaped video-stimulated comments, audiotaped comments recorded in private by each participant at the conclusion of the interaction, solicited comments handwritten by participants of focus groups prior to their discussions, and audiotaped focus group discussions. For the purpose of this chapter, only the first two are relevant.
3. This ideal resonates with the protocol of cognitive psychologists who investigate subjects' cognitive processes while the subjects' perform solo tasks, for example solve a problem, make a decision, or read a text. Those psychologists study cognitive processes by instructing subjects to 'think aloud' while performing clearly defined tasks [Ericsson and Simon, 1993 #102].
4. In a study by Daly et al. [Daly, 1989 #103] participants were asked to talk aloud their thoughts as they interacted. This was possible because the participants were not interacting face-to-face; they interacted by typing their messages to one another on networked computers.

5 From paradigm to prototype and back again: interactive aspects of 'cognitive processing' in standardized survey interviews

Nora Cate Schaeffer and Douglas W. Maynard

Survey researchers have long been interested in the process by which answers to survey questions come about (see Schaeffer and Maynard, 2002b; Maynard and Schaeffer 2002b). The last two decades have seen considerable research on this subject. Most of this research has drawn heavily and fruitfully on social-information-processing models of the question-and-answer process, which are fundamentally psychological. These approaches commonly use one of several variants of a four-stage model of the process of responding to questions; according to the description in these models the respondent interprets the question, retrieves the requested information, evaluates the information for the purposes of reporting it, and finally maps his or her answer onto the response categories and reports an answer (see Cannell, Miller and Oksenberg, 1981; Sudman, Bradburn and Schwarz, 1996; Tourangeau, Rasinski and Rips, 2000). Such models present 'cognitive processing' as a psychological process that takes place within the respondent. Research based on this model has also contributed to the development of methods – such as cognitive interviewing – for improving the design of survey questions that are rooted in this psychological perspective and model. For example, the cognitive interviewing techniques of paraphrasing and 'think-alouds' that are used to study comprehension and information retrieval draw on psychological models to seek evidence of the cognitive processing that respondents perform, which would otherwise remain invisible (for examples, see Presser et al., 2004; Schwarz and Sudman, 1996).

A complementary approach that obtains indirect evidence of respondents' cognitive processes does so by considering interactional aspects of the survey interview in a particular way. This approach does not actually examine the interaction between interviewers and respondents directly, but uses theories about interaction to predict how survey questions affect answers. This approach can be illustrated by referring to research about the effects of question order. Schwarz and others (see review in Schwarz, 1994) draw on descriptions of the norms governing conversation (Grice, 1975), to predict and explain how the order of questions influences answers. Following Grice, they argue that respondents will use the sequence of questions as informative and design their answers to be relevant, to provide new information, and so on. Split-ballot experiments that vary the order of questions for randomly assigned groups of respondents then allow researchers to examine when the answers respondents give are actually affected by features of the questions. When a split-ballot experiment shows that the order of survey questions does affect answers, researchers working in this paradigm then interpret the effect as indirect evidence of respondents' cognitive processing and an illustration of the influence of conversational norms – a particular set of social and interactional practices – on mental processes. The interpretation of such studies thus describes the respondent as 'interacting with' or 'reacting to' the features of survey questions, but the role of interviewer and the actual interaction between the participants is not examined.

In the present chapter we take a different view of cognition and examine the interaction between the interviewer and respondent directly in a specific genre of interview – the standardized survey interview. In the *paradigmatic*, and probably most common, interactional sequence in standardized survey interviewing, an interviewer asks a question as written and a respondent answers in the format (e.g., 'yes' or 'no'; a specific quantity, etc.) implied by the question. We call such a sequence paradigmatic in the sense that it is the ideal sequence from the standpoint of survey design. Because such sequences display no special 'problems' in the interaction, an observer might infer that the stages of cognitive processing required to produce an answer occur 'inside the respondent's head'. But in our view, the process of 'cognition' is not so individualistic.

Consider the first stage in the information-processing model, the respondent's act of interpreting the question. To understand the 'point' of any question, a respondent must understand at least two things: the type of information that constitutes an adequate answer and the form in which he or she should provide that information. How does the respondent come to know and understand these two matters? When the interviewer simply reads a question and the respondent quickly produces an answer, it is easy – though not necessarily correct – to conceive of this process of understanding as internal to the respondent. However, when the interaction between the interviewer and respondent goes beyond the paradigmatic sequence, the interaction may give clues about the requirements for such knowledge and understanding. Indeed, interviews in which there are 'deviations' from the standardized script and the paradigmatic question-answer sequences make visible the ways in which answering a question – and what might otherwise be labelled as the respondent's 'cognitive processing' – can be fundamentally interactive and collaborative. Therefore, in the conclusion, we address assumptions about what *is* paradigmatic and what is deviation with regard to interaction in the survey interview. We propose that the *prototypical* question-answer sequence involves an organized set of activities in which the contribution of the interviewer goes beyond merely reading questions; many times the actions of the interviewer form an integral part of what a psychological perspective would identify as the respondent's cognition and answering.

Interaction in the interview cannot provide a window to the internal processes – that might be labelled cognitive – of the participants. Our analysis parallels the critiques in Edwards and Potter (1992), Potter and Wetherell (1987), and elsewhere that challenge 'the assumption that cognition is exclusively an individual act, clearly distinguishable from external social processes that may influence it' (Levine, Resnick and Higgins, 1993, p. 588). Instead, when we observe the interaction between the interviewer and respondent, we see activities that show participants orienting toward the task at hand. What might be conceptualized as 'cognitive processing' from the psychological perspective is visible in the interaction between participants and is not reducible to the 'cognitive processing' of either party. Thus, we locate the immediate site of what might be labelled joint 'cognition' in the interaction between interviewer and respondent and in the way parties exhibit the 'interactional substrate' of standardized interviewing (Maynard and Marlaire, 1992). At various points in our analysis we note in passing that behaviours we observe might be interpreted as indirect evidence of internal cognitive processing by one of the participants. However, such an approach is different from ours, which focuses on how the participants jointly accomplish the task at hand (obtaining and recording information and opinions) through their practical actions and interactions.

Survey researchers use standardized questions and interviews as part of a set of practices (that include probability sampling) that have as their goal taking measurements that meet certain requirements in order to describe a population (see Schaeffer, 1991; Maynard and Schaeffer, 2000). Many proposals to replace the standardized survey interview with a different sort of interaction would have the consequence of sacrificing that goal (see, for example, Mishler, 1986; Widdicombe and Wooffitt, 1995), and we do not make such a proposal. Furthermore, in this analysis we are agnostic about the matter of individual 'cognitive processing' as it is invoked in the research tradition described above. However, we recognize that activities we observe and analyze below would be labelled as concerned with 'comprehension' or other cognitive tasks by researchers who use social-information-processing models of the response process. Thus, when we refer to 'cognitive processing' in the analysis, we mean to show how the concept might be used in discussing the phenomena we describe. Our own focus is on the orientations and characterizations of participants as revealed in their talk and actions; and we argue that individualistic notions of the respondent's cognitive processing are insufficient to describe what we observe in the interaction between the interviewer and respondent. Although notions of shared cognitive processing are closer to the approach we take here, we focus on what can be observed in the interaction, how the participants treat each other's contributions, and what this tells us about participants' concerns. Our analysis shows how the structure of concerted participation in the interview, including the behaviour of interviewers, radically enters into what some researchers assign to the respondent as 'cognitive processing'. We also suggest implications our analysis has for improving the design of survey questions.

The analysis and data

The interviewer's behaviour in survey interviews is constrained by the rules of standardized interviewing, which are requirements of the interviewer's role. Several of those constraints are particularly relevant to this analysis: to read the question as worded, to obtain an answer that can be seen to be produced by the respondent and not the interviewer (compare Button, 1987), to probe nondirectively, and to maintain a cooperative relationship for the duration of the interview (see, for example, Brenner, 1985; Fowler and Mangione, 1990). These constraints are relevant because interviewers are trained to follow these rules, are supervised and evaluated according to how well they accomplish them, and can be seen to orient to the rules in their interaction with the respondent (e.g., by saying, 'I need to read the question as it appears on my screen'; Houtkoop-Steenstra, 2000). Proper standardization sometimes requires the interviewer to ask a question with an 'obvious' answer – an answer that uses information the respondent has already volunteered or that seems to be a reasonable inference from previous answers. Repeatedly asking such obvious questions may make the interviewer seem inattentive or socially inept, and so threaten her cooperative relationship with the respondent. To help mitigate such role conflict, Census Bureau interviewers can use a practice called 'verification'. In this procedure, an interviewer verifies both that she has correctly heard and remembered information already provided by a respondent and that the information is the correct answer to the question. For example, if a respondent has already mentioned her age, the interviewer could, instead of asking a question about age, say something like, 'I think you said you are 24 years old. Is that the age I should record for you?' or 'How old were you on your last birthday? I think you said you were 24. Is that correct?' The situations in which a verification might be useful and appropriate are highly varied, and the techniques interviewers use for verifications are similarly diverse. Although we have not studied them closely, it seems that most verifications are constructed both to show that the interviewer has 'heard' the respondent and to show that the answer is the respondent's own. In listening to actual interviews, however, it is sometimes difficult to determine whether the interviewer has changed the wording of a question as part of an acceptable verification or for some other reason that may have less justification under the rules of standardization.

Standardized survey questions also constrain acceptable answers (compare Fowler and Mangione, 1990; Suchman and Jordan, 1990). Questions may be designed and formatted to obtain a 'yes' or 'no' answer, a specific number or piece of information, one of a set of response categories, or a relatively free-form description (see Dohrenwend, 1965). Accordingly, there are different question-answer 'idioms' (Marlaire and Maynard, 1990), which are probably familiar to most survey respondents from other interactional contexts. To hold some features of question structure constant in this analysis, we study just one survey item that presents the respondent with a complex set of categories to choose from. In this question, the respondent is asked to report about herself and to give proxy reports for other members of the household.

Our analysis presumes, but does not analyze in detail, the basic three-part structure of the question-answer-acknowledgement sequence (see Cannell and Kahn, 1968, p. 572; for parallels see Mehan, 1979, pp. 52–3 and Marlaire and Maynard, 1990, p. 89). Often, in survey interviews – as in the testing sequences Marlaire and Maynard (1990) studied – the acknowledgement is followed by a silence. During the acknowledgement and this silence, the interviewer is engaged in recording one answer and preparing to ask the next question (see Maynard and Schaeffer, 2002b on the 'interviewing sequence').

The data we analyze are provided by audiotapes of twenty-four Computer Assisted Telephone Interviews (CATI) by US Bureau of the Census interviewers for a test of redesigned questions about labour force participation in the Current Population Survey. The information available to us on the audiotapes approximates that available jointly to participants speaking on the telephone. The tapes were not screened or selected using any criteria; they constitute a haphazard collection of interviews. The tapes include only the portion of the interview concerned with labour force participation, and four different versions of the labour force participation questions appear on the tapes. Although the interviewer's identification number is not recorded for all interviews, it appears that there are two pairs of interviews in which the same interviewer conducted both interviews.

Conversation analysis provides a theory about how interactional sequencing makes utterances and associated interactional objects understandable (Heritage, 1984a; Maynard and Clayman, 1991). Conversation analysis also offers a body of prior research and methodological procedures that enable systematic, close examination of interactional detail in the interview. Such examination permits identifying conversational practices – elements of the interactional substrate – that persist in the relatively constrained environment of the standardized interview. Interviews are not conversations and standardized interviews are not job interviews or ethnographic interviews, but all interviews are talk-in-interaction (see Maynard and Schaeffer, 2002b; Schegloff, 1990). More generally, analysis of these practices shows how the organization of interaction enters into the production of social science data (Maynard and Schaeffer, 2000; Schaeffer and Maynard, 2002b).

The Question as it is to be read: paradigmatic sequences

Our analysis concerns the relatively simple question in Figure 5.1, which shows the question as it appears on the interviewer's screen. This question is intended to elicit a choice among the four categories. (The notation '[blind]' means that the categories are available for the interviewer to use but do not appear on the screen and are not read to the respondent.)

Test CPS, Versions C and D, Q25B-2
    Is this business or organization mainly manufacturing, retail trade, wholesale trade, or something else?

      Manufacturing
      Retail Trade
      Wholesale Trade
      Something else
[blind] Don't know
[blind] Refused

Figure 5.1

In the terms used by the social-information-processing model described above, the principal cognitive difficulties posed by this question appear to involve interpreting the question and mapping an answer onto the response categories. If the respondent has relevant information, retrieving it and deciding whether or not to report it would appear to be relatively straightforward. Our analysis focuses on the potentially ambiguous category, 'something else', which can be heard in at least two possible ways, as the excerpts from the interviews below will illustrate. There are eight instances of this question in our tape recordings in which the category 'something else' appears to be the relevant answer.[1] These eight instances account for half of the sixteen occasions when this question was asked (or should have been asked) in nine different interviews.[2]

Extract 1[3] represents an administration of this question that approaches what we call paradigmatic standardized interviewing: the interviewer reads the question (lines 72–4) as it appears on the screen and the respondent chooses one of the four response categories, 'something else', with minimal hesitation (line 76), whereupon the interviewer acknowledges and records the answer (line 77) and then moves on to the next question (lines 77–8).

Extract 1   [Interview 024c, Version D]

```
62  IV:    Sam and friends?
63  MR:    Yes ma'am
64         (2.0) ((typing))
65  IV:    .hh what kind of business or industry is it. {q25B}
66  MR:    Uh beautician
67         (3.8)
68  IV:    .hh Alright and the place where she at she's uh at Is
69         this a beauty shop? or a beauty salon? or
70  MR:    Uh:: Beauty salon
71         (2.1)
72  IV:    .hhh Alright and is this business or organization mainly
73         manufa:cturing retail trade wholesale trade or something
74         else {q25B-2}
75         (1.3)
76  MR:    Uh:: something el(h)se hh::
77  IV:    heh hal::right .hhhH What kind of work does she
78         usually do at this job that is what is her occupation?
```

There is no evidence for the interaction of how the respondent comes to realize the type of information required and the form in which to report it. A similarly unremarkable administration of the question appears in one more of our eight cases (not shown).

Respondents' solicitations of interviewer help

If extract (1) accords with the ideal of standardized interviewing, extract (2) shows a departure from the ideal because of the possible ambiguity of 'something else' in the question.

Extract (2) [Interview 007c, Version C]

73	MR:	Insurance Company
74		(13.0) ((typing))
75	IV:	And what kind of business or industry is this?= {q25B}
76	MR:	=the insurance industry
77		(7.0) ((typing))
78	IV:	Is this business or organization mainly manufaturing
79		retail trade wholeta- wholesale trade or something
80		else? {q25B-2}
81		(1.0)
82	MR:	It's a service industry
83		(1.8)
84	IV:	So it'd be under::?
85		(2.0) ((3rd voice whispers 'something else'))
86	MR:	Well: it wouldn'- wouldn't be manufacturing or retail or
87		(0.9)
88	MR:	or anything like that it's:
89		(0.7)
90	MR:	I don't know how- I don't know what you'd (.) classify
91		it=
92	IV:	=Under something else=
93	MR:	=Yeah:
94		(1.0)
95	IV:	And what kind of work do you usually do at this job that
96		is (.) what is your occupation. {q25C}

This extract illustrates how understanding the point of a question can be fundamentally interactive rather than a problem for the respondent alone. With two small errors in pronunciation, one of which she repairs, the interviewer reads the question accurately (lines 78–80). The respondent, after a slight delay (line 81), provides an answer, 'It's a service industry' (line 82), which suggests that he heard 'something else' as an indirect request to produce a category taxonomically consistent with the categories previously read (for a discussion of indirect requests, see Clark, 1979).[4] However, the interviewer's probe ('So it'd be under::?,' line 84) does not accept the answer, and asks for one that uses the categories rather than adding to them. Now the respondent delays for two seconds[5] and then produces an extended turn of talk (line 86–91) that is not formatted as implicitly requested by the probe. The response reviews material from the interviewer's initial question ('manufacturing or retail trade', line 86) in the order in which it was originally presented and ends with a formulation of uncertainty (lines 88, 90–1). From a psychological perspective this response could be taken to exhibit cognitive processing – it could be a spontaneous retrospective think-aloud displaying how the respondent arrived at his original answer. But that perspective neglects the fundamentally interactive character of the response. In sequential terms, the turn appears to solicit guidance or help.[6] It invites the *interviewer* to produce a candidate answer; note how the interviewer (line 92) treats the respondent's utterance by proposing one of the original categories as a possible answer. The respondent's agreement ('Yeah', line 93) accepts the proposal and ends the verbal exchange.

In summary, extract (2) shows how a respondent may treat 'something else' as a request to produce a new category rather than as one of several categories from which to choose. As it is written, the category 'something else' is potentially ambiguous, and this respondent's initial answer activates the ambiguity, although he has no way of knowing this. Clarifying the point of the question and the form the answer is to take requires coordinated activity by both parties. Thus, this extract also demonstrates how we can understand utterances-in-context as something other than evidence of such cognitive processes as 'interpreting' the question. Rather, turns and their component utterances play fundamentally interactive roles such as soliciting help or guidance with answering a question. And, although the interviewer's probe at line 92 might be judged leading, she is using her knowledge of the structure of the question to respond to a strong solicitation by the respondent. Put differently, actual talk and its related non-vocal content (such as silence) may exhibit something more fundamental than an answering party's cognitive processing. Such fundamental interactive phenomena reflect intricate coordination between the interviewer and respondent in yielding a codable answer.

Extract (3), shows another example of the respondent soliciting the interviewer's help in answering the question. After verifying that 'Certi-Cleaner' is a janitorial service (lines 243–6), the interviewer reads question 25B-2 at lines 248–9. But she omits the category 'manufacturing', providing a possible example of how interviewers use information respondents have previously provided to modify question wording (Houtkoop, 1991/4). That is, the interviewer may have decided that a 'janitorial service' would not be considered 'manufacturing', and so does not read that category.

Extract (3)   [Interview 019c, Version C]

```
243    FR:    Certi-Cleaner of Bigelow
244           (6.2) ((typing))
245    IV:    O:: kay:: and you said this was a (.) janitorial service? {q25B-1}
246    FR:    Yes
247           (7.5) ((typing))
248    IV:    Ohhkay (uh:) would this be considered (.) retail trade
249           whole (.) tale (.) trade or something else.    {q25B-2}
250           (3.5)
```

```
251  FR:    Well (.) Like I say it's just a janitoral service that
252         cleans (.) businesses
253         (0.5)
254  FR:    [when they]'re closed
255  IV:    [Uh  Okay]
256         (3.0)
257  IV:    O : : : : kay : :
258         (1.2)
259  IV:    And let's see what kinda work does he usually do at his
260         job .hh uh:: [(ju-)]   {q25C}
```

After the question reading, the respondent hesitates, producing a long silence (line 250). Previous research has treated response latency such as this as evidence that cognitive processing is taking place (see Bassili, 1996). The respondent's next utterance (lines 251–4) is not formatted as an answer to the question. From a psychological perspective, this utterance might show that the respondent is having trouble understanding the point of the question and as such might display the respondent's 'uncertainty'. But this kind of answer can also be a deployment of 'tentativeness' as an interactive resource (Schaeffer and Maynard, 2002a; cf. Marlaire and Maynard, 1990), which is a characterization of how the participants themselves proceed. Rather than selecting from among the offered categories, the respondent marks her utterance as a repeat ('Like I say', line 251) of the type of business in which her son is engaged ('janitorial service', line 251), adds one descriptor ('that cleans businesses' lines 251–2) and then, after a brief pause (line 253), another ('when they're closed').[7]

The respondent appears to be doing something akin to what Drew (1984) describes as 'reporting' in invitation sequences. Reporting is a way of providing details relevant to answering an invitation without stating an acceptance or rejection, and it allows a co-participant to determine the 'upshot' of the reporting. Analogously, the respondent here avoids answering the question with a category, but provides possibly relevant information the interviewer could use in selecting a proper category or deciding on the next question to ask. The three-second silence at line 256, the acknowledgement at line 257, the next silence at line 258, plus the interviewer's proceeding to the next question (lines 259–60) all indicate that she does precisely this. That is, the silences, acknowledgement and moving on suggest that the interviewer herself has constructed a codable answer from the material provided by the respondent. In short, in a manner similar to that used by the respondent in extract (2), the respondent here solicits the interviewer's help with answering, and the interviewer accedes to that solicitation. (See also the more detailed analysis in Schaeffer and Maynard, 2002a).

Interviewers' offers of help for answering questions

We have seen that an interviewer's help can be solicited, but interviewers can also *offer* help. We examine below four instances of interviewers making increasingly strong offers of help. In these sequences, the help the interviewers offer may make use of information they have already obtained from a respondent:

Extract (4)   [Interview 018c, Version C]

```
104   FR:   The University of North Georgia
105   IV:   Oka:y
106         (5.8) ((typing))
107   IV:   ((tch)) An:d what kind of a business or industry is
108         this? {q25B}
109   FR:   It's a
110         (0.3)
111   FR:   college
112         (0.3)
113   FR:   [ uni]versity
114   IV:   [(uh)]
115   IV:   Okay
116         (4.0)
117   IV:   And is this business or organization mainly
118         manufacturing retail trade wholesale trade or would you
119         (.) consider that something else {q25B-1}
120   FR:   Something else=
121   IV:   =I would too [heh heh heh]
122   FR:                [hhhhhhh]
123   IV:   .hhh and uh (.) what kind of work do you usually do at
124         this job that is (.) what is your occupation? .hhh
125         [ and ] I think- {q25C}
```

Recall that the item on the computer screen reads, 'Is this business or organization mainly manufacturing, retail trade, wholesale trade, or something else?' At lines 118–19 in extract (4), the interviewer modifies the end of the item from '. . . or something else?' to '. . . or would you consider that something else?' The question is intended to get the respondent to choose one of the four categories, but this modification results in *two* questions being asked. The initial question presents a choice of categories to the respondent, while the second is formatted for a 'yes-no' answer. While the modification is slight, it is interactionally significant. The interviewer has shaped the overall item in a way that draws on the conversational preference for contiguity and for agreement (Sacks, 1987). With two questions in a single turn of talk, the preference for contiguity obliges a respondent to answer the second question first. Here, when the interviewer changes 'or something else?' in the standardized question to 'or would you consider . . .', she has restructured the item to elicit an answer to this question immediately.[8] The preference for agreement involves formatting the question to indicate that the speaker expects a particular answer. In extract (4), even as the interviewer employs the 'something else' category, her preface ('would you consider that . . .'), indicates that she expects the respondent to confirm the category as the correct answer. The preface also clarifies that 'something else' is a category, so that the phrase is less likely to be interpreted as it was in extract (2), as a request for a category return. The respondent then gives the preferred answer without hesitation, producing an agreeing answer (line 120) that is a codable category.

Of course, the previous interaction suggests that the question modification is itself occasioned, because the interviewer has learned that the respondent works at a university and knows that a university is to be classified as 'something else'. Therefore, the interviewer's understanding of information already supplied by the respondent and her training about proper coding may lead her to hypothesize an answer for the respondent as she does here (Houtkoop, 1991/4). Following the respondent's confirmation (line 120), the interviewer comments on the answer, laughingly affirming the respondent's answer in a way that exhibits her prior knowledge. The respondent joins in with the laughter (line 122).

In some – possibly most – cases, then, the interviewer has already heard enough about the respondent's job by the time they reach question 25B-2 to infer the answer, and the interviewer may simply verify this prior inference. In our next excerpt, the interviewer does so in a way that redesigns the question (see lines 179–81 below) more extensively than it was in extract (4):

Extract (5)   [Interview 011c, Version C]

```
168  MR:   Children's Hospital
169          (6.8)
170  IV:   What kind of business or industry is this {q25B}
171          (1.2)
172  MR:   It's a- It's a hospital eh heh heh=
173  IV:   =uhkay I have to ask the questions as [they] come up on=
174  MR:                                        [(  )]
175  IV:   =the screen
176  MR:   Tha(h)t's fine.
177  IV:   Uhkay:
178          (2.6)
179  IV:   A:nd so this business or organization would not be
180          manufacture retail trade wholesale trade it would be
181          something else? {q25B-2}
182  MR:   Yeah °sompin else°
183  IV:   .hhhh And what kinda work does she usually do at this
184          job that is what is her occupation {q25C}
```

Prior to the focal question, the interviewer had asked what kind of business or industry the respondent's place of work ('Children's Hospital', line 168) is, and the respondent reiterated her answer and laughed (line 172). As Jefferson (1979) argues, laughter that ends an utterance invites the recipient of the laugh to laugh in return (see Lavin and Maynard, 2001 for an extended treatment of laughter in invitations and responses in the survey interview). However, the interviewer here declines that invitation, and instead seriously pursues the topic, explaining that she must read the questions as they appear on the screen (lines 173–5). As he acknowledges this, the respondent again laughs (line 176). The placement of the laughter may suggest to the interviewer the reason her questions amuse the respondent. In lines 179–81, we can notice how the interviewer's redesign of question 25B-2 displays an analysis of the humorous response as being due to the obviousness of the questions. That is, she formats the question in a way that proposes its answer, incorporates her prior knowledge of the respondent's work setting, and requires only agreement from the respondent (line 182). This redesign of the question as a verification is more extensive than that in extract (4) (and contradicts the interviewer's own claims at lines 173–5, although the respondent would not know this). By presenting 'something else' as a candidate answer, this redesign exhibits that 'something else' is a category rather than a request to categorize. Therefore, although the respondent does 'answer' the question (line 182), the *interviewer's* understanding of both the question and information already provided by the respondent clearly play a central role in his 'comprehension' and answering of the question.

In extracts (4) and (5), the interviewer redesigns the question in a way (via the preference for agreement) that elicits a particular categorical answer from the respondent. Nevertheless, the other possible categories (or most of them) are still visible in the questioning of the interviewer. In our next extract, the interviewer redesigns the question to present only one category to the respondent.

Extract (6)   [Interview 024c, Version D]

```
139   MR:    Jack's (.) Refrigeration
140          (5.2) ((typing))
141   IV:    .hh What kind of business or industry is this? {q25B-1}
142          (0.6)
143   MR:    Uh : : :'s a refrigeration (.) company
144          (1.6)
145   IV:    .hh Would that be for retail sale wholesale or
146          manufacturing?
147          (0.8)
148   MR:    Uh : : : retail
```

```
149            (4.0)   ((typing))
150    IV:     And (.) what particular products do they sell would that
151            be a refrigerator?
152    MR:     Uh: n- air conditioning (.) Uh
153            (1.5)
154    MR:     and refrigeration
155            (0.7)
156    MR:     repair products
157            (13.5) ((typing))
158    IV:     .hh Alright and your believe you said this (in-) uh (.)
159            business organization was mainly b- retail trade is that
160            correct? {q25B-2}
161            (1.2)
162    MR:     Uh retail and service
163            (0.7)
164    IV:     Al[righ-  ]
165    MR:        [But (.)] retail fitting in with the parts and
166            equipment that we sell yes
167            (0.9)
168    IV:     Alright (4.0).hh What kind of work do you usually do at
169            this job that is what is your occupation? {q25C}
```

After probing the respondent to determine the type of business or industry for which he works (lines 141–57), the interviewer modifies question 25B-2 to take this information into account. The question at lines 158–60 seeks and prefers confirmation from the respondent that the business is 'retail trade'. The respondent first hesitates (line 161) and then suggests that two categories may be relevant, retail and service (line 162).[9] After the interviewer's brief silence, which the respondent may take as implying disagreement (Pomerantz, 1984a), the interviewer starts to acknowledge the respondent's answer (line 164), and the respondent starts an utterance in overlap (line 165). Because it is marked as a contrast ('But . . .') and reasserts and justifies the 'retail' category, the utterance can be heard as a stronger alignment with the interviewer's original proposal. The interviewer acknowledges this utterance with 'Alright' at line 168 and proceeds to the next question.

In this extract the interviewer omits any mention of the other categories in question 25B-2. Furthermore, in fashioning an answer for the respondent to confirm, the interviewer virtually appropriates from the respondent's cognitive realm certain decisions about relevant and possible answers. Still, the interviewer does produce a 'question' for the respondent to 'answer', and the respondent does so. The codable answer, then, can be seen as the respondent's. This is much less true in extract (7), where the interviewer not only eliminates several answer categories but almost entirely appropriates the respondent's work of answering:

Extract (7)   [Interview 014c, Version C]

111 IV: Now I have a few questions about y- where you work what
112   is the name of the company of which <u>for</u> which you work
113   {q25A}
114   (0.5)
115 FR: Richard W. Barr (.) em dee
116   (9.5)
117 IV: .hh and uh he is a (.) what type of doctor is [he]
118 FR: [fam]ily
119   practice
120   (8.0)
121 IV: O::ka:y and he would de- uh
122   (1.0)
123 IV: (As) a <u>ser</u>vice company okay {q25B-2} and what kind of work do <u>you</u>
124   usually do there= {q25C}
125 FR: =Secretary

Although the interviewer starts question 25B-2 (line 121), she quickly abandons it. This may be partly in response to the respondent's speed; note that the respondent's answer overlaps the interviewer's talk at lines 117–18. But the interviewer still manages to suggest, in a very compact way, the three-part question-answer-acknowledgement structure described earlier: the question is indicated by 'and he would de- uh' (line 121), the answer by '(As) as <u>ser</u>vice company', and the acknowledgement and beginning of a new question by 'okay' (line 123) (see Beach, 1993). The interviewer presumably records 'something else' as the answer. At first glance, the appearance of the phrase 'service company' is surprising – it is not a codable category, and we saw it rejected as a candidate answer by the interviewer in extract (2). But here the phrase announces the interviewer's understanding of the type of company the respondent works for and gives the respondent at least some opportunity to object to associating 'Richard W. Barr, M. D.' and 'service company'. The announcement thus constitutes a minimal 'verification' of the answer to question 25B-2, and might almost permit the ultimate answer to be seen as the respondent's own. The interviewer presumably makes the translation from 'service company' to 'something else' when she records the answer. Note that if the interviewer had used the codable category 'something else' in her utterance at line 123, both the announcement and any subsequent acceptance by the respondent might have been less informative than the actual sequence, and might have provided less justification for regarding the answer as the respondent's own. (Such an utterance might also have led the respondent to ask for clarification, and thus have used some of the time a verification can save.) The interviewer appears to be using an extended taxonomy like that referred to by the respondents in extracts

(2) and (6) to construct a verification that, at the least, skirts the edge of acceptability under the rules of standardized interviewing. In this example, the interviewer substitutes her understanding of the question and knowledge of the respondent's biography for the respondent's own cognitive processing *and* answering.

Conclusion

As interviewers, through interaction, acquire information about respondents, see indications of uncertainty and diagnose comprehension problems, they customize questions, engage in verification protocols, accept answers, omit questions or answer categories, and the like. Given the variety of ways in which the interviewer's behaviour may shape an interaction, it seems that in many cases the interviewer performs work that the individualistic psychological model of cognitive processing locates in the respondent, such as interpreting the question and even mapping the respondent's answer onto a response category. Interviewers draw on their tacit knowledge to diagnose problems in understanding, offer help and negotiate clarity sufficient for the purposes at hand. For example, the redesign 'or would you consider that something else' in extract (4) projects a possible ambiguity that the respondent's biography to that point in the interview makes potentially relevant and neatly fashions a pre-emptory clarification of the potential ambiguity of 'something else'.

The 'reporting' sequences produced by some of these respondents play an important role in this process. Behaviour coding of standardized interviews shows that respondents do not often explicitly request clarification of a question. For example, in a study that coded behaviours in sixty interviews, the mean percentage of administrations in which the respondent requested clarification, computed across sixty questions, was 10 per cent (Okensberg, Cannell and Kalton 1991, p. 354). In only one of the six nonparadigmatic cases examined here does the respondent produce a strong solicitation for help from the interviewer and even that solicitation is indirect (extract (2), 'I don't know *what* you'd (.) classify it'). 'Reporting' potentially relevant information may be more common than direct requests as a method for soliciting clarification (see Schaeffer et al., 1993). Recognizing the role of this activity of respondents is important in at least two ways: questions that frequently elicit such reporting may require redesign. In addition, because it is typically the job of the interviewer to diagnose and correct (or repair) misunderstandings by the respondent, interviewers may need further training in interpreting and responding to such reports within the constraints of standardization.

Our analysis also raises more general issues. The traditional approach to cognitive processing has been individualistic and psychologistic. Consequently, when there are departures from the paradigmatic question-answer sequence, researchers are tempted to see these departures as 'deviations' that index the respondent's own problems in cognition. Our interactional analysis suggests a different approach. In most situations, even when interviewers attempt to be standardized, language is flexible, rather than rigid. And interactants have available to them resources in the interactional substrate that they readily use to negotiate the clarity they need for the purpose at hand (see, for example, Schegloff, 1991a, p. 155). Thus it is not surprising that the interviews we analyzed include fewer paradigmatic than deviant enactments of question 25B-2 and that the interviewer plays a prominent role in deviations from the paradigm. Our analysis of these deviant instances suggests that seeing the point of a question and the relevance of its answer categories is, *in the first place*, an interactional accomplishment: in the face of anticipated and actual problems, participants regularly resort to orderly activities of heightened co-involvement in which the interviewer's contributions to the respondent's answer become intensified. If answering a survey question requires thinking by the individual, it also requires interaction.

To be technically precise, in extract (2), we see a respondent who apparently takes 'something else' in Question 25B-2 as a request for further categorization rather than as a category. When the interviewer does not accept the respondent's answer, the respondent solicits the interviewer's help in obtaining one. In extract (3), the respondent displays uncertainty in answering the question, yet reports information that allows the interviewer to gather the upshot for purposes of coding an answer. An interviewer can also offer help without being invited. Moreover, as extracts (4), (5), (6) and (7) show, the interviewer can do this more or less strongly. In extract (4), the interviewer redesigns the latter part of 25B-2 to prefer agreement with the 'something else' category, while in extract (5), the interviewer modifies the entire format of 25B-2 to propose 'something else' as the correct answer. In extract (6), the interviewer eliminates certain categories from her question, whereas in extract (7), the interviewer eliminates all codable categories from the question and then answers for the recipient, eviscerating the respondent's cognitive contribution almost entirely. Accordingly, we have suggested that the interviewer can be *invited* to participate or can *offer* to participate in answering a question, and hence make some degree of interactive contribution to what is usually seen as a respondent's own or sole efforts at cognitive processing. That this occurs attests to the strength of the interactional substrate and the orderly, socially organized skills and activities of which it consists.

If there is a socially organized tendency to construct answers interactively, departures from the *paradigm* are nevertheless *prototypical*. Indeed, we would argue that the paradigmatic question-answer sequence – the simple version of interviewer asking and respondent answering in an immediately codable way – is itself a 'deviation'. Although respondents may be engaging in an individualistic form of cognitive processing in paradigmatic sequences, such sequences are a devolution from interactional structures to which participants resort at the first indication of trouble. This view of what is prototypical implies a nontraditional approach to question design. Questionnaire writers usually seek to avoid or to *minimize* disorderly departures from the paradigmatic question-answer sequence from the outset. This is the approach taken, for example, by versions of behaviour coding that rely only on the behaviour codes themselves to evaluate questions (e.g., Oksenberg, Cannell and Kalton, 1991). But it may be more effective to begin with the prototype – i.e., with actual, plainly collaborative (including interviewer-dominated), orderly episodes of asking and answering questions. Then the problem would be to *maximize* deviation from the prototype – i.e., to streamline it – in order to obtain more instances of the paradigm.

As just one instance, reconsider how, in extract (2), the respondent had difficulty with interpreting the status of 'something else'. We argued that its placement in a particular sequential context led to the respondent's hearing it as a request to categorize rather than as a category to choose. After offering an inappropriate answer, and after hearing the interviewer's rejection, the respondent then solicited and obtained the interviewer's help in constructing the answer. All of these features of the episode attest to ordinary, organized – prototypical – practices of the interactional substrate. Furthermore, the specific actions of the respondent and interviewer locate the problem, the conditions under which it appears to be a problem and suggest possible solutions: changing the sequential context of 'something else' in a new version of question 25B-2 could make the prototypical practices of the participants unnecessary and thereby enhance the probability that respondents would produce the simpler paradigmatic question-answer sequence. Although this particular problem is a relatively simple one, characterizations of more complex problems and their solutions can be similarly based on an approach that relates cognitive processing to interactional sequences and activities.

Acknowledgements

This chapter is adapted from Schaeffer, Nora Cate and Douglas W. Maynard, 1996. 'From Paradigm to Prototype and Back Again:

Interactive Aspects of Cognitive Processing in Standardized Survey Interviews'. Pp. 65–88 in *Answering Questions: Methodology for Determining Cognitive and Communicative Processes in Survey Research*, edited by Norbert Schwarz and Seymour Sudman. San Francisco, CA: Jossey-Bass Publishers. Copyright ©1996 by Jossey-Bass, Inc. This material is used by permission of John Wiley and Sons, Inc.

The research reported here was partially supported by the Ameritech Foundation Fellowship Program through the Research Committee of the Graduate School of the University of Wisconsin, Madison. Initial transcription and analyses of these data were supported by a Joint Statistical Agreement (90–45) with the US Bureau of the Census. Computational support was provided by the Center for Demography and Ecology, which receives core support from the National Institute for Child Health and Human Development (HD05876). Chris Fassnacht pointed out the link between the argument made here and that in the literature on shared cognition. The views expressed in this chapter are the authors' and not those of the funding agencies.

We thank the US Bureau of the Census for permission to analyze the Current Population Survey test interviews. In the excerpts from the interviews, all names of persons, businesses and locations are fictitious.

NOTES

1. In the other instances the respondent chooses another category (four times), the interviewer verifies with another category (two times), or the interviewer does not ask the question and appears to code another category (probably 'retail') based on information already provided by the respondent (two times). There is no interaction around the category 'something else' in any of these cases, except that the interviewer omits reading it in one of the instances in which the respondent chooses 'retail'.

2. The question was asked twice in each of four interviews and four times in one interview. When the question is asked multiple times in a single interview, one administration asks about the respondent and the other administrations ask for proxy reports about the jobs of other members of the household. In some situations the question was not asked when it should have been; the interviewer probably filled in the answer based on information previously provided by the respondent.

3. The transcripts use the following notation: MR indicates a male respondent and FR a female respondent, parentheses around spoken material indicate that it was spoken softly, equals signs indicate that speakers' utterances are linked, square brackets indicate material overlapping speech, a colon indicates that a sound is drawn out, '.h' indicates an audible inbreath, and '(.)' indicates a pause with each '.' indicating about a tenth of a second. Timed pauses (in seconds) are shown in parentheses between turns. Question numbers from the CPS instrument appear in curly brackets. The transcripts show material

immediately preceding the question of interest to illustrate the kind of information already available to the interviewer. The line numbers are from the transcript of the entire audiotaped extract.

4. As Sacks (1992a, p. 726) has argued, the 'position of an item on a list is relevant to hearing what that item is', which suggests a sequential basis for what Grimshaw (1980) identifies as 'partial' understandings and 'mishearings'. For the way that sequencing can lend to misunderstandings, and even incorrect answers, in standardized testing, see Maynard and Marlaire (1992, p. 183).

5. The voice at line 85 appears to be someone at the CATI telephone facility. Neither the interviewer nor respondent gives any indication that they have heard the voice.

6. Indeed, before the interviewer responds at line 92, the respondent 'invites' the interviewer to talk at two other places. At line 86, the respondent names and rejects two items from the list of possible categories and then hesitates with 'or' and the silence at line 87. This is a place where the interviewer could have offered the respondent some help in answering. After the interviewer passes this opportunity (line 88), the respondent 're-starts' (with another 'or') a generalized third item ('or anything like that . . .'), which now appears (because of this re-start) as a third item on his list of rejected possible categories; and it is a generalized third item. According to Jefferson (1990, p. 79), such 'weak' third parts (e.g., an item that is weakened by being generalized) can accomplish a variety of interactional tasks, one of which is to invite co-participation in assembling a list. In fact, this generalized third part may be a dispreferred alternative to what the interviewer might have been invited (at line 86) to produce as a specific third part. When, at line 89, the interviewer again passes the occasion to take a turn at talk, the respondent issues what we call his formulation of uncertainty. In the context of the two prior offered opportunities for the interviewer to talk and, more specifically, to help the respondent with his displayed difficulties, line 90 is a third and possibly *exacerbated* request for help.

7. The interviewer appears to delay responding to the respondent's utterances at lines 251–2 long enough that the respondent begins to add to her utterance (line 254) in overlap with the interviewer's acknowledgment (line 255).

8. Sacks (1987) shows how the recipient of two questions answers the second question first and the first question second. Here, had the answer to '. . . or would you consider that something else?' been negative, the preference for contiguity implies that the respondent would have said 'No', and then tried to choose one of the prior categories. Because the answer is affirmative here, however, the first question need not be answered.

9. The category 'service' industry was also referred to by the respondent in extract (2). The category was not referred to in previous questions in the interview, but appears to be part of an extended native taxonomy of types of businesses that some respondents are familiar with. The interviewer in extract (7) seems to presume such knowledge.

6 A cognitive agnostic in conversation analysis: when do strategies affect spoken interaction?[1]

Robert Hopper

Introduction

In a cartoon I find hilarious[2] there is an egg with hands and feet reaching to take a ticket from one of those number-dispensing machines that you see in bakeries or post offices. The other side of the cartoon shows a hen in the same posture. This cartoon suggests that we might finally be provided with empirical data to address the classic problem in mundane philosophy: which came first, the chicken or the egg?

This chicken-egg question is an English proverb referring to a variety of difficult-to-resolve disputes. For example, since my graduate education I have considered language and thought puzzles to be chicken-egg questions. But this analogy understates the empirical problems we face when we study the mutual interpenetration of talk and cognition. Let us consider what this chicken-egg cartoon, and its attendant proverb, teaches us.

- The cartoon suggests that an action which '*comes first*' enjoys explanatory priority. The social actor who obtains the first number at the post office thereby documents a place in a temporal queue ahead of any other claimant. Or in talk, if one event-type precedes another (e.g. first and second greetings) we sometimes characterize that which came second as consequential from that which came first. Does thought come before talk in this way? How could we test this notion in empirical discourse analysis?

- The cartoon suggests that actors (and not just theorists) routinely encounter problems in detailing which came first. The take-a-number machine is a refinement in our cultural software for standing in a queue, devised to solve just such problems.

- The cartoon is humorous in its application of this machine to the classic 'chicken-egg' proverb, which highlights some irreducible reflexivity between two temporally related empirical manifestations within the same life cycle.

- The cartoon suggests that firstness should be decided empirically. If we focus on empirical traces of cognition in speech, the question, 'Which came first?' is a question of *when*.

And here is the rub: chicken and egg are two time-stages in a poultry life cycle and they both appear as observable stuff. Talk and cognition are not quite so empirically comparable. Surely cognition happens from time to time, and is linked to talk-in-interaction. But a critical question is *when* thought happens. Some of the frustrations that arise in dealing with *when* questions help to explain an agnostic stance about cognition in the writings of some conversation analysts.[3] I hope to focus on these *when* questions.

The seductiveness of 'before'

My dad was a careful man, an engineer. After some occasions in which I ran my youthful mouth and got into trouble Dad could emit a silence to help me reflect on my actions. He showed in his own infrequent but literary speech, in his stories for instance, evidence that each word had been carefully edited. On one painful occasion he shared with me this engineer-speak maxim: '*Engage brain before putting mouth into gear*'. I take this to be a cognitivist maxim. Let me unpack this maxim.

- The maxim prescribes thought before speech as a preferable and attainable order of things. This maxim optimistically invokes the social engineer's hope that, if one thinks, one can exhibit a high degree of strategic control over speech – and hence over outcomes of speech events.
- The maxim invokes a monologue view of communication, much like Shannon's model (1948): that there is a source for talk (purposeful thinking), and talk proceeds from purpose to effect. There does exist certain talking that follows such constraints: the public oration is one prototype. There should be (and often is) thinking about a central idea and a speech outline before an orator engages recipients. Since the oration shows strategic thought before talk I label it a *pre-strategy when* utterance-type. Some writers (Saussure, Sanders) distinguish purposeful, or calculative (*pre-strategy*) speech from the rest. But most of us, and even these writers, may muddy the waters by letting things we can infer about cognition-driven talk apply to a vague but larger class of interactive moments.
- The maxim, '*engage brain before putting mouth into gear*' presupposes there is one other main alternative to thought-before-speech, that is: speech before thought, or thoughtless communication – rash-unplanned running of the mouth. However, we should find a third alternative to *late-strategy* v. *pre-strategy* in speech: that much speech-thought

is reflexive in principle. Sometimes one foot (the one in our mouth) seems to lead. Sometimes we lead from the other foot (the one we hope is in the mind). But in empirical lived experience we only hear the mouth's talk. How we go about documenting the mind's strategy from the appearances in talk is a line of thought in which Garfinkel has boldly gone before, at least in principle, with his 'documentary theory of interpretation.' But how may we follow up this insight with empirical analyses of discourse?

If our view of cognitive theorizing is thought-first, when we overstate the frequency and importance of calculated speech, we portray the social actor as resembling a computer programmer or a business planner. But Moerman (1988) suggests that the social inter-actor is more like a surf-boarder or skier. Heritage suggests that the conduct of speaking turns is like playing tennis. He contrasts a tennis serve (which seems similar to calculated speech in being a first action determined largely by strategy) with volleying shots (undertaken at a crowded interactional moment and displaying arrays of micro and macro skills).[4] Computer programmers or business planners are *pre-strategy* professionals. Whereas the when of strategy in surfing, tennis or skiing seems problematically distributed in time, sportspersons, or social actors, are *emergent-when* professionals.

I am agnostic about the applicability of models of calculated speech to the conduct of mundane social interaction. I do not deny the importance of or existence of cognition. Rather, I report how some conversation analysts have tracked carefully what talk in interaction shows us about that kind of thought called strategy. I attempt:

- To show conversation analytic advances along the margins of talk and strategy.
- To reformulate these advances in terms of *when* questions about strategic cognitions displayed in talk.
- To test this reformulation against the repetitive/formulaic telephone calls of Lyndon Johnson's first week as US President in 1963.

Why need this train of words concern us? One importance is in the domain of social engineering, whether it is self-help for managers, advice for intimates, or instructional programs for incipient bilinguals. Practitioners in these arenas often prescribe practices for the management of talk-in-interaction – practices that presume that actors have a high degree of conscious control over the strategic deployment of talk through clarification of thinking.

A second importance involves the domain of theory, and especially our models of the social speaker-listener. We should distinguish between calculated speech and most social interaction. As we review this research it also becomes important to distinguish what actors do from what theorists may infer – especially in a series of encounters.

Conversation analysts on talk and strategy

One area that raises questions about the when of strategy is research about pre-sequences (Terasaki, 1976; Schegloff, 1980; Drew, 1984). Sometimes the way that pre-sequences unfold leads actors to believe that the initiator of the 'pre' has a strategic destination in mind from the start, but just gently leads the other along.

Extract (1)   [Field note]

	Alice:	Hello?
	Fred:	Hello, Alice?
	Alice:	Hi Fred.
→	Fred:	Hi, what are you doin
	Alice:	Nothin, what's up.
	Fred:	How about if I come over in a while.
	Alice:	Great, I'd love to see you.
	Fred:	Okay, I have a paper that needs typing.

When Fred begins this pre-sequence, he apparently misdirects Alice to expect a social invitation. But later Fred seems a manipulative cad who planned to mislead his conversational partner. This seems a case of pre-strategy – though one could quibble about this. The grounds of such a quibble show in extract (2), a pre-sequence that leads where Alice probably thought Fred was heading in extract (1):

Extract (2)   [UTCL D8.3]

Jeff:	Have you eaten yet?
Sid:	No: I haven't
Jeff:	You hav(h)n?
Sid:	No:.
	(0.2)
Jeff:	U:m dyou have Billy's car:?
Sid:	Yeah I do
Jeff:	Y'wanna go to Kerbey? ((A restaurant))

This instance may also display pre-strategy, that is, Jeff might have thought: I'm hungry, I need a car to get to Kerbey, I wonder if Sid has a car, I'll invite Sid to supper. But it is possible that Jeff just called his friend, asked what was up, and they muddled towards a plan together. How we might distinguish among those possibilities in extract (2), I haven't a clue. I intuit that extract (2) gives more appearance of pre-strategy than does extract (3):

Extract (3)   [NB:11:14] (simplified)

Emma: Whatiyih doin.
         (0.9)
Nancy: What am I [doin?
Emma: [Cleanin?
Nancy: I'm ironing, wouldju believe that?
Emma: Oh bless its [heart
Nancy: [In fact i: ir; I started ar'ning and I'd I.
         Somehow or another ironing jis kind of leaves me co:ld
Emma: Yea:h.   Wanna come dow'n have a bite of lu:nch with
         me?

This instance resembles extract (2) in pre-sequence structure. In both instances pre's lead to reportings that make the invitations appropriate and indicate some sense of readiness to accept an invitation, should one be offered (Drew, 1984). In extract (3) the instance occurs many minutes into a chatty call, whereas extract (1) and extract (2) are right after the telephone opening, marking these pre-sequence goals as a probable reason for calling. In extract (3) Nancy, in response to enquiry, happens to indicate boredom with what she is presently doing. This makes an invitation appropriate; but if proffering that invitation had been Emma's invitation prior to the call, that plan gets nicely disguised as an instance of emergent-strategy.

These instances provide grounds for remaining agnostic about when strategy gets planned during the enactment of pre-sequences. The sequences themselves – at least their initiatory 'pres' – seem sequentially ambiguous. That is, when one says 'What are you doin' one might be initiating an invitation sequence, or simply asking the other for assurance that one is not eating supper or doing some other activity that would compromise a phone chat. Or one might suspect that the other was on call-waiting. These possibilities get sorted out in the sequences that follow, and this sequential organization houses an ecological wisdom of protecting the actors from face threat. All this gets done precisely by hiding just when strategic thoughts occur. As Schegloff phrases this issue in describing pre-pre sequences:

It does not appear that these several uses (some of which can be co-operative in a segment of talk) are discriminated and differentially prefigured in the form or placement of the action projection. Which use is being made of an action projection is something worked through by the parties in the ensuing talk. (1980: 135)

Schegloff's term 'action projection' implies that some action is likely to emerge out of a pre-pre in progress, but the nature of that action remains to be worked out. Therefore, if the actor has planned a strategy, the conversational structures used to reveal that strategy to the other are, in principle, ambiguous. Therefore, it is often difficult for actor or analyst to show when an intention to invite occurred.

Pomerantz (1980) takes a similarly agnostic stance about the when of strategy in her discussion of 'my side tellings' as 'fishing devices':

Extract (4)   [Frankel, TC](simplified)

→   S: I was trying you all day. And the <u>line</u> w'z busy fer like
          <u>hours.</u>
    G: Oh::: oh:::, We::ll, I'm gonna come over in a while to help
          yer brother ou:t
    S: Good
    G: Cuz I know he needs some he::lp
    S: Yeah. Yes he'd mention that today
    G: Um hm
→   S: Um, ˙hhh Who were yih ta:lking to.

Pomerantz argues in this instance that G, in the first utterance in extract (4), may be fishing for information about what S has been doing during the time G has previously called and received a busy signal. The final line in this segment shows S probing for such information, which had not been forthcoming earlier:

If the telling is an attempt to have G volunteer information, it fails . . . A few turns later, S directly asks for the information with 'Who wih yih ta:lking to'.(1980: 187)

Pomerantz remains agnostic about *when* the intention to seek further information about G's phone call first occurs. Was this intention pre-strategy or emergent-strategy? (See discussion of this instance in Heritage, 1990/91: 317.) Attempting to resolve this agnostic stance, Drew (1995) argues a distinction between emergent v. pre-[5] strategic trajectories in conversation. He classifies all three pre-invitations [1] to [3] as likely indicating pre-strategy, at least when compared to those involved in the 'po-faced receipts of teases'.

Extract (5)   [Campbell 4:5 (Drew, 1987, pp. 224; 236–7)] (simplified)

1→   B: I'm still gettin:g you know, stomach pains I sp<u>ew</u>ed last
          ni:ght...<u>Chronic</u> diar well, just before I went to bed and ..
          .. I've been getting funny things in front of my <u>eyes</u>
          actually. A bi:t, just slightly, Li:ght flashes. But uh (0.3)
2→   A: Well you probably got at least a week.
          (0.4)
3→   B: What of this:.
          0.3)
     A: <u>No</u> a week before you die

Drew argues that a three-stage trajectory occurs during this segment: (1) an overbuilt complaint by B elicits (2) a tease from A, which in turn elicits (3) a po-faced response by B. Drew (1987) argues that this sequential pattern is an interactive phenomenon relevant to the participants.

However, no participant anticipates or plans this pattern. Rather, the speakers generate the sequence out of the normal turn-by-turn course of interaction. The pattern turns out to be a kind of found art for analysts and to some degree for actors. But this is emergent-strategy, something that comes up along the way. Since analysts' descriptions should be no more definite than what participants do; we may remain agnostic about speakers' purposes or conscious strategy during preliminary phases of interactive sequences and series.

Evidence from a series of events

Heritage (1990/91), who reviews the literature noted above, suggests that we may track cognitive strategizing in talk by analyzing a series of encounters during which some objects recur. Heritage argues that in the second of these calls, an analyst (but not the participants) may locate the caller's strategy by making analytical reference to similar conversational objects in the prior call. I reconsider Heritage's arguments in terms of a more numerous series of telephone calls during which Lyndon Johnson accepts congratulations on his first speech as US President (November 27, 1963). President Johnson develops and refines several tropes over the course of these phone calls and the evolution of these tropes may be used to refine Heritage's arguments and cautions about the interplay of talk and strategy. Heritage distinguishes two concepts of strategy:

- Strategy (cs) 'has close affinities with commonsense outlooks on the nature of choice and rationality and it has largely been developed from them' (ibid.: 314). I re-label this as pre-strategy.
- Strategy (cog) 'arises out of cognitive psychology and has been increasingly used by students of interactional data' (ibid.: 314). Examples: a reader's switching from a holistic to an item-based heuristic, or alternation of politeness strategies. In these formulations small actions 'are coordinated as sub-plans with respect to the achievement of some overall goal. In none of these cases are we tempted to attribute these strategies to the conscious awareness of an agent (ibid.: 315). I re-label Heritage's strategy (cog) as emergent-strategy to emphasize the problem of *when*.

Hereafter I substitute my terms for Heritage's as I summarize his position. Heritage notes that in the move from (pre-)strategy to emergent-strategy we lose 'the notion of conscious goal direction in all but the most macro sense of the term – e.g., the goal of reading the sentence'. Pre-strategy *guides* behaviour, whereas an 'emergent-strategy' is a description of behaviour patterns (ibid.: 315).

In talk-in-interaction, Heritage argues, actors 'treat one another as agents, who assume that one another's talk is under 'voluntary control' and who hold one another morally accountable for what they say. These

conditions create an endlessly fluctuating borderline' between what analysts may claim as pre-strategy and as emergent-strategy (ibid.: 315).

Heritage applies this distinction to two conversations from the NB
corpus, the first of which connects two sisters, and the second of which
connects one of these sisters with her friend. The common partner in
these two conversations emits (in each of them) a touched off narrative
connecting her to the recent assassination of Robert Kennedy. In each
case Emma describes her brush with this great event, that Kennedy's
coffin left Los Angeles on a chartered plane that took off from the same
place that she had occupied when she and her husband had flown to
Hawaii. Heritage argues that we might find pre-strategy in the second of
these two narratives, by virtue of what we (as analysts, not the actors!)
may observe of the two interactions together. Here are transcriptions of
the two extracts, in the order in which they occurred.

Extract (6)   [NB:11:1:R:3] (Sisters) (simplified)

Emma:	This's rilly been a <u>wee:</u>k hasn'it,
Lottie:	Oh: Go:d a lo:ng wee⌈k. Yeah.
Emma:	⌊Oh: my God I'm (.) glad it's over.
	I won't even turn the teevee o⌈-:n
Lottie:	⌊I won'<u>ee</u>ther.
→ Emma:	Oh no. They drag it out so. THAT'S WHERE THEY WE TOOK
	OFF on ar chartered flight that sa: me spot. Didju see
	it' (0.7)
	When they took him in [the airpla:ne,
Lottie:	[n:N<u>o</u>:::.
	Hell I wouldn't even watch it.

Extract (7)   [NB:11:2:R:2] (Friends) (simplified)

Emma:	((about golf friends who cancelled))
	There wz a death in their family <u>so</u>:
Nancy:	Aww:::.
Emma:	THE:Y gosh hu <u>this</u> is really been a wee:k ha:sn't it?=
Nancy:	Oh:: it rilly ha:s. ((Sadly))
	((About 20 lines omitted))
Emma:	Yeah, in the church yesterday thih ˙hhh flas:hin the
	cameras on um when theh w'r there yihknkow went
	in tuh <u>pr:a:y</u> and an' Go:d g- (.) [Jah-
Nancy:	[Ah think it's
	terrible-
→ Emma:	˙hh Jackie <u>looked</u> <u>u:p</u> Hey that wz the <u>same</u> <u>spot</u> we
	took off fer Honolulu.

About this second instance, which (in ways not shown here) gets a better hearing than the first instance, one finds no particular evidence of
pre-strategy. However, when Heritage takes into account the evidence
from the preceding call he finds the second call more (pre-)strategic than

otherwise. Emma in each call undertakes 'an almost identical series of actions to arrive at the same point – the mention of her relationship to the post-assassination events' (ibid.: 321). For example, 'this has really been a week' serves as Emma's precursor to the narrative in both cases, and in each case, stepwise topic transitions occur toward this disclosure about the take-off place – hence of Emma's proximity to the events of the great and famous dead. Presumably, the use of stepwise transitions might be only emergent-strategy but the goal of introducing the take-off story seems to Heritage to exemplify pre-strategy (ibid.: 322–4). However, Heritage mutes this claim by observing that the conversational devices by which Emma brings off her disclosure (e.g., stepwise transitions) cannot be matters of pre-strategy. On these bases Heritage charges that many cognitivist psychologists claim (pre) strategy far too often.

Heritage, in summary, is plenty agnostic about the circumstances in which one might employ my term pre-strategy. But I see even his description of Emma's 'intention' to bring up the take-off story as too interactive a thing to describe in terms of pre-strategy. In part I reach this conclusion by way of exposure to a remarkable series of phone calls that will allow us to meditate on the nature of strategies that President Lyndon B. Johnson (LBJ) deploys within each call and across the series of calls. This remarkable trove of repetitive phone calls might allow a more extensive discussion of 'when' questions in telephone strategy.

Strategies in the LBJ congratulation calls

As sort of an *hors d'oeuvre* indicating the perils of such an analysis of single versus multiple calls, let us consider a call from LBJ to Senator John Pastore, at the start of which LBJ congratulates Pastore on a recent panel show appearance, then (in an apparently touched off way attached to the closing) LBJ asks for Pastore's support in his giving an award to scientist Robert Oppenheimer. Question: When did LBJ formulate the strategic intention to ask Pastore about Oppenheimer? I show only part of the closing portion here:

Extract (8)   [11/29/63 LBJ 11.04.]

	LBJ:	Hope you had a happy Thanksgiving and 'hhh I look forward to seeing em the first time they're down her bring em in I want to see em again=
	JP:	=Alright thank you very very much=
→	LBJ:	=Johnny I'm giving this award to Oppenheimer that the President-planned for him
	JP:	[Yes?
	LBJ:	[I- (0.2) I don't- I thought I oughta carry it on through.

LBJ's raising the topic of Oppenheimer, like Emma's raising the location of Robert Kennedy's plane in extract (7), is packaged to appear to be touched off. In this case, the event appears to be touched off by the pre-closing in progress, a sequential (and cognitive) place to mention a previously-unmentioned mentionable (Schegloff and Sacks, 1973). But most listeners for whom I have played this tape (or given performances based on it) believe that LBJ's reason for this call was precisely to talk to Pastore about Oppenheimer. The compliments about the talk (not shown above) are, on this view, just a disingenuous way to put his interlocutor at ease before raising a potentially sensitive issue. Listening to this call by itself I'm not unsympathetic to portray the Oppenheimer trial balloon as pre-strategy – though direct evidence for this analysis is limited.

However, as it happens, there is counter-evidence for this position in the series of calls of which the Pastore call is the fourth. LBJ called each of the panellists who appeared on this show. Yet only with Pastore does he mention Oppenheimer. Does this external context alter our hearing of the Oppenheimer trial balloon? Once again we confront a difference between what an analyst might claim and what a participant might claim. Perhaps Pastore thought the mention of Oppenheimer had been the reason for the call (i.e. pre-strategy). But with the series of four calls before us, I take an agnostic view on this matter.

With these perplexities in mind let us turn to the main series of calls I have pondered in preparation for this seminar. On 27 November, the fifth day of his presidency, about lunchtime, LBJ spoke to Congress and to a live nationwide audience in his first formal appearance as post-funeral president. This speech was a remarkable performance, a speech sometimes referred to as 'let us continue', after one of the refrains in the speech. The phone calls which I have been studying in detail happened during the afternoon following that speech. In these calls, some of which LBJ placed and some of which he received,[6] the president responded to a number of compliments. His compliment responses seem thematic: at least as repetitive of prior calls as Emma's narrative – and as repetitive in sequential environment, here, the compliment response slot (Pomerantz, 1978). Here are a few examples of LBJ's responses. All the compliments occur within the first few seconds of the call, unless noted.

Extract (9) [LBJ Compliment Responses 11/27/63 1:35 pm LBJ 63.11.03.5] (Nellie Connally, LBJ is caller, 40 seconds in)

C→ NC: I have never been prouder of anybody than I was of you a
                  while ago.
                  (0.3)
        LBJ: Well (0.2)
        NC: Can you hear me?

CR→   LBJ: I sure can and I've always been mighty proud of you
                 darlin n I appreciate it

[11/27/63 2:00 pm LBJ.63.11.03.10] (rough transcript) Jim Haggarty,
(Ike press sec.), LBJ is caller.

C→   JH   ... That was a fi:ne (.) talk to Congress today.
CR→   LBJ: Well, ˙hhh they were very good to me ah ah ˙hhhh on both
                 sides I thought, and I˙hhhh appreciate it.

[11/27/63 3:25 pm LBJ 11.03.21] (rough transcript from LBJ lib) Gene
Pulliam, Pulliam is caller.

C→   GP: ...you've always had my heart in my hand and you still
                 do.
CR→   LBJ: I know that Gene and I appreciate it very much. God bless
                 you

Now these are not the complete set of early-afternoon compliment
receipts, but these are the ones that run most to type. (A larger set of
these calls appears in the Appendix.) Yet one would be hard-pressed to
argue, based on the similarity of these instances, that LBJ formulated a
pre-strategy for receiving compliments and followed it consistently. First,
there are some counter-instances (see calls with Louis Selzer and Adam
Claton Powell for two different receipts). Second, any mature member
has a wealth of experience in accepting compliments – especially someone
in public life for as long as LBJ.

On this afternoon, LBJ, after receiving many compliments, begins to
play with his response formula. He first does this in a call from his old
friend, columnist Joe Alsop. This playful gambit was tried out twice in
two calls close together in a way that reminds me of Emma's two stories
about RFK's airplane location:

Extract (10)   [11/27/63 4:01 pm; LBJ.63:1 1.3.23] (Joe Alsop (Columnist), Alsop is caller)

        LBJ: I wanted to tell you how grateful I am for that most
                 beautiful wonderful article I don't deserve it but I
                 appreciate it you know ˙hhh I'm not as frustra-=
        JA: = Yes sir I mean
→   LBJ: I'm not as frustrated as that Baptist preacher in Te-
                 uh when the:y showed up one morning they gave him
                 a ↑car. ˙hhhh and he got up in the pulpit and he didn't
                 know what to sa:y, and he didn't expect em to give
                 him a: Ford automobile, poor little ↑church, and he said
                 uh˙hh I just want ya'll to kno:w that I don't appreciate it
                 but I do deserve it [hunh hunh heh heh heh heh heh
        JA: [hunh hunh hunh hunh hunh
        LBJ: But I do appreciate it and I don't deserve it

Here, LBJ apparently does not wait for a compliment on the speech itself,[7] but compliments Alsop on a column. Since the column was apparently a compliment, however, this is still an occasion of receipting a compliment. On this occasion LBJ tells an odd and self-deprecating story. This story weaves in the 'appreciate it' theme used in prior compliment receipts in ways suggesting that the story's occurrence is related to the string of compliments he has been receiving all afternoon.

A bit later, LBJ rolls out a slightly more polished and effective version of this odd joke:

Extract (10a)   [11/27/63 5:00 pm LBJ 11.3.29]? (Roscoe Drummond columnist, etc)

```
C→    RD:    I watched you:r speech toda:y, and I knew that the hand
             of God was in it. (0.3) and Mister President I kno- your
             my President and (0.3) I'm very proud of the way you're
             doing it.
             (0.3)
CR→   LBJ:   We:ll uh you have through the ye:ars uh (0.4) been uh
→            (0.5) unusually uh charitable with me: and uh (0.4)
             I'm kinda like the preacher (0.5) that was surpri:sed
             when they gave him a Ford automobile the congregation
             one Sunday (0.4) he got up somewhat frustrated and he
             said I don't appreciate it but I do deserve it
      RD:    gheh gha ha ha ha ha ha ha uhhhh
CR→   LBJ:   I don't deserve it but I do appreciate it =
```

Was this second telling of the preacher joke done as pre-strategy derived from the prior version? I remain unsure how to put this question. Certainly the prior occurrence makes the joke poetically available to LBJ (Jefferson, 1996). LBJ receipted the first few compliments in a routine way, but then shows other evidence that he is playing with the formulaic response to compliments. Certainly, my intuitions are ruffled by the dubious strategic value of this story (as they are by Emma's story in extract (5) and extract (6)). But LBJ acts more like a skier or tennis player here, responding to new exigencies with old tropes and skills; than like a computer programmer, planning either the first or second version of this joke. Maybe LBJ is rattled by the pressures of the long day and the long week. He shows signs of lapsed taste in a receipt immediately after the Drummond call:

Extract (11)   [11/27/63 5:01 pm LBJ 63.11.03.20?] (Rough transcript from LBJ lib, Bill White, LBJ is caller)

```
C→    BW:    ...I think your speech today was the greatest ever heard
             in my life. I think that not for the substance alone but
```

		for the manner of delivery, and I tell you I don't normally get terribly emotional, maybe I do, but I was crying there at the end, myself
CR→	LBJ:	Well, you're mighty good. Homer Thornberry came in crying and poor old boy from the Cleveland Press, Louie Seltzer, called me up and he was crying ... ((Continues self-praise))

LBJ begins with a standard return compliment, but then – stimulated perhaps by the word 'crying' – LBJ notes that his close friend (a Congressman) had cried (which is both embarrassing to Thornberry and praise to himself; see Pomerantz, 1978). Then LBJ ridicules a prior caller (see Appendix for Selzer's call in which the compliment is overbuilt). Whatever the reason, the move away from self-deprecation toward self-praise that emerges in extract (11) gets further elaborated in the very next call:

Extract (12) [11/27/63 5:10 pm LBJ 63.11.03.31] (Gould Lincoln (newsman), LBJ is caller, 30 seconds in)

	DKG:	Well I put- I only put t in the mail this afternoon.
	LBJ:	Well I'll get it then, she'll get it to me tomorrow
		I jus- I was up til two thirty last night on the speech an=
C→	GL:	=0h yeah I think you did a wonderful job today
		(0.5)
LBJ:		[.hhh We:ll?
	GL:	[I was up there and uh (1.0) and I- I -I really thought the content of your speech, and the delivery was (0.6) .hhh well I thought it was fine.
CR→	LBJ:	· hh This's off the record. I don't want anything said about it but Bob Anderson called and said that · hhhh that General Eisenhower could give me some suggestions I talked to him a lot but he said he was up with a group of businessmen there today and said that · hhhh 'hey jus didn't think that this could happen. That uh, said hell if he does that we're gonna hafta support him. ↑huh huh huh [huh huh huh
	GL:	[hah hah

Not only does LBJ praise himself in this compliment response, he seems perhaps to fish for the compliment itself by making reference to staying up late to work on the speech.

Perhaps chastened by his interpersonal excesses in the last few calls, LBJ becomes modest to a fault in the last compliment receipts in this record. Here is one:

Extract (13)   [11/27/63 5:13 pm LBJ 63.11.03.32] (rough transcript).
(Spessard Holland (Florida Senator), LBJ is caller, the topic is the naming
of Cape Kennedy, then about 4 min. in)

C→	SH:	I thought your message today was <u>very</u> fine
		(.)
CR→	LBJ:	Well u:h-

What may we infer about strategy in this series of calls? Not a great
deal, and perhaps the nature of the event, and the responsive position
in which LBJ found himself is not one conducive to pre-strategy. But
my evolving sense of these records is that each momentary compliment
response seems not only reflective of the momentary complement, but
bears traces of and resemblances to prior events in the series. These
resemblances seem as much poetic (Jefferson, 1996) as strategic.

But there is another slice of these same materials that could be more
strategic, perhaps even (pre-)strategic, though our analysis is by no means
complete. This involves LBJ's frequent mention of *thrift* and related
terms, largely during compliment responses. Here is a sampling of these
moments, which make LBJ seem like a very effective strategic politician:
but in which sense of that term?

Extract (14)   [11/27/63 2:00 pm LBJ.63.11.03.10] (rough transcript,
Jim Haggarty (Ike's press secretary), LBJ is caller; 10 seconds after
compliment)

	LBJ:	I had Bob uh 'hh Anderson in, and the General and uh
	JH:	Yes I know
T→	LBJ:	you saw the prudence and the thrift huh huh the dollar
		value for the dollar spent and so forth

[11/27/63 2:10 pm LBJ 11.03.13?] (rough transcript, Otis Chandler, LBJ
is caller; begins about 10 seconds into call)

C→	DC:	... congratulations on what I thought was a magnificent
		performance this morning.
CR→	LBJ:	Well, I did the best I could.
C→	OC:	Well, I thought it was just exceptional (.) really
CR→	LBJ:	Bob Anderson and General Eisenhower did say (.) they're
T→		glad we were talking about economy and prudence and
		watching the dollar ((LBJ continues))

[11/27/63 2:15 pm LBJ.63.11.03:14] (Walker Stone, Stone is caller)

	LBJ:	Hello?
C→	STN:	President I saw you today, and I'm proud of you.

T→   LBJ: Well I just hhuh wanted to talk to my frugal thrift:y
             friend who believes in gettin' a <u>do</u>llar's value out
             of a dollar spent.
STN: Well done. even Harry Byrd applauded you

[11/27/63 2:45 pm LBJ 63.11.03.19] (rough transcript from LBJ lib,
(Louis Seltzer (newspaper editor); one minute in)

C→   LS: ... Now the reason I picked this telephone up to call
             you is that I do not remember in all of my time (.) when
             any President of the United States (.) so recently
             assuming his very heavy responsibilities (.) did so
             impressive and tremendous a job as you did just a few
             moments ago (.) and I could not resist the temptation of
             calling you. That's the sum total of my call.
CR→ LBJ: Well you don't know how much strength that gives me (.)
             not only because of my high regard for you but I was up
             till two thirty this morning (.) and I tried so hard to
             pay just tribute and still let the country know that I
             had some thoughts of my own and that we were going to be
T→   prudent, frugal, progressive people but we were (.) going
             to be in charge.

[11/27/63 3:25 pm LBJ 11.03.21] (rough transcript from LBJ lib,
Gene Pulliam, Pulliam is caller)

C→   GP: You made a wonderful speech today (.) it was absolutely
             wonderful
             (.)
T→   LBJ: I was thinking of you when I talked about thrift and
             frugality.

[11/27/63 5:10 pm LBJ 63.11.03.31] (Gould Lincoln (newsman), LBJ is
caller, 40 seconds in)

     LBJ: ·hh This's off the record. I don't want anything said
             about it but Bob Anderson called and said that·hhhh
             that General Eisenhower could give me some suggestions
             I talked to him a lot but he said he was up with a group
             of businessmen there today and said that ·hhhh 'hey jus
             didn't think that this could happen. That uh, said hell
             if he does that we're gonna hafta support him.
             ↑huh huh huh [huh huh huh
     GL: [hah hah Well uh-
             [hh hh
     LBJ: [·hhh but   [he- he wa- he-
     GL: [well uh I hh think I think that's true=
T→   LBJ: =.hhh When I started talking about frugality and thrift
             and gettin a dollars worth of value out of a dollar
             spent and sayin how I was gonna tighten up on things an
             watch what we were doin and try to .hhhh do some of these
             things, why he said that they just broke into appl(h)ause

Of these seven references to thrift, the first two and the last one invoke former President Eisenhower as a source to the speech's remarks about thrift. The four references in between allow the implication that LBJ credits his current interlocutor as having been his partner in talk about thrift. Now, possibly each of those people had mentioned thrift to LBJ recently. But LBJ seems to be campaigning for the principle of thrift and his co-implication of various conversation partners in this value is an astute way to build consensus on an issue by implicating many people as affiliated with the idea – and with its expression in the President's first speech. Thus Johnson gives these conversation partners a sense of entitlement to the works of a great man, and at the same time promotes one of his key political agendas (shrinking the national budget). Is this evidence of pre-strategy, or is LBJ simply performing the gift of glib on frugality. Frugality does in the days that follow become a major theme of his phone calls (and I believe of his public presidency).

Conclusions

I hope to have shown that conversation analysts are attentive to a critical set of *when* questions about strategy in talk. Strong evidence of pre-strategy seems relatively rare and to the extent that it occurs it usually cannot be located precisely in time. LBJ got well-greased at accepting compliments during this afternoon, and he gave off a sense that thrift would become a theme of his administration. What would it add to this analysis if we were to know that at 3:12 pm on 11/27/63 President Johnson made an actual decision to emphasize thrift? Some clear cases of pre-strategy undoubtedly occur, but are these typical of most talk-in-interaction? Some clear cases of late-emerging-strategy may also occur. But in the widest array of cases (those I find most paradigmatic of human interaction) evidence of strategy seems widely distributed across the surface appearances of talk. Analytic *when* questions turn up recurrent ambiguities in regard to communicative strategy.

I have studied some repetitive speech events that Heritage's NB analyses suggest might shed light on pre- versus emergent-strategy. These instances convince me of the widespread distribution of strategy development over a spate of repetitive encounters, and of the multiple strategic characterizations that can seem to become the 'reason for calling' – to congratulate, to ingratiate, to tell a joke, to consult about an award, to promote one's political value of frugality. This series of LBJ calls show a Burkean braid of savvy political motivation. It is amazing to listen as this guy operates. But I hear LBJ's strategies as growing in uncertain emergent ways across the sets of calls. I am optimistic about claims that see strategy as something cumulative across encounters, such as:

- Johnson's subsequent calls seem to utilize fragments from prior calls as improvisation rehearsals of material that may get more effectively formulated in later calls than earlier calls.
- The series of preacher stories grows from, and eventually settles back to a modest and apt formulation recalling the compliment receipts with which the series started: 'I appreciate it but I don't deserve it'.

But I remain agnostic about claims such as:

- Johnson pre-strategized to tell this preacher story a second time.
- Johnson called Senator Pastore to check out the Oppenheimer problem, and the prior congratulation about the panel show was incidental and gratuitous.

I advocate future research on numerous ways of doing being cognitive, that is, of signalling to an interactive partner that one is, e.g.:

- changing directions strategically or a-strategically (touched off)
- doing thinking it over, either in meta-talk (let me think) or in dispreferred-shape second-pair parts. (For example, it is striking how often student analysts hear a dispreferred-shape second-pair part as 'thinking it over'.)

Furthermore, a feature of these indicators of cognition is their routine disingenuousness. That is, being strategic may be falsified, distorted, simulated, or otherwise performed in various fictive ways (see Jefferson, 1996; Bateson, 1972). What is remarkable in all this is the actor's faith that we can document and know what other people are undertaking strategically. If this is all a postmodern version of the old mind-body problem, Descartes versus Leibnitz; I guess I come down as a theoretical monist. Surely there is a subject matter 'cognition' to be investigated. But as one dedicated to empirical inquiry, I start from the point of embodied actions and see what I can construct. (I claim pre-strategy for myself in this regard.) Let me conclude with a shaggy dog story that's not terribly funny, but seems worth some thought. On the plane to Montreal yesterday I happened to sit next to this francophone fellow in weird old clothing. We fell to talking and he seemed pretty intellectual, so I introduced myself by name, and admitted to being a scholar giving a talk about cognition. He said he used to speculate on some of these matters. Then he smiled and said 'Je m'appelle Rene Descartes'. I was trying to figure out whether to take this guy seriously, when the airline hostess came by and asked: 'Professor Descartes, would you like something to drink'. There was a short pause, then he answered: 'I think not'. And as soon as he said this, he disappeared.

The historical Descartes bequeathed us some of our current discourse analytic problems when he doubted his own existence. He tried empirical approaches to his existential agnosticism, like pinching himself, but still he doubted the evidence from these experiences. He could have been dreaming that he pinched himself. What he could not doubt was that he was thinking about his doubts. Aha: *cogito ergo sum.* I'm thinking, I must be real.

We do seem to think. Yet the when of thinking is a difficult thing to get empirical about. So, as a conversation analyst, I start with the empirical bits and try to reason from there about human experience. In my view, if you say 'I think not', you don't disappear. In fact, such a statement may not change much in our understanding of human communicative action and agency.

When I examine human talk I often get convinced that people are thinking about stuff as and in their talk. Sometimes I even suspect that people are being (pre-)strategic. In some kinds of speech events: private manipulations or swindles, and in the public manipulative swindles we call public policy, politics and scholarship, there is even sometimes evidence in the discourse that people follow my father's dictum and engage in pre-strategy – that is, doing thinking before the events in which I hear them putting their mouth into gear.

Appendix

LBJ Phone Fragments: 11/63
Theme indicators

T→	thrift mentioned (e.g. frugality and thrift, prudence and thrift)
C→	compliments to LBJ on his 'Let us continue' speech
CR→	compliment responses by LBJ
P→	preacher story (a way of receipting compliment)

[11/27/63 1:35 pm   LBJ63.11.03.5]
(Nellie Connally (Mrs. Gov. John Connally), LBJ is caller)

SEC:	Missus Connally on nine three?
	(1.6)
LBJ:	I'm so proud of your boy when he was up here 'n I'm sittin' here in- in my office with
	Ladybird 'n' Lucy and Linda and (0.2) we wanted to find out how our- (0.3) <u>boy</u> was getting along
NC:	Now wait a minute I know this is irreverent to tell the president to <u>hush</u> but I want to tell you I have <u>never</u> been prouder of <u>any</u>body than I was of <u>you</u> a while ago.
	(0.3)
LBJ:	Well (0.2)
NC:	Can you hear me?
LBJ:	I sure <u>can</u> and I've always been mighty proud of you

CR→		darlin n I appreciate it I'd rather hear that from <u>you</u> than nearly anybo[dy
	NC:	[I was just tryin to decide whether to try
C→		to get in touch with you or not but I - uh- Lyndon you just made me feel so wonderful
CR→	LBJ:	Well you're a wonderful gir: l, how's my boy.
	NC:	He's doin <u>real</u> well.

[11/27/63 2:00 pm   LBJ63.11.03.10] (unfinished transcript Bob Kintner and Jim Haggarty (Ike's press secretary), LBJ is caller)

C→	BK/JH	... That was a fi:ne (.) talk to Congress today
CR→	LBJ:	Well, 'hhh they were very good to me ah ah 'hhhh on both sides I thought, and 'hhh appreciate it.
	BK/JH	Well- as I say, God bless and there's anything I can do to help any of your staff I most certainly would be
		[(glad to)
	LBJ:	[Come in the first time you⌡re down here will ya
		(0.2)
	JH:	Anytime you say Mister Pres[ident.
	LBJ:	[Well, I'll- I'll just um 'hhh got this one
		by me now and I don't want you to make a <u>spe</u>cial trip
		but when you're here I want you to come and just (.) chew the rag a
		little bit then
		(.)
	JH:	Any time you say [(you say)
	LBJ:	[I had Bob uh 'hh Anderson in, and the General
		and uh
	JH:	Yes I know
T→	LBJ:	you saw the prudence and the thrift huh huh the dollar value for the dollar spent and so forth and [uh
	JH:	[Yes sir
	LBJ:	I thought that we got some (0.2) uh 'hhh we we had a pretty good statement [and
	JH:	[Yes it[was
	LBJ:	[And now I want all the help of all Americans (.) and particularly yours cause I've been your admirer a long time

---

[11/27/63 2:10 pm   LBJ63.11.03.13?] (rough transcript Otis Chandler, LBJ is caller, about 10 seconds into call)

C→	OC:	Yes sir. We'll do everything we can and congratulations on what I thought was a magnificent performance this morning
CR→	LBJ:	Well, I did the best I could
T→	OC:	Well, I thought it was just exceptional (.) really
CR→	LBJ:	Bob Anderson and General Eisenhower did say (.) they 're

T→		glad we were talking about economy and prudence and watching the
		dollar (LBJ continues)

[11/27/63 2:15 pm   LBJ63.11.03.14] (Walker Stone, Stone is caller)

	LBJ:	Hello?
C→	WS:	President I saw you today, and I'm proud of you
T→	LBJ:	Well I just hhuh wanted to talk to my frugal thrift:y friend who
		believes in getting' a dollar's value out of a dollar spent.
	WS:	Well done. even Harry Bird applauded you
CR→	LBJ:	(uh ha ha ha) hh well thank you W- Walker I just wanted to thank you
		for being with me these uh (.) last few days
T→		that have been so:(0.2) uh so much of a trial tribulation and Marshall
		(0.4) 'hhh u:h came called me and was uh real wonderful and hh
CR→		I:uh don't deserve it but hh I: do appreciate it.
		(0.7)
	WS:	Well hh well call anytime Lyndon.

[11/27/63 2:22 pm   LBJ63.11.03.15]
(Adam Clayton Powell (Harlem congressman), caller unknown, 1 minute into call)

	LBJ:	I- I pointed em out did I do alright on civil rights?
		(0.2)
	ACP:	My friend I just finished with CBS, and tellin them it was (.)
C→		it was unequivocally the finest that uh I said uh it was more than I
		hoped for
		(0.4)
		And uh the finest that anyone could say forthright (.) it was really
		wonderful you know you were at your best today absolutely superb- I
		don't know when you get the time to ↑do it though.
CR→	LBJ:	Well they had thirty four- ya:'ll were gunners you had thirty four
		applauses in twenty minutes
C→	ACP:	I knew you had good ghostwriters but brother that was Lyndon Baine
		Johnson that wasn't any ghostwriter that- speech was absolutely
		magnificent.
CR→	LBJ:	Well thank ya and I'll- I'll get in touch with this and I'll be back in
		touch with you.

[11/27/63 2:45 pm   LBJ63.11.03.19] (rough transcript from LBJ library
Louis Selter (Newspaper editor), 1 minute into call)

C→	LS:	... Now the reason I picked this telephone up to call you is that I do
		not remember in all of my time (.) when any President of the United
		States (.) so recently assuming his very heavy responsibilities (.) did so

impressive and tremendous a job as you did just a few moments ago
(.) and I could not resist the temptation of calling you. That's the sum
total of my call.

CR→   LBJ: Well you don't know how much strength that gives me (.) not only
because of my high regard for you but I was up till two thirty this
morning (.) and I tried so hard to pay just tribute and still let the
country know that I had some thoughts of my own and that we were
going to be

T→   prudent, frugal, progressive people but we were (.) going to be in
charge.

[11/27/63 3:25 pm   LBJ63.11.03.21] (rough transcript from LBJ library
Gene Pulliam, Pulliam is caller)

LBJ: Hello. I've been thinking of you, and I've had some trials and
tribulations these last few days but I want to thank you for your
friendship and all you've done for me and I hope that the first time
you're this way we'll get together.

GP: I wrote you a letter (.) you won't get it (.) ask Reedy to get it to you (.)
I said you know you'v always had my heart in my hand and you still
do.

LBJ: I know that Gene and I appreciate it very much. God bless you
(.)

C→   GP: You made a wonderful speech today (.) it was absolutely wonderful (.)

T→   LBJ: I was thinking of you when I talked about thrift and frugality.

[11/27/63 4:01 pm   LBJ63.11.03.23]
(Joe Alsop (Columnist), Alsop is caller, a few seconds into call)

LBJ: I wanted to tell you how grateful I am for that most beautiful
wonderful article I don't deserve it but I appreciate it you know 'hhh
I'm not as frustra-=

JA: = Yes sir I mean

P→   LBJ: I'm not as frustrated as that Baptist preacher in Te- uh when the: y
showed up one morning the gave him a ↑car. 'hhhh and he got up in
the pulpit and he didn't know what to sa: y and he didn't expect em to
give him a: Ford automobile, poor little ↑church, and he said uh 'hh I
just want ya'll to kno:w that I don't appreciate it but I do deserve it
[hunh hunh heh heh heh heh heh

JA: [hunh hunh hunh hunh hunh

LBJ: But I do appreciate it and I don't deserve it

JA: Well- all I can sa:y is I (0.4) I- I didn't want to bother you I was trying
to get you a (1.0) a wor:d to to a (.) uh through Bill Moyers and I sent
a wor:d to Lady Bird that (you'll be so) watching you there n (0.4)
that they're thinking about Phil, and a couple of my colleagues who
were (0.2) uh started out- you know eager to (0.4) see a

C→   failure and um 'hhh remained to applaud a triumphant success. (0.4)
and um (0.2) I came back to lunch with (0.2) Ka:y and (0.2) all I can
say is that we both had a darn good ↑cr:y.=

LBJ: = Don't let- don't let the governor get away from me there now Bill?
'hh alright go go- [go ahead what?

JA: [We both had a darn   [good

CR→   LBJ: [Well I 'hh I've had to
restrain myself all during the period uh 'hh you and Phil, uh Jackie
came over and visited me this afternoon 'hh and told me about being
at your house one night at dinner and hh 'hh how (.) what- you and
Phil had said about me and how touched she was and how she
remembered it. and what the President had said her several times
about it 'hhhh we just kinda had a hhh 'hh real lovely session for thirty
minutes here, we're gonna name Cape Canaveral Cape Kennedy
(0.6)
[an:d (.) so

JA: [u:h (.) yeah
(0.4)
Kay and I after your speech this morning she lunched with me:, and
uh (1.0) hhh we both had a sort of ridiculous cr:y.
(0.2)
because Phil wasn't there to to:uh (.) see how right he'd been.

LBJ: Did uh did you see u:h what she sent me that he had written
(0.8)

JA: No I didn't

LBJ: I'll have tu[::h she was (merry) some night-

JA: [but uh

LBJ: some [night when

C→   JA: [the speech was a triumphant success, Lyndon
(0.2)

CR→   LBJ: Was it, well

[11/27/63 5:00 pm   LBJ63.11.03.29]
(Roscoe Drummond, columnist, etc.)

RD: Well Mister President I'm: just gratified and I (0.3) I

C→   watched you:r speech toda:y and I knew that the hand of God was in
it. (0.3) and Mister President I kno- you're my President and (0.3)
I'm very proud of the way you're doing it.
(0.3)

CR→   LBJ: We:ll uh you have through the ye:ars uh (0.4) been uh (0.5)

P→   unusually uh charitable with me: and uh (0.4) I'm kinda like the
preacher (0.5) that was surpri:sed when they gave him a Ford
automobile the congregation one Sunday (0.4) he got up somewhat
frustrated and he said I don't appreciate it but I do deserve it

RD: gheh gha ha ha ha ha ha ha uhhhh

CR→   LBJ: I don't deserve it but I do appreciate it
      RD: [Well I think you do
      LBJ: [Roscoe and I never needed you more than I do now

[11/27/63 5:01 pm   LBJ63.11.03.30] (rough transcript from LBJ library)
(Bill White, LBJ is caller)

C→   BW: ... I think your speech today was the greatest ever heard in my life. I think that not for the substance alone but for the manner of delivery, and I tell you I don't normally get terribly emotional, maybe I do, but I was crying there at the end, myself

CR→   LBJ: =Well, you're mighty good. Homer Thornberry came in crying and poor old boy from the Cleveland Press, Louie Seltzer, called me up and he was crying... (continues self-praise)

[11/27/63 5:10 pm   LBJ63.11.03.31]
(Gould Lincoln (newsman), LBJ is caller, 30 seconds into call)

      GL: Well I put- I only put t in the mail this afternoon.
      LBJ: Well I'll get it then, she'll get it to me tomorrow I jus- I was up till two thirty last night on the speech an=
C→   GL: =Oh yeah I think you did a wonderful job today
           (0.5)
CR→   LBJ: [.hhh We: ll?
      GL: [I was up there and uh (1.0) and I- I- I really thought the content of your speech, and the delivery was (0.6).hhh well I thought it was fine.
      LBJ: 'hh This's off the record. I don't want anything said about it but Bob Anderson called and said that 'hhhh that General Eisenhower could give me some suggestions I talked to him a lot he said he was up with a group of budnismen there today and said that 'hhhh 'hey jus didn't think that this could happen. That uh, said hell if he does that we're gonna hafta support him. ↑huh huh huh [huh huh huh
      GL: [hah hah Well uh-
             [hh hh
      LBJ: ['hhh but   [he- he wa- he-
      GL: [well uh I hh think I think that's true
T→   LBJ: .hhh When I stared talking bout frugality and thrift and getting a dollars worth of value out of a dollar spent and sayin how I was gonna tighten up on things an watch what we were doin and try to .hhhh do some of these things, why he said that they just broke [into appl(h)ause
      GL: [Uh?
      LBJ: hah [hhh hh?
      GL: [huh? (0.2) Well that's true.

[11/27/63 5:10   pm LBJ63.11.03.32] (rough transcript)
(Spessard Holland (Florida Senator), LBJ is caller, ~4 minutes into call,
(topic is the renaming of Cape Canaveral Cape Kennedy))

	LBJ:	I can make a check with the governor too before we take any action
		(0.2)
C→	SH:	I thought your message today was <u>very</u> fine
		(.)
CR→	LBJ:	Well u:h-
C→	SH:	And I especially thought your (0.4) your uh recognition of uh (0.4)
		the legislative branch, and the words you used about it uh (0.4) were
		splendid (0.4) and I don't see how you could 've done a better <u>job</u>. (.)
		I've already made that comment to the press and I want to tell you
		personally (.)
		[to that effect
	LBJ:	[go ahead
CR→		You've been a gra::nd and devoted (0.2) uh 'hhh uh loyal friend and
		I'll never forget you my friend I app<u>re</u>ciate it.

[11/29/63   LBJ63.11.04.??]
(John Pastore (Rhode Island Senator), LBJ is caller, 1 of 4 about panel
show)

LBJ:	Ah 'hhh what I called you: about was t tell you that uh my Texas::s 'hh
	uh friend's in toda:y He'd come up here t get my will and two or three
	little ol things and 'hh he said that the best program he'd ever saw was
	you on some ↑panel, And he said that- 'hh I think he met you when
	you came down there in that (.) rain that day and hh 'hh Judge
	Morsund and he said that u:h just the best he ever ↑sa:w. And uh I: I
	hadn't known about it and I just told him to get a hold of ya and tell ya:
	how much I loved ya and I:ho:w appre- how much I preciate it
JP:	Well that's so wonderful of you as busy as you a:(h)re.
	Just typical of ↑you:.
LBJ:	Well
JP:	Well (0.4) uh Lyndon I: I- I did say one thing and I repeat it to you that
	uh (0.3) Excuse me for saying Lyndon I- (0.2) I gotta get used to it=
LBJ:	=huh huh huh huh huh [huh ↑huh huh huh=
JP:	[Mister President
LBJ:	= 'hhh well [you been sayin it a long ti:me.
JP:	[I think that one of thee:(..)
	legacie:s that uh (0.5) that John Kennedy left to the American people is
	when he chose Lyndon Johnson.
LBJ:	Well [thank you.
JP:	[(in control)
	(0.4)

LBJ:	'hh I'm not worthy of it, but I'll try to be
	(0.7)
JP:	Thank you so much for calling=
LBJ:	=Give your sweet wife and your lovely children my lo:ve=
JP:	=I: certainly will, and they'll appreciate it very very much
LBJ:	Hope you had a happy Thanksgiving and 'hhh I look forward to seeing
	em first time they're down her bring em in I want to see em again=
JP:	=Alright thank you very very much=
LBJ:	=Johnny I'm giving this award to Oppenheimer
	that the President- planned for him
JP:	[Yes?
LBJ:	[I- (0.2) I don't- I thought I oughta carry it on through.

Editors' note

We have kept as closely as possible to Hopper's original manuscript. This reflects its original presentation to a pre-conference on Cognition and Discourse organized for the International Communication Association in Montreal, 1997.

NOTES

1. This paper is very much research in progress. I gratefully acknowledge Senem Sayrak's contributions to the analyses of the LBJ calls.
2. Geo Wilson 'Take a number', *The New Yorker*. July 18, 1994: 49.
3. For general discussions of conversation analysis methods, see Jacobs (1988), Wieder (1988), Zimmerman (1988), Hopper (1988, 1989, 1990/91), Pomerantz (1990), Heritage (1984a).
4. '. . . easily accessible conversational actions for which accounts of meaning shaped in terms of consciousness and intention simply will not do. But the complex procedural resources for engaging in interaction permeate every aspect of its realization . . . .

   For the lay observer of tennis, the difference between a well positioned topspin serve and a reflex volley is that the first is the product of conscious intent while the second is a product of unconscious skill. But *both* actions . . . embody an immense reservoir of unconscious skilled practices. In interaction, actions can emerge which look most like a skilled serve in tennis. On these occasions, the conscious intentionality of an action can seem obvious and inescapable. Yet . . . The carefully designed conversational action is also based on layer upon layer of unconsciously learned and mobilized capacities ' (Heritage, 1990/91: 326).
5. Emergent and pre-strategic are my terms for Drew's distinction (Hopper, 1992).
6. The power distinction between caller and called (Hopper, 1992) is somewhat effaced for a President, who is always the most powerful person in these calls, and whose call openings are inevitably mediated by others.
7. This could be incorrect. The first few seconds of the call were not preserved on the recording.

Part II

Cognition in action

7   Is *confusion* a state of mind?

Paul Drew

Introduction

First, some preliminaries, to clear the decks. There are, of course, good reasons for detaching the study of interaction from that of cognition and treating the *interaction order* as an autonomous field of conduct.[1] Most radically, some have rejected the dualism between mind and action, proposing for instance that it makes no sense to regard action as the embodiment or manifestation of some putative prior mental state (Melden, 1961; Ryle, 1963; Coulter, 1979). However, those who study conversation have what are perhaps less radical reasons for rejecting a cognitive approach to conversational action. First, we cannot know from speakers' behaviour in conversation, that is from what is said, what they were thinking or feeling as they spoke. Their mental states are opaque in their verbal conduct. Second, the organization of conduct in conversation and talk-in-interaction generally, can be shown to be systematically *socially* organized independently of the predispositions – and hence personality and other mental constructs – of the individuals who happen to participate in any particular interaction.

The opacity of cognition in conversational (inter)-action and the autonomy of the social organization of conduct (and the sequences associated with conduct) in talk-in-interaction, taken in combination with one another, suggest that the practices of verbal conduct are independent of the cognitive states of individual participants. Some brief examples may help to illustrate this, and begin to show something of the complexity of connecting action and mind. Consider the construction of turns in which speakers decline invitations, as in this instance.

Extract (1)   [SBL:1:1:10:17]

```
1  Ros:   And uh the: if you'd care tuh come ovuh, en visit u
2         little while this morning I'll give you [cup a'coffee.
3  Bea:                                           [ khhh
4  Bea:   Uhhh-huh hh Well that's awf'lly sweet of yuh I don't
5         think I can make it this morning, hheeuhh uh:m (0.3)
```

6   'tch I'm <u>running</u> an <u>a</u>:d in the <u>pa</u>per and an:d uh hh I
7   have to st<u>ay</u> near the ph<u>o</u>::ne,

The key property of Bea's declination here – in which she does an appreciation of Rose's invitation (line 4), a (mitigated) declination (lines 4–5) and an account – is that it is built to indicate that she would have accepted, had she been free to do so. Accounts for rejecting, declining and so on are generally constructed in terms of constraints, through formulating circumstances which prevent the speaker from accepting (Heritage, 1983, 1988). In this example these circumstances are adumbrated in the declination component, in *don't think I can make it*, and are then detailed in her account for why she cannot leave the house that morning. Taken together, these components convey Bea's willingness to accept, had she been able to do so.[2]

Now we cannot tell whether *in fact* this is how Bea regards the invitation. It may or may not be true that she's running an ad in the paper that day; and if she is, there might be someone else at home who could deal with enquiries or take a message, or she might leave the answer-phone on. She might have gone for coffee and figured that people would ring back later. We know that circumstances, even if they are 'real', can be glossed in a variety of ways to suit speakers' *interactional* purposes[3] – that descriptions of 'reality' can be formulated not to reflect one's actual state of mind, but rather in accordance with the conventions of declining an invitation. So that, for example, one constructs as a constraint circumstances which might perfectly well not prevent one doing something – as a convenient fiction, to avoid having to accept, but in a way which suggests one *would rather have* accepted. Constructing declinations in this way can enable speakers to disguise their actual states of mind (what their actual intentions are, how they really feel etc.). Of course this is speculative, and relies largely on what we know, introspectively, we do from time to time: we bend 'reality', or lie, in order to avoid doing something we would rather not do, whilst conveying the opposite (though it should be noticed that this possibility is the basis for participants themselves speculating about, and commenting on, whether or not an account given for not doing something is 'genuine').

Here is a second example illustrating a possible disjunction between action and cognition: Emma begins to close the conversation with her sister with the canonical device used to close telephone calls – refering to a future getting together (Schegloff and Sacks, 1973). However, the form of that device which Emma uses in lines 4/5, 'Ah:ll (.) pob'ly <u>SEE</u> yih one a' these da:<u>ys</u>,' is susceptible to being heard as – and is heard by Lottie as – a complaint.

Extract (2)   [NB:1:6:8]

```
1   Lot:   °Oh I love tuh gee I ride mine all [th' ti:me.°
2   Emm:                                      [°Ye:ah.°
3   Lot:   I love it.
4   Emm:   .hhh WELL honey? ( ) Ah:ll (.) pob'ly SEE yih
5          one a' these da:y[s,
6   Lot:                    [Oh: Go:d yeah [(ah wish)]=
7   Emm:                                  [ehh huh ]=
8   Lot:   =But I c- I jis [couldn' git do:w[n (      )
9   Emm:                   [Oh-u            [Oh I know=
10  Emm:   =I'm not as[kin yih tih] c'm dow-]
11  Lot:              [Iee : z i z] I mean  ] I jis
12         (0.2)
13  Lot:   I didn' have five minutes yesterday.
```

In her response in lines 6 and 8, Lottie evidently treats Emma's reference to seeing her *one of these days* as complaining that Lottie hasn't been to see her. Lottie provides an account for not having been down to see Emma (again, one formed as a constraint, *couldn't get down*, rather than what she'd like to have done; see *I wish* at the end of line 6). As Lottie begins this account (seemingly going to strengthen the account from *but I couldn't* to *I just couldn't* in line 8), Emma disavows that interpretation of her closing remark: that's to say, she claims in lines 9/10 that she had not been implying anything (complaining) about Lottie not having been to see her (note that *I'm not asking you* in line 10 is a formulation of her prior closing turn). Here we have, in effect, quite different understandings or versions of Emma's intention in referring to seeing Lottie *one of these days*. Lottie understands Emma to have been complaining about her not coming to see her; whilst Emma, in disavowing that understanding, is claiming the 'innocence' of her remark. Emma's formulation of what she intended does not of course settle the matter of what she may or may not originally have intended in making that remark (and it doesn't settle the matter for them, interactionally, since Lottie continues in line 13 with her defensive explanation for not coming down).

A final illustration of the possible disjunction between action and cognition: laughter would seem very directly to betoken a state of mind, one associated with the humour of a situation or what had been said. Setting aside for the present the systematic occurrence of laughter in environments (by which I mean, places or positions in conversation) in which humour seems not to figure,[4] research shows that participants are prompted to laugh at something someone has said by that speaker laughing in the course of, and especially towards the end of, their turn. Laughter is thereby occasioned by having been 'invited' (Jefferson, 1979;

Glenn, 1992; 2003). This is primarily a social interactional organization or process, rather than the simple manifestation of a cognitive state.

Furthermore, there is evidence that people may thereby be invited or prompted to laugh, in the absence of their having found anything funny.

Extract (3) [Holt:X(C):1:1:3:4–5] (re Philip's daughter's holidays) (Jefferson, 1997)

```
1    Phil:      She's having three weeks 'n staying here one week I
2               think [(is it)]
3    Les:             [Y e : s]=
4    Les:       =[Y e s
5    Phil:  +   [eh-heh-he[h
6    Les:   +             [he-huh he-huh.
```

Lesley's initial response to Philip's report of how long his daughter is staying at home during her holiday is a fairly minimal acknowledgement (lines 3 and 4). It is only in response to Phil beginning to laugh (chuckle) in line 5 that Lesley comes to laugh (line 6). Since there is no 'new information' between her initial non-laughing response and her subsequent laughter, and only his laughter which can have generated hers, we can surmise that as Lesley didn't find anything humorous in his report, she comes to laugh only because he has done so, and not as an expression of anything she has found amusing (Jefferson, 1997). Once again then, conduct appears to be generated by an interactional organization, rather than any state of mind on the part of the one whose conduct is being examined.

These three examples help to illustrate that there is no necessary congruence between verbal conduct and a speaker's cognitive state. Whilst the verbal conduct might correspond with the mental state with which that conduct is usually associated (in extract (1)), there is no guarantee that that is the case. In extract (2) the conduct in question, a form of call closing, is consistent with two quite different 'intentions'; whilst in example 3, there is some evidence that the speaker (Lesley) specifically does not possess the cognitive state with which her behaviour (laughing) is usually associated. In each of these ways, the organization of behaviour in interaction is to be treated analytically as being independent of any supposed cognitive states on the part of participants, especially since there is evidence that there may be a disjunction between conduct and the cognitive state which it might be taken to represent or express. Certainly behaviour is not reducible to being the manifestation of states of mind. These examples illustrate why, in investigating the organization and practices of talk-in-interaction, we have generally done so without attempting to connect these organizations and practices to cognition.

Nevertheless, despite the autonomy of the organization of (verbal) behaviour, ways have been found to address cognitive issues through the analysis of talk-in-interaction – albeit by re-specifying the kinds of questions which are asked and issues which are addressed. In the next section I shall outline briefly two of the directions this research has taken, as a preliminary to suggesting and illustrating another avenue we might take in exploring the connection between talk-in-interaction and cognition.

Mental States as an interactional resource

The study of conversation seems to lie at the intersections between linguistics, psychology and sociology; and increasingly research at these intersections is transforming the kinds of questions which can be asked about traditional areas and issues within these disciplines. For instance the study of grammar is being transformed by investigating grammar-in-use, and particularly the role of grammar in interaction (eg. Ochs, Schegloff and Thompson, 1996). In this view grammar is a practice, or rather sets of practices, constituting resources which may be mobilized in the course of interactional projects. As a result grammar and interaction are viewed as symbiotic: 'Grammar is not only a resource for interaction and not only an outcome of interaction, it is part of the essence of interaction itself. Or, to put it another way, grammar is inherently interactional' (Ochs, Schegloff and Thompson, 1996: 38). This focus on grammar and/in interaction has begun to involve a quite radical re-specification of the object of enquiry.

Similarly, explorations at the intersection between psychology and interaction/discourse have transformed the kinds of questions about mental or cognitive states which are being addressed (for a review see Edwards, 1997). Traditionally verbal conduct has been regarded as 'overt manifestations of the mind in action . . . windows to both the content of the mind and its ongoing operations' (Chafe, 1990:79, quoted in Edwards, 1997:269), a view which rests on the assumption that cognition determines behaviour in interaction. The examples discussed above serve only to remind us how mistaken is that assumption. For these and other reasons (again, see Edwards, 1997), and in parallel with transformations in the study of grammar, one direction which research in this field has taken has been to focus on how mental states are employed as resources in interaction, through the *attributive use* of mental/cognitive states (a term borrowed, perhaps loosely, from Edwards, 1997; but see also Levinson, 1996). 'Emotion words and other mental predicates (are) *ways of talking*' (Edwards, 1997:296; emphasis in original): so that the repertoire of terms describing both cognitive and emotional states can be regarded as a folk psychology which speakers employ to account for what has happened or is happening, to describe states of affairs, in the course of their interactional and discursive projects. Hence the focus shifts to participants' situated uses of terms such as *thinking, angry, surprise, jealous, intend, understand, realize*, and so on. The attributional work which such terms are employed to perform offer a variety of directions for analysis, some of which were proposed by Coulter (1979) among others, and which have been taken by the discursive psychologists, including Edwards 1997.[5]

These directions include investigating both the rhetorical uses made by participants of terms describing mental states, as well as ways in which claims to and attributions of mental states may work to organize more fine grained aspects of interaction. For instance, Goodwin (1987) showed that displays of forgetfulness or uncertainty operated as requests to 'knowing' participants (one who knows about the events or experiences being talked about) to collaborate in the production of some ongoing narrative or sequence. This 'provides resources for dealing both with systematic problems faced in talk by parties, such as couples, who share many of their experiences, and with local contingencies that emerge in the midst of interaction. With such a request, a speaker can attempt to rearrange the structure of the current interaction' (Goodwin, 1987:128). The *rhetorical/attributive* and *interactional* approaches to the use or display of, or claims to, mental states have in common that descriptions or depictions of mental (cognitive and emotional) states are analyzed as resources mobilized by participants in their engagement in interactional projects or activities.[6] (For another 'discursive' approach deriving from the rejection of cognitivism, focusing on the factuality of descriptions, see Potter, 1996 and 1998.)

Cognition in interaction

Both the approaches I have just described rely on the visibility of participants' orientations to and treatments of mental states, manifest either in their reference to such states, or their behaviourial expression of them (for instance, Goodwin, 1987 investigates an instance in which one speaker asks 'What was that guy's name', thereby claiming, at least, to have forgotten). By contrast, I want to begin to consider whether, and how, cases can be identified in which cognitive states appear to be 'real' but only incipient – and in some fashion oriented to by participants though not acknowledged by them in any very explicit way. My purpose in reviewing these instances is to suggest a direction which connects with and complements both the attributional and interactional approaches, but which stands as an alternative to the 'cognition as resource' standpoint which underlies them. In particular it explores the kind of behaviourial manifestation of cognitive states adumbrated in Goodwin's analysis.

Something which seems to support the 'preference for self-correction' (Schegloff, Jefferson and Sacks, 1977) is that from time to time we realize that someone we're talking with has made a mistake, but we let it pass. We know what they mean, and it's not sufficiently important to hold up the conversation for; or, they're non-native speakers of our language and making a good enough fist of it – why rub their face in it by correcting every small error they make over pronouns or syntax or the like. We recognize this situation in our daily lives – introspectively. And therein lies the problem for empirical research – introspection is not a satisfactory basis for the analysis of conduct. We cannot begin to build an analytic science on the basis of intuitions about what we ourselves do, or what might have happened in an interaction. But then if we were to explore speakers' overt conduct at such possible moments (i.e. moments at which one speaker lets another's error pass), there is a difficulty. A transcription of such a moment in conversation would reveal . . . nothing! Speaker A takes a turn, in which we might see there's an error: speaker B responds, but without correcting or otherwise drawing attention to A's error. Neither the error, nor the possibility that B realized that A was mistaken but let it pass, comes to the interactional surface. Did B realize that A made an error, but let it pass; or did B not spot A's mistake? Who knows? It seems impossible from the data, on the basis of B's observable conduct, to tell anything about their cognitive state.

We can find cases in which the one who made an error, speaker A, realizes they made a mistake and corrects it, *after* B has responded – suggesting that B had an *opportunity* to correct A's mistake. But here too we cannot be sure if B let A's mistake pass, or just didn't see it.

Extract (4)   [Heritage:1:5:3–4]

```
1   Dorothy:    But (0.4) uh::m:: (0.9) uh-:: (.) if:: .h.h uhw he
2               won't do whatchu want him tuh do: t-.h twice a
3               week with you'n twice a wee:k with me.
4   Edgerton:   We:ll we[: we-
5   Dorothy:            [Uh twice a:, a month.
6   Edgerton:   Well we've got to we've gotta talk to him about
7               it. I haven' mention'it to him yet.
```

In lines 1–3 of this extract from a telephone conversation, Dorothy is talking about having spoken with her son Edgerton's gardener about coming to do some work in her garden; and she refers to him doing 'twice a week with you' (i.e. with Edgerton). Edgerton begins to respond (line 4), whereupon Dorothy corrects her mistake, 'twice a:, a month'. Did Edgerton realize Dorothy had made a mistake and chose not to correct her (he ought, after all, to know how often his gardener comes), or was he day dreaming – did it escape his notice? There's no evidence in the data to decide it either way.

It might be suggested that since his mother's mistake does not appear to be salient to Egerton's conduct, then it's not relevant to know (or to speculate about) whether or not he realized that she had made a mistake. In certain respects, that is quite right. When we are documenting sequential patterns such as the one illustrated here (in which a speaker self-corrects in third turn), it is not necessary to consider speakers' cognitive (or affective) states. Indeed, for the reasons outlined in the introductory section, generally we set aside questions about participants' psychological states, since these have no part to play in the *socially* organized practices of talk-in-interacion. It is important that we continue to focus analysis principally on the autonomous organizations, practices and devices through which social actions are conducted, and through which also the coherence of talk is achieved. Nevertheless, we can expect that these organizations will, in ways that we do not yet properly understand, intersect in some fashion with individual consciousness. We need therefore to begin to explore these possible intersections – including here, for instance, the possibility that what we know introspectively that we do, let pass another's error, might be manifest in the details of observable conduct. In other words one can begin to explore and document how a cognitive or other psychological state might come to be salient for an organized pattern of conduct.

Some evidence for supposing – empirically rather than introspectively – that participants may be aware of another's mistake, but let it pass without correcting it, was reported by Jefferson (1988). Here's an instance of the kind she identified.

Extract (5)   [NB:II:4:8]

```
1    Emma:   .t .hhuh W'l I TELLYIH uh; BUD MI:GHT go BA:CK UP
2            tih the BOA:T HE'S OUT RIDIN a BI:KE NOW EN'E
3            THOUGHT EE'D [GO UP'n getta PA:PER,
4    Nancy:                [O h : : : : :.
5    Emma:   .hh[hhhhh
6    Nancy:     [Oh'e wasn' going 'ee din'go fishi-
7            eh deh-e [didn: go GO:Lfing then huh?
8    Emma:             [O h I CAN'T go Oh:: God I can't go inna boat
9            for a long time'e siz no boating er no::,
10           (0.2)
11   Nancy:  Aw:::
12   Emma:   [GO:LF,
```

13   Nancy: [Bud wasn't playing go:lf?
14   (0.2)
15   Emma: No:
16   Nancy: Oh::.

It appears that Nancy is surprised to learn from what Emma says in lines 1–3 that her husband (Bud) is at home with her, albeit out riding a bike: from line 7 we see that Nancy thought Bud would be out playing golf (she's called to ask Emma to go shopping with her). Her surprise that he's not playing golf is manifest in her exclamation in line 4, and her enquiry in lines 6/7 (I shall for the present pass over the cognitive ascriptions that I, as an analyst, am making in describing Nancy as *surprised*). But in response to Nancy's enquiry about Bud, Emma answers about herself; she has just had an operation to remove a toenail, and *he says* in line 9 is a version of 'doctor's orders'.[7] Emma has made a mistake, whether genuine (arising from not having heard or understood Nancy correctly[8]) or otherwise (simply deciding to talk about herself; Jefferson [1988] provides another very similar case). Nancy's initial reaction is sympathy, 'Aw:::' (line 11). However, in line 13 she re-asks her original question. Repeating her enquiry[9] about Bud in this way serves as evidence that she treats Emma's first response (in lines 8/9) as not having answered the question she asked. And showing that Nancy *treats* Emma as not having answered the question she asks, reveals, in effect, a cognitive state – that Nancy recognizes that Emma did not answer her question (and therefore presumably made a mistake when responding). This is empirical evidence that she saw her co-participant had made a mistake: without correcting her (which is Jefferson's 'non-correction' phenomenon), she nevertheless rectifies Emma's mistake by asking the original question again – thereby revealing that she knew Emma had not answered the question she asked.

A couple of points to highlight. Nancy's first responding in an appropriately sympathetic manner and subsequently re-asking her original question is evidence that she *realized* Emma had made a mistake. She doesn't correct it (and in that respect lets it pass), but nevertheless Nancy's recognition or awareness of Emma's mistake is *salient* to Nancy's conduct. Second, though salient, and though visible in the details of this sequence, one could hardly say that the error or Nancy's recognition of it rose to the interactional surface of the talk. The cognitive salience of (her recognition of) Emma's mistake is only *latent* in the talk: it is not referred to, addressed or in any other way explicitly manifest in Nancy's conduct. In this respect a cognitive state is visible in the talk, but in quite a different way than forgetfulness is manifest in the enquiry 'What was that guy's name'. In that example, 'forgetting' is *displayed in* the enquiry. By contrast Nancy's conduct in extract (5) makes *visible* her recognition of Emma's mistake, but does not display it – insofar as 'display' engages the co-participant in a response to a (claimed) cognitive state, whilst 'visible' does not do so.[10]

With those points in mind, I want to consider a kind of case in which cognitive states manifestly come to the interactional surface, although they are not overtly expressed. These states are *observably relevant* to the participants, though neither refers to or addresses cognition explicitly. Recall that we saw in extract (1) that a speaker declines an invitation by constructing a turn which, typically, consists of three components, an [Appreciation] + [(mitigated) Declination] + [Account]. Consider what happens in the following extract in which Emma invites Nancy over for lunch.[11]

Extract (6)   [NB:II;2:17]

```
1  Emm:         Wanna c'm do:wn 'av [a bah:ta] lu:nch w]ith me?=
2  Nan:                            [°It's   js] (      )°]
3  Emm:         =Ah gut s'm beer'n stu:ff,
4               (0.3)
5  Nan:  -->    Wul yer ril sweet hon: uh:m
6               (.)
7  Emm:  -->    [Or d'y] ou'av] sup'n [else °(      )°
8  Nan:         [L e t-] I :   ] hu.   [n:No: i haf to: uh call Roul's
9               mother, h I told'er I:'d call'er this morning . . .
```

It will be recalled that in extract 1, Bea's [Appreciation] is prefaced with *well*, 'Well that's <u>awf</u>'lly <u>sweet</u> of yuh'. Here too Nancy begins her response to Emma invitation with a nearly identical *well*-prefaced appreciation (line 5). Before she can go any further (though simultaneously with her about to go further), Emma anticipates that Nancy might have something else (line 7), and therefore might be going to decline the invitation. She does that on the basis of the delay before Nancy begins to respond (the pause in line 4) and Nancy's beginning with a *well*-prefaced appreciation.[12]

This is a 'cognitive moment', in a double sense: in order to make that move, before Nancy makes explicit her declination, Emma has to have *realized* that Nancy might be going to decline her invitation; she thereby *reads Nancy's mind*, attributing that *intention* to her. Her realization/ anticipation is made possible by her orientation to the structure of the design of declinations: in this respect the structure of declinations is an intersubjective phenomenon – and intersubjectivity can be regarded as itself a cognitive dimension (Schegloff, 1991a). In conversation analysis we sometimes use 'orient to' in a way which perhaps stands for (disguises?) a cognitive state: Emma's anticipation that Nancy may be about to decline her invitation makes visible her realization or recognition of what Nancy's appreciation foreshadows. This realization is interactionally salient insofar as her conduct – stepping in to forestall what she anticipates, and formulating that specifically as likely to be a declination – is contingent on that mental state. In that respect Emma's realization is observably relevant to the interaction. But nothing about their respective cognitive states is articulated or explicitly referred to in their talk. Neither makes any attributional reference to cognition, and neither uses the display of a cognitive state as an interactional resource.

One could provide many other similar examples of sequences in which the action of at least one of the participants is contingent on a cognitive state, and hence in which that cognitive state is interactionally relevant to conduct. These examples however, and others which might have been given, have three features in common:

- The conduct which is contingent on a cognitive state – *realizing* that her co-participant made a mistake, and that the other is about to decline – is nevertheless socially organized. The sequential patterns of which those actions are a constitutive part are systematic and recurrent, and thus in every respect are social rather than individual or psychological phenomena.

- A cognitive state is not made visible or manifest in any display of that state, and therefore does not become salient to the interaction in terms of its being employed as an interactional resource.

- A cognitive state is interactionally generated in the talk. The speaker's *realization* in each case here has been generated by the prior turn(s) of their co-participant, and is the basis of their next action/response (hence the contingent nature of that response).

Confusion

The features outlined above connect, in various respects, with the analysis both of the (rhetorical) attribution of cognitive states in discourse, and of how displays of cognitive states can serve as interactional resources. They suggest a complementary but alternative analytic route, which I want to consider further by exploring a cognitive state which participants seem not infrequently to experience in conversation, that of *confusion*. Like all such mental predicates, *confusion* is, perhaps in the first instance, a lay or folk category (as discussed in Edwards, 1997). It is a term which people frequently use when accounting for their own or others' conduct, especially where that conduct is problematic in some fashion. So *confusion* is an attributive term used in accounting for conduct. An example is the following.

Extract (7)   [Holt:88U:2:4:9]

```
1    Car:   This mo:rning she did say oh isn't a pity. when we knew
2           about the baby[(that (.) he) wasn't here I [mean that=
3    Les:                 [.tlk Oh: ↓ye:s.            [.hhh
4    Car:   =wz my fir:st thought too-: sort of thin[g I=
5    Les:                                           [.hh
6    Car:   =[m e a n  I  f e e : l
7    Les:   =[Well you should've said-
8           (.)
9    Les:   .mt I'm sure 'ee knows all abou[t i:t.↓
10   Car:                                  [Well yes quite. Now I didn't
11          say that to her because that might confu(hh)se 'er. hih
12   Les:   hOh ye[s. huh huh
13   Car:         [(      ) eh ↓he-he-↑he-he-he-e
14          (0.3)
15   Car:   However I'm sure (h)ih(h)yes.
16          .
17          .
18          .
19   Car:   Yes she-: she's got her own little faith it's quite (0.2) a
20          simple one but it's quite deep seated I think
```

Carrie has telephoned Lesley to announce the birth of her granddaughter. Just before this excerpt, however, they have been talking about the
recent death of her (Carrie's) husband, and particularly the reaction to
his death of her adult daughter (Megan) who lives at home with her, and
who it appears has learning difficulties. Immediately before this they have
been wondering to what extent Megan has fully comprehended his death.
And it's in this context that Carrie reports Megan's poignant remark to
her this morning, about her father not living to see his granddaughter
(lines 1/2).

Both Carrie and Lesley are active Christians: just before this extract
Carrie mentioned how comforting the hospital chaplain had been when
her husband died, and that Megan had also found the prayer he said for
them comforting ('she said to me (0.3).hh That wz a nice little prayer
Mummy (.) uh helped me no end. So: (.) she's there alri:ght'). Their talk
in this excerpt is of course imbued with their belief in an afterlife (see also
Carrie's remark about Megan's faith, lines 19/20). In particular, Lesley's
response to Carrie's report, suggesting that she (Carrie) should have said
to Megan that her father would *know all about it* (i.e. the baby's birth)
(lines 7–9) quite overtly invokes an afterlife – Carrie's belief in which is
clear from line 11 (note the contrastive stress on 'say' in line 11, and her
affirmation that she's sure he will, line 15). Now Carrie accounts for her
not having said that to Megan in terms of the likelihood that that would

confuse her (lines 11/12): she might not be capable of understanding the concept of an afterlife, and might instead take *knowing all about it* rather literally. Having just become used to the idea of her father not being there, she might be confused by something that would seem to rest on his still being 'present'.

Thus I think that if we were exploring this attributional use of *confuse*, the meaning of the term which might be derived from this situational use would be something like the following. Suggesting to Megan that her father will *know all about it* runs the risk that she'd be likely to understand that literally, thereby implying that he is present after all – which would not be consistent with her having come to understand that her father is not there (dead). She would be incapable of squaring one with the other; and therefore her understanding would be compromised or jeopardized. Put more simply still, for someone who could not handle the complexity and metaphorical character of the afterlife, the suggestion that her (dead) father will know about the baby's birth would seem to be contrary to what she has come to understand.

The attributional use of a cognitive state here rests on the person concerned being be unable to reconcile what she knows or expects, with some other apparently inconsistent information. When we examine instances where people are evidently confused in conversation, we similarly find just this collision between what they (previously) know or expect, and some subsequent and contradictory information – something which runs counter to what they had understood thus far. Here is another instance, in which *confusion* is a self-attribution.

Extract (8)   [Holt:O88:1:8:2]

```
1    Les:   Would ↑you mind if: u-uhm:: I went first or second
2           t'morrow night,h
3           (0.6)
4    Joy:   ↑YES. [↓Su:re.
5    Les:         [Is that alri:ght,
6    Joy:   [Ye:s.
7    Les:   [Cuz: then Skip'll pick me up after the soft mat bowling.
8           (1.1)
9    Joy:   .t.hhhh ↑Oh:: that dzn't matter. Listen. I'm confu:sed
10          utterly confused. .hh I thought you w'r talking about
11          N.W.R:.
12          (0.2)
13   Les:   I ↑a:m. Yes. He['ll pick me up. a[fter-.hh
14   Joy:              [.hhh          [Oh ↑I ↓see
```

It seems that Joyce might be momentarily uncertain when responding to Lesley's request to go *first or second tomorrow night* (lines 1/2): having delayed responding (line 3), her sudden pitch rise and increased loudness on '↑YES'. seem to betoken her now having understood what Lesley is asking about – that understanding being embedded in her agreeing to Lesley's request (lines 4 and 6). But then Lesley continues with something further about the arrangement (that if she goes first or second then her husband can collect her). It becomes apparent that this information causes Joyce to revise whatever understanding of Lesley's request she had previously arrived at. This is evident principally in three features of Joyce's turn in lines 9–11. First, she indicates a change in her understanding though the turn initial *Oh* (on *Oh* as a change-of-state token, see Heritage, 1984) (notice that the change in the way she agrees to Lesley's request, comparing *Yes sure* in line 4 with *That doesn't matter* in line 9 is consistent with this manifest change in understanding). Second, she says explicitly that she *thought* Lesley had been talking about the NWR, where *thought* contrasts with what she now knows/realizes.[13] Third, she refers to herself as being *confused, utterly confused* – thereby accounting for having mistakenly understood that Lesley was referring to one thing (the NWR), when from what Lesley said subsequently she realizes Lesley meant something else. Note that it makes no difference that, as it happens, her initial understanding turns out to have been correct (lines 13–14), and her subsequent understanding (whatever that was, in line 9) incorrect: Joyce's sense of confusion arises directly from the way in which the detail which Lesley gives in line 7 disconfirms, or does not support, Joyce's earlier understanding of what she (Lesley) is referring to/asking about.

The attributional use of the cognitive state, *confusion*, is something like an accounting device. It is one which rests on the further attribution that the person in question would be unable to reconcile what she (thought she) knows or expects, with some other apparently inconsistent information. When we come to examine instances where people are evidently confused in conversation, we find just this collision between what they (previously) know or expect, and some new and contradictory information – something which occurs in the interaction which runs counter to what they were expecting. This is particularly visible in some instances of repair initiation.

For example, Jefferson and Lee report 'an utterly recurrent sort of interchange between agency personnel and various parties phoning on behalf of a stricken person' (Jefferson and Lee, 1992:538), in which callers recurrently found themselves confronted by the agency wanting information about the caller, but did not want the same information about the sick or injured person. Here are just two examples of this phenomenon.

Extract (9)   [FD:I:14] (Jefferson and Lee, 1992: 540)

1	Desk:	May I have your name please,
2	Caller: –>	My name?
3	Desk:	Yes.
4	Caller:	This is Missuz McCoughlin.
5		.
6		.
7	Desk:	I-n. Okay. Your first [name
8	Caller: –>	[And the lady's name is Miss[uz-
9	Desk:	[Your
10		first initial.
11	Caller:	My n- my name is uh Beth, B-e-t-th,

Extract (10)   [FD:IV:3] (Jefferson and Lee, 1992: 540)

1	Desk:	What was your first name please,
2	Caller: –>	Mi:ne? Eleanor.
3	Desk:	Eleanor, Baxter.
4		(Pause)
5	Caller: –>	My first name? (.) or her first [name.
6	Desk:	[Yours.
7	Caller:	Ya::h, Eleanor, hhh
8	Desk:	O:ka::y,

It seems in these instances that the callers cannot quite comprehend whose name – theirs (caller's), or the victims – the desk has asked for. We cannot tell whether they are not certain, or do not believe, whose name has been requested. Either way, in initiating repair in extract (9) line 2 and extract (10) lines 2 and 5, the callers quite evidently did not expect to be asked their name, but rather to be asked the name of the victim (whose name the caller begins to volunteer in extract (9) line 8). In initiating repair, callers manifest their confusion: they expected to be asked the victim's name, but instead appear to have been asked for their own name – and they check before answering (in extract (9) line 2); and even having answered, 'double' check that they were correct (extract (10) line 5).Thus their expectations are confounded by the desk's question, and their resulting confusion is visible in their uncertainty.

Once again, these examples illustrate a recurrent and systematic pattern which can be identified quite independently of the cognitive states of individual callers. However, the cognitive state involved here – uncertainty and confusion – is more explicitly manifest, and more salient to the interaction, than were the states described in extracts (5) and (6). Where those did not come to the interactional surface, here they do, given expression in the repair initiations; it is the *expression* of uncertainty and confusion which is characteristic of the way in which this cognitive state comes to the interactional surface in those cases. This is consistent with the interactional approach to cognitive states outlined above; but here the expression given to confusion does not serve as an interactional resource. Rather it is the manifestation of an interactional moment which has generated a cognitive state: the question was not the one which a caller expected, and this confuses her. Instead of taking cognition and other mental states to determine conduct, what I am pointing to in these cases is that conduct in the interaction appears to generate a cognitive state.

This happens very plainly in this extract from a conversation in which Lesley is telling Joyce about her morning in a local city, which included shopping.

Extract (11)   [Holt:M88:1:2:6]

```
 1  Les:   .pk An' I got s'm nice cott'n ↓to:ps:: I'm
 2         not g'nna[tell Skip     ].hhh
 3  Joy:           [↑Oh did ↓y]ou:
 4  Les:   Ye::s. u-I meant (.) only to get one or two.hhh but
 5         they're- (0.2) iyou kno:w I mean if I stock up ↓now
 6         then I don't need t'do it again do I
 7         hhe[h heh h]a-[: .hhhhh
 8  Joy: + [Ye:↓ah.]  [°Ri:ght,°
 9  Les:   Yes.[°(   )°
10  Joy: + [Oh weh:- what (.) duh-aa-ou:ter-: wear: tops you
11         mean
12  Les:   .hhh Well no: some I c'n wear underneath::.
13  Joy:   ↑Oh:.
14  Les:   You see::? d-against my skin,hh
15  Joy:   Oh:[:,
16  Les:      [.hhh An' some ↓↓I c'n wear on top.↓↓.hhh But the
17         ↑thing was I couldn't get eh:m: .p.t I couldn't get a
18         (.) cott'n: (.) pettycoat or(p) (.) p- cott'n slip
19         any ↓where.
20  Joy:   Coul[↓d'n you[:
21  Les:       [.h h h   [No: they're all: this polyester mos'ly,
```

Joyce's confusion about what Lesley reports in lines 1–6 is evident in her responses in lines 8 and 10/11. Notice that Lesley seeks confirmation (support for) her account for 'stocking up', when at the end of line 6 she asks 'do I'. A's strongly supportive confirmation of that might take the form of a partial elliptical repeat, something along the lines of *No you don't*, or *That's right you don't* (or even at a pinch the highly elliptical *That's right*). Instead, Joyce's response in line 8 consists of two quite minimal acknowledgements, which do not readily or enthusiastically confirm

Lesley's account. Neither does she reciprocate Lesley's pronounced chuckling laughter in line 7; she appears not to have seen what's amusing. Furthermore she already sounds very uncertain in these acknowledgements (both are articulated softly, with downward intonation on the first, and the second spoken especially quietly). So Joyce does not respond with any conviction to Lesley's report about what she bought; neither does she confirm or support her account for stocking up.

The reason for the lack of conviction in line 8 becomes apparent in her subsequent turn (lines 10/11), from which it's clear that she's unsure now what it was that Lesley bought. In her repair initiation, 'Oh weh:- what (.) duh-aa-ou:ter-: wear: tops you mean', she returns to the first part of Lesley's report, the part she (thought she) understood. Her uncertainty in lines 10/11 is reflected both in the repair initiation itself, which takes the form of *What, x you mean?*, as an attempted understanding of what Lesley had bought; and in the delivery of the repair initiation, including the false start and the articulation of 'ou:ter-:'. The transcription only inadequately captures the abrupt halting, almost foreclosure, of the word which she is offering as her understanding of what Lesley meant.

It is worth looking closely at how it is that Joyce comes to do the repair initiation which reveals her uncertainty in lines 10/11. I have mentioned that her previous response in line 8 lacks conviction. In three respects it is not an appropriate response: it is a positive token, delivered in response to a negatively framed question (hence the suggestion that a more appropriate response might have been *No, that's right*); she doesn't reciprocate Lesley's laughter; and they are minimal tokens, which do not display having understood or agreed with Lesley. In all these respects, Joyce *fails to confirm* the advantage of stocking up on them. There is now a momentary misalignment amounting to a hiatus. In line 9 Lesley produces a post-confirmation confirmation, 'Yes', but in a position where the previous speaker's turn was *not* a confirmation. Lesley's post-confirmation confirmation passes the next slot back to Joyce. The effect of this sequence (request for confirmation/*non*-confirmation/ post-confirmation confirmation, passing it back to Joyce) is to leave the topic of her shopping suspended, in a position where neither has found a satisfactory way to continue or close the topic. Joyce's uncertainty or non-understanding (and note the difference between non-understanding, and misunderstanding) thereby becomes exposed in this hiatus: yet they need to find a way to continue. Joyce's repair initiation in lines 10/11 is the solution resolving this hiatus.

The point here is that it's not simply the case that Joyce is uncertain or confused: instead a sequential position arises in which her uncertainty becomes exposed. What is she going to do in her next turn following Lesley's 'pass'? The importance of this is that it's not the cognitive state itself which is driving the interaction, or determining behaviour. One can be confused 'in one's mind', but avoid revealing that confusion – not acknowledging it, disguising it, and hoping perhaps that the matter will be clarified by what the other goes on to say (all of which, again, one knows only through introspection). However, here the interaction has come to a point where Joyce may need to take a turn, and what kind of turn depends on understanding what Lelsey meant. The interaction has generated a moment, a slot, in which Joyce's confusion comes to the surface. This is akin to what happens in extracts (8) and (9): the desk has asked the caller a question: the caller's reply is contingent upon having properly heard/understood whose name they were asked. So we can regard a 'cognitive moment' in interaction as a point at which, not merely is a participant in a certain (cognitive) state of mind (e.g. confused), but the interaction has generated a slot in which that speaker needs to make a move (take a turn). And what he/she does/says in that slot is contingent in some way upon that cognitive state. The visibility of a cognitive state has been occasioned by the interactional sequence.

But equally, the interactional sequence generated that cognitive state in the first place. Joyce's uncertainty or confusion arises from an incongruity in the design of Lesley's report. When she announces that she *got some nice cotton tops*, she adds that she's not going to tell her husband. This plainly trades off a kind of marital joke: wives go shopping and don't tell their husbands what they've bought or how much they've spent, and husbands complain about how much their wives spend.[14] Now this works for 'big' or expensive items – dresses, coats, hats, classy shoes and the like: I don't think it works for socks or handkerchiefs or knickers. So that the expectation generated by the conspiratorial fashion in which Lesley confides that she's not going to tell her husband is, that the *nice cotton tops she's got* are . . . well, expensive – involving the kind of cost that it would be worth hiding from one's spouse (even, of course, if she's no intention whatever of hiding the cost from him). Perhaps this is part of the 'script' for this kind of marital jiggery-pokery (on scripts, including their use in accounting for aspects of marital relations, see Edwards, 1997, chapter 6). In her repair initiation in lines 10/11 it is apparent that by *nice cotton tops* Joyce first understood Lesley to mean *outer wear tops*. Hence Lelsey's announcement in lines 1/2 has generated that expectation on Joyce's part, that she bought that kind of garment.

However, Lesley adds to this that, although she intended to buy only one or two, 'if I stock up ↓now then I don't need t'do it again'. Herein lies the incongruity. Whatever it is one would purchase but not tell one's husband about, including outer wear tops, would not be the kinds of garments one would stock up on (to last for some time), this possibly for two reasons – cost, and particularly fashion. With respect to the nature of the garments which she's bought, there is an inconsistency between her saying that she's not going to tell her husband, and subsequently that she stocked up on them. This then results in the uncertainty and confusion which Joyce manifestly experiences in lines 10/11.

We can discern in this account of *confusion* in interaction a number of points which I think suggest a view of cognition, a kind of focus, which complements but which is distinctive from the approaches which investigate how cognitive states are attributed by participants (the lay or folk use of cognitive descriptions), and how displays of cognitive states serves as interactional resources.

Form and cognition

As was mentioned earlier, Schegloff (1987) has underlined the independence of the form of repair initiation, from the nature of the trouble source. There is no determinant correspondence between the design or type of repair initiation, and the problem which a speaker is having, where that 'problem' is in some respects a cognitive state the nature of which generally cannot be known. A co-participant may treat that problem as having been *x*; but neither that, nor the first speaker's concurrence with that analysis of their problem, proves that indeed that had been their difficulty. So forms of repair initiation do not signal a particular cognitive state: for this reason I don't mean to suggest that the form which Joyce employs here, *X you mean?*, corresponds to *confusion*. That form may, and is, used in circumstances where the trouble may be quite otherwise. Similarly, other repair (initiation) forms may manifest a speaker's confusion.

One consequence of this is that the exploration of the sequential organization of repair, and patterns associated with various forms of repair initiation, is a quite autonomous enterprise: it does not connect with the psychology of those participants who happen to animate these organizations in particular sequences of action, such as the sequence in extract (11).

The 'meanings' of mental predicates

When in extract (7) Carrie accounts for her conduct in terms of not wishing to confuse her daughter – an attributional use of the predicate – she refers to an inconsistency which might arise were her daughter to be told that her father will know about the baby's (his granddaughter's) birth. She would understand that literally (suggesting that he therefore is still alive), when she has now come to understand that his death means that he is no longer present. Her expectations about his absence would then be confounded by this 'new' information, that he'll know about the baby. The same feature of *confounded expectations* was apparent in the interactional manifestations of confusion in extracts (8), (9), (10) and (11) – and the self-attribution in extract (8). This begins to explore the 'meaning' of confusion, in ways which might be consistent with and complement the discursive approach outlined by Edwards (1997, especially chapter 7).

Cognitive states manifest in the details of talk

In each of extracts (9), (10) and (11) *confusion* on the part of one of the participants was manifest in that speaker initiating repair: hence a cognitive state was manifest in the details of the talk. Of course not any piece of verbal conduct will reveal that person's state of mind: indeed generally it will not. These cases are perhaps exceptional. But they suggest an approach to connecting the details of behaviour to cognition, in certain specialized cases.

One respect in which these are specialized is that whilst the cognitive state of being uncertain or confused is *manifest* in their repair initiations, the display of a cognitive state need not serve as an interactional resource, as is reported in Goodwin (1987). It seems in these cases that the confusion needs to be resolved (hence the repair initiation) in order for the interaction to proceed (or, as in extract (10) line 2 where the caller first checks *My name?* but gives it without waiting for confirmation, that an uncertain understanding/hearing is the basis for proceeding in this way – that uncertainty being manifest in her asking again in line 5). Thus the repair initiations are a resource only for resolving the confusion, the manifestation of which does not serve any further interactional function (as far as I can tell).

Salience to participants

The cognitive state concerned is salient to participants only insofar as it becomes interactionally relevant – the confusion needs to be resolved in order to continue, for the talk to proceed, where a next turn/move is in some way contingent upon that cognitive state. It is not salient in the more explicit sense that participants orient to that as a cognitive state as such: they don't remark on one another's confusion, as participants do in the kinds of instances in which the attributional uses of cognitive terms may be explored (as for instance in extract (8), where one participant does explicitly refer to being confused).

Interactionally generated

The confusion which speakers manifest in their repair initiations in these examples is interactionally generated. It is the result of the other saying/ asking something which confounds their expectations (in extracts (9) and (10)), or having said something which appeared inconsistent (the expectation deriving from what was originally said being confounded in what was said next, as in extract (8)). Thus instead of regarding cognition as determining action, we can view interaction as a source of cognition. It is in the course of interactional sequences, and speakers' moves and actions within those sequences, that cognition may be shaped – and in this way interaction becomes a context for cognition (to reverse Potter's 1998 title, though not the thrust of his argument).

Conclusion

I have focused on *confusion* to illustrate that I think we can identify cognitive 'moments' which are generated in interactions, out of the verbal activities in which speakers are engaged. They are independent of participants explicitly acknowledging a given cognitive or mental state (for instance by attributing mental states to themselves and others), and in this respect they are not treated by participants as cognitive events. However, insofar as they are manifest in the talk, they are relevant to the interaction. But they are not designed as displays of mental states, in the way that for example 'trying to recall' a name is a display of having forgotten – and thus they seem not to serve as a resource in the interaction.

The moments which have been considered in this chapter, especially those associated with repair initiation, seem to involve the intersection between interaction and cognition. But the interactional sequences in which they may occur and of which they then happen to be a part are *social* organizations, the properties of which are unaffected by the diversity of cognitive or other psychological states which may be experienced by participants as these interactions unfolded in real time (and which at best can only be discerned imperfectly in the talk). So the practices of repair, for example, are organized without respect to what (if anything – recalling Ryle, Melden and others) was in any individual's mind at the moment he or she initiated repair. The action (the repair initiation, whatever) is driven by the interaction and the sequence organization, and not by an individual's cognition.

And my answer to the question posed in the title of this chapter is that whilst *confusion* may be a state of mind, it is not one which exists independently of its interactional generation and its interactional 'moment'. The uncertainty which underlies it is simultaneously created by what has been said, and is occasioned by interactional contingencies in the talk (that an appropriate response should be forthcoming, that a question should be answered etc.). We come back, therefore, to Goffman's insight about the manifestation (presentation) of self: whilst confusion may be a private state, its manifestation in talk is subject to what participants choose or are required to do as next moves in interaction.

NOTES

1. As Goffman did, to begin with most explicitly in referring to 'The *Presentation of Self Everyday Life*' (Goffman, 1959); and at the end of his life, in his presidential address to the ASA (Goffman, 1983). See Drew and Wootton, 1988.
2. That they do indeed convey this – to Rose – is evident from Rose's response to Bea's declination.

   [SBL:1:1:10:17]

   ```
   6   Bea:    'tch I'm running en a:d in the paper 'nd an:d uh hh I
   7           haftih stay near the pho::ne,
   8   (R):    (°Ya[h°)
   9   Bea:         [hhhh
   10  Ros:    Alright?=
   11  Bea:    = hh A[nd
   12  Ros:          [Well *eh ˆsometime when you ˆare ˉfree, h give ˆme
   13          a ˉcall becuz ah'm not alwiz ho:me.
   14  Bea:    Mm hm
   15  Ros:    hh[hh
   16  Bea:      [Why I'd like ˆto en thanks a lo*::t.
   ```

   In leaving the invitation open for 'ˆsometime when you ˆare ˉfree,', Rose treats Bea as only unable to accept, and not therefore as unwilling to do so.
3. On which see for instance Jefferson, 1986.
4. For instance, when patients laugh in response to turns in which a doctor has mentioned something which is discrepant with a patient's prior version, which might be regarded, cognitively, as more akin to 'nervous' laughter; see Haakana, 1999, 2001.
5. For a different but complementary view about the fundamentally 'attributional' character of interaction, see Levinson, 1995.
6. And in some respects just as attributions of mental states may be regarded as constitutive properties of the interactional events in the service of which they are employed, so too (and recalling here the symbiotic relation between interaction and grammar noted above) the interactional work into which

service given attributions are pressed become constitutive properties of the meaning of such attributive terms.

7. Jefferson did not include this example in her chapter, because the self-repair in Nancy's enquiry, in which she begins to ask if Bud went *fishing*, and then changes that to *golfing*, results in their talking in overlap, lines 7/8. However, when Emma begins her response it's already clear that the enquiry is about *he* i.e. Bud (line 6), even if it's not yet quite clear what Nancy is asking about him.

8. The grounds for Emma misunderstanding or mishearing Nancy can readily be seen, in Nancy's starting to say *fishing* and changing that to *golf* (this already after a self-repair, from *wasn't going* to *didn't go*) – by which time Emma has already begun to answer the enquiry about going fishing (see the overlap between their turns in lines 7/8). However it came about, Emma is nevertheless answering about herself, in response to a question about her husband.

9. Nancy's enquiry in line 13 is a repeat in the sense of re-asking the question: it is not a straight repeat of that first enquiry. She replaces the proterm with Bud's name, and changes the verb form slightly.

10. For another account of a connection between repair – in this case 'third position' repair – and cognition, via intersubjectivity, including repairs associated with memory troubles, see Schegloff, 1991a.

11. For more extended treatments of this extract, and of some of the issues discussed here, see Davidson, 1984 and Drew, 1984.

12. Nancy's softly articulated *It's just* in line 2, which might appear from the transcript to be a very prompt, indeed premature, response to *Wanna come down*, is in fact connected with the prior topic. Emma has moved abruptly from the previous topic, to introduce her invitation (data not shown).

13. *Thought* is akin to one of those class of verbs which Sacks referred to as 'incomplete', such as *I tried to*, where what that indicates is that I tried but failed. *I wanted to* or *I was going to* can work in a similar fashion. Sacks also referred to these as 'first verbs', in that when one of these verbs is used, it says that another verb will be used, which will indicate how it is that one failed (to do what one tried, or wanted etc.). See Sacks, 1992b:180–2. *Thought*, as here in line 10, is not so much an incomplete or 'first' verb, but rather a contrastive one. It contrasts what one (wrongly) believed with what one now knows; but where what one now knows does not need to be articulated in a 'second' verb, but instead is implicit in a preceding action/turn, here in line 9.

14. Women who earn independent incomes can be heard saying this, or couples in which the woman earns an income (sometimes in excess of the man) joke about the man earning the money and the wife spending it shopping. So evidently the joke, if joke it is, doesn't depend on the woman relying on the man to pay; it's become so ingrained in the culture of marriage/partnership that it works without respect to the financial realities of their particular relationship.

8 Cognition in discourse

John Heritage

Introduction

The objective of this chapter is to describe some of the ways in which the issue of cognitive process surfaces in talk as an explicit, or relatively explicit, matter that the participants are dealing with in the talk itself. I will begin with some brief comments on how participants represent cognitive process in their descriptions of everyday experiences and events. Subsequently I will look at the embodiment of cognitive process in interaction, focusing on the response particle *oh*, which is virtually specialized to the task of this embodiment. I will conclude with some basic observations about the treatment of cognition in the domain of ordinary interaction.

Portraying cognitive process

While attention, cognition and memory are central topics of psychology, they can also be matters of significant concern in the way events are portrayed by those who report them. Representations of cognition, and especially of cognitive process, are commonly driven by a desire to evidence the normality and reasonableness of the objects of cognition (Garfinkel, 1967; Sacks, 1984; Jefferson, forthcoming).

Consider the following interaction in which a mother is presenting her eleven-year-old daughter's upper respiratory symptoms to a paediatrician. The time is Monday afternoon and the daughter has not attended school. The mother begins with a diagnostic claim (lines 1–2, 5) which strongly conveys her commitment to the veracity of her daughter's claims about her symptoms, and may imply the relevance of antibiotic treatment (Stivers, 2002; Stivers et al., 2003; Heritage and Stivers, 1999):

Extract (1)

```
1 MOM:     .hhh Uhm (.) Uh- We're- thinking she might have an
2          ear infection? [in thuh left ear?
3 DOC:                    [Okay,
4 DOC:     Oka:y,
```

```
 5  MOM:       Uh:m because=uh: she's had some pain_
 6             (.)
 7  DOC:       [Alrighty?
 8  MOM:       [over thuh weekend:. .h[h
 9  DOC:                             [No fever er anything?,
10  MOM:       Uhm[:
11  DOC:          [Mkay:[:?
12  MOM:               [An' uh sore throat_
13             (0.2)
14  MOM:       An:' like uh (.) cold.
15             (.)
16  DOC:       Wow.
17  MOM:       (An' thuh)/(Kinda thuh) cold symptoms, huhhh.
18  DOC:       Was it like that over thuh weekend too?
19             (0.2)
20  MOM: →     Uh:m: When did you notice it.
21             (.)
22  MOM: →     <Yesterday you mentioned it.
23  PAT:       Yesterday.
24  DOC:       M[kay.
25  MOM:        [It started yesterday. (          )/(0.5)
26             (0.2)
27  DOC:       °#Lemme write that i:n,#°
```

After some elaboration of the child's cold symptoms (lines 12–17), the doctor asks about their duration (line 18), and the mother refers the question to her daughter at line 20 ('Uh:m: When did you notice it'.). The verb form – 'notice' – that she uses here conveys a quite distinct notion of attention and cognition. It suggests that the child's perception of her symptoms emerged in an unlooked for and, hence, unmotivated way. Its use is a second way in which the mother conveys her commitment to the facticity of her daughter's symptoms, and especially works against any possibility that they were fabricated as a means of not attending school – an issue that can hang heavily over Monday visits to the paediatrician! Subsequently the mother distinguishes between the child's noticing her symptoms and 'mentioning' them – thus opening up the possibility that the child has endured them for longer than 24 hours, which would further underwrite the unmotivated nature of their discovery and report. Here then what is at issue is how the 'discovery', and the process of the coming to recognize, 'medical symptoms' is to be portrayed (see Halkowski (forthcoming) for an extended discussion of this subject).

A more elaborate presentation of cognitive process is contained in the following telephone call to a police emergency number in the central United States. Here the caller has a possibly police-relevant problem to describe to her local emergency service. Her report contains a number of references to attention, cognition and memory, almost all of which are designed to convey the objectivity, probity and disinterestedness of her description.

Extract (2)

```
 1  Dis:  .hh Midcity emergency.
 2  Clr:  .hhh Yeah uh(m) I'd like tuh:- report (0.2) something
 3        weir:d that happen:ed abou:t (0.5) uh(m) five minutes
 4        ago, 'n front of our apartment building?
 5  Dis:  Yeah?
 6  Clr:  On eight fourteen eleventh avenue southeast,
 7  Dis:  Mm hm,=
 8  Clr:  =.hh We were just (.) uhm sittin' in the room 'n'
 9        we heard this cla:nking y'know like (.) someone was
10        pulling something behind their ca:r.='N' we
11        looked out the window'n .hhh an' there was (this) (.)
12        light blue: smashed up uhm (1.0) .hh station wagon
13        an',=.hh A:nd thuh guy made a U-turn,=we live on
14        a dead end, .hh an:d (0.2) thuh whole front end of
15        the- (.) the car (is/w'z) smashed up. .hhh And (.) >he
16        jumped outta the car and I (r)emember< 'e- (.) he tried
17        to push the hood down (with/er) something and then he
18        jus' (.) started running an' he took o::ff.
19  Dis:  Mm hm,
20  Clr:  .hh A:nd we think that maybe 'e could've (.) you know
21        stolen the car and aba:ndoned it. er something,
22  Dis:  What kinda car is it?
23  Clr:  .hh It's a blue station wagon.=hhh .hhh
24        (0.2)
25  Clr:  We just (.) have seen it from the window.
26  Dis:  We'll get somebody over there.
```

Consider, for example, the preface (lines 2–4) with which she begins her account. She undertakes to offer a 'report' on an event which she then characterizes as 'something weir:d'. This juxtaposition of terms is most interesting: viewed in the abstract, there is a strong contrast between the word 'report' with its overtones of objectivity and 'official' probativeness, and the vague and highly vernacular description of the object of that report as 'something weir:d'. Yet, in context, the purpose of this juxtaposition seems clear enough: the caller cannot classify the event she's reporting on as a 'robbery', 'car accident', or some other police relevant event, and she needs some generalized description of the event that can serve as a referential placeholder for the narrative in which its particulars will be disclosed. In context, the term 'report' and the cautiously anxious 'something weir:d' convey the stance of a concerned caller who is reluctant to jump to conclusions. Also noteworthy as elements of this opening turn conveying objectivity and trustworthiness are the time reference of the event ('five minutes ago') which conveys that she considered the situation before calling, and 'n front of our apartment building?' which not only conveys her legitimate interest in her local environment (Whalen and Zimmerman, 1990; Zimmerman, 1992) but also, with the word 'our', suggests that there was another witness to the event – something that is confirmed at line 8.[1]

The subsequent narrative then describes how the caller's attention was drawn to the incident she reports. Here the caller goes to some trouble to portray how she came to be looking out of her apartment window at a point when she could observe the car and driver. As it is described here, the caller's observations have some parallels with the simple 'noticing' of the first example. She portrays herself as engaged elsewhere ('We were just (.) uhm sittin' in the room'), and having her attention drawn to an unfamiliar sound 'cla:nking y'know like (.) someone was pulling something behind their ca:r'. The shift in attention and the action of going to look out of the window is specifically legitimated by the unusual sounds she describes herself as having heard. In this way, the caller portrays her coming to see the incident as 'innocent' and as 'unmotivated' by anything beyond the specifics of the occasion.

In the later part of her account, which is designed to be complete at line 18, the caller persists with the reporting policy which she began with her use of 'something weir:d': she avoids interpreting the motivation of the events she describes. It is only after she is prompted by the police dispatcher's continuer at line 19, that she describes the event in police relevant terms, and then with much caution: '.hh A:nd we think that maybe 'e could've (.) you know stolen the car and aba:ndoned it. er something'. It is significant that this final suggestion is not embedded in the caller's earlier descriptions, which are entirely free of motive attributions, and instead emerges as a 'prompted' inference, the withholding of which until 'prompted' in itself embodies the caution, probity and objectivity that the caller has consistently sustained by reporting 'just the facts' of what she has seen.

While both of these examples are comparatively ordinary and mundane, they illustrate two fundamental points: (1) cognitive process can be and often is the object of particular, careful and detailed handling in reports of events, and (2) this handling is not 'unmotivated': it is ordinarily driven by efforts to underwrite the objectivity and legitimacy of what is claimed to be the case and, no matter how outlandish the claim, the ordinariness, disinterestedness and normality of the person who witnessed it (Sacks, 1984). In sum, the portrayal of cognitive process in discourse is substantially driven by normative (or 'moral') conventions which delimit the kinds of factual claims that can be made by witnesses of particular types (Garfinkel, 1967; Pollner, 1987; Heritage, 1984b; Edwards, 1997).

Cognitive process as an interactional event

Cognitive process is not something which speakers simply report, it is also something which they embody in talk-in-interaction. This embodiment takes a wide variety of forms, but a particularly common and significant one involves the deployment of the particle '*oh*'. This particle is effectively specialized for the expression of cognitive process since it functions as a 'change of state' token used to 'propose that its producer has undergone some kind of change of state in his or her locally current state of knowledge, information, orientation or awareness' (Heritage, 1984b:299). *Oh* is heavily deployed in interactions involving information transfer and in interactional events that involve the embodiment of cognitive events such as noticing, remembering and understanding.

Oh is frequently deployed in interaction sequences in which a participant needs (or wishes) to embody the experience of recollection. For example, in extract (3) a story teller suspends a story in progress while some participants leave the room:

Extract (3)   [Goodwin: G91:250]

```
1   A:      Yeah I useta- This girlfr- er Jeff's gi:rlfriend,
2           the one he's gettin' married to, (0.9) s brother.=
3           = he use'to uh,
4           .... ((13 lines of data omitted. Some potential story
5           .... recipients leave the room))
6           ....
7   A:      What was I gonna say.=
8   A:   →  =Oh:: anyway. She use'ta, (0.4) come over
```

At line 7, the story teller undertakes to resume the story with a display – 'What was I gonna say.=' – that he is searching for the point at which to resume it. At line 8, his resumption of the story is prefaced with 'Oh:: anyway', by which he conveys that this search has been successful, and that he has remembered the point at which the narrative was previously abandoned and should be resumed. The resumption picks up the very words ('used to') at which the narrative was previously abandoned (see line 3). In extract (4) recollection is also associated with the production of '<u>oh</u>'. Shirley's offer of a 'place to stay' (in San Francisco) is rejected by Geri with the account that she 'has Victor' – the person she was apparently intending to visit (line 12). At this point Shirley emphatically displays her recollection that this is true: '↑OH that's ↑RI:GHT.' and 'I FER↑GO:T Completely'. (lines 11 and 13).

Extract (4)   [Frankel TC1]

```
 1  Shi         .hhhhhh Mike en I er thinking about going.
 2              (0.3)
 3  Shi:        and if we do:, (.) we're g'nna stay et her hou:se.=
 4  Ger:        =M-[hm,
 5  Shi:           [.hhhh So: it's a four bedroom house.
 6              (0.2)
 7  Ger:        M-[hm,
 8  Shi:           [.hhh So if you guys want a place tuh sta:y.
 9              (0.3)
10  Ger:        .t.hhh Oh well thank you but you we ha- yihknow Victor.
11  Shi:    →   ↑OH that's ↑RI:GHT.=
12  Ger:        =That's why we were going[(we)
13  Shi:    →                           [I FER↑GO:T. Completely.
14  Ger:        Ye:ah. Bec'z, .hhh he called tih invite us,
```

Here, as in extract (3), the production of *oh* is clearly associated with an explicit effort to convey a cognitive event – an interactionally engendered 'remembering'. A 'change of cognitive state' – produced by the informing – is conveyed by *oh* and thereby injected into the interaction, as part of the interaction's own process and contingencies. That Shirley 'remembers' about Victor here, rather than simply 'registering the new information' is crucial. Participants keep rather exact score over what each knows, and is entitled to know, about the social worlds of others. To fail to register 'remembering' here would be to deny knowledge that Geri has presumably conveyed to Shirley in the past. To fail to register 'information change' (for example by just acknowledging the account with 'Okay'), would be to treat the account as 'already known' and, hence, to be visibly guilty of a pro forma or 'phony' invitation – one that the inviter knew would have to be rejected. 'Remembering' is therefore the only means by which Shirley can respect the fact that she previously knew about 'Victor' and his availability as a person to be visited, while also embodying the claim that her original invitation was genuine rather than phony or pro forma.

At this point in the discussion, it might be tempting to think of *oh* as simply the outward expression of an inner psychological event – an expression like 'Ouch' which provides a voluntary or perhaps even involuntary 'window into the mind' (Goffman, 1981). However, this perspective is complicated by cases like extract (4) above in which cognitive claims are implicated in the management of social relationships. It is also complicated by the fact that the display of a 'change of state' is something that may be required by virtue of an interactional logic that organizes the social relations that obtain between different speaking roles.

For example in extract (5) below, the caller, Carrie, has 'good news' to impart to her recipient:

Extract (5)   [Field U88:2:4:1]

```
 1  Les:    Hello↑:?h
 2               (0.2)
 3  Car:    Oh Les-lie [it's Carr[ie.]
 4  TV:             [( )    [( ]    [ )
 5  Les:                          [.t hOh: ↑Carrie: ↑Yes
 6          he↑llo[↓:.hh .hh hh
 7  Car:          [I: ↑thought you'd like to know I've got a little
 8          ↓gran'daughter
 9  Les:  →  .thlk ↑Oh: how love↓ly.
10  Car:    ↓Ye:s? bo:rn th's <early hours'v this ↓morning.
11  Les:  →  .k↑Oh: joll[y goo:d,[h
12  Car:          [↓Ye:s  [↑Christi:ne ↓Ru[th.
13  Les:  →                      [.hhhhh -hOh:: that's
14          ↓ni::ce:.h What a nice name.
```

At the risk of belabouring the obvious, Lesley's response to each piece of news is managed through an [*oh*] + [assessment] format. This is a format in which *oh* – the part of the turn concerned with acknowledging the status of the information as 'news' – always precedes the assessment of the news itself. Thus in this sequence each prior turn is first addressed as 'news' and only subsequently as 'good' (or 'bad') news. This is a pattern which is, of course, very general.

The situation in extract (5) can be compared with that in extract (6) in which Shirley has bad news to tell Geri:

Extract (6)   [Franket TCI]

```
 1  Shi:    In any eve::nt?hhhhh That's not all thet's ne:w.
 2  Ger:    W't e:lse.
 3  Shi:    .t.hhhhh W'l Wendy'n I hev been rilly having problems.
 4  Ger:    M-hm,
 5  Shi:    ((voice becomes confiding)) .hh En yesterday I talk'tih
 6          her. .hhhh A:n' (0.3) apparently her mother is terminal.
 7               (0.5)
 8  Ger:  →  .tch Yeh but we knew that befo[:re.
 9  Shi:                      [.hhh Ri:ght. Well, (.)
10          now I guess it's official.
11  Ger:    Mm-hm.
12  Shi:    .t.hhh So she's very very upset.
```

Here, what is projected as news is met, not with *oh*, but with '<u>Y</u>eh' and 'but we knew that befo:re', which underscores that this is not 'news' for Geri. Shirley's unhappiness with this response, which denies the 'newsworthiness' of what she had clearly projected as 'news' is highlighted in her response: '.hhh Ri:ght. Well, (.) now I guess it's official'. This response is designed to salvage the significance of what she has just said as news by describing it in terms of a shift in how 'publicly' Wendy's mother's terminal cancer is being treated, though Geri declines to acknowledge this as 'news' either (at line 11).

Oh is also used to index a cognitive shift in the context of answers-to questions. In this context the questioner, who by asking the question has committed to a position of non-knowing (K−), may be obligated to acknowledge an answer to a question by indexing a change of cognitive state from nonknowing to knowing (K+). This possibility is illustrated in the next few examples. In extract (7) this simple interactional logic informs Jenny's production of '*oh*' at line 6.

Extract (7)   [Rah:II:1]

```
1  Ver:       And she's got the application forms.=
2  Jen:       =Ooh:: so when is her interview did she sa[:y?
3  Ver:                                                  [She
4             didn't (.) Well she's gotta send their fo:rm
5             back. Sh[e doesn't know when the [interview is yet.
6  Jen:   →           [O h : : .                [Oh it's just the form,
```

Jenny's initial question (about a mutual friend's job application) clearly presupposes that the friend's application has progressed to the point where an interview for the job is the 'next step'. It is this presupposition which Vera's response undercuts, and is this undercutting which Jenny's *oh* acknowledges. The information that Vera provides is evidently 'surprising' to Jenny, and it might be held that this example involves a similar yoking of inner cognitive event (surprise – a drastic change of cognitive state) and outer behavioural display that is arguably central to the earlier cases of remembering. Yet it can also be argued that someone who has experienced this degree of cognitive shift is under an *interactional* obligation to embody it, and that this obligation is also implicated in Jenny's response at line 6.

Support for this second line of thinking comes from cases where the information given in question-answer sequences is less 'surprising' to the questioner and *oh* production is more likely driven by the external demands of interaction rather than the internal pressures of cognitive expression. In extract (8) for example, there is a much more fine-grained information transfer. Shirley asks her friend Geri about when her academic term ends, using what survey methodologists would describe as a closed ended (alternative) question:

Extract (8)   [Frankel:TC]

```
1  Shi:       .hh When do you get out. Christmas week or the
2             week before Christmas.
3             (0.3)
4  Ger:       Uh::m two or three days before Ch[ristmas,]
5  Shi:   →                                    [ O h : ,]
```

Here Geri's answer falls well within the parameters set by Shirley's question, yet Shirley still acknowledges the information conveyed with an *oh*-carried change of state token.

Still more fine-grained is extract (9) in which Jenny questions Ivy's work plans by describing a third-party's claim that Ivy will be working tomorrow:

Extract (9)   [Rah:12:4:ST]

```
1  Jen:       Okay then I was asking and she says you're
2             working tomorrow as well,
3  Ivy:       Yes I'm supposed to be tomorrow yes,
4  Jen:   →  Oh:::,
```

Ivy's response simply confirms what Jenny reports, yet Jenny still acknowledges that confirmation with *oh*, indicating a change in her state of information. And here too there is after all a change: information from a third party has been confirmed by a first party: its certainty has been increased. It is this shift which is being acknowledged.

A sequential-interactional logic is implicated in this registration of a cognitive change of state. By the act of questioning, a questioner proposes to be 'uninformed' about some matter, and by the same act, projects the recipient to be 'informed' about it. Inbuilt into this sequential logic is the notion that the answer to a question by an answerer who was projected to be informed, should impact the state of knowledge of the questioner, changing it from 'uninformed' to 'now informed'. It is just this shift which *oh* is deployed to acknowledge. Moreover, by that deployment it also reconfirms the basic relationship of non-knowing (K−) and knowing (K+) that the roles of questioner and answerer embody.

The use of *oh*-receipt to sequentially 'lock down' the K−/K+ relationship of questioner and answerer is also strongly supported by counter-examples. Teachers do not receipt answers to 'known answer' or 'exam' questions with *oh* because they have not been 'informed' by them. Legal counsel and news interviewers do not *oh*-receipt the answers to their questions, in part at least, because it is not their obligation to support the truthfulness or adequacy of an answer in the way that an *oh*-receipt (with its claim of a K− > K+) inevitably does.

Related considerations are in play in the following case example from ordinary conversation. Nancy is talking to her friend Hyla about Hyla's new boyfriend in San Francisco:

Extract (10)   (HG:II:25)

```
 1  Nan:   a->   .hhh Dz he 'av 'iz own apa:rt[mint?]
 2  Hyl:   b->                            [.hhhh] Yea:h,=
 3  Nan:   c->   =Oh:,
 4                (1.0)
 5  Nan:   a->   How didju git 'iz number,
 6                (.)
 7  Hyl:   b->   I(h) (.) c(h)alled infermation'n San
 8         b->   Fr'ncissc(h) [uh!
 9  Nan:   c->                [Oh::::.
10                (.)
11  Nan:         Very cleve:r, hh=
12  Hyl:         =Thank you [: I-.hh-.hhhhhhhh hh=
13  Nan:   a->              [W'ts 'iz last name,
14  Hyl:   b->   =Uh:: Freedla:nd. .hh[hh
15  Nan:   c->                        [Oh[:,
16  Hyl:                                 [('r) Freedlind.=
17  Nan:   d->   =Nice Jewish bo:y?
18                (.)
19  Hyl:   e->   O:f cou:rse,=
20  Nan:   f->   ='v [cou:rse,  ]
21  Hyl:           [hh-hh-hh]hnh .hhhhh=
22  Nan:         =Nice Jewish boy who doesn'like tih write letters?
```

Here, in a series of three Q-A-*Oh* sequences, Nancy interrogates her friend about her new *amour*, and at line 17 seemingly begins a fourth with the question-intoned declarative 'Nice Jewish bo:y?'. Although this turn could readily be understood as a continuation of this line of questioning, it is noticeable that Nancy's acknowledgement of Hyla's response at line 20 does not involve a change of state claim. To the contrary, it echoes Hyla's answer 'O:f cou:rse' in such a way as to treat that answer as having been quite specifically 'nonews'. This receipt has the effect of recalibrating how Nice Jewish bo:y? is to have been understood. Instead of a declarative question, it was intended as a 'comment' – an obvious enough inference from a common Jewish family name – and its 'confirmation' is not therefore to be treated as 'informative'. Here then the presence or absence of *oh* has consequences for how knowledge and information are understood to be possessed and trafficked by these conversationalists. With an *oh*-receipt, Nancy would have acknowledged a transfer of information but, with it, she would have also acknowledged a certain lack of savoir faire about the boyfriend. With the 'v cou:rse', receipt, Nancy lays claim to that knowledge and, perhaps, to the inner mechanics of Hyla's choice of boyfriend.

The upshot of these observations is twofold. First, interactional participants keep rather exact track of who knows what at each and every moment of an interaction. They do so in some substantial measure through the use of *oh* as a means of acknowledging 'changes of state' of knowledge and information, and they are attentive to this task because it is mandated by the terms of many of the sequences in which they participate. Second, the use of *oh* to keep track of the distribution of knowledge and information is remarkably economical. *Oh* merely enacts 'changes of state', but whether the change of state enacted involves a change of attention, memory, orientation or knowledge is left to be inferred from the context in which the *oh* is produced. Similarly, whether the knowledge accrued in a particular informing that is acknowledged with *oh* is significantly new (as in extract (7)) or merely incrementally confirmatory (as in extract (9)) is likewise inferred, though intonational and other resources may be used to discriminate the weight and unexpectedness of the information involved (Maynard, 2003).

Grasping the meaning of referents

Oh is also systematically deployed in sequences of interaction where issues of understanding are at issue. Consider extract (11) below, which follows just after Sam (S) has invited Fran's (F) daughter to visit his children at their beach house.

Extract (11)   [NB:III:1:2]

```
1  F:        When didju want'er tih come do::w[n.
2  S:                                        [.hhh Oh any time
3            between: now en nex' Saturday, hh
4  F: ->     A wee:k from:: (0.3) this coming Saturdee.
5  S:        Yeah.
6            (.)
7  F: ->     .hhhh Oh:::.
```

Our sequence begins as Fran asks about a date for the projected visit (line 1), and Sam's response contains a residual ambiguity concerning how 'next Saturday' is to be understood – the immediately next Saturday (about two days hence) or the Saturday that is still nine days away. Fran deals with the ambiguity by offering an understanding check – a 'best guess' about the Saturday referred to – and, when this is confirmed, she acknowledges that confirmation with *oh* (line 7). Two points can be made about this sequence. First Fran withholds the *oh*-carried claim of understanding, until *after* Sam has confirmed her understanding check. The displayed 'moment of understanding' is deferred until her 'best guess' is confirmed. Second, by this means, the understanding check at line 4 is presented as having been deployed in pursuit of a genuine and currently experienced ambiguity. Line 4 was truly and only a 'best guess' at what Sam intended, 'enlightenment' did not arrive until line 5, and was only registered at line 7.

This situation contrasts rather pointedly with extract (12), in which there is a very similar type of ambiguity about the meaning of 'Monday':

Extract (12)   [DA:2:2]

```
 1  M:        How long yih gunna be he:re,=
 2  B:        =.hhhh Uh:t's (.) not too lo:ng. Uh:: just'ntil:
 3            uh::uh think Monday.
 4            (1.0)
 5  M:    →   Til, oh jih mean like a week tomorrow
 6  B:        Yah.
 7            (0.3)
 8  B:        Mm:hm,=
 9  M:    →   =Now you told me you ehw-u-where are yuh.Are
10            you u-ut uh:, Puh-uh: (.) Palos uh::
```

Here Betty's response to Mary also seems to have a residual ambiguity, but the context of the conversation, which happens on a Sunday, leads Mary to believe that if Betty had meant the immediately upcoming Monday, she would have used the term 'tomorrow' and hence that she must mean the following Monday. All of this she unpacks with 'Til, oh jih mean like a week tomorrow'. In this case, the *oh*-carried change of state that conveys 'understanding' occurs *before* Mary delivers on the actual understanding she has achieved. In this way she indicates that 'then and there', prior to confirmation by Betty, is the moment at which she has become enlightened. It can be further noticed that after Betty has confirmed this understanding at line 6, Mary does not further acknowledge this confirmation with *oh*. Line 5 was the point at which understanding was reached, not line 7 or line 9. And Mary successfully conveys that her utterance at line 5 was not an 'understanding check' in primary search of confirmation, but rather a display that she had correctly understood what her co-interactant had intended. Across these two parallel cases, it is clear that *oh* is implicated showing the moment at which understanding is reached as an integral part of the process through which the exact status of the 'understanding check' is displayed.

Tracking the ownership of knowledge: *Oh*-prefaced turns in second position

Interactants not only keep score on who knows what, they also keep rather close watch over the relative rights that each may have to know particular facts. *Oh* is also involved in this process. *Oh*-prefaced turns are often used to convey what might be termed 'ownership' of knowledge and with it, epistemic supremacy in relation to other interactants. Consider the following interview in which Sir Harold Acton, a noted English aesthete, is interviewed by the British broadcaster Russell Harty. The interview has turned to a discussion about the manners of the Chinese and some work that Acton was doing in Beijing – teaching modern poetry at Beijing University. Sir Harold Acton's reply to the question 'Did you learn to speak Chinese' is *oh*-prefaced:

Extract (13)   [Chat Show:Russell Harty-Sir Harold Acton]

```
 1   Act:              ....hhhh and some of thuh- (0.3) some of my students
 2                     translated Eliot into Chine::se. I think thuh very
 3                     first.
 4                     (0.2)
 5   Har:              Did you learn to speak (.) Chine[:se.
 6   Act:    →                                        [.hh Oh yes.
 7                     (0.7)
 8   Act:              .hhhh You ca::n't live in thuh country without speaking
 9                     thuh lang[uage it's impossible .hhhhh=
10   Har:    →                  [Not no: cour:se
```

Here, given that Acton taught modern poetry and that his students were the first to translate T. S. Eliot's work, the interviewer's question is clearly vulnerable to the charge that it is questioning the obvious. Acton's responsive 'oh yes' manages to convey just that, treating it as evident that he would have learned the language. Subsequently both parties topicalize the self-evident nature of the point. Acton goes on to explain briefly why it was essential to learn the language to live in China (lines 8–9). And this explanation, in turn, is acknowledged by the interviewer (with 'Not no: course' [line 10]) in a way that treats the answer to his question as, after all, having been quite self-evident.

In this example and others like it (Heritage, 1998), this process of challenging the relevance or appropriateness of a question by *oh*-prefacing the response exploits the 'change-of-state' meaning of 'oh' to indicate that the question has occasioned a *shift of attention*. In the case of questions, conveying a shift of this kind can imply that a question was inapposite and, hence, that the respondent is experiencing difficulties with the question's relevance, appropriateness, or presuppositions. In this way, a respondent

can challenge or resist the relevance of a question and the course of action
that the question may be implementing.

An important feature of this practice is that, through it, the respondent can convey that *their own point of view* is the basic framework
from which the issue is to be considered, and does so inexplicitly yet
insistently (Heritage, 1998:291–6). In treating their own point of view
as the perspective from which some matter should be considered, *oh*-
prefacing respondents index (and reaffirm) a claim of epistemic authority
or supremacy over their questioners.

A similar process is involved in *oh*-prefaced agreement and disagreement. In the following case, for example, Gay is giving Jeremy a German
telephone number. After she has given eleven digits of the number, thus
exceeding the norm (during the 1980s) for a (British) intra-country call,
Jeremy comments (line 13) on the length of the number, prefacing his
comment with 'Gosh', an expression which indicates that, for him, this
is something new, notable or surprising. Here Gay could have responded
with a simple agreement which would have conveyed that her agreement
was grounded in the 'here and now' common experience of an inter-
minable telephone number. Instead, her *oh*-prefaced response – 'Oh it
doe:s' – treats his remark as reviving an earlier observation of the same
type that she had made independently of this occasion, and she thereby
conveys that, in contrast to Jeremy, she finds it unsurprising. By this
means she also manages to indicate that she is an 'old hand' at phoning
abroad, at least relative to Jeremy:

Extract (14)   [Heritage:0I:7:3]

```
 1  Gay:        So the -number is (0.2) oh: one oh::.
 2  Jer:        Oh one oh:,
 3              (1.0)
 4  Jer:        Yeup,
 5  Gay:        ↑Four ni:ne,
 6              (0.5)
 7  Jer:        Ri:ght?
 8  Gay:        Sev'n three, u-six o:ne?hh
 9              (0.6)
10  Jer:        Sev'n three: six o:ne?
11              (0.3)
12  Gay:        Ei:ght ni:ne,
13  Jer:    →   °Gosh° it goe:s (.) goes on'n on
14  Gay:    →   Oh it doe:s Germany doe:s.
```

It may also be noticed that Gay adds a turn component that appears
designed to further suggest her expertise about foreign telephone
calls. Her postpositioned 'adjusting' component ('Germany doe:s.')

recalibrates the referent of her response from this particular telephone number to German telephone numbers in general, and also works to convey a degree of prior knowledge on the topic. Moreover, with its hint of a further contrast with telephone numbers in other foreign countries, it implies a still broader expertise in the matter of placing telephone calls abroad. Shortly afterwards, Gay underscores her expertise, informing Jeremy that the 'ringing' sound on a German phone sounds like a 'busy' signal on a British phone (data not shown).

Here then the second speaker, Gay, has used an *oh*-preface in her response to convey that Jeremy's remark has induced a shift in her attention to something previously known and taken for granted. In this way she conveys that she has *previously and independently* arrived at the conclusion that her co-interactant verbalizes. Here, although both parties are in agreement about the length of the telephone number, the expression of their agreement is managed such that Gay asserts epistemic superiority over Jeremy in the matter of 'phoning abroad' (Heritage, 2002).

Oh-prefaced agreements are common in environments where the second, *oh*-prefacing speaker has primary access to the state of affairs being assessed, and/or primary rights to assess it. In this context, *oh*-prefacing continues to index 'independent access' to the referent, and as indexing the epistemic authority of the second speaker.

In the following instance, for example, two dog breeders – Norman and Ilene – have been talking about the readiness of one of Norman's younger dogs to have a first litter. At line 9, Ilene ventures a comment about one of Norman's other dogs (Trixie), who apparently began breeding at a young age:

Extract (15)   [Heritage 1:11:4]

```
 1  Ile:        No well she's still a bit young though isn't [she<ah me]an:=
 2  Nor:                                                    [S  h  e  :  :]
 3  Ile:        =uh[:
 4  Nor:           [She wz a year: la:st wee:k.
 5  Ile:        Ah yes. Oh well any time no:w [then.]
 6  Nor:                                      [Uh:::]:[m
 7  Ile:                                              [Ye:s.=
 8  Nor:        =But she[:'s (              )]
 9  Ile:    →           [Cuz Trixie started] so early [didn't sh[e,
10  Nor:    →                                         [°0 h : : [ye:s.°=
11  Ile:        =°Ye:h°=
```

Here Norman's *oh*-prefaced agreement (line 10), in conveying the independence of his assessment from Ilene's, also alludes to his epistemic priority with respect to the information in question. At the same moment,

Ilene's tag question (line 9) downgrades the epistemic strength of what would otherwise be a flat assertion.

In extract (15), the epistemic priority of the second, *oh*-prefacing speaker is available from the topic and context of the interaction, and inexplicitly indexed in the talk. In the following cases, the priority between first and second assessors is directly established in the sequence prior to the *oh*-prefaced second assessment. In extract (16) Jon and Lyn are talking to Eve, Jon's mother. After Jon's announcement about going to the movie 'Midnight Cowboy', Lyn asks Eve if she has seen it. She replies that she did not and goes on to account for this by reference to a friend, 'Jo', who reportedly said that the film 'depressed her terribly' (lines 5–6):

Extract (16)   [JS:II:61:ST]

```
1  Jon:          We saw Midnight Cowboy yesterday -or [suh- Friday.
2  Eve:                                               [Oh?
3  Lyn:          Didju s- you saw that, [it's really good.
4  Eve:                                 [No I haven't seen it
5                Jo saw it 'n she said she f- depressed her
6  Eve:          ter[ribly
7  Jon:    →        [Oh it's [terribly depressing.
8  Lyn:    →                 [Oh it's depressing.
```

Here both Jon and Lyn agree with Eve's friend's opinion, but both their agreeing assessments are *oh*-prefaced, thus indexing the independence of their access to the movie, and in this context that, relative to Eve, they have epistemic priority: direct, rather than indirect, access to the movie. Once again, in a sequence that is clearly occupied with agreement about the film, the 'terms of agreement' – who has epistemic priority in the film's assessment – is also being addressed (Heritage and Raymond forthcoming).

The use of *oh*-prefacing is far from being the only resource through which this kind of epistemic supremacy is indexed. For example, in the following sequence, Lesley is the one with direct access to her daughter's dental problems, and Mum downgrades her access to the referent with the evidential verb 'sounds' (Chafe, 1986), and the following tag-question:

Extract (17)   [Field X(C)-1-2-7]

```
1  Les:    .hh An' I'll: get her fixed up with a de:ntist too:,
2          (0.7)
3  Mum:    Oh w't a ↓nuisance isn't ↓it. Is it ↓ey:e tee:th?
4          (0.4)
5  Les:    .hh ↑Well the den: u-her dentist says °no:t.°
6          (0.2)
```

```
 7  Mum:     [↑Hm:.
 8  Les:     [.hh But I:'ll send 'er to ↓my den:tist I thi[nk
 9  Mum:                                                  [Sounds
10            ↓like it ↑dzn't[↓it.
11  Les:                     [.hhh It does rather yes:
```

Lesley matches this downgrade with an upgrade managed through a deferred agreement 'It does rather yes:'. While Mum's tag-question (line 10) invites a 'type-conforming' 'yes' or 'no' response as the *first* component of any response (Raymond, 2003), Lesley's initial declaratively formed partial repeat 'It does' manages to *confirm* Mum's evaluation prior to 'responding to the question'. This confirmation embodies the claim that she previously and independently held this position, and treats this as an interactional issue to be dealt with as a matter of priority.

Discussion: informational terrain and cognitive process in conversation

This chapter has offered some illustrations of several interrelated conversational phenomena that bear on the issue of cognition in discourse.

First, and most basic, is the observation that participants in conversation hold one another to strict standards of accountability concerning such matters as who knows what, when, and with what degree of epistemic priority relative to others in the interaction. The examples in this chapter indicate that social interactants address these matters with considerable economy and precision through the way turns are designed and timed. By these means each participant maintains, and is socially accountable for maintaining, a range of informational territories. For example, there is personal information which a person properly knows, and has rights to know better than others because it concerns his or her life, experience and property. Persons can 'know best' about working in China, or phoning Germany, because they have lived through such experiences. They can know best about particular dogs and children because they own them, and with that, they own the rights to describe them. This kind of cognitive terrain is bound up with social identity, and both the assertion of, and defence of, priority claims in this terrain can often be co-terminous with the assertion (and defence) of identity itself (Raymond and Heritage, 2004). Or again, there is information which a person properly knows by virtue of having been told it by another. This is information that a person is often held accountable for as a condition of achieving understanding of turns at talk, as some of Garfinkel's (1967) experiments illustrate. It is information that a person can be enjoined to 'remember'. It is information which one should not be repeatedly told (Maynard, 2003; Terasaki, forthcoming; Schegloff, forthcoming). Then there is information that is acquired in the here and now, whose registration as 'new information' is mandated as a matter of sequence-specific priority.

Second, this chapter has illustrated the corollary to this first point: the specificity and exactness with which cognitive process is both *represented* and *embodied* in interaction. These features are commensurate with the importance with which cognition and cognitive process are invested in conversation. As this chapter has illustrated, the meaning of actions qua actions, their implications for the nature of social relations and their import for identity itself can be, and frequently is, embedded in their treatment in terms of cognitive process. Considerable interactional resources are dedicated to this treatment.

However, these issues raise a third: what is the status of the 'cognitive processes' that are somehow indexed by *oh* and the other procedures discussed here. As noted earlier, it might be possible to think of *oh* as directly tied to the experience (and the neuropsychology) of undergoing a 'change of cognitive state', such that the utterance of '*oh*' indexes the arrival of such a state as its outward marker. Perhaps *oh* and 'ouch' and other similar response cries – 'signs meant to taken to index directly the state of the transmitter' (Goffman, 1981:116) – have a direct psychological reality. Such a conception is not without its attractions: most readers will have produced an *oh* at the very moment of some dawning understanding or realization and, when interaction is examined, it is clear that many *ohs* are produced very close to the point at which the information-content of prior talk was conveyed – see, for example, extracts (5) and (7) above. Yet it is clear that this conception has some difficulties: the utterance of *oh* is a point event, whereas a change of cognitive state is likely a processual one that dawns, emerges and consolidates. Additionally, like 'ouch', *oh* can be withheld in the face of its corresponding cognitive event, or produced in the absence of such an event – both of these sins (of omission and commission) representing forms of conduct associated with the manipulation of symbols, rather than the direct expression of cognitive states. Moreover like pain and other forms of distress behaviour (Heath, 1989; Whalen and Zimmerman, 1998), the production of *oh* is accommodated to the exigencies of interactional decorum, being mainly produced at the boundaries of turn-constructional units where turn-transfer becomes an option, rather than an 'online' reaction to information as it is produced. All of this points to the symbolic conventionalization of *oh* which is specifically conveyed in Goffman's characterization of 'response cries' as 'signs *meant to be taken* to index directly the state of the transmitter' (emphasis added). Then, further, there is the additional conventionalization of the semantics of *oh* in many *oh*-prefaced usages which are also distanced from the experiential states that their utterance might otherwise claim.

In his later writings, Emile Durkheim (1915) made frequent reference to the idea that the control and regulation of knowledge was simultaneously the control and regulation of social relations between persons. In this chapter I have suggested that this idea may have some value when we examine how cognitive processes are represented and embodied in social interaction. In the lay world of interaction, attention, cognition and memory are far from being abstract topics of purely scientific interest. On the contrary they are matters of relentless social concern and personal accountability. At the same time, communication processes which can be plausibly conceived to have a relatively primitive psychological substrate have undergone a level of conventionalization and domestication that permits their 'semantic' deployment. The result is enhanced human capacity to regulate experiential and informational territories that are substantially more distant, and sophisticated, than the simple exclamations with which we began.

NOTE

1. The invocation of third parties to bolster the objectivity of descriptions is commonplace, especially when they are potentially questionable (Wooffitt, 1992; Potter, 1996; Heritage and Robinson, frth).

9   From process to practice: language interaction and 'flashbulb' memories

Robin Wooffitt

Introduction

To make significant strides in reworking traditional understanding of cognition we need to engage cognitive scientists: we have to show that we can speak directly to the concerns which animate their disciplines. And this demonstration must not rest in theoretical or conceptual arguments, important as these are; instead, it is necessary to show how the results of empirical analyses mesh with, and have real implications for, research agenda and methodological developments in cognitive science.

To this end, I'm going to talk about a type of memory which has come to be known as flashbulb memory. These kinds of memories have been the subject of a substantial amount of research in cognitive psychology, particularly in the United States. In recent years some researchers have begun to reflect critically on the methodology of their research. Equally, there has been a willingness to question some of the core premises which have traditionally motivated their research. Finally there has been an openness to explore analytic techniques and data which would hitherto have been considered inappropriate for research in cognitive science. And it is at this juncture that the orientations and findings of conversation analytic and discourse analytic studies become relevant.

To begin, then, I'll give a brief account of the origins of the concept of flashbulb memory and outline some of the main themes which run through research on this topic. But I want to show that the kinds of issues I'll be raising are not limited to the flashbulb memory, but might have a broader compass, in that they have implications more generally for autobiographical memory, self and identity.

Flashbulb memory

In their seminal paper, Brown and Kulik (1977) were concerned with the way in which it seemed that memories of hearing significant news seemed more detailed, vivid and less likely to fade than other kinds of memories.

They observed that their own personal recollections of the assassination of President Kennedy in 1963 seemed to be qualitatively different from other types of memory. They had a primary 'live' quality that is almost perceptual. Indeed, it is very much *like a photograph that indiscriminately preserves the scene* in which each of us found ourselves when the flashbulb was fired. (Brown and Kulik, 1977: 74; emphasis added.)

It was argued that 'flashbulb' memories occurred not only in the recollection of receiving dramatic news, but in any case where the individual undergoes an unusual or traumatic experience which is personally consequential (Brown and Kulik, 1977; Pillemer et al., 1987). They suggested a neurophysiological explanation: upon recognizing the personal significance of an event or experience, neural mechanisms within the brain which lead to information encoding and storage are triggered. Brown and Kulik argued that because this 'Now Print!' mechanism is activated under conditions in which the organism is in a considerable state of arousal or surprise, the subsequent memory is resistant to deterioration and more accessible to conscious recall. (See also Gold, 1992.)

There was another enduring feature of flashbulb memories that puzzled Brown and Kulik: why was it that people seemed to be able to recall the more trivial and mundane features of their circumstances at the time of hearing dramatic news, or having a traumatic experience? As far back as 1899, F. W. Colegrove asked subjects to try to recall when they first heard the news that President Lincoln had been assassinated, an event which happened thirty-three years before the study (Colegrove, 1982;[1899]). His respondents were able to provide detailed information of their routine circumstances at the time. For example:

'I was standing by the stove getting dinner; my husband came in and told me'
'I was setting out a rose bush by the door. My husband came in the yard and told me. (Colegrove, 1982 [1899]: 42.)

Anticipating the Brown and Kulik explanation, Colegrove had surmised that there must be a psychological facility which captures the mundane, routine and trivial features of the speaker's environment at the time of the dramatic event. Brown and Kulik's neurophysiological account provided the mechanism: cortical activities lead to the formation of a record of not only the stimulus event, but also any other information being processed by the brain, consciously or unconsciously, as part of its routine monitoring of the organism's state and environment.

Brown and Kulik's paper has certainly been influential. Brewer (1992) suggests its status is due largely to the fact that, when it was published, research was focused mainly on rote memory and semantic memory. And it is certainly true that it:

identified an aspect of autobiographical memory that had received scant attention from cognitive psychologists – memory for one's own personal circumstances
(such as location, ongoing activities, and feelings) when receiving important
and shocking news . . . as opposed to memory for the newsworthy event itself.
(Pillemer, 1992: 236)

But it advanced other claims which generated further research: for example, that there may be a distinct memory formation mechanism; and that
these kinds of memories are more vivid than other forms, and less likely
to decay.

However, while there are psychologists who still support the idea that
there is a distinct mechanism behind the formation of flashbulb memories
(for example, Conway, 1995) there has been sustained criticism.

Perhaps the major criticism of Brown and Kulik's neurophysiological
account is that we can have flashbulb memories which are simply wrong.
In 1986 the Space Shuttle *Challenger* exploded shortly after launch. This
provided the possibility of collecting 'ecologically valid' data regarding the stability and vividness of flashbulb recollections on first hearing
of this tragic accident. For example, Neisser and Harsch (1992) adminis-
tered a questionnaire to first year United States undergraduate students
the day after the explosion. These respondents were required to write a
description of how they first heard of the accident. Two and a half years
later the same students were again contacted and asked to write another
account of their first awareness of the disaster. Neisser and Harsch's
comparative analysis suggested that flashbulb occasions can be recalled
incorrectly. (See also Bohannon, 1988; McCloskey *et al.*, 1988; Neisser,
1982b; Neisser *et al.*, 1996.)[1]

A telling critical assessment came from the cognitive psychologist, Ulric
Neisser, who proposed an alternative account for the organization of
flashbulb memories. Rejecting the idea that there is a cognitive of neurophysiological basis for them, he argued:

they seem to be like narrative conventions. . . . News reporters and novelists, myth-
makers and autobiographers have a fairly consistent idea of how events should be
described, of what readers and listeners want to know. Everyone in our culture is
at least roughly aware of these conventions. In effect, we have a *schemata* for the
arrival of important news . . . (Neisser, 1982b: 47; original emphasis)

He suggests that we remember the details of 'flashbulb occasions' because
they provide a link between our own individual biographies and the pro-
cession of historical events unfolding around us. Moreover, he suggested
that these recollections appear to be vivid and resistant to decay because
they are rehearsed and repeated: we anticipate telling how we came to

hear significant news, and then we tell these stories to others. Indeed, Neisser goes as far as to say that the truth of the memory is one of the least significant aspects of it: 'It is the very existence of the memory that matters, not its content' (1982b:48).

While these arguments reflect Neisser's broader concerns to promote ecological approaches to remembering, autobiographical memory and the self (Neisser, 1988; Neisser and Fivush, 1994; Neisser and Winograd, 1988), they also suggest intriguing lines of research which invite sociological consideration. First, he draws attention to the significance of producing memories in social contexts. Second, his suggestion that there is a schemata which informs the ways in which we produce accounts of our memories leads us to consider the recurrent systematic properties of the discourse which surrounds and informs memory production in talk. Finally, his writings suggest that research on the production of memories and their social contexts is at least as important as the study of the veridicality of these memories, or the neurophysiological mechanisms supposedly involved in their formation, storage and retrieval.

Many of these themes are developed by Pillemer (1992) in his functional analysis of flashbulb memories. He argues that there has been too much emphasis upon examining the accuracy of flashbulb memories. The research agenda should be expanded to include memory functions hitherto not considered in cognitive psychology. He lists three: the directive, psychodynamic and the communicative functions. His discussion of the directive functions considers how flashbulb memories provide prescriptions for present and future behaviour. The psychodynamic functions range from the healing effects of reporting traumatic experiences through to the evolutionary advantage of being able to form vivid mental images. (See also Hyman, 1999 for an evolutionary account of the formation of false autobiographical memories.)

But it is in his discussion of the communicative functions where Pillemer invites sociological attention, sometimes explicitly. He states that:

The act of recounting a detailed personal memory to others communicates meaning that transcends the surface content of the particular recollection, and this specialized form of communication appears to be rule governed. (1992:236)

He considers two themes: first, he discusses what he calls the rules of memory sharing. He observed that the simple act of telling of one's own memories, and hearing those of others, performs functions beyond the mere transmission of information. He cites two studies to illustrate his case. The first is a study by Tenney (1989) of the way in which new parents inform friends of the birth of their child. Tenney argues that what gets reported owes more to social and interactional norms rather than any memory of the events being reported. Research by Barsalou (1988) is also cited as evidence that people's narrative styles are more likely to reflect cultural conventions than underlying memory organization.[2]

Similar themes emerge when Pillemer considers the meanings of memory sharing. He argues that the production of detail adds authenticity to a memory. Moreover, he claims that the production of vivid recollections adds emotionality, intimacy and immediacy: recounting such memories may be a sign of the speaker's openness, thus encouraging others to reciprocate and thereby strengthening interpersonal bonds.

To communication researchers, especially those influenced by scholars such as Goffman, Sacks and Garfinkel, these may not seem like radical claims. But they are significant in that they represent an attempt by cognitive scientists to encourage research which takes account of communicative competencies, and the socially organized normative conventions which they embody, in examination of the production of memories in real life settings. Moreover, Pillemer's discussion of the meanings of flashbulb memories focuses on the interpersonal consequences of reports of memories, and also echoes many themes in the study of factual language (Edwards and Potter, 1992; Potter, 1996; Wooffitt, 1992).

So what are the relevant points from this discussion of flashbulb memory? Several developments are clear.

- The emphasis upon examining the veridicality of flashbulb memories is diminishing; it is proposed that memories can serve functions even if some of the recollections are imprecise or plain wrong.
- This meshes with a move within cognitive psychology to explore ecologically valid data. However, although recollections of hearing about the *Challenger* disaster provided a natural laboratory for research, the memories themselves were still elicited through traditional experimental means.
- There is an interest in the ways in which prototypical characteristics of the memory (detail, vividness, etc) perform interpersonal functions.
- Functional analysis of flashbulb memories, and memory more generally, invites contributions from sociolinguistics, communication studies, the analysis of textual materials and so on.

Clearly then, there are points of convergence between cognitive psychological research on flashbulb memories and conversation analytic and discourse analytic studies of talk and texts. In the next section I will consider how a CA concern first, to describe formally the detailed production of utterances and, second, with the examination of inferential work accomplished by utterance design, may flesh out some of the projects sketched by Pillemer and other cognitive psychologists.

Describing anomalous human experiences

Some years ago I examined a corpus of recordings in which members of the public described their encounters with a range of paranormal or parapsychological phenomena. Inspired in part by Sacks' (1984) analysis of doing 'being ordinary' and Jefferson's (1984) subsequent development of his ideas in her analysis of 'At first I thought . . .' formulations, I was primarily concerned to see what kinds of resources were used to warrant the factual status of the account and the authority of the speaker as a competent reporter. These data were not collected in the first instance to allow examination of memory formulation. Invariably, however, the data I had collected were not simply accounts of events: they were accounts of recollections of events.

A recurrent property of these recollections was that speakers used a two-part format by which to introduce into the account the first experience of their respective phenomenon (or in the case of phenomena which were experienced more than once, every particular episode). This format can be identified as 'I was just doing X . . . when Y', where the 'X' component is used to describe the speakers' activities at the time, and the 'Y' component reports the speaker's first awareness of the phenomenon or its impact upon the speaker. Here are some examples. In the first, the speaker is describing one of a series of violent encounters with a poltergeist.[3]

Extract (1)   [ND 22:159]

```
1        anyway I got to the kitchen door an as ah hh
2        I had the teapot in my hand like this and I walked
3        through the kitchen door (.5) hhh
4   X    as I was going through the doorway
5        (.7)
6   Y    I was just (.) jammed against the doorpost (.) like
7        this with the teapot sti(h)ll stu(h)ck
8        out in front of me
```

In the following extract the speaker is describing an apparition of her husband, who had been a pilot in the RAF. He had a military funeral service which was held in an aeroplane hanger.

Extract (2)   [EL 4:29]

```
1        an' I went in there (.) er:m w- with my mother in
2        law and uhm: (.4) friends that were with me
3        (1.3)
4   X    hhh (.) and I was just looking at the coffin
5   Y    and there was David standing there (.3)
6        he was in Blues
7        (1)
```

8   hh he wasn't wearing his hat his hat was on the
9   coffin and he was there

There are some strong parallels with flashbulb memories. First, these were accounts of events which were sometimes profoundly significant for the individual. Second, the speakers formulate a recollection of what they were doing *just before* the onset of their first experience with the phenomenon. In extract (1) the speaker claims that he encountered an invisible presence which forcibly pressed him against a door frame. He describes this as happening 'as I was going through the doorway'. In extract (2) the speaker is reporting her first awareness of an apparition of her deceased husband; this is described as happening as she 'was just looking at the coffin'. These are precisely the kinds of mundane details which have intrigued cognitive psychologists. Indeed, it was the apparent recollection of such trivial matters that prompted Brown and Kulik to consider the need to invoke a special mechanism to account for their occurrence. More recently, in his study of flashbulb memories of the attempted assassination of President Reagan, Pillemer pondered 'why these mundane private experiences are remembered *at all*' (1984: 77; emphasis added).

Extracts (3) and (4) provide further examples of descriptions of mundane activities prior to a reference to the initial encounter with an anomalous phenomenon. In extract (3) the speaker is reporting one in a series of apparitions; in extract (4) the speaker is recounting an apparition which occurred while she was watching a video of her husband's funeral service.

Extract (3)   [REW52]

```
1        so I I think I remember I 'ad a dish in hand I was out
2        in the kitchen it was different like (.) y' know (.)
3        to this sort've flat (.5) an' it ws' like a (.) big
4        entrance hall (.7) with one (.) door (.5) and then it
5        came straight the way through there was a door there
6        and a door there (.5) a door there an (.5) it was a
7        kitchen
8        (1)
9        and I was right by this unit part
10       (1.5)
11       an'
12       (.)
13    X  I were lookin' out that way
14    Y  an' it seemed to be like a figure (.) coming through
15       the |hall (.7) all I could see was the ah (a-)
16       the top part
```

Extract (4)   [EL5:39]

```
1         I also wanted it video'd for my children: who were
2         (1.7)
3         two and four at the time they didn't come to the
4         funeral
5         (2.4)
6         and so perhaps a week later
7         (1.3)
8         >must've bin about< a week afterwards h I:: (.5) put
9         the recording on and was watching it
10        I was obviously extremely upset
11        (.8)
12   X    and I was sat on a chair (.) uhnd
13        (.5)
14   Y    when I looked down David was (.)
15        kneeling at the side of me
```

The first part of the 'X when Y' format is used to refer either to an activity or a place: for example, in extract (4) the speaker produces the description 'I was sat on a chair', thus reporting her activity (sitting) and her location (on a chair). Again, these data contain features which meet two of the canonical categories by which Brown and Kulik identified flashbulb memories: recall of *where* the person was and *what they were doing* at the time of the traumatic event. There are, then, good grounds for treating these memory formulations as naturally occurring instances of flashbulb memories.

For cognitive psychologists the question had been: why are these apparently trivial matters available for recall? However, analysis of the structure of these utterances suggested that they are not simply verbal renditions of non-narrative imaginal states somewhere in the head; they exhibit design features: they are built to have the properties of triviality mundaneity and so on. There are three kinds of evidence.

First, there is a relationship between the activity used in constructing a description of the circumstances of the experience, and the nature of the phenomenon or event being reported. In extract (1) the speaker's experience consisted of being pressed against the frame of a door by an invisible agency. His description of the mundane things he was doing prior to this is 'as I was going through the doorway'. There is, then, a 'fit' between the activity selected and the type of experience he had. This occurs also in extract (2), in which the speaker saw an apparition of her recently deceased husband standing next to his coffin at the funeral. Her formulation of what she was doing prior to seeing the apparition is 'I was just looking at the coffin'.

There is, then, a contingent relevance between the activities indexed in the first part of the format and the paranormal or unusual event referred to in the second. The activities reported in the first part are not coincidentally related to the subsequent experience, as we might expect if they are recollections composed of events randomly recorded by cognitive processes at the time. That is, it is not that they are mentionable because they were happening and then something extraordinary happened. Rather, the descriptions of these activities are designed to elevate features of the speakers' experiences made relevant by the subsequent event. They attain a reportable status by virtue of what the event turned out to be.

Second, Pillemer (1992: 246) has argued that one way in which speakers can make their flashbulb memories more vivid is through the use of the historical present verb tense. Thus 'walking', 'looking' and 'standing' preserve the active, on-going quality of the action being described. This was common throughout the data I had collected. But the use of tense not only enhanced the drama of the narrative, but established a contingency of one event upon another.

When constructing routine state formulations speakers have a choice between verb tenses; descriptions of mundane circumstances which employ passive tenses are routinely abandoned in favour of formulations which display the historical present. For example, from extract (1)

```
1       anyway I got to the kitchen door an as ah hh
2       I had the teapot in my hand like this and I walked
3       through the kitchen door (.5) hhh
4    X  as I was going through the doorway
5       (.7)
6    Y  I was just (.) jammed against the doorpost
```

And in the following extract the speaker is reporting an experience which happened while she was on a public demonstration.

Extract (5)   [EMA 10:86]
```
1       but my experience was
2       I got to a certain point in
3       the (.3) circle s:circle and the chant
4    X  we kept going round slowly
5       in a circle without stopping
6    Y  hh all of a sudden
        ((goes on to report onset of experience))
```

In the section from extract (1) the speaker formulates the activity 'walked through' which is then displaced by 'was going through'. In extract (5) the speaker replaces 'I got to a certain point in the s: circle' with 'we kept going round'. In both extracts the speakers provide two consecutive utterances which address ostensibly with the same issue – their activity at the time; and in both instances the information in the first version is repackaged in the second. The reformulated version, however, employs the historical present tense.

Pillemer suggests that the use of the historical past tense is a way of demonstrating that a speaker is not merely recalling an experience, but reliving it (1992: 246). But there is a more pragmatic explanation. One feature of the historical present is that its use implies the relevance of some other event which occurred while the activity described by the verb was itself taking place, especially when used in conjunction with 'as', 'just' and so on. Its use clearly suggests that the activity described in this way is contingent upon some other, as yet unstated occurrence, thus heightening an expectation of further narrative developments. We will return to this later.

Finally, the designed quality of 'X' formulations becomes apparent when we consider instances in which they are used to provide some form of summary of prior talk. Heritage and Watson (1979) examined how participants in news interviews provided gists or upshots of other people's prior talk and the interactional tasks accomplished through such formulations. Their analysis revealed that such characterizations allowed the speaker to constitute reflexively the character of the preceding talk. When employed as 'X' formulations, gists and upshots served similar functions in accounts of paranormal experiences.

Extract (6)   [DM 7]

```
1         un' I was thinkin' about religion un' eh (.5) I was
2         thinkin' well (.4) (     ) on the lines of it (.3)
3         I(t)- i- it must be very easy to be Saint Paul because
4         yuh get yer blindin' light on the road to Damascus
5         sort u(v) thing un' eh hh (.6) you've no problems (so
6         you) you:: know as far as you're concerned
7         you measure all things according to that experience
8         the experience was exterior to yourself an' so
9         therefore
10        (1.3)
11        you viewed it (.7) as a star:t (.5) (>yu know<) >yeah<
12   X    I were just thinkin' (.3) er:m
13   Y    and then suddenly I was aware of (.7) almost (.) the sensation
14        was almost as if a veil was lifted
```

Extract (7)   [EL1:6]

1   a::n: deh (.) they drove me (.) to (.) Angelsey
2   (1.5)
3   a: nd
4   (.5)
5   **X**   we were all sat round (.) ehm in a room
6   (.6)
7   and I know >thut< (.3) I know it sounds silly but
8   **Y**   I knew that David was there he was behi: nd me hh

In extract (6) the speaker provides an account of a religious or mystical experience. In the first part of the extract he provides a lengthy description of some of the thoughts which were occupying him prior to the experience. These concerned his reflections on personal faith which results from a direct personal encounter with a mystical presence. Yet in building a gist of this prior talk he deletes the more evocative aspects of his prior talk and constructs the more mundane state formulation 'I were just thinkin'. Similarly, in extract (7), the speaker has been reporting how she was met by Royal Air Force officials who informed her of her husband's fatal accident, and then driven to a nearby military base. In the light of the traumatic news events which she had just experienced, and to which she had just referred, the formulation 'we were all sat round (.) ehm in a room' is conspicuously routine. In each case, then, speakers actively design their 'X' formulations as gists or upshots of materials they had provided earlier. In doing so they gloss over or discard those features of their prior talk which are non-ordinary, emotive or traumatic to furnish only the routine character of their circumstances at the time.

Reports of the speakers' mundane states or activities prior to the onset of paranormal experiences are not merely verbalized reports of information secreted somewhere in the head. They are utterances which, first, form part of a recurrent device which exhibits robust properties. Moreover, they are built to establish and display the mundane environment of the experience. But why? In the following sections we explore some of the inferential or pragmatic work addressed in the design features of this class of flashbulb memory formulations.

Contrastive organization and narrative development

Many cognitive psychologists have noted that flashbulb memories can be reported in such a way as to enhance their vividness and the drama of the story; Pillemer's discussion of the role of verb tense is one example. However, it is invariably the case that these stylistic flourishes are viewed as embellishments to a set of cognitively stored information. The assumption is that there are a set of details – for example, the recall of the mundane circumstances of the experience – and then the narrative colouring which is added later. But if we take a conversation analytic approach we can see that the production of mundane details is itself a form of rhetorical organization.

In the two parts of the 'X then Y' device speakers describe first the 'normal' and then the 'paranormal'. Consider the relevant sections from the first four data extracts.

```
6    X    as I was going through the kitchen door
7         (.7)
8    Y    I was just (.) jammed against
9         the doorpost

4    X    and I was looking at the coffin
5    Y    and there was David standing there

12   X    I were just thinkin' (.3) er:m
13   Y    and then suddenly I was aware of (.7) almost (.) the sensation
14        was almost as if a veil was lifted

13   X    and I was sat on a chair (.) uhnd
14        (.5)
15   Y    when I looked down David was (.)
16        kneeling at the side of me
```

In each case the onset of the paranormal experience is offered by way of contrast with the routine events immediately preceding its onset.

The use of contrast pairs has been investigated in a variety of occasions of natural language use (Atkinson, 1984; Heritage and Greatbatch, 1986; Pinch and Clark, 1986; Smith, 1978). These studies have shown the various ways in which the contrast structure is employed as a persuasive device. In Atkinson's work on political rhetoric, for example, this device not only projects a point at which the audience can begin to applaud, but also highlights the difference between the two positions or cases addressed through the contrastive pair.

In the paranormal data two parts of the 'X then Y' device are used to report an ordinary activity which is interrupted by something truly extraordinary. The juxtaposition of these images ensures that the character of each component is affirmed in relation to the other. Thus the mundane environment is enhanced by virtue of the contrast to what happened next, while the strangeness of the phenomenon is made inferentially available through its rupture of the everyday and routine. The very drama of the experience is not reflected in the recall of the mundane circumstances of its occurrence: it is at least partially constituted in the very design and organization of the subsequent account.

'X' formulations and scepticism

Research on interaction in a variety of contexts has shown that participants may design their utterances defensively in circumstances in which the co-participant(s) may be hostile to, sceptical or suspicious of, or simply unsympathetic to, what the speaker is saying. For example, Pomerantz (1986) shows how speakers in everyday conversation may build formulations of their 'points of view' to guard against the likelihood of a recipient being able to undermine the basis of their claims or opinions. In courtroom interaction also, utterances produced by counsel, witness and defendant will be designed to influence the range of inferences which the overhearing jury will arrive at (Atkinson and Drew, 1979; Drew, 1990; see also, Drew, 1978). Equally, young people who are members of youth subcultures may provide accounts in which descriptions of activities and events are designed to deflect the criticism that they attract trouble by virtue of their unusual appearance (Widdicombe and Wooffitt, 1995). Finally, people who espouse racist or extreme opinions may design their talk to minimize unsympathetic responses (Potter, 1996; Wetherell and Potter, 1992). Thus, where speakers are in an inauspicious environment, their descriptions can be designed to circumscribe the range of negative or unsympathetic inferences which may be drawn by a recipient. 'I was just doing X . . . when Y' formulations are a device by which speakers may address a range of potential sceptical responses to the reporting of extraordinary events.

One feature of the inauspiciousness of reporting anomalous events is that, due to the prevailing scepticism, there is always the possibility that recipients may try to formulate explanations of the reported experience so as to recast them as ordinary. (This is quite often a strategy which sceptics employ when they appear in television documentaries or talk shows about the paranormal.) All manner of personal characteristics can be inspected to 'reveal' what it is about a person that makes them believe they have had the experience they claim.

Consider extract (6) again.

Extract (6)

1	un' I was thinkin' about religion un' eh (.5) I was
2	thinkin' well (.4) ( ) on the lines of it (.3)
3	I(t)- i- it must be very easy to be Saint Paul because
4	yuh get yer blindin' light on the road to Damascus
5	sort u(v) thing un' eh hh (.6) you've no problems (so
6	you) you:: know as far as you're concerned
7	you measure all things according to that experience
8	the experience was exterior to yourself an' so
9	therefore

```
10        (1.3)
11        you viewed it (.7) as a star: t (.5) (>yu know<) >yeah<
12   X    I were just thinkin' (.3) er: m
13   Y    and then suddenly I was aware of (.7) almost (.) the sensation
14        was almost as if a veil was lifted
```

Here the speaker is describing a transcendental experience which led to religious conversion. When he is describing his activities prior to the onset of the actual experience, he explicitly reports that he had been thinking about religious conversion through an encounter with a numinous presence. Moreover, he was pondering that such experiences provide people with a certainty for their religious beliefs. His subsequent experience, however, was exactly that type of revelatory mystical encounter. On the basis of his own prior talk it would be entirely feasible for a hearer to draw the inference that the actual experience was a form of wish-fulfilment: the phenomenon was the product of the speaker's implied desire to have personal faith validated by an encounter with an objective spiritual presence.

In the next extract the speaker is describing an experience which occurred during a near fatal bout of pneumonia in his childhood.

Extract (8)   [YB 3:13]

```
1         so:: anyway (.5) when you're in bed that length o' time you don't
2         sleep regular hours like (.3) when you normally go to bed at nighty
3         yu' know if you've been up all day you go to bed you go to sleep (.)
4         hhhh an' you wake up in the morning (.)
5    X    an' ah musta bin do:zin' there or somethin'
6    Y    un u(h)r: suddenly this: light a very small light (.) must've started
7         playing s:i:lly devils
```

Prior to reporting the onset of the experience (in this case, a light which grew into an apparition of his dead father), the speaker has been reporting how prolonged illness disrupts everyday sleeping patterns. From this information it would be simple to claim that the experience was not an objective event, but the product of a illness-induced delirium, or a particularly vivid dream state caused by disrupted sleep patterns.

In each case, then, the speaker has furnished materials which could be cited as the warrant to dismiss the claim to have experienced something genuinely supernatural: the accounts themselves provide the basis for an alternative story which advances a non-paranormal explanation. The provision of the 'X' formulation, however, allows the speakers to do pragmatic work to minimize this possibility. So, by describing their routine circumstances, speakers ensure that a description of the phenomenon is not introduced directly after their own prior talk. Thus the material which could support a damaging assessment of the objectivity of the experience does not constitute an immediate narrative context for the first reference to the paranormal event. Furthermore, in these extracts the speakers have reformulated their own talk so as to provide for the routine character of their circumstances. And by emphasising the everyday features of their circumstances at the time they delete or transform precisely those materials from which a sceptical interpretation could be drawn. So for example, a lengthy report of contemplations about the evidential value of a direct encounter with a numinous force is summarized as 'I were just thinkin' And 'ah musta bin <u>do: zin</u>' there or somethin' is offered as the upshot of an account of the effects of a serious illness.

So far, we've looked at a class of recollections which certainly meet main criteria of flashbulb memories: recall of mundane circumstances at the time of the event and personal consequentiality of the experience. But close analysis of the actual descriptions indicates that the mundane character of circumstances at the time is an achievement. Moreover, this design property facilitates certain kinds of inferential work relevant to the production of warrantable claims about truly unusual and sometimes traumatic experiences. Both of these sets of observations seem to mitigate against an account of flashbulb memories as simple verbal representations of images or information stored passively in cognitive processes. However, it is important to bear in mind that X formulations are just the first part of a two part device. This broader structural organization provides further resources by which speakers can address the sceptical concerns about the objectivity of the phenomenon and their status as credible reporters.

Insertions in the 'I was just doing X . . . when Y' device

In the paranormal accounts corpus, there were a number of instances in which the speakers produce the first part of the 'X . . . then' device, but do not then move directly to the second part. Instead, either they extend their description of what they were doing at the time, or introduce new material. Only then do they complete the device with a reference to the paranormal phenomenon, or what turns out to be an anomalous event. Inspection of these inserted materials reveals that they are invariably designed to bolster the 'paranormality' of the story, either by defusing possible sceptical assessments of the story, or addressing alternative, non-paranormal accounts of the events being described.

For example, the veracity of a paranormal account may be questioned by raising the possibility that the experient simply misperceived mundane events and thus interpreted them to be indications of paranormal activity. Insertions between the two parts of the device can be used to address this. In the following case the speaker introduces the claim that she was 'right in front' of a part of her house relevant to the event being reported, thus establishing that she was in the best possible position to obtain a clear view.

Extract (9)   [HS 17]

```
1            ah came home from work at lunchtime
2            (1)
3            an' I walked into the sitting room door
4            (.)
5     X      in through the sitting room door
6            (1.5)
7            an::
8     ins.   right in front of me (.) was a sort of alcove (.)
9            and a chimney breast (.) like this (.7)
10    Y      and a photograph of our wedding
11           (1)
12           came off the top shelf (.2) floated down to the ground
13           hh completely came apart But didn't break
```

And again in the next case, the speaker inserts material which demonstrates that he was ideally positioned in the house to hear clearly the onset of what transpired to be a series of poltergeist activities.

Extract (10)   [ND 7:49]

```
1     S1     and then the disturbances started
2            (2.4)
3            the first thing we
4            (1.3)
5            really noticed was: (.5)
6            one night
7            (1.3)
8            in (.7)
9            I would think September
10    S2     yeah September -seventy six=
11    S1              -September
12    S2     =it would be
13    S2     yeah that's right
14           (1.5)
15    X      we were laid (.7) in the front bedroom
16    ins.   which was below the front attics
17           (1.5)
18    Y      and we heard a noise (.5)
19           like someone throwing gravel across
20           a piece of (.) hollow hardboard
```

As the previous extract shows, paranormal events sometimes occur when the experients are in bed getting ready to sleep. In such cases, the speakers' claims are vulnerable to the suggestion that the events they report are not objective and rooted in external reality, but vivid dream states or hypnogogic imagery at the onset of drowsiness. Inserted materials can be used to establish that although the speakers were indeed in bed, they were fully sentient at the time of the experience.

Extract (11)   [AN 17:31]

1		but <u>this</u> particule h) (er) it was- when ah had me he-
2		u- (.) b- bedhead (.) at that end so the m- window (.)
3		was behind me (we:r) so hh
4	**X**	an' (.) as I (.) was laid in bed (.7)
5	**ins.**	yuh know (.) sort uv propped up (.4)
6		>an ah thou (hh) ght< (.)
7		and it was <u>dark</u> (.) yuh know
8		i (t) sws er: I hadn't me curtains
9		drawn or anything
10	**Y**	hhh and (.) I saw this <u>glo:</u>w: (.3)
11		on the (ws) got rea<u>:lly</u> (.3)
12		glow (.3) on the wall up above

Extract (12)   [EM B 10]

1		I mean a simple example which everybody's had
2		something similar to hhhh I was living in uhm (.)
3		inglan years ago:
4		and all of a sudden
5	**X**	I was sitting in bed one night (.)
6	**ins.**	getting ready to go to sleep
7	**Y**	and I decided to write to a friend I hadn't seen
8		for four years (.) in Massachusetts (.) a:nd
9		I found myself congratulating her
10		on (.) the engagement of her oldest daughter

In these extracts the speakers construct 'X' formulations in terms of their position in bed: 'an' (.) as I (.) ws laid in bed' (extract 11, line 4), and 'I was sittin' in bed one night (extract 12, line 5). Both speakers then provide additional information: 'yuh know (.) sort uv propped up' (extract 11, line 5) and 'getting ready to go to sleep' (extract 12, line 6). This material is designed to reveal that the speakers were awake: for example, 'getting ready to go to sleep' orients to a stage of activity prior to sleep; also, 'propped up' in bed is the type of position in which one might read, but it is less likely to be a position in which one might sleep.

Why is it that such defensive materials are being inserted between the two parts of this device? There is a 'sensitive' character to the business dealt with by the production of these insertions: overt attempts to make the strongest and most plausible case for the truth of an account could itself be taken to imply that the account is, in some ways, intrinsically weak or unreliable. However, the 'X when Y' sequence is a single device, designed to be heard as a unit of two related utterances: the provision of an X component sets up the expectation of the forthcoming provision of the Y component. And, as we discussed earlier, this is one consequence of the use of the historical present tense over more passive tense formulations. This expectation ensures that directly after the provision of the 'X' component is an advantageous position in which to introduce sensitive material. Disrupting the format at this point ensures that material which is crucial to the account being produced acquires the character of 'parenthetical' or 'incidental' information. Thus insertions in the 'X then Y' device allow speakers to deal with issues relating to the credibility of the account, or the reliability of the witness, in such a way as to lessen the risk that the witness may be viewed as trying too hard to present a persuasive case.

Discussion

In this analysis we have examined what appears to be a class of flashbulb memory formulations from a perspective which emphasises the action oriented nature of language. It is worth spelling out how this approach begins to address many of the substantive and methodological issues raised by cognitive scientists working in this area of autobiographical memory.

Ecological validity of data

We noted earlier that a recurring theme in much of the recent cognitive science literature on flashbulb memories was the need for ecologically valid data: recollections which are not artificially produced via laboratory or experimental procedures. And although some may argue that the accounts of paranormal events are hardly naturally occurring, in that they were derived from informal interviews, the flashbulb memory formulations were unsolicited components produced as part of the broader activity of the telling of an extraordinary personal event. The speakers themselves employed these formulations to introduce into the narrative their first awareness of the phenomenon, or the onset of the experience.[4] The interviews were not organized to harvest instances of this form of description. The corpus thus provide instances of flashbulb memories in their natural environments: they are real life instances of the phenomenon in question.

The corpus of paranormal stories is unusual by virtue of the strange nature of the experiences being recounted; but it is utterly normal in that its collection provides the possibility to analyze hitherto unanticipated kinds of discourse practices, such as memory accounts.

The emphasis on naturally occurring data in conversation analysis and other approaches to discourse studies has resulted in the collection of several corpora of recordings of everyday telephone calls and face-to-face interaction. Many of these corpora have become widely available. Researchers have access to these established corpora, in addition to other data sets collected for their own research purposes. There is, then, a vast stock of data which can be investigated to identify memory formulation and the ways in which they are produced and managed. Equally, these data provide rich materials for the analysis of the ways in which interactional matters attendant upon memory recollections are addressed (see for example, Drew, 1989). But these kind of data are uncompromising: participants are concerned with their matters, and talk about things of consequence to them, and in ways relevant to them, not the researcher. But careful attention to these data sets can yield dividends.

The following extract comes from a corpus of naturally occurring telephone conversations recorded in England in the late 1980s. The participants, L and T, are having an ordinary chat about friends, relatives, and so on: the features of this conversation are quite spontaneous. Immediately prior to this extract, L has asked about T's 'haunting', a reference to mysterious events in a house belonging to one of T's friends. T replies that nothing untoward has occurred recently, but then goes on to say:

Extract (13)   Holt: J86:1:2:4]

T:		It's quite funny actually cuz there's someb'dy up the road I wz talking to an' uh (.2) sh'reckoned tha(.)t uh: he he bought th'house b't'er bought it off his sister.
		(.5)
T:	**X**	A-n' iz sister wz: uh gettin' ready one night t'go out.
L:		-Yes.
T:	**ins**	She hadn't been hhinking hhh
	Y	an' the hairspray apparently lifted itself up 'n went t'the other side a' the dressing table.

There are several interesting features of this extract. First, this is an instance of the 'X then Y' device produced by a speaker when recounting *someone else's* paranormal experience. This certainly attests to Neisser's (1982b) argument that formulations of the flashbulb type owe more to culturally organized communicative competencies than information stored away in the brain by neurophysiological processes. Second, this is a very neat conversational instance of the 'X when Y' device which exhibits many of the features identified earlier. There is, for example, an instance of the contingent relationship between the design of the state formulation and what the paranormal experience turned out to be. That is, 'gettin' ready one night t'go out' is neatly fitted to the phenomenon of the levitating hairspray, an item likely to be at hand when a young woman is preparing for an evening out. And there is also an insertion between the two components of the device which is transparently designed to minimize the possibility of a sceptical response to the story: it works to preserve the integrity of the event as a tellable story.

Corpora of conversational interaction are fairly easy to obtain. Certain kinds of institutional data sets can be recorded from television or radio broadcasts. These materials provide real instances of memories being produced in various kinds of interactional circumstances. There is no guarantee that the data will even contain instances of memory production. Moreover, what instances there are will have to be located through careful examination of tapes and transcripts. But there can be no more ecologically valid source of data for cognitive scientists interested in verbal reports of autobiographical memories.

The functions of memory formulations

Pillemer's (1992) discussion of the functional aspects of flashbulb memories argued first that there has been too much emphasis upon the apparent accuracy of the recall and not enough attention paid to the ways in which they can be used as a form of persuasion. At the heart of his argument is the claim that we use flashbulb memories to achieve specific kinds of interpersonal or psychodynamic goals. Crucially, he supports Barsalou's claim that people may employ narrative styles in verbal recollections that 'do not reflect underlying memory organisation but instead reflect various cultural and linguistic conventions' (Barsalou, 1988:217). This is a bold step but we can take it further: why bother with underlying memory organization at all? If we are seriously concerned with ecologically valid data then we have to focus on recollections produced in naturally occurring settings, be they verbal or textual. Given the vast array of events which may be recalled, the cognitive scientist has little chance to verify the accuracy of any particular memory formulation with the event itself. If verification is impossible, it makes little sense to try to track the cognitive operations which might lead to the internal codification and storage of information. But more important, the analysis in this chapter indicates that, at least for flashbulb formulations which occur in stories of paranormal phenomena, their defining characteristic is that they are usable resources to deal with latent or actual scepticism attendant upon claims to have experienced supernatural phenomena. In various ways, they allow the speaker to warrant the credibility of the story, either by establishing the objectivity and 'out-there-ness' (Woolgar, 1980) of the phenomenon, or by portraying themselves as ordinary reporters of extraordinary things.

And this use of the 'X then Y' formulations is not restricted to accounts of paranormal occurrences. The following extract appeared in a newspaper story compiled by a war correspondent who witnessed the death of one of his colleagues, and was dictated by him over the telephone to the newspaper.

They were just relaxing when another car-load of journalists arrived. It was a Dutch crew: Cornel Lagrouw, a cameraman . . . with his wife Annelise. . . . We all knew each other so it was fun to see them.
[X] We were just taking pictures of the guerillas,
[Y] when all of a sudden gunfire rang out . . .
(S. Wallace, 'The Guardian', 21 March, 1989:24.)

The X and Y flashbulb formulation is utterly enmeshed in the subtle dynamics of interpersonal business. It is designed to have the features it displays because this is one method for doing 'being ordinary' (Sacks, 1984).

Until recently memory research has focused on the veridicality of memory processes. However, cognitive scientists such as Neisser, Pillemer and Barsalou are pressing for a more sustained analysis of the ways in which memory formulations are produced in discourse and the kinds of functions they are designed to achieve. Given their overriding focus on the action orientation of language and interaction, conversation analysts and other discourse scholars are best placed to contribute to, and indeed carry forwards this work.

Towards a 'grammar' of memorial expression

In his discussion of the various functions of flashbulb memories, Pillemer suggested that:

Effective communication requires that memories be shared in accordance with a system of rules, a *grammar* of memorial expression, that has yet to be fully described. (Pillemer, 1992: 242; original italics)

We might not be able to locate a grammar of memory production in the same way that we can identify the determinate formal rules which govern sentence structure. But discourse scholars can begin to describe the system of socially organized communicative compentencies which inform the ways in which verbal expressions or memory formulations are produced as part of the weave of everyday discourse. Thus we can begin to locate the discursive contexts of memory production: what kinds of discursive activities occasion memory formulations; and how do these formulations shape the subsequent trajectory of interaction? Moreover, we can begin to get a sense of the normative and inferential orientations which are embodied in the production of memory formulations.

This raises intriguing possibilities. Flashbulb memories are one type of autobiographical memory: and to borrow the title of Barclay and DeCooke's (1988) article, such ordinary every day memories in narratives are 'some of the things of which selves are made' (Barclay and DeCooke, 1988: 91–125).

In recent years, there have been a number of studies which have examined how categorizations of self and others be accomplished with respect to interactional and inferential concerns generated from the trajectory of verbal exchanges (Antaki and Widdicombe, 1998; Hester and Eglin, 1997; Stokoe and Smithson, 2001; Widdicombe and Wooffitt, 1995). Within this literature, however, there has been little explicit attention to the ways in which accounts of memories may be used as resources by which to do identity work. A conversation and discourse analytic investigation of the way in which constructions of identity are managed by autobiographical memory formulations would significantly advance our understanding of the ways in which identity concerns are managed in everyday discourse.

Conclusion

We have, then, an opportunity to fashion anew the study of a defining feature of human behaviour. Conversation analytic methods, and the orientations of discursive psychology, allow us to develop the lines of enquiry suggested by researchers in cognitive science. There can be no better kind of ecologically valid data than instances of memory formulations which occur spontaneously in naturally occurring everyday interaction and institutional discourse. There are no methods of analysis better suited to the need to examine the functional or dynamic nature of verbalized recollections. And no other analytic approach seeks a systematic description of the web of normative, socially organized competencies which inform ordinary conduct: the everyday grammar of memorial expression. If we begin to analyze memory work, rather than the cognitive basis of information storage and retrieval, then we will be taking a key step towards a postcognitive understanding of memories.

NOTES

1. However, Conway, 1995, offers a critical analysis, arguing that the stimulus event has to be *personally* consequential to the respondents/subjects, and that this was not established in the *Challenger* studies.
2. There is also growing focus on the influence of conversation roles on the production of memories. See Hirst and Gluck, 1999; Hirst and Manier, 1996; Keenan *et al.*, 1982.
3. For a more detailed treatment of this phenomenon see Wooffitt, 1992, pp. 117–54.
4. Besides which, these informal interviews are precisely the kinds of data collected as part of parapsychological projects on spontaneous happenings: for example, see Hufford, 1982.

10 'My memory has been shredded': a non-cognitivist investigation of 'mental' phenomena

Michael Lynch and David Bogen

Introduction

In the cognitive sciences, activities like seeing, remembering, recognizing, learning, problem solving and decision making tend to be treated as individual processes for recording, retrieving and configuring information. Everyday actions are regarded as surface behaviours which are caused by underlying mental and neurological processes; processes that are often masked by the contingencies of everyday situations and the referential ambiguities of ordinary language. Technological advances in the ability to visualize the interior of the skull have reinforced the tendency to pursue cognitive processes into the recesses of the mind-brain.

Although fuelled by impressive neuroscientific breakthroughs, the philosophy of mind that animates cognitive science has been criticized for more than a half century by Wittgensteinians and ordinary language philosophers. In his later philosophy, Wittgenstein (1958) rejects the presumption that thinking, knowing, giving reasons, looking, seeing, and so forth, are products of internal mental mechanisms. He does not propose a competing causal explanation of thought, mind and knowledge, but instead he explicates how 'mental' concepts (like other everyday concepts) are grounded in communicative actions produced by competent members of a linguistic community. To the extent that they pay any attention to such arguments, proponents of cognitive science typically dismiss them as out of date and unscientific, but as Button et al. (1995) argue, Wittgensteinian and ordinary language arguments are as pertinent as ever. It is not our purpose to review such arguments, but we believe they have profound implications for empirical investigations of the embodied and discursive activities through which persons look for things, report what they see, recall the past, or forget significant details. The approach we recommend does not necessarily comprise an alternative sociological or discursive approach to *cognition*, because it challenges the very idea that a coherent array of abstract processes subsumes the range of actions and expressions associated with seeing, thinking, knowing, remembering, and so forth. In this chapter we take up a common topic of cognitive research – memory – and we suggest a non-cognitivist way to investigate particular situations in which recollections and failures to recall become perspicuous and contentious. This investigation does not compete with cognitive science. Instead, it takes up a topic that has been appropriated by that science and gives it a radically different treatment. Our programmatic attitude toward cognitive science is one of indifference, not competition.

Investigating everyday cognition

Not all psychologists share a narrow view of cognition as internal mental states and/or neurological processes. In fact, some of the most influential investigations address visual perception, remembering, and other so-called cognitive processes in naturalistic and 'ecological' settings (Gibson, 1986; Neisser, 1982; Loftus, 1979). Hutchins' (1995) recent efforts to capture cognition 'in the wild' by studying the collective, communicative production of tasks like ship navigation, represents a further move in the direction of an anthropology of cognitive activities. In a reciprocal movement, a growing number of social interactionists, discourse analysts, activity theorists and conversation analysts have investigated communicative practices in which perception, memory, classification and learning are situated (Chaiklin and Lave, 1993; Bowker and Star, 1999; Edwards and Potter, 1992; Goodwin and Ueno, 2000).

Despite this convergent interest in everyday cognition, the common terrain is hotly contested: where cognitivists tend to stress the primacy of an underlying information processing system, sociologists and anthropologists stress discourse, communicative action and cultural practice. While we tend to side with those who take a pragmatic and communicative approach, we hold that a deeper problem is obscured by contests over the appropriate empirical site, or unit of analysis, for addressing cognition. In our view, it is not enough to *relocate* perception, memory, classification, and the like, from a neuropsychological space to a socio-communicative space. What is in the offing is not 'an alternative geography of cognition' (Goodwin, 2000b: 33), because the concept of 'cognition' itself is likely to be dissolved in the course of the displacement from an abstract space of mental representation to a contexture of communicative practices. In this chapter we examine actions and locutions associated with memory in a particular organizational and historical setting. Memory is, of course, one of the main topics of cognitive science. The point of the investigation is not to place 'cognition' in a social, as opposed to psychological, domain, but to elucidate contextual uses of remembering and forgetting, the intelligibility of which owes nothing to an overarching concept of 'cognition'. Our empirical approach derives from ethnomethodology (Garfinkel, 1967; 1991) and studies of everyday interaction (Sacks, 1992). In summary, the approach involves three strategies for addressing selected 'cognitive' topics: (1) investigate one or more of the topics associated with cognitive science (perception, memory, etc.) by locating organized social settings in which those topics feature as perspicuous phenomena (Garfinkel and Wieder, 1992), (2) examine how the intelligibility of actions and expressions associated with these phenomena are bound to interactional, pragmatic and political contexts, and (3) treat assessments about what goes on in a speaker's mind as themselves part of the social interactional field of production.

(1) National scandals and perspicuous phenomena

In recent decades, US national politics have involved a series of public scandals: Watergate, the Iran-Contra affair, the Impeachment and Senate trial of President Clinton, and, most recently, the contest over the results of the year 2000 Presidential election. Each of these scandals involved one or more nationally broadcast tribunals, and it is fair to say that the scandals, and the media spectacles that accompanied them, have become a primary means of conducting US politics. Such spectacles are sometimes characterized (optimistically to be sure) as 'civics lessons'. Incidentally, perhaps, they also provide public tutorials on topics of interest to ethnomethodology: a field that investigates the ways in which members of a society accomplish and reflexively address the practical 'methodologies' through which their social affairs are organized (Garfinkel, 1967; 1991). In this chapter, we focus upon the 1987 Joint House-Senate investigation of the Iran-contra affair (see Lynch and Bogen, 1996). The investigation involved nationally televised hearings in which various US government officials gave testimony about covert weapons sales by the US to Iran, and the 'diversion' of profits from those sales to aid counterrevolutionary forces in Central America – both of which were charged with contravening official US policies. The Iran-contra hearings highlighted the 'memories' of particular witnesses by providing a public occasion for witnesses to recall past events. Equally important for our purposes, the dialogues between interrogators and witnesses included enquiries into, and explications of, 'memory'. Unlike the Watergate hearings a decade and a half earlier, in which former White House counsel John Dean gave profuse testimony (whether accurate or not) about scandalous dealings, the key Iran-contra witnesses, and especially Oliver North, seemed to have very bad memories for certain key events. Moreover, as North admitted openly to doing, he and some of his colleagues shredded a mass of White House documents, presumably containing memoranda that would have been material to the committees' investigation. Consequently, Oliver North's testimony provided a perspicuous example of a common, if perverse, political grammar of (non)recollection. Our investigation of this perspicuous phenomenon demonstrates how actions and expressions associated with memory are logically organized, practically managed and dialogically orientated.

(2) Contextual organizations of memory in testimony

There is a heterogeneous array of expressions for remembering, forgetting, recollecting, reminding and recalling. Though less confusing, perhaps, than the impressively large array of perceptual verbs, which range from seeing, looking and scrutinizing, through to ogling, peering and perusing (Coulter and Parsons, 1991), 'memory' concepts also exhibit striking grammatical and contextual differences. To a limited extent, psychologists like Bartlett (1932), Loftus (1979) and Neisser (1981) recognize that memory is not a simple mechanical process analogous to the operations of a tape recorder or camera, and they pursue naturalistic investigations of the modes and modalities of remembering, forgetting and recounting the past. However, their research retains the idealization of memory as a coherent group of internal mental processes, and they neither investigate, nor show much interest in, the conceptual differentiation of terms and the contextual organization of practices associated with remembering, forgetting, recalling, etc.

Neisser's (1981) study of John Dean's recollections during the Watergate hearings provides an instructive case. Neisser was able to review Dean's testimony about meetings at the White House with President Richard Nixon and compare Dean's recollections to tape recordings of those meetings that had been secretly recorded at Nixon's behest, and later released to Watergate investigators after a protracted struggle. Neisser demonstrates convincingly that Dean's recollections differed substantially from the relevant tape recordings, but he does not fault Dean for the discrepancies. Nor does he excuse Dean's inaccuracies by reference to the normal fallibility of human memory. Instead, he questions the adequacy of the idea that memory is organized like a camera or tape recorder, and he argues that Dean retrospectively reconstructed the gist of specific meetings in a way that, for the most part, was adequate and honest, if not literally accurate. The White House tapes had not yet been released to the investigating committees, and so Neisser had a material advantage that Dean's interrogators and audiences lacked at the time. Neisser used the tape recordings of the meetings as an accurate record of the meetings that Dean professed to recall. This correspondence procedure worked effectively to expose numerous differences between tapes and recollections of the 'same' events, and it enabled Neisser to develop a strong criticism of simpler, mechanical models of memory. What his procedure failed to elucidate was how Dean's interrogators and audience elicited, tested and assessed his testimony. Dean's interrogators did make use of (arguably) independent records and other testimonies to elicit, challenge, test, impugn and corroborate Dean's testimony, and such moves were constitutive of the testimony itself (Molotch and Boden, 1985). However, unlike Neisser, who was able to compare two historical documents (transcripts of Dean's testimony and the White House tapes), Dean and his interrogators generated an ongoing, and highly contentious, dialogue, which was made up of avowals of recall, references to independent documents, and claims and counterclaims about gaps and contradictions. Memory was a highly salient theme in the dialogue, but it came into play in connection with a circumstantially specific array of methods for describing, documenting and challenging stories about the witness's past. Though valuable for purposes of criticizing a 'memory drum' model in the psychology of memory, Neisser's analytic procedure bypasses an investigation of how avowals and assessments of recall were embedded in the surface of testimony. He performs a detached and idealized assessment of Dean's accuracy and honesty that parallels, and to an extent competes with, the contentious assessments that animated the very dialogues he analyzed (Edwards and Potter, 1992). It is the latter, constitutive investigation of 'memory' that interests us in our examination of Oliver North's testimony at the Iran-contra hearings.

(3) Assessments of 'mind' as internal to dialogue

Unlike Neisser, we are in no position to compare Oliver North's testimony at the 1987 hearings with the meetings and other events described in his testimony. The official investigations of the Iran-contra affair, and numerous journalistic sources, furnished documents and testimonies that could be used to impugn many of North's stories, but for the most part there was nothing comparable to the detailed records supplied by the White House tapes in the case of Dean's Watergate testimony. Like virtually all other official and unofficial auditors of North's testimony, we had no independent access to his past experiences. This lack of independent access was not simply a disadvantage, however, as it alerted us to a characteristic feature of testimony. For us, and presumably for many in North's audience, there is no way to check his testimony against some independent record of correspondingly real events, or to assess the extent to which his descriptions faithfully reported what he saw 'in his mind's eye'. Nevertheless, his testimony was intelligible and susceptible to a variety of methods for assessing its sincerity, veracity and rhetorical effectiveness.

Given the absence of independent access – a common situation for the audience in a tribunal – our comprehension of what North said about the past did not depend upon an ability to trace his words back to contents of his mind or to compare them to actual incidents in the world outside the courtroom. Instead, we heard what he said in relation to what he had been asked and the possible implications of possible answers for his (or his party's) 'case'. The salience of memory, and the credibility of what he recalled, was situated in a field of organizational logics and relevancies. Clearly, the open texture of relevancies that came into play would confound any effort to make strictly controlled observations. However, ambiguity did not simply preclude certainty about the contents of North's testimony. Instead, his production and uses of ambiguity, and his interrogators' pursuit of (alleged) ambiguities, were themselves constitutive of the testimony. Consequently, we were able to examine the shifting fates of memory claims, and to describe the interactional and textual leverage used by interrogators and witnesses to highlight and suppress particular relevancies. To the extent that machineries, devices or procedures came into play, they were not mental or even interpretative, but discursive and interactional.

The 'contra-mantra': non-recall and plausible deniability

Many of the key witnesses at the Iran-contra hearings repeatedly answered interrogators' questions by saying that they could not recall the relevant incidents and details. A popular magazine dubbed this recurrence of non-recall 'the contra mantra'. In North's testimony, for example, there are numerous instances of such phrases as 'I don't recall', 'I don't recall at all', 'I can't recall a specific date', 'I don't have a specific recall of that at this time point', 'I guess- and I don't remember', 'I don't think so, I mean you may refresh my memory', and most famously, 'My memory has been shredded'. Not unreasonably, many commentators suspected that North and his National Security Council staff colleagues were dissembling. The problem was to judge whether or not any given recollection, or non-recollection, was credible.

Howard Horwitz (1988: 788) noted that 'as is typical in conspiracy investigations, faultiness of memory was frequent testimony that summer and was the Reagan administration's main defence strategy', and he added that 'the reliance of memory, so resolutely unreliable, along with the destruction of evidence which made vagaries of memory so crucial, obstructed reconstructing and interpreting events, and ensured the hearing's close would resound with the sentiment that, we will probably never know what really happened in the affair'. This conclusion later was underlined with the release of the Special Prosecutor's report (Walsh, 1994), which was widely heralded as having turned up little 'new' information after years of expensive effort to secure documents, leverage testimony from key parties and draw definite conclusions about the involvement of the key administrative figures. As Horwitz (1988: 788) put it, it seemed as though '[h]istory was not, as it were, happening'.

Together with the destruction of documents that permitted 'deniability' (the fabrication of minimally plausible cover stories), avowals of non-recall facilitated a familiar evasive strategy. An interesting thing about this strategy is that the parties involved in its operation were able to deny – often in the most self-righteous way – *that* they were evading or were conducting a strategy. Even more interestingly, parties who admitted having set up 'plausible deniability', also managed to deny (plausibly?) that it covered the particular things that they were just now saying. North, for example, at one point reacted to a remark by his interrogator John Nields, after Nields suggested that North had shredded records from his office 'so that you can later say you don't remember, whether you had 'em, and you don't remember what's in 'em'.

> Nouth: I came here to tell you the truth. To tell you:: and this committee, and the American people the truth, and I'm trying to do that Mister Nields, and I don't like the insinuation that I'm up here having a convenient memory lapse, like perhaps some others have had. (North testimony, 7 July 1987, ML/DB transcript)

Despite his ringing invocation of truth, the fact that key documents were unavailable for inspection, because they were shredded by North and his colleagues in anticipation of just this sort of enquiry, seriously compromised the Committees' 'fact-finding' work. It is in this sense that North can be credited with being an applied deconstructionist who, having placed a documentary field 'under erasure', is then in a position to testify to the undecideability of that field's substantive historical reality.

The social logic of memory

In a courtroom hearing (or in this case a congressional tribunal) non-recall presents a difficult problem for interrogators, because it defeats the binary logic of yes-and-no type questions (cf., McHoul, 1987). This fact is not lost on defendants and their legal representatives. A perspicuous instance of this is described in an anecdote from a book about prison life. Roger Braithwaite is described as a 'shrewd jail-house lawyer . . . a gravel-voiced, gray-haired, forty-nine-year old armed robber who looked and spoke like a college professor'. He was a lay advisor for inmates in disciplinary committee hearings within the penitentiary.

If he went to court and the committee chairman denied his request to speak on his client's behalf, Braithwaite had other ways of communicating. He stroked his beard to tell a client to say 'yes', he tugged his ear for 'no', and drummed his fingers on the table for 'I don't remember'. (Hoffman and McCoy, 1981: 139)

When reduced to such a gestural code, 'yes', 'no', and 'I don't remember' become tokens in a primitive language game. By calling this game 'primitive', we do not mean to attribute atavistic qualities to Braithwaite and his clients, but to speak of a simplified, restricted and recurrent form of language-use. Wittgenstein (1958: para. 5) recommends that it 'disperses the fog to study the phenomena of language in primitive kinds of application in which one can command a clear view of the aim and functioning of the words'. Unlike 'yes' or 'no', the answer 'I don't remember' neither confirms, nor denies the event in question. In legal terms, the witness becomes 'practically unavailable' (Graham, 1978: 170), for the moment withdrawn from the task of generating substantive testimony. The following fragment from the North testimony exemplifies and explicates the logic of this 'practical unavailability'.

Nields: Did you suggest to the Attorney General that maybe the diversion memorandum and the fact that there was a diversion need not ever come out?
North: Again, I don't recall that specific conversation at all, but I'm not saying it didn't happen.
Nields: You don't deny it?
North: No.
Nields: You don't deny suggesting to the Attorney General of the United States that he just figure out a way of keeping this diversion document secret?
North: I don't deny that I said it. I'm not saying I remember it either.

(North,1987:33)

As North so clearly states, he is neither confirming nor denying the description of the event presented to him. This does not give the witness a completely free hand. As Ekman observes, a 'memory failure is credible only in limited circumstances'. He gives the example of a doctor, who when 'asked if the tests were negative can't claim not to remember' (Ekman, 1985: 30). Ekman adds that in order to be plausible, such a claimed memory loss must be associated with a relatively insignificant event (as viewed by the witness at the time), combined with an appropriate passage of time between that event and the present testimony. Some events, according to Ekman (1985: 31), are so extraordinary that 'anyone would be expected to recall [them] no matter when they happened'.

Ekman's account is suggestive, but it misses some key considerations. Significance is often contestable. North and other witnesses often claimed that particular meetings, documents, and the like, which seemed highly significant in light of the later scandal and investigation, were not significant at the time they occurred. In this case a conception of what would have been salient for the particular persons involved in the original scene may be less pertinent than an assessment of the public responsibilities assigned to relevant types of actor. The question is not 'what might North have remembered or forgotten'; rather, it is 'what can he get away with saying'. Instead of imputing a lay psychology of memory to North's overhearing audience, it might make more sense to speak of a lay sociology of occupational categories and moral responsibilities. The doctor in Ekman's example 'can't claim not to remember' the results of particular tests, because it is a doctor's legal and professional responsibility to keep a record of such tests and to report them in a timely fashion to the relevant parties. To claim to forget under such circumstances does not effectively contest the conventional understanding of what a doctor should do. This has less to do with psychology than with legal regulations and public standards of accountability that apply to particular occupational categories and their record keeping practices.

It may seem natural for Ekman to draw a connection between what a speaker says and the operations of that individual's memory, but saying that one forgets or does not remember something often implies more about the 'something' in question than about the 'state' of the speaker's memory. In some contexts saying 'I don't recall' differs significantly from saying 'I forget' or 'I forgot' (although it does seem equivalent to 'I don't remember'). As Coulter (1985: 132) points out, saying that one forgot something makes a retrospective knowledge claim. For example, saying 'I forgot that today is our anniversary' acknowledges the substantive existence and relevance of *what* had been forgotten. Saying, 'I don't recall that we've met', makes no such presumption about a past meeting; indeed, such an utterance may strongly imply that there was no such meeting.

Although it may be the case that Ekman confuses a (lay) psychology of memory with the conventional and legal demands on specified categories of social actors, it is also the case that such a confusion was encouraged by Iran-contra participants when they were asked to recall particular meetings and actions in which the arms sales to Iran and related actions may have been discussed and approved. Reagan and others gave variants of what might be called 'the breakfast defence': 'How would you be expected to know what you had for breakfast on a particular date six months ago?' Such a defence relies upon a credulous audience to forget that the relevant mode of recollection for a bureaucratic official is to consult the files and retrieve the appropriate records. (At the White House, even what the President has for breakfast on a given morning is likely to be recorded for posterity.) In the particular case of the Iran-contra hearings, the plausibility of the breakfast defence (in accordance with the policy of plausible deniability) was perversely aided and abetted by the prior shredding of possible minutes for key meetings, authorizing documents and other memoranda. Such destruction amounted to a particular kind of forgetting. The point is that lay and professional assessments of witness's 'memory' need to be placed in the context of a social-logic of testimony, where category-specific avowals of rights and responsibility establish what can or cannot be recollected.

Memory is a key theme in testimony, but the immediate issue is not how a witness's mind actually operates. Instead it is what the witness *says* he remembers, forgets, remembers only in part, or remembers in light of later events, and what the audience accepts or rejects as credible and plausible. Some witnesses (like John Dean, of Watergate fame, and John Poindexter, of Iran-contra) were reputed to have very fine, and even 'photographic', memories, whereas others (like President Reagan) were not, and such reputations became relevant to public assessments of their testimony. In the context of a tribunal, individual memory is relevant, but only in connection with an open array of normative judgements.

Counterfactual conditionals and the moral grammar of recall

A witness's failure to recall loosens the logical constraints imposed by a series of yes-and-no type questions, but interrogators are still able to press on by raising normative claims about what a witness – or just this particular witness – *should* or *should not* recall about their own pasts. An assessment of a witness's credibility, and of the plausibility of what he recalls, is tied to public criteria, arguments and moral judgements. These do not necessarily make up a stable and inflexible body of normative standards shared by members of a community, because they are brought into play singularly, rhetorically and contestably. However definite or uncertain, their relevance is such as to complicate a cognitivist explanation of particular instances of remembering and forgetting. This is because the salience of memory per se is subordinate to the social-logic of testimony. Consider, for example, the role of counterfactual conditionals in speakers' recollections of the past. In his discussion of the ability to extend a number series (such as 2, 4, 6, 8, . . .) Wittgenstein observes that when we speak of what we knew in the past, we are not always recalling a concrete incident or experience.

When you said 'I already knew at the time . . .' that meant something like: 'If I had then been asked what number should be written after 1000, I should have replied "1002".' And that I don't doubt. This assumption is rather of the same kind as: 'If he had fallen into the water then, I should have jumped in after him.' (Wittgenstein, 1958: §187)

Wittgenstein draws analogies between a knowledge claim ('I already knew at the time . . .'), an arithmetical competency, and a disposition to perform an appropriate action under the circumstances. None of these dispositional claims *represents* an actual past experience; rather, each asserts what the speaker was able to do, or would have done, but in fact did not do at the particular time. The example, 'If he had fallen into the water then, I should have jumped in after him', is especially relevant to the present discussion, because we can imagine the speaker saying it to defend against an accusation of negligence in the aftermath of a drowning. The speaker acknowledges that he did not in fact jump in the water after the victim because, e.g., he arrived too late or had left the scene before the victim took the plunge. This defence takes the form of a counterfactual conditional: an avowal of what the speaker would, should, or could have done under conditions that did not in fact obtain at the time. Counterfactual conditionals are often used when persons speak of what they understood, intended, knew, or were disposed to do, under conditions that did not in fact occur (Budd, 1984: 312).

Witnesses often use counterfactual conditionals when responding to interrogators' questions about the past. Such conditional expressions do not simply bring memories into play, but they are relevant in a broader sense to what can be recalled about one's past. They implicate a speaker's entitlements to experience and responsibilities for past activities. By closely examining how recall is performed in testimony, we can begin to see that recalling the past is not limited to accurate or inaccurate recounting of experienced events. Especially in an adversary interrogation, the parties to the interrogation struggle to place the witness in a past that implicates differential entitlements, responsibilities and implications of guilt or innocence. The recollected details may attain a stable or temporary status as memorable, inferential, speculative and contestable, but the overall sensibility of an assemblage of details is inescapably moral. For example, consider the following sequence from North's interrogation:

(7 July 1987, Afternoon Session, ML/DB transcript):

Nields: Were you ever told that the president had authorized the TOW shipment to proceed?
North: I was at some point, yes
Nields: To the best of your recollection, when?
          (2.0)
North: Well, I know I was told that in eighty-six as I was preparing the chronologies, I was probably told that in eighty-five or I would've asked more questions than I did about it.
          (1.4)
Nields: (Who)
          [
North: I don't recall specifically.

Here we find North working backwards from an acknowledged event ('I was told that in eighty-six') to an earlier time where he infers what he knew on the basis of what he would have done if he had *not* known ('I was probably told that in eighty-five or I would've asked more questions than I did about it'). By his account, if he had not known in 1985 that the President had authorized the TOW missile sale to Iran, he would have enquired about the warrant for executing the deal. The matter of fact – or in this case the matter of probable fact – is implicated by what he recalls *not doing*. This is a variant of Wittgenstein's example 'if he had fallen into the water then, I should have jumped in after him'. In this case North can be paraphrased as saying 'if I had not known at the time that the deal was authorized, I would have asked more questions about it'. Although the utterance takes the form of a recollection, it is not a recollection of an experience. Rather, it is a reconstruction of a past catalyzed by a counterfactual claim to the effect that the speaker *would have been* disposed to act appropriately in the situation. In this case North's recollection is crystallized around a moral claim to the effect that he is not the sort of person who would act without first securing proper authorization.

Even when witnesses do not use counterfactual conditionals when formulating their answers, an utterance like 'I don't remember' or 'I don't recall' may be intelligible as a conditional expression, rather than an acknowledgement of a faulty or incomplete memory of a past event. Take, for instance the following sequence of testimony from a rape case described by Paul Drew (1992: 478) ('C' is counsel for the defence, and

'W' is the witness/victim under cross-examination).

C: An a' tha: t <u>time</u> (0.3) he: asked ya to go ou:t with yu (0.4) isn't that c'rect.
      (2.1)
W: Yea[h
          [
C: [with h<u>i</u>m. Isn't that so?
      (2.6)
W: Ah don't remember

Drew argues that in this instance 'I don't remember' side steps any implication of the event having been a significant occurrence (if it occurred at all).

Quite apart from what cognitively one can or can't remember, stating that one doesn't remember such details can be to treat them as details one wouldn't remember. By saying that she is unable to recall them now, in court, the witness can exhibit her having taken no account of such matters *at the time*. They are not recallable now because then they were not things she noticed: which is to say that 'not remembering' something gives a kind of status to it, as unmemorable because it was unnoticed. (Drew 1992: 479)

That the event was unmemorable-because-unnoticed can imply that it was unnoticeable, perhaps because it became significant only in light of later events or because it never happened in the first place. To say 'I don't remember' thus can act as a display of innocence. As Drew (1992) points out, such a disavowal can imply the standpoint of an innocent observer who at the time the event occurred had no idea of its later significance. Moreover, if it is assumed that this witness, or any witness like her, should have noticed and remembered something as significant as 'being asked out', the disavowal of recall can imply that the event never occurred. Less charitable suppositions can also apply. A juror might, perhaps, decide that the witness was so blasé about her sexual relationships that getting asked out on a date would mean nothing special to her. In such a case, her failure to recall would be taken as prejudicial to her identity as a classic rape victim. Audience complicity is required for upholding the plausibility of an 'innocent' standpoint, since the display of innocence implied by the story can seem credible or incredible depending on the audience's overall assessment of the case.

Conclusion

In this brief discussion, we began with a particular 'cognitive' theme – memory – and situated it in a particular investigative context. This context was 'investigative' in a double sense: in the first instance, the Iran-contra hearings *consisted* of an investigation in which parties solicited, produced, examined and disputed written memoranda and spoken recollections, and, secondarily, it was a topic for our investigation in this chapter. Instead of delving into the mental origins of a witness's recollections and assessing their accuracy, we described how they were bound up with the procedures and moral assessments of an interrogative investigation. Such assessments were moral in the commonplace sense that they involved claims and judgements about the witness's character (how he *would* act, as well as how he had acted) and about what someone like him *should* have recalled as well as what he, singularly, did or did not recall. We argued that there are certain things that, in particular circumstances, incumbents of agent-categories *cannot* (are not allowed to) forget. The possibilities of remembering and forgetting are thus logically bound to assessments of particular persons and agent-categories, and are associated with judgements about plausibility and credibility and defences against accusation.

We also mentioned how commonplace understandings of what plausibly could be recollected or forgotten entered into the production and assessment of testimony. Only in certain respects did this involve folk psychology, since it included understandings of what someone might be talking about, what such a person could legitimately claim to know, and what the person is entitled to do as a member of specific cultural categories. This was as much a matter of 'mundane reasoning' as of folk psychology (Pollner, 1987).

The particular study we described is only one of a large number of studies that, in Garfinkel's (1991) terms, aim to 'respecify' familiar topics in the study of social order, so that they become perspicuous phenomena in specific situations of action. This injunction can be extended to cover the recurrent topics of cognitive science: perception, attention, memory, learning, problem solving, reasoning, representation, etc. (Coulter, 1991). To respecify them means to show how these topics feature in actual conduct, not just as situated 'acts' of remembering and forgetting, but also as situated inquiries, and strategic anticipations of such inquiries, on the workings and vagaries of recall.

Investigations of situated activities – in this case, of a witness under interrogation recollecting the past – are instances of 'epistemic sociology' (Coulter, 1990). These are not investigations of 'cognition' in the established sense of that term, because they do not respect the integrity and topical coherence of a 'cognitive' domain. 'Cognitive' actions like remembering and forgetting are of a piece with other communicative actions like answering questions, telling stories and demanding explanations for problematic conduct. Although such actions can be interesting in their own right, and challenging to explicate, there is no necessity to isolate them in an abstract domain that traces back to a mental and/or neurological substrate. Consequently, our approach is both more and less inclusive than a cognitivist investigation of memory. It is more inclusive because it treats memory in relation to an open range of organized activities. It is less inclusive because it does not examine memory as an entire domain, but instead examines specific interactions in which spoken recollections and written memoranda are used as accountable features of an organized setting.

Ethnomethodological studies of activities in science and daily life describe complex language games, organizational circumstances, record keeping practices and distributions of knowledge (see Garfinkel, 1967; Lynch, 1985; Suchman, 1987; Button, 1993). It is difficult to integrate this line of research with cognitive science, because the nominal points of contact (remembering, seeing, etc.) are embedded in entirely different understandings of what is relevant to investigate and how an investigation should proceed. Moreover, ethnomethodological studies *topicalize* as well as pursue investigations. In this chapter, for example, we examined interrogations designed to elicit and 'test' a witness's testimony about the past. What he recalled or failed to recall was responsive (or not) to what he was asked, accountably orientated to the possible consequences of an answer for the ongoing investigation. By describing selected features of the logical and moral grammar of such recollections in testimony, we contributed nothing of substance to an aspiring science that would causally explain the workings of memory. It might be said that we have stolen the topics of cognitive science in order to incorporate them into a very different form of analysis, but we prefer to say that we have taken those topics back home to the organizational circumstances in which they have lived all along.

11   Discursive psychology, mental states and descriptions

Derek Edwards and Jonathan Potter

Introduction

Our aim in this chapter is to show how discursive psychology (DP) deals with psychological states and characteristics. We do this in several ways: by defining what DP is, by demonstrating it analytically, and by discussing various criticisms and misunderstandings of it. As for defining it, DP works in three closely related ways:

1. *Respecification and critique.* Standard psychological topics are respecified as discourse practices. Topics recognized in mainstream psychology such as 'memory', 'causal attribution', 'script' knowledge, and so on, are re-worked in terms of discourse practices. We study how people ordinarily, as part of everyday activities, report and explain actions and events, how they characterize the actors in those events, and how they manage various implications generated in the act of reporting. DP often generates a critical stance on cognitive psychology. For example, cognitive theory and measurement of 'attitudes' is criticized and replaced by the study of argumentative and evaluative practices in discourse (Billig, 1987; Potter, 1998a; Potter and Wetherell, 1987; Wiggins, 2002; Wiggins and Potter, 2003). Similarly, cognitive methods and theory on 'causal attribution' are critically opposed by analyses of how people manage accountability in everyday talk (Antaki, 1994; Edwards and Potter, 1992a, 1993).

2. *The psychological thesaurus.* DP explores the situated, occasioned, rhetorical uses of the rich common sense psychological lexicon or thesaurus: terms such as angry, jealous, know, believe, feel, want, and so on. For example, expressions such as 'I don't know', or 'your angry stage' are examined for the local contrasts and interactional work for which they are used (e.g., Edwards, 1995; Potter, 1998b). By grounding such studies in empirical materials, we are able to explore the ways in which concepts such as 'know' or 'angry' are used interactionally and rhetorically, with regard to specific, locally relevant alternative descriptions. We develop some examples in this chapter.

241

3. *Managing psychological implications*. DP examines discourse for how psychological themes are handled and managed, without necessarily being overtly labelled. We explore how agency, intent, doubt, belief, prejudice, commitment, and so on, are built, made available, or countered 'indirectly', through descriptions of actions, events, objects, persons and settings. In fact, this has been a key feature of the kinds of 'respecification' done in DP type 1, where attributions of intent and blame are shown to be handled, not by overt descriptions of intent or motive, but through what look like (or are produced as) straightforward event descriptions. This is the basis of DP's explorations of 'fact and accountability' (Edwards and Potter, 1992b; Potter and Edwards, 2001), where we show how factual descriptions are used to implicate a range of psychological states and attributions, and vice versa. Again, this kind of psychologically implicative use of factual descriptions is closely tied, in actual talk and its analysis, to participants' uses of the 'psychological thesaurus'.

This is a good point at which to address a recurrent misunderstanding about DP. It is sometimes assumed that DP is concerned only with overt talk about mental states, what we have just listed as DP type 2. For example Coulter summarizes Edwards (1997) to the effect that in DP 'the "mental" is thus to be construed solely in terms of what people say about it' (1999: 166). We will return to Coulter's characterizations of DP later in this chapter. Similarly, Drew (this volume) identifies DP with what he calls the 'attributional' approach, which is the study of 'the rhetorical uses of terms describing mental states' (p. 00). But exploring uses of the psychological thesaurus is only part of DP. DP also explores how mental states feature as talk's *business*, rather in the way that CA deals with the relevance of institutional settings and social structures. Psychological categories are analyzed as matters being handled, managed, produced, made relevant (etc.) in the talk, rather than as something sitting outside of the talk, for analysts to use in explaining it (Edwards, 1997; Potter, 1998b; cf. Drew and Heritage, 1992).

One further point of clarification: when we use the term 'psychological', we do so under the auspices of DP. We use it provisionally, commonsensically, bracketed off for respecification, or else as DP re-defines it, but not as any kind of commitment to an inner life of the mind, nor to individualism, nor to whatever else academic psychology might assume or propose. Yet the main thrust of DP is not to close down psychology departments, but to counter and invert what mainstream psychology has done *with discourse*, which is to treat it as the *expression of* thoughts, intentions and cognitive structures. The 'inversion' offered by DP is to start with discourse itself, and to see how all of those presumptively prior and independent notions of mind, intention, motive, etc., are topicalized, categorized and, in various less direct ways, handled and managed within discourse itself.

So, DP focuses on person and event descriptions in talk and text. It examines how factual descriptions are assembled, how they are built as solidly grounded or undermined as false, and how they handle the rational accountability (or otherwise) of actors and speakers. We focus particularly on what we (provisionally) call 'mind and reality' – on how people deploy common sense notions of an 'external' reality as a kind of setting for, and evidential domain for inferences about, a range of mental states and personal characteristics.

We also emphasize *rhetorical organization*, how descriptions and their inferences routinely (and not only in adversarial contexts) attend to possible or actual counter versions. Descriptions are *constructive* of their objects. This is not to say that talk brings things into the world, but rather, that descriptions are categorizations, distinctions, contrasts; there are always relevant alternatives available. This permits descriptions to be *performative*; they offer one construction rather than another, produced in sequential and rhetorical contexts, where the specifics matter for the actions being done.

Again, this is a suitable juncture for some clarification. The sense of 'construction' that we are using here, is what we have called 'epistemic' rather than 'ontological' (see, for example, Edwards, 1997: 47–8). In his review of various sorts of discursive psychology, including the latter volume, Coulter glosses DP as 'a thesis which proposes that the human mind and its various properties are generated in and through discourse: in essence, the 'mind' is revealed in and through analyseable features of the things that people say and do through their talk' (1999: 163). In fact, the DP that we promote here, and that Coulter reviewed, is programmatically opposed to any of that. The term 'epistemic' construction is designed to distinguish DP from 'constructivist' developmental-psychological theories such as Piaget's, Vygotsky's and Bruner's in which 'actual minds' (Bruner, 1986) are produced and shaped through language and action. Similarly, Coulter's further gloss on DP, that minds are 'revealed' in discourse, is clearly repudiated in DP; indeed that repudiation is virtually the essence of it. It is probably the most salient characteristic of DP, at least as we practice it, that it rejects the cognitivist assumption that minds are revealed or expressed in what people say. To use a vernacular expression, it is where we came in! Coulter has blended together a range of different and sometimes opposed approaches that have adopted the term '(social) construction', rather as he did, in his major work *The Social Construction of Mind* (Coulter, 1979).

While opposing the cognitivist assumption that talk is driven by the workings of an inner life of the mind, that is not the end of the matter. The status of it as a poor general theory of language and mind does not prevent people from making use of it as a way of talking. This is not merely a matter of people making false theoretical assertions such as 'I think in my head' (Coulter, 1999: 166), but of talking *as if* that were the case, as part of talk's everyday practices. There are practical, common sense uses of such a notion, that a person's words may be produced or taken on occasions, *to be* expressions of a private and prior realm of mental life. This can be a practical basis for talking and doing things with words, whose *investigation* requires no commitment to mentalism on the analyst's part.

Descriptions, inferences and not knowing

In our three-way typology of DP, we distinguished between investigating uses of the psychological thesaurus, and studying how event descriptions may be produced for their psychological implications. But even the overt labelling of psychological states needs to be analyzed within the descriptive, narrative and turn-by-turn sequences where they occur, where inferences about intentions, thoughts, feelings, motives (and so on) are made available and countered in how events are told.

Extract (1)   [DE-JF:C2:S1:p.9]

```
 1    J:    And uh:: (1.0) Connie had a short skirt on
 2          I don'know.
 3          (1.0)
 4          And I kn<u>ew</u> this- (0.6) uh ah- maybe I had
 5          met him.
 6          (1.0)
 7          Ye:h. (.) I musta met Da:ve before.
 8          (0.8)
 9          But I'd heard he was a bit of a la:d (      ).
10          He didn't care: (1.0) who he (0.2) chatted
11          up or (.) who was in Ireland (.) y'know
12          those were (unavailable) to chat up with.
13          (1.0)
14          So Connie stood up (0.8) pulled her skirt
15          right up her side (0.6) and she was looking
16          straight at Da: ve (.) >°like that° < (0.6) and
17          then turned and looked at me (1.2) and then
18          she said w- (.) turned and then (.) back to
19          Dave and said (.) by the way that wasn't
20          for you.
```

Let us start with how descriptions of things, actions and events can provide for psychological inferences. This is a small, specific illustration of a very general feature of everyday discourse. Extract (1) is part of an extended sequence from an hour-long counselling session, in which a husband and wife ('Connie' and 'Jimmy') are recounting their problems with each other. Connie has described Jimmy as an endemically jealous person, prone to recurrent and unreasonable fits of jealousy.[1] The descriptive detail in line 1, 'Connie had a short skirt on', depicts her (and her subsequently narrated actions build on this) as dressed in a sexually relevant or provocative way. It is part of how Jimmy builds his wife's character and motives as flirtatious (and therefore making his jealousy reasonable), along with directing her behaviour on this particular occasion at a reputed 'bit of a lad' named Dave (line 9), in which Dave is positioned as a recipient of Connie's actions and appearance. The descriptive details work, not only through what they include, but through what they might well have mentioned but do not. Of all that she wore, it is only the 'short skirt' that is mentioned (here or elsewhere in the session), and of all the skirt's describable characteristics, only its brevity is remarked on.

The sequential positioning of the description is also important. It occurs immediately before (and thus hearably relevant to) the introduction of Dave. We can hear Connie's motivation and character being set up here, as flirtatious, sexy and targeting Dave (explicitly, in lines 15–16). The specific words that *we* are using, 'sexy' and 'flirtatious', are ours and not definitive (though they are used later by the counsellor as formulations of what Jimmy was saying), but the point is that *something like that* is implicitly conveyed. It is done not by overtly calling his wife sexually motivated and flirtatious, but by making those kinds of characteristics *inferentially available*, as categories that a hearer of these descriptions can infer for themselves. Indeed, they are categories that Connie herself orients to in a similarly indirect manner (in a subsequent turn not presented here), by providing alternative, contrastive descriptions of the length of her skirt, what she did with it, and at whom she was looking. So Connie's character, motives and intentions (psychological matters) are built and countered by descriptions of witnessable things – her skirt and her actions, the proximity of those things to the descriptions of Dave, and their place in the narrative sequence.

Consider now the use of an overt psychological term, 'I don'know', in line 2. It would be a mistake to hear this as simply an assertion of ignorance or uncertainty, or even as an 'assertion' at all (it is said parenthetically, with no explicit object). What it does, like the rest of the sequence in which it occurs, is attend to Jimmy's own character, as a purportedly jealous and suspicious husband who may be prone (in this case) to some kind of obsessive monitoring of the details of his wife's clothing and behaviour. The use here, and *just* here, of 'I don'know' counters that. It implies that he wasn't paying particular attention, and does not have a lot hanging on it. In fact, this kind of interpersonal use of 'I don'know' or 'I dunno' (used in this parenthetical, framing kind of way, rather than as a bald answer to a factual question), recurs across a range of discourse materials as a way of handling, or playing down, the speaker's stake or interest in the content of a description (Potter, 1998b; see also Beach and Metzger, 1997).

Clearly, any such uses of 'I don't know' are not independent of what 'know' signifies as a 'concept'[2] or its dictionary definition. However, what Jimmy does with it is not well catered for by this 'conceptual' understanding. Indeed, his subsequent narrative conveys his close attention to the details of Connie's skirt, its length, and what she did with it. Expressions such as 'I don't know' can do interactional work of this kind, attending to potential common sense inferences and rhetorical alternatives at stake in the interaction; such as, in this case, that he is a suspicious, over-jealous husband prone to persecuting his wife over small, exaggerated things that are more in his head than in the world, more a reflection of his own preoccupations than of his wife's actual clothing, actions or character. Clearly, the way that discourse handles psychological categories is not just a matter of using overt psychological labels.

What makes these kinds of analytic observations more than merely ad hoc comments on particular stretches of talk, is that they are recurrently applicable to a wide range of materials. Motives and intentions (vernacularly understood) are built inferentially out of descriptions of actions and events; they are built to contrast with alternatives; they attend to matters local to the interactional context in which they occur; and they attend reflexively to the speaker's stake or investment in producing those descriptions. There is also a range of devices through which this kind of thing is done, including situated uses of 'I don't know', and various linguistic ways of establishing a person's recurrent actions as implying motive and character (see Edwards, 1994, 1997 on 'script formulations').

Knowing, telling and wanting

Wittgenstein (1958) argued that what we are calling 'mental state avowals' (i.e., descriptions of one's own thoughts and feelings) do not and could not obtain their meaning from 'referring to' privately experienced mental states. Bilmes (1992) has suggested that folk may nevertheless actually, and reasonably, consider themselves to be doing that, or may talk as if they were doing that. Coulter's (1992) basic response is that Bilmes and the lay public are wrong about it, at least as a theoretical explanation, or conceptual analysis, of what they are doing. Yet we have suggested that the *concept* of private mental states, and of the ability to provide experiential reports about them (which is clearly a meaningful idea, if only to allow Coulter and ourselves to call it 'cognitivism' and oppose it!), may be a rhetorically useful way of talking. We can ask how, when, and in the performance of what kinds of actions, do people talk as if they were in possession of a privately available mental life, which their words may either truthfully or falsely express?

A routine account for not telling something is not knowing it. Indeed we can invert that, and say that handling the practical accountability of not telling something, where telling is called for, is a routine environment for formulations of not knowing. So 'not knowing' is analyzable for what it does, not just for what it says about states of mind. However, in extract (2) 'W' must rely on a different kind of account for not telling, given that it is his own recent actions that he is talking about. Here he *knows* but is *not saying*. 'W' is a witness being questioned by a police officer (P1) about the theft from a shop, and the subsequent 'selling on', of some cigarettes: a theft to which W has confessed.

Extract (2)   [DE:West:p. 10]

```
1    P1:    So: (.) where were they sold to
2           (1.2)
3    W:     In a pub in Pen.
4           (2.4)
5    W:     I'm n'gonna tell y'the name a the pub.
6           (1.8)
7    W:     B'cause: I jus don' want the person in there
8    W:     (0.2) involved (.) the- manager in- involved
9           in any a this,
10          (0.4)
11   P1:    Right,
```

The notion that W might normatively be expected to tell what he relevantly knows, at least under questioning in this setting, concerning the disposal of stolen goods, is oriented to by the fact that W *accounts for* it (lines 7–9). Note how the initial response 'in a pub in Pen' (line 3) answers the prior question, but in a manner that would not allow the police officer to specifically identify the place. W's statement, that he is not going to provide specific identifying information (line 5), and the account that follows it (lines 7–9), are provided only after delays in lines 4 and 6 that W may be taking as signs that his answers are insufficient. The delay in line 10, prior to P1's receipt of the account, is notably shorter.[3]

Clearly in this case, knowing and telling are handled under recognizable and recognized (line 11) normative auspices.

The content of W's account for not telling includes another common sense psychological avowal, *not wanting* (line 7). Again, what W may or may not want is produced as part of a normative order, recognized by P1 in line 11, not to get someone else into trouble. Avowals of this kind, of knowing and wanting, are produced not simply as reports on mental states, as if for interest's sake, but as claims that are recognizable and somewhat confirmable within a conventional framework. There is a kind of intersubjectivity at work, in which thoughts and wishes are made plausible in context, with regard to what a person might be expected to think, do or feel under the circumstances. Of course it works both ways, and this is important in W's general uses of it. Given the availability of circumstantial, normative warrants for psychological avowals, those psychological avowals can work reflexively, to establish W's version of 'circumstances' (the events he is describing) as precisely what happened.

W makes regular use of mental state avowals and their normative reportability, in building factual versions of the events that those mental states are 'about'. This is done while attending to his own accountability in, and through, reporting some things and not other things that he is being questioned about. Extract (3) is an example parallel to extract (2).

Extract (3)   [DE:West:p. 22]

```
1  P1:   Who are you owin the money to?
2        (2.6)
3  W:    I don' wanna h (0.3) give you his name because
4        a the(h) the £e(h)nd a the day he's a dealer?£
5        (0.3)
6  P1:   Yeh
```

Again, W accounts for not providing the requested information, an account also based on not wanting to get another person into trouble, and again P1 acknowledges it (line 6).[4] There is an additional relevance beyond this short extract, in that owing money is W's repeated account for stealing the cigarettes and selling them on; he claims to have needed the money to pay a debt for some cannabis, and was being threatened by the dealer if he did not pay up. So W's failure to substantiate that story is less incidental than it might appear in the extract. As seen in extract (2), refusal (not inability) to comply with a request is accounted for in terms of a normatively overriding, indeed somewhat laudable, desire or motive to protect another individual. The fact that the individual concerned is a drug dealer probably heightens rather than softens the obligation, given the kind of trouble they would be in with the police, and perhaps the trouble that W might be in with the dealer. W's laughter (the (h) signs) and smiling delivery (bracketed by the £ signs) orient to that problem, as perhaps both obvious and ironic, but in any case recognizably to P1. W and P1 are using, as part of practical accountability, a common sense notion that what we know is tellable, but sometimes may and should remain a private matter, within a field of normatively recognizable motives and circumstances.

Further uses of *wanting, hoping* and *liking*

A person's wishes, motives, likes or wants can play a crucial part in establishing or undermining contested versions of events as factual. In DP we have called this 'stake management' (Edwards and Potter, 1992a; Potter, 1996). Claiming that a person has some kind of stake, interest, wish or motive in favour of their particular version of events, can be a way of undermining that version. As a corollary, people routinely work at defining preferred versions as disinterested, or even as contrary to their hopes and interests ('stake inoculation'). More broadly, we are dealing with the common sense play-off between reality and mind, within forms of practical reasoning and accountability. Avowals of hoping and wanting, and other psychological states, work in concert with, or in contrast to, factual descriptions of circumstances and events, particularly in environments of scepticism or dispute.

Extract (4)   [DE:West:p.16]

```
1    W:    (...) I didn' push the woman or nothin, (0.5)
2          I really did not do that.= I'm not that type
3          of person y'know what I me:an. .h Fair enough
4          I stole the ciggies, (0.9) I wouldn' hurt an
5          old lady.
6          (0.5)
7    P1:   [Right.]
8    W:    [No.  ]
9          (.)
10   W:    Not a chance.=
11   P1:   =What I'm saying is that this (0.5)
12   W:    I hope there's a Ceet- a camera at the shop=
13   P1:   =There i[s.
14   W:            [security [camera      ]
15   P1:                     [There were] cameras in the
16         shop, but I'll tell y' now that the cameras
17         (0.7) weren't (1.1) functionin, (.) at that
18         particular time.
19   W:    Bit coincidental innit?
```

The factual dispute is displayed in the opening lines. W is denying a version previously put to him by P1, citing the 'old lady' shopkeeper's testimony, that he came across the shop counter and pushed her, causing an injury, turning the admitted theft into a more serious crime ('robbery'). W emphatically denies this, using the extreme expressions (Pomerantz, 1986) 'or nothin', 'really', and 'not a chance' (lines 1, 2 & 10). He ties his denial to a claim about himself as a kind of person (lines 2–5), using the practical logic of scripts and dispositions (Edwards, 1995, 1997), building the case that he did not do it on this particular occasion because he would not do it on any occasion. Again, we have psychological formulations working alongside contentious event descriptions, building one version and undermining another.

We can now focus on something for which these opening lines provide a relevant setting: the mental state avowal 'I hope' (line 12), and its object. One would not generally expect a person to *hope* to see the evidence of their crime on videotape. It is not merely that the video evidence is potentially decisive. In fact W may already know that there is no such evidence; it becomes clear earlier in the interview that W has been briefed by his solicitor on the content of the shopkeeper's testimony. It is the *hoping* that works rhetorically here. It signals, in the absence of the tape recording, the *truth of the object* of that hope, the factual content of what any such tape would reveal, which of course corresponds to W's contested version of events. W's 'I hope' is a mental state avowal at work in a rhetorical environment of stake and interest (cf. Edwards and Potter, 1992a), where W's contended version of events risks being heard as functional, self-serving, inaccurate, motivated. What W hopes for (the existence of a video recording) counters an alternative motivational story, alive in the interrogation by P1, that he is lying in order to downgrade the seriousness of his crime. So mental state avowals *can* work to reify their objects – the states of affairs, as described, to which they pertain.

In extract (5) a second police officer, P2, is asking about the possible involvement of an accomplice named Alan.

Extract (5)   [DE:West:p.24]

```
1  P2:    When did Alan come into the shop with you then.
2         (1.8)
3  W:     I didn' wan im in the shop.
4         (1.5)
5  W:     Didn' wan im in the shop.
6         (0.2)
7  W:     Jus told im to walk down I said I'll be back
8         now I'm goin to get ciggies.
9         (1.8)
```

It has been a major and repeated feature of the interview up to this point, that W consistently denies the shopkeeper's version, repeatedly put to him by P1 or P2, that he committed the theft with an accomplice, Alan. W has insisted that Alan never came into the shop and took no part, but rather continued on down the road and waited for him. So P2's question in line 1 is hearable against that background of repeated proposal and denial. W's response is not simply to deny it again, but to offer a mental state description that provides a credible basis for that denial – he did not *want* Alan in the shop. W goes on soon after to explain this as a feature of his routine modus operandi when stealing cigarettes from shops, that it just complicates things: '>The enda the day< it's easier for me to get away on me own than havin t'look out for somebody else as well'. But by reporting on his state of mind with regard to the matter, W provides a credible basis for his contested (and otherwise uncorroborated) version of events. Those events are again the intentional object of the not wanting – i.e., having 'him in the shop' (lines 3 & 5). As with extract (4), W's mental state avowals work closely with his event descriptions, establishing the factual plausibility of his version of events within a normative order of mind and reality – of how one *would* think, what one *would* want or hope for or expect, given the truth of events as he tells them.

Later in the same interview (see extract (6)) W is again referring to Alan's (lack of) involvement in the theft from the shop.

Extract (6)   [DE: West: p. 37]

```
1    W:    this is truly, (0.5) right, (0.3) from the
2          bottm me he*art, (0.5) he was not with me,
3          (0.6) >know waramean<, (0.3) ↑tell the  truth
4          I don' even ↑like the lad, (0.8) he's
5          implicated me (.) ↓in some'in.
6          (0.5)
7    W:    Right?
8          0.4)
9    W:    In a burglary (0.6) ↑that I've had no (.) no
10         part of?
11         (1.4)
12   W:    I don't really like im, he's more of an
13         acquaintance >y'know waramean.<
14         (0.4)
15   W:    But (.) he (.) did not have nothin to do with
16         this
17         (0.3)
18   P2:   If you don' like im you've been (.) you've put
19         im up in your flat haven' you.
```

Not liking Alan (lines 4, 12), whom W has been consistently defending as not involved in the crime, serves as a *stake inoculation* (Potter, 1996). Note various details of W's talk: the term 'even', in 'I don' even ↑li̲ke the lad' (line 4) signals the rhetorical, contrastive nature of this avowal, working against what might be assumed, which is that W has a motive to lie, in order to protect a friend. Again, the category 'acquaintance' is introduced in the same contrastive way; Alan is 'more of' an acquaintance (lines 12–13). The distancing between W and Alan is further brought off by referring to him impersonally as 'the lad' (line 4). So the whole construction, 'I don' even ↑li̲ke the lad', works together, through all its detailed components (including contrastive stress on 'like'), to inoculate W from any motive he may be imputed with, to lie on Alan's behalf. Further, W actually claims a *contrary* motive to implicate Alan, as a piece of quid pro quo for Alan's having 'implicated' W in another crime of which W was innocent (lines 4–10). So again, as in extracts (4) and (5), we have a mental state avowal (not liking) serving to reinforce the factuality of a particular, disputed version of events.

The avowals in extract (6), occurring in an environment of contestation and scepticism, are accompanied by emphatic claims to sincerity: 'truly', 'from the bottom of my heart', 'tell the truth', 'really'. These expressions exploit one of the features of mental state avowals, which is their common sense (if philosophically disputed) reference to private mental states, that are the speaker's privilege to know and report. W is claiming to speak sincerely from within, indeed from the bottom of his heart. One useful thing about talking in this manner, is that it can counter evidence to the contrary, though of course its rhetorical uses against such evidence do not guarantee success. That is what we see in extract (6), where P2 counters W's avowals to dislike this mere acquaintance, on the grounds that W has acted in a manner associated with friends, putting him up at his flat. In membership category terms, such actions are associated with friends rather than disliked acquaintances.

We are not pursuing here the consequences of this dispute between W and P2. Rather, the important things are the conceptual, discursive resources through which the dispute is conducted. Descriptions of witnessable events in the world (what happened in the shop, W's putting Alan up for the night) are offered in support of, or against, mental state avowals. Similarly, and as a corollary, claiming a mental state or psychological disposition (liking, hoping, wanting, etc.) can be used to build or refute a particular version of external events. Within these common sense descriptive practices, mind and world are invoked in concert or in contrast with each other. Whereas one can justifiably argue that all words, including mental state avowals, can be meaningful only via their public uses and ratifications, it remains part of such public uses, that people talk as if there is a world of inner experience that can be reliably reported on by the experiencer and set against evidence to the contrary.

Some situated uses of *thinking*

A cognitive conception of *thinking* is that it refers to mental cogitation, ideas occurring in the mind, a process of ratiocination, information processing, or mental problem solving, whether conscious or unconscious. Of course the term can be used that way in everyday talk, to propose that some train of ideas is passing through our minds (whatever that might, in turn, amount to). Billig (1987, 1999) suggests that thought is intrinsically more social than psychologists have generally taken it to be, that it is better characterized as argumentative and ideological in nature. Also, the earliest definitions of *think* in the *Oxford English Dictionary* (2002) specify it as deriving from old English and Anglo-Saxon, with an initial sense of 'to seem, appear'. This provides for a function in the 'discourse of mind and world' that we are discussing in this chapter: a contrast between how things appear, or are assumed to be, and how they turn out. So we are able to say 'I thought so!' when saying that assumptions are confirmed, or else 'At first I thought . . .' when saying that things turned out otherwise (see Sacks, 1992: 787ff; and Wooffitt, 1991, for useful observations on that). Extract (7) is rich in uses of the verb *think*, including echoes of this ancient sense of proposing alignment or misalignment with events in the world.

Extract (7)   [Holt:1:1: p.7]

```
1   L:    .hh Oh m:Mum, I ↑↑thought she wz gon'send'im
2         mon↓e:y.
3   M:    She told me she was.
4         (0.3)
5   L:    Oh:::::.
6         (1.4)
7   L:    .hh I think I'll 'aftuh tell'er in the letter
8         not tuh send any mo::re.
9         (1.4)
10  M:    ( ) that w'd be a good i:dea
11        (.)
12  L:    Yes. You don't think she'll take umbrage,
13        (.)
14  M:    No::,
15        (.)
16  M:    N-o:?
17        (0.2)
```

```
18   M:    Uh: ↑no: if you jus'say thet uh (0.5) uh if yuh
19         (0.3) tha- thank her very much'n say thet (0.2)
20         but Gordon doesn't wear that sort'v thi:ng=
21   L:    =mn::↓Ye:s.
22         (0.4)
23   M:    I think that'd be a good idea.
24   L:    Ye:s. I ↓think so:↓
```

In extract (7) Lesley (L) and her mother (M) are talking about the prospect of Ann (named elsewhere) sending a gift for Gordon, L's son. It is a gift that Ann has sent on previous occasions (line 8), some white T-shirts with a company logo on them, items that Gordon reportedly (line 20) never wears. The thing of interest is the ways in which notions of 'thinking' are occasioned and accountable in this public way, rather than merely reports of a private life of the mind. One feature of their account-ability is projected by past or present tense, 'thought' versus 'think'. As Sacks (1992: 787–8) noted, both tense and intonation are important to the factual status of whatever was thought. 'I thought' (line 1), together with the emphasis and falling pitch on 'money', signal that what was thought turned out *not* to be the case; money was not sent. Using past tense, saying what one 'thought' can be a way of setting up what actually happened as something normal, routine, deviant, unusual, indicative of the actors and current speaker, and so on. Further, in the event that such thoughts turned out to be wrong, it is an accountable matter why the mis-take was made. Accounts may take the form of how unusual the events were, and/or how reasonable the presumptions. In this case, a reasonable basis is provided by M (line 3): it is what Ann said she would do.

On the other hand, present tense uses of 'think' (lines 7, 12, 23, 24) are used here to project actions and events that are as yet unknown, or have not happened. These are: the proposal to tell Ann not to send any more t-shirts (lines 7–8), and the consequence that Ann might 'take umbrage' (line 12). L's telling M what she is 'thinking' is a way of sounding M out (occasioning a 'second assessment' from her: cf. Pomerantz, 1984) on the delicate matter of rejecting a gift and anticipating Ann's possible reaction. As with making false predictions (I thought X but Y happened), rejecting a gift is an accountable matter. The accounts provided here are: (1) that it *has* to be done (line 7), where 'have to' routinely contrasts with what anyone might freely choose to do (cf. Drew, 1984, on 'inability accounts' in invitation refusals); (2) that it is a good idea (lines 9, 22, 23); and (3) that Ann will anyway not 'take umbrage' (lines 12–14) if it is properly done, with some normative restitution consisting of a thank you and an account (lines 18–20). So the various 'mental state' terms in extract (7) are made subject to public ratification, as being reasonably grounded or appropriate. Note M's various interventions throughout the extract, corroborating L's thoughts and assessments, and in lines 18–20 providing an account, when prompted by L, of how and why Ann's umbrage might be avoided.

Extract (7) displays a rich interplay of mental states, normative actions and factual descriptions. Although we have provided no systematic analysis of these uses of 'think' and 'thought' here, for which a range of cases would be required, the analysis illustrates DP's central concern with how psychological avowals, attributions and implications work in conjunction with factual descriptions and normative accountability (Edwards and Potter, 1992a). False ideas, ones that do not correspond with a given reality, along with non-normative actions, are treated as requiring accounts. Relationships between psychological states and the nature of the world to which those states pertain, feature in discourse as part of the normative order of social life and conversational interaction, as central elements in what talk does.

Discussion

We can distinguish three theoretical versions (there may be others) of what is going on when someone says how they feel, what they think, want or believe.

1. Utterances of that kind might be taken as reports from within, expressions of mental states. This is what Harris (1981) has called the 'telementation myth', that thoughts and feelings occur in our minds, and (then) we express them in our words. It is the starting point of a wide range of philosophy, psychology, clinical assessment, interviewing and general research methodology. Within this perspective, talk need not be a straightforward reflection of mind. People can lie, be wrong about themselves, strategic, or inarticulate. So caution is always required when finding mind behind words, and sometimes special procedures are deployed to reduce unreliability. But according to this approach, the expression and communication of thoughts is basically what talk does.

2. A contrasting approach argues that descriptions of mental states are best analyzed in the manner recommended by linguistic philosophers such as Ryle and Wittgenstein. Here, the notion that words such as 'think' or 'feel' express or refer to mental states is rejected in favour of an analysis of how those words are properly used, in publicly ratifiable ways. Anyone, whether philosopher or lay person, who claims to be using such words to refer to an essentially private mental experience is making a conceptual error. This approach often takes the form of

analyzing assertions or propositions, often single sentences, that people might be imagined to make, such as 'I feel unhappy' or 'I believe in ghosts'. Empirical study of recordings of conversation plays a minor role, if any.

3. While acknowledging the arguments in extract (2), a third approach recognizes that there is nevertheless some substance to the idea of referring to private mental states, though *not* as the analyst's favoured theory of language and mind. The very idea of reference to mental states is at least conceivable, if only for it to be attributed by their critics to cognitivists and misguided lay persons. In this third approach, the status of reference to internal mental states is not something to be refuted, even though it is conceptually refutable, but rather, studied as a practice within public forms of life. People may sometimes talk as if, or on the *proposed and oriented-to basis*, that their words are expressing inner thoughts and feelings. It is a basis and orientation found in clinical psychology for example, if we approach clinical attributions as studiable practices rather than rival theories. But it is found also in everyday talk, where again it is available for study as a social practice. It is also something that can be countered, not only by philosophical argument, but as part of everyday practices. People may point to inconsistencies, or to evidence to the contrary, or to disagreements, or to the speaker's proposed strategic aims, and thus challenge any claim that they are merely reporting what they think.

DP rejects position (1), in the main aligns theoretically with position (2), but mostly develops position (3), by approaching mentalistic claims as performative rather than merely erroneous (cf. the invocation of 'indifference' in Lynch and Bogen, this volume). The notion that mental states are private and reportable emerges as *part of*, rather than merely refuted by, their public sense and ratification.

There are, therefore, two different kinds of relationship between DP and cognitive psychology. One relationship is that of opposition and critique, in which DP is a rival way of understanding what is going on when people talk, or 'remember', or 'attribute causes', or 'express their attitudes and feelings', or whatever; it is a rival approach to discourse (Edwards, 1997 is an example of this style of DP). The second relationship is that of studying cognitive and social cognitive psychology as a form of life like any other, studying the set of scientific concepts and practices through which the nature of the 'cognitive' is produced (examples of such work include: Antaki et al., 2000; Edwards and Potter, 1992b; Puchta and Potter, 2002). Neither approach entails any kind of endorsement of cognitivism.

Critical reactions to DP range from defences of traditional cognitive psychology (e.g., Conway, 1992), to the kind of politically grounded critique (e.g., Parker and Burman, 1993) that is commonly also directed at CA. Rather than engaging with those alternatives here, we focus instead on a discussion by Coulter (1999) that deals critically with DP more directly in its own terms and has more direct ramifications for the issues raised in this volume. In distinguishing his own 'praxiological' approach from DP, Coulter characterizes DP in ways that align it with position (1) above. This characterization is wrong. However, rather than dwell on that here (see Potter and Edwards, 2003 for an elaborate rebuttal), our concern is with the different practices of DP and Coulter's approach, as well as the different materials that are the focus of study. We shall explore that a little bit here, given its central relevance to DP as a project and given the significance of Coulter's own contribution to the development of a non-cognitivist approach to mind, which we have acknowledged elsewhere, and do again here. We hope that our discussion will clarify some quite subtle issues.

Coulter mistakenly interprets Edwards (1997) as studying 'the 'mental' . . . solely in terms of what people say about it' (1999: 166). This is in turn conflated with 'members' lay . . . theorizing' (ibid.). We have already noted that DP is not solely concerned with what people *say about* 'the mental'; but nor does the latter amount to 'lay theorizing', and this is a significant point of contrast worth highlighting. Coulter goes on (ibid.: 166–7) to discuss the status of someone 'asserting'[5] 'I think in my head'. Even when DP *is* concerned with overt uses of psychological concepts (DP type 2), it is not concerned with members' disembedded quasi-theoretical 'assertions'. In fact, it is not clear how, when, and doing what, people might make such assertions. Our reaction as analysts of discourse to such an example is to ask what anyone might be *doing by* uttering it somewhere. Rather than being concerned that such a person has a mistaken understanding of themselves, or of the concepts that they use, we would investigate what kinds of work such utterances might do, how and when they may occur, what they are used in contrast with, indeed what makes them locally intelligible things to say. This contrasts with Coulter's use of such an item as a kind of hypothetical interview response, a proposition to refute.

We do not have to hand a case of somebody asserting 'I think in my head', but extract (8) includes a situated use of a similar expression (lines 6–7). It comes from a counselling session with a husband and wife, 'Jeff' and 'Mary'.

Extract (8) [DE-JF:C1:S1:p.5]

```
1  J:      And I TR↑I:ed, befor yo- I dunno a couple o'
2          days it might work [(     ) and all] of a=
3  M:                         [ ((coughs))   ]
```

```
4  J:      sudden I'd- (0.9) youknow I'd (.) I'd ↑go to
5          wor:k or: I'd be on my ow:n, (0.4) somewhere
6          an:d (0.4) all these thoughts would fill my
7          hea:d and the anger would build up< and next
8          >time I see Mary I'd have a go at her you see,
```

Jeff is responding to a complaint by Mary, that he is spoiling her efforts
to get closer to him, following an extramarital affair she had, because of
his continuing bad feelings about it.[6] Jeff tells how he does make genuine efforts (lines 1–2) but they are thwarted by a kind of process he
undergoes, that he cannot help, that happens to him against his best
efforts, 'all of a sudden' (lines 2–4). His expression 'all these thoughts
would fill my head' serves as a kind of observational report on things
happening within him, where a notion of passively and reluctantly undergoing mental experiences is something other than performing actions
for which he might be blamed. Note how it is nicely situated in contrast to his concerted efforts ('I TR↑I:ed', line 1). Jeff is using a familiar,
common sense mind-as-container metaphor (cf. Lakoff, 1987). What
it does here is enable him to say and feel bad things about Mary, to
avow and express anger and resentment, and not be very receptive to
her overtures, without those being actions that he culpably does. So
reporting on 'in the head' experiences is a culturally recognizable practice in talk, that has its uses. Of course, analyzing it in this way, as an
intelligible practice of accountability, implies no ontological endorsement on our part of what Jeff claims about events in his head, any more
than if we were analyzing the uses of Azande oracles (Evans-Pritchard,
1937).

Other issues with Coulter are discussed in Potter and Edwards (2003).
In this chapter have used his critique as an opportunity to clarify the
discursive psychological position on mental states, and to correct some
misleading claims before they become too established.

More generally, in this chapter we have tried to sketch out the contours
of an approach to psychology, mind, cognition, psychological states and
so on which is both non-cognitivist and empirical. We have illustrated
this approach with a set of examples. They point the way to the kind of
analysis that would appear in full DP studies, but should be treated as
no more than illustrations so far. Up to now research in discursive psychology has developed three themes: (1) respecification of psychological
topics; (2) studies of the practical use of the psychological thesaurus; (3)
studies of psychological orientations. Cognitive psychology and cognitive science are huge fields employing hundreds of researchers, working
in close relation to applied disciplines such as human computer interaction, ergonomics and cognitive neuroscience. The implications of a

respecification of cognition along discursive psychological lines would be immense.

NOTES

1. Connie described Jimmy a couple of minutes earlier as 'extremely jealous. Extremely jealous person. Has always been, from the day we met . . . it was totally ridiculous the way he goes on, through this problem that he has'. Extract (1) is part of Jimmy's extended response to that and other things. See also Edwards (1995, 1997).
2. Our scare quotes round 'concept' are to distance us from the common cognitive interpretation of concepts, which treats them, roughly speaking, as mental meaning packets associated with words. In a sense our enterprise will, and should, generate major problems for a traditional understanding of what a concept is.
3. 'Notably shorter' is reflected in its being well inside Jefferson's (1989) normatively 'standard maximum silence' of one second, whereas the pauses in lines 4 and 6 are well beyond that.
4. The minimal nature of that acknowledgement, as in extract (2), serves as a receipt of what W is saying that stops short of what might, for a police officer, be a problematic endorsement of it.
5. The use of this speech act category 'asserting' is itself interesting, and rather typical of philosophical analysis, where people are imagined to 'assert' things, uttering definitive theoretical statements, and so on. Ironically, it is the very stuff of cognitivism to deal with objects of that kind, which readily lend themselves to a notion of people saying what they think; it is a way in which psychological, philosophical and linguistic treatments of language often get off on the wrong foot right from the start.
6. Mary's complaint included: 'I feel every time I try to get closer to him he's hurting me, and then it makes me distant again'.

References

Antaki, C. (1994). *Explaining and Arguing: The Social Organization of Accounts.* London: Sage.

Antaki, C., Houtkoop-Steentra, H. and Rapley, M. (2000). 'Brilliant. Next question . . .': high-grade assessment sequences in the completion of interactional units. *Research on Language and Social Interaction,* 33, 235–62.

Antaki, C. and Widdicombe, S. (eds) (1998). *Identities in Talk.* London: Sage.

Atkinson, J. M. (1984). Public speaking and audience responses: some techniques for inviting applause. In J. M. Atkinson and J. Heritage (eds), *Structures of Social Action: Studies in Conversation Analysis* (pp. 370–409). Cambridge University Press.

Atkinson, J. M. and Drew, P. (1979). *Order in Court: the Organisation of Verbal Interaction in Judicial Settings.* London: Macmillan.

Barclay, C. R. and DeCooke, P. A. (1988). Ordinary everyday memories: some of the things of which selves are made. In U. Neisser and E. Winograd (eds), *Remembering Reconsidered: Ecological and Traditional Approaches to the Study of Memory* (pp. 91–125). Cambridge: Cambridge University Press.

Barsalou, L. W. (1988). The content and organization of autobiographical memories. In U. Neisser and E. Winograd (eds), *Remembering Reconsidered: Ecological and Traditional Approaches to the Study of Memory* (pp. 193–243). Cambridge: Cambridge University Press.

Bartlett, F. C. (1932). *Remembering.* Cambridge: Cambridge University Press.

Bassili, J. N. (1996). The how and why of response latency measurement in telephone surveys. In N. Schwarz and S. Sudman (eds), *Answering Questions: Methodology for Determining Cognitive and Communicative Processes in Survey Research* (pp. 319–46). San Francisco: Jossey-Bass Publishers.

Bateson, G. (1972/1951). *Steps to An Ecology of Mind.* San Francisco: Chandler.

Beach, W. A. (1993). Transitional regularities for 'casual' 'Okay' usages. *Journal of Pragmatics,* 19, 325–52.

Beach, W. A. and Metzger, T. R. (1997). Claiming insufficient knowledge. *Human Communication Research,* 23, 562–88.

Benoit, P. J. and Benoit, W. L. (1986). Consciousness: the mindlessness/mindfulness and verbal report controversies. *Western Journal of Speech Communication,* 50, 41–63.

Best, J. B. (1999). *Cognitive Psychology* (5th edition). Belmont, CA: Wadsworth.

Birch, S. A. J. and Bloom, P. (2003). Children are cursed: an asymmetric bias in mental-state attribution. *Psychological Science*, 14, 283–6.

Billig, M. (1987). *Arguing and Thinking: A Rhetorical Approach to Social Psychology*. Cambridge: Cambridge University Press.

Billig, M. (1999). *Freudian Repression: Conversation Creating the Unconscious*. Cambridge: Cambridge University Press.

Bilmes, J. (1992). Referring to internal occurrences: a reply to Coulter. *Journal for the Theory of Social Behaviour*, 22, 253–62.

Bloom, L. (1973). *One Word at a Time: the Use of Single Word Utterances before Syntax*. The Hague: Mouton.

Bohannon, J. N. (1988). Flashbulb memories for the Space Shuttle disaster: a tale of two theories. *Cognition*, 29, 179–96.

Bowers, J. S. (2002). Challenging the widespread assumption that connectionism and distributed representations go hand-in-hand. *Cognitive Psychology*, 45, 413–45.

Bowker, G. and Star, S. L. (1999). *Sorting Things Out: Classification and Its Consequences*. Cambridge, MA: MIT Press.

Brenner, M. (1985). Survey interviewing. In M. Brenner, J. Brown and D. Canter (eds), *The Research Interview: Uses and Approaches* (pp. 9–35), London: Academic Press.

Brewer, W. F. (1992). The theoretical and empirical status of the flashbulb memory hypothesis. In E. Winograd and U. Neisser (eds). *Affect and Accuracy in Recall: Studies of 'Flashbulb Memories'* (pp. 274–305). Cambridge: Cambridge University Press.

Brown, P. and Levinson, S. C. (1987). *Politeness: Some Universals in Language Usage*. Cambridge: Cambridge University Press.

Brown, R. and Kulik, J. (1977). Flashbulb memories. *Cognition*, 5: 73–99.

Bruner, J. (1975). The ontogenesis of speech acts. *Journal of Child Language*, 2, 1–19.

Bruner, J. S. (1986). *Actual Minds, Possible Worlds*. Cambridge, MA: Harvard University Press.

Bruner, J. S., Roy, C. and Ratner, N. (1982). The beginnings of request. In K. Nelson (ed.), *Children's Language*, vol III (pp. 91–138). New York: Gardner Press.

Budd, M. (1984). Wittgenstein on meaning, interpretation and rules. *Synthese*, 58, 303–23.

Button, G. (1987). Answers as interactional products – two sequential practices used in interviews, *Social Psychology Quarterly*, 50, 160–71.

Button, G. (ed.). (1993). *Technology in Working Order: Studies of Work, Interaction and Technology*. London: Routledge.

Button, G., J. Coulter, J. R. E. Lee and W. W. Sharrock (1995). *Computers, Minds and Conduct*. Oxford: Polity.

Cannell, C. F. and Kahn, R. L. (1968). Interviewing. In G. Lindzey and E. Aronson (eds), *The Handbook of Social Psychology* (pp. 526–95). Reading, MA: Addison-Wesley.

Cannell, C. F., Miller, P. V. and Oksenberg, L. (1981). Research on interviewing techniques. In S. Leinhardt (ed.). *Sociological Methodology* (pp. 389–437), San Francisco: Jossey-Bass.

Chafe, W. (1990). Some things that narratives tell us about the mind. In B. K. Britton and A. D. Pellegrini (eds), *Narrative Thought and Narrative Language*. Hillsdale: Erlbaum.

Chafe, W. (1986). Evidentiality in English conversation and accademic writing. In W. Chafe and J. Nichols (eds), *Evidentiality: the Linguistic Coding of Epistemology* (pp. 261–72). Norwood NJ: Ablex.

Chaiklin, S. and Lave, J. (eds) (1993). *Understanding Practice: Perspectives on Activity and Context*. Cambridge and New York: Cambridge University Press.

Chomsky, N. (1957). *Syntactic Structures*. The Hague: Mouton.

Chomsky, N. (1959). A review of 'Verbal Behaviour' by B. F. Skinner. *Language*, 35, 26–58.

Chomsky, N. (1965). *Aspects of the Theory of Syntax*. Cambridge, MA: MIT Press.

Cicourel, A. (1974). *Cognitive Sociology: Language and Meaning in Social Interaction*. NY: Free Press/Macmillan.

Clark, H. H. (1979). Responding to indirect speech acts, *Cognitive Psychology*, 11, 430–77.

Clark, H. H. (1996). *Using Language*. Cambridge: Cambridge University Press.

Colgrove, F. W. (1982). The day they heard about Lincoln. In U. Neisser (ed.), *Memory Observed: Remembering in Natural Contexts* (pp. 41). San Francisco: Freeman. (Originally published in *American Journal of Psychology*, 10, 228–55, 1899).

Conway, M. (1992). Developments and debates in the study of human memory. *The Psychologist*, 5, 439–55.

Conway, M. (1995). *Flashbulb Memories*. Hove: Lawrence Erlbaum.

Coulter, J. (1979). *The Social Construction of Mind: Studies in Ethnomethodology and Linguistic Philosophy*. London: Macmillan.

Coulter, J. (1983). *Rethinking Cognitive Theory*. London: Macmillan.

Coulter, J. (1985). Two concepts of the mental. In K. J. Gergen and K. E. Davis (eds), *The Social Construction of the Person* (pp. 129–44). New York: Springer-Verlag.

Coulter, J. (1990). *Mind in Action*. Oxford: Polity.

Coulter, J. (1991). cognition: Cognition in an ethnomethodological mode. In G. Button (eds.), *Ethnomethodology and the human sciences* (pp. 176–195). Cambridge: Cambridge University Press.

Coulter, J. (1992). Bilmes on 'internal states': A critical commentary. *Journal for the Theory of Social Behaviour*, 22, 239–252.

Coulter, J. (1999). Discourse and mind. *Human Studies*, 22, 163–181.

Coulter, J. and Parsons E. D. (1991). The praxiology of perception: Visual orientations and practical action. *Inquiry*, 33: 251–272.

Daly, J. A., Weber, D. J., Vangelisti, A. L., Maxwell, M. and Neal, H. (1989). Concurrent cognitions during conversations: Protocol analysis as a means of exploring conversation, *Discourse Processes*, 12, 227–44.

Davidson, J. (1984). Subsequent versions of invitations, offers, requests, and proposals dealing with potential or actual rejection. In J. M. Atkinson and J. Heritage (eds.), *Structures of Social action*. Cambridge: Cambridge University Press: 102–28.

Deutscher, I. (ed.) (1973). *What we say/what we do: Sentiments and Acts.* Glenview, IL: Scott, Foresman.

Deutscher, I., Pestello, F. P., Frances, H. and Pestello, G. (1993). *Sentiments and Acts.* New York: Aldine de Gruyter.

Dohrenwend, B. S. (1965). Some effects of open and closed questions on respondents' answers, *Human Organization*, 24, 175–84.

Drew, P. (1978). Accusations: the occasioned use of members' knowledge of 'religious geography' in describing events, *Sociology*, 12, 1–22.

Drew, P. (1984). Speakers' reportings in invitation sequences. In J. M. Atkinson and J. C. Heritage (eds), *Structures of Social Action: Studies in Conversation Analysis* (pp. 129–51). Cambridge: Cambridge University Press.

Drew, P. (1987). Po-faced receipts of teases. *Linguistics*, 25, 219–53.

Drew, P. (1989). Recalling someone from the past. In D. Roger and P. Bull (eds), *Conversation: An Interdisciplinary Perspective* (pp. 96–115). Clevedon and Philadelphia: Multilingual Matters.

Drew, P. (1990). Strategies in the contest between lawyer and witness in cross-examination. In J. Levi and A. G. Walker (eds), *Language in the Judicial Process* (pp. 39–64). New York: Plenum.

Drew, P. (1992). Contested evidence in courtroom cross-examination: the case of a trial for rape. In P. Drew and J. Heritage (eds), *Talk at Work: Interaction in Institutional Settings* (pp. 470–520). Cambridge: Cambridge University Press.

Drew, P. (1995). Interaction sequences and 'anticipatory interactive planning.' In E. Goody (ed.), *The Social Origins of Human Intelligence* (pp. 111–38). Cambridge: Cambridge University Press.

Drew, P. and Heritage, J. C. (1992). Analyzing talk at work: an introduction. In P. Drew and J. Heritage (eds), *Talk at Work: Interaction in Institutional Settings* (pp. 3–65). Cambridge: Cambridge University Press.

Drew, P. and Wootton, A. (1988). *Erving Goffman: Exploring the Interaction Order.* Cambridge: Polity.

Durkheim, E. (1915). *The Elementary Forms of the Religious Life.* London: George Allen and Unwin.

Edwards, D. (1991). Categories are for talking: on the cognitive and discursive bases of categorization. *Theory and Psychology*, 1, 515–42.

Edwards, D. (1994). Script formulations: a study of event descriptions in conversation. *Journal of Language and Social Psychology*, 13, 211–47.

Edwards, D. (1995). Two to tango: script formulations, dispositions, and rhetorical symmetry in relationship troubles talk. *Research on Language and Social Interaction*, 28, 319–50.

Edwards, D. (1997). *Discourse and Cognition.* London and Beverly Hills: Sage.

Edwards, D. (1999a). Emotion discourse. *Culture and Psychology*, 5, 271–91.

Edwards, D. (1999b). Shared knowledge as a performative and rhetorical category. In J. Verschueren (ed.), *Pragmatics in 1998: Selected Papers From the 6th International Pragmatics Conference, vol. 2* (pp. 130–41). Antwerp: International Pragmatics Association.

Edwards, D. and Middleton, D. (1987). Conversation and remembering: Bartlett revisited. *Applied Cognitive Psychology*, 1, 77–92.

Edwards, D. and Potter, J. (1992a). *Discursive Psychology*. London: Sage.

Edwards, D. and Potter, J. (1992b). The chancellor's memory: rhetoric and truth in discursive remembering. *Applied Cognitive Psychology*, 6, 187–215.

Edwards, D. and Potter, J. (1993). Language and causation: a discursive action model of description and attribution. *Psychological Review*, 100, 23–41.

Edwards, J. C. (1990). *The Authority of Language: Heidegger, Wittgenstein and the Threat of Philosophical Nihilism*. Tampa: University of South Florida Press.

Ekman, P. (1985). *Telling Lies: Clues to Deceit in the Marketplace, Politics, and Marriage*. New York: Norton.

Ericsson, K. A. and Simon, H. A. (1993). *Protocol Analysis: Verbal Reports as Data*. (Revised Edition). Cambridge, MA MIT Press.

Evans-Pritchard, E. E. (1937). *Witchcraft, Oracles, and Magic Among the Azande*. Oxford: Clarendon Press.

Fiske, S. T. and Taylor, S. E. (1991). *Social Cognition* (2nd Ed.). New York: McGraw Hill.

Fodor, J. A. (1975). *The Language of Thought*. New York: Thomas Crowell.

Fodor, J. A. (1983). *The Modularity of Mind*. Cambridge, MS: MIT/Bradford Press.

Fodor, J. A. (1988). *Psychosemantics*. Cambridge, MA: MIT Press.

Fowler Jr., F. J. and Mangione, T. W. (1990). *Standardized Survey Interviewing: Minimizing Interviewer-Related Error*. Newbury Park: Sage.

Gardner, M. (1985). *The Mind's New Science*. New York: Basic Books.

Garfinkel, H. (1967). *Studies in Ethnomethodology*. Englewood Cliffs: Prentice-Hall.

Garfinkel, H. (1990). A conception of, and experiments with, 'trust' as a condition of stable concerted actions. In J. Coulter (ed.), *Ethnomethodological Sociology*. Vermont: Edward Elgar.

Garfinkel, H. (1991). Respecification: evidence for locally produced, naturally accountable phenomena of order, logic, reason, meaning, method, etc. in and as of the essential haecceity of immortal ordinary society (I) – an announcement of studies. In G. Button (ed.), *Ethnomethodology and the Human Sciences* (pp. 10–19). Cambridge: Cambridge University Press.

Garfinkel, H. (2002). *Ethnomethodology's Program: Working Out Durkheim's Aphorism*. New York: Rowan and Littlefield.

Garfinkel, H. and Sacks, H. (1970). On formal structures of practical actions. In J. C. McKinney and E. A. Tiryakian (eds), *Theoretical Sociology: Perspectives and Developments* (pp. 337–66). New York: Appleton-Century-Crofts.

Garfinkel, H. and Wieder, D. L. (1992). Two incommensurable, asymmetrically alternate technologies of social analysis. In G. Watson and R. M. Seiler (eds). *Text in Context: Contributions to Ethnomethodology* (pp. 175–206). London: Sage.

Garson, J. (2002). Connectionism. In E. N. Zalta (ed.), *The Stanford Encyclopedia of Philosophy* (Winter 2002 Edition). <http://plato.stanford.edu/archives/win2002/entries/connectionism/>.

Gergen, K. J. (1994). *Realities and Relationships*. Cambridge, MA: Harvard University Press.

Gergen, K. J. (1999). *An Invitation to Social Construction*. London: Sage.

Gibson, J. J. (1986). *The Ecological Approach to Visual Perception*. New York: Lawrence Erlbaum.

Glenn, P. (1992). Current speaker initiation of two-party shared laughter. *Research on Language and Social Interaction*, 25: 139–62.

Glenn, P. (2003). *Laughter in Interaction*. Cambridge: Cambridge University Press.

Glenn, P. J., LeBaron, C. D. and Mandelbaum, J. (eds) (2003). *Studies in Language and Social Interaction: In Honor of Robert Hopper*. Mahwah: Lawrence Erlbaum.

Goffman, E. (1959). *The Presentation of Self in Everyday Life*. Garden City, NY: Doubleday.

Goffman, E. (1967). *Interaction Ritual: Essays on Face-to-Face Behavior*. New York: Anchor Books.

Goffman, E. (1981). Response cries. In E. Goffman (ed.), *Forms of Talk* (pp. 78–123). Oxford: Blackwell.

Goffman, E. (1983). The interaction order. *American Sociological Review*, 48, 1–17.

Gold, P. E. (1992). A proposed neurobiological basis for regulating memory storage for significant events. In E. Winograd and U. Neiser (eds), *Affect and Accuracy in Recall: Studies of 'Flashbulb Memories'* (pp. 141–61). Cambridge: Cambridge University Press.

Goodwin, C. (1987). Forgetfulness as an interactive resource. *Social Psychology Quarterly*, 50, 115–30.

Goodwin, C. (1995a). Seeing in depth. *Social Studies of Science*, 25, 237–74.

Goodwin, C. (1995b). Co-constructing meaning in conversations with an aphasic man. *Research on Language and Social Interaction*, 28 (3, Special Issue, *Co-construction*, S. Jacoby and E. Ochs, eds), 233–60.

Goodwin, C. (1997). The blackness of black: color categories as situated practice. In Resnick, L. B., Säljö, R., Pontecorvo, C. and Burge, B. (eds), *Discourse, Tools, and Reasoning* (pp. 111–40). Berlin: Springer.

Goodwin, C. (2000a). Action and embodiment within situated human interaction. *Journal of Pragmatics*, 32, 1489–522.

Goodwin, C. (2000b). Practices of color classification. *Mind, Culture and Activity*, 7, 19–36.

Goodwin, C. (2000c). Practices of seeing: visual analysis: an ethnomethodological approach. In T. van Leeuwen and C. Jewett (eds), *Handbook of Visual Analysis* (pp. 157–82). London: Sage.

Goodwin, C. and Goodwin, M. H. (1996). Seeing as situated activity: formulating planes. In Y. Engeström and D. Middleton (eds), *Cognition and Communication at Work* (pp. 61–95). Cambridge: Cambridge University Press.

Goodwin, C. and Goodwin, M. H. (1997) Contested vision: the discursive constitution of Rodney King. In B.-L., Gunnarsson, P. Linell and B. Nordberg (eds), *The Construction of Professional Discourse* (pp. 292–316). London: Longman.

Goodwin, C. and Ueno, N. (Guest eds), (2000). *Vision and Inscription in Practice*. Special Double Issue of *Mind, Culture and Activity* 7, 1–163.

Gottman, J. M. and Levenson, R. W. (1985). A valid procedure for obtaining self-report of affect in marital interaction. *Journal of Consulting and Clinical Psychology*, 53, 151–60.

Graesser, A. C., Gernsbacher, M. A. and Goldman, S. R. (1997). Cognition. In T. A. van Dijk (ed.), *Discourse Studies: A Multidisciplinary Introduction, Volume I: Discourse as Structure and Process* (pp. 292–319). London: Sage.

Graham, M. H. (1978). The confrontation clause, the hearsay rule, and the forgetful witness. *Texas Law Review*, 56, 152–205.

Green, D. W. (1975). The effects of task on the representation of sentences. *Journal of Verbal Learning and Verbal Behavior*, 14, 275–83.

Greene, J. and Burleson, B. (eds) (2003). *The Handbook of Communication and Social Interaction Skills*. Mahwah: Erlbaum.

Greene, J. O. (1984). A cognitive approach to human communication: an action assembly theory. *Communication Monographs*, 51, 289–306.

Greene, J. O. (1995). Production of messages in pursuit of multiple social goals: action assembly theory contributions to the study of cognitive encoding processes. In B. R. Burleson (ed.), *Communication Yearbook* 18 (pp. 26–53). Thousand Oaks, CA: Sage.

Grice, H. P. (1957). Meaning. *Philosophical Review*, 66, 377–88.

Grice, H. P. (1975). Logic and conversation. In P. Cole and J. L. Morgan (eds), *Syntax and Semantics 3: Speech Acts* (pp. 41–58). New York: Academic Press.

Grimshaw, A. D. (1980). Mishearings, misunderstandings, and other non-successes in talk – a plea for redress of speaker-oriented bias. *Sociological Inquiry*, 50, 31–74.

Haakana, M. (1999). *Laughing Matters: A Conversation Analytic Study of Laughter in Doctor-Patient Interaction*. Doctoral thesis, Department of Finnish Language, University of Helsinki.

Haakana, M. (2001). Laughter as a patient's resource: dealing with delicate aspects of medical interaction, *Text*, 21, 187–219.

Halkowski, T. (forthcoming). Realizing the illness: patients' narratives of symptom discovery. In J. Heritage and D. Maynard (eds), *Practicing Medicine: Structure and Process in Primary Care Consultations*. Cambridge: Cambridge University Press.

Harré, R. (2002). *Cognitive Science: A Philosophical Introduction*. London: Sage.

Harris, R. (1981). *The Language Myth*. London: Duckworth.

Harris, R. (1988). *Language, Saussure and Wittgenstein*. London: Routledge.

Heath, C. (1989). Pain talk: the expression of suffering in the medical consultation. *Social Psychology Quarterly*, 52, 113–25.

Hepburn, A. (in press). Crying: notes on description, transcription and interaction. *Research on Language and Social Interaction*.

Heritage, J. (1983). Accounts in action. In G. N. Gilbert and P. Abell (eds), *Accounts and action* (pp. 117–31). Farnborough: Gower.

Heritage, J. (1984a). *Garfinkel and Ethnomethodology*. Cambridge: Polity.

Heritage, J. (1984b). A change-of-state token and aspects of its sequential placement. In J. M. Atkinson and J. Heritage (eds), *Structures of Social Action* (pp. 299–345). Cambridge: Cambridge University Press.

Heritage, J. (1986). Exposed working on understanding in conversation and news interviews: unpublished.

Heritage, J. (1988). Explanations as accounts: a conversation analytic perspective. In C. Antaki (ed.), *Understanding Everyday Explanation: A Casebook of Methods* (pp. 127–44). Beverly Hills, CA: Sage.

Heritage, J. (1990/91). Intention, meaning and strategy: observations on constraints in interaction analysis, *Research on Language and Social Interaction*, 24, 311–32.

Heritage, J. (1998). Oh-prefaced responses to inquiry. *Language in Society* 27(3): 291–334.

Heritage, J. (2002). Oh-prefaced responses to assessments: a method of modifying agreement/disagreement. In C. Ford, B. Fox and S. Thompson (eds), *The Language of Turn and Sequence* (pp. 196–224). Oxford: Oxford University Press.

Heritage, J. and Raymond, G. (forthcoming). The terms of agreement: indexing epistemic authority and subordination in assessment sequences. *Social Psychology Quarterly*.

Heritage, J. and Robinson, J. (forthcoming). Accounting for the visit: patients' reasons for seeking medical care. In J. Heritage and D. Maynard (eds), *Practicing Medicine: Structure and Process in Primary Care Consultations*. Cambridge: Cambridge University Press.

Heritage, J. and Stivers, T. (1999). Online commentary in acute medical visits: a method of shaping patient expectations. *Social Science and Medicine* 49, 1501–17.

Heritage, J. and Watson, D. R. (1979). Formulations as conversational objects. In G. Psathas (ed.), *Everyday Language: Studies in Ethnomethodology* (pp. 123–62). New York: Irvington.

Heritage, J. and Greatbatch, D. (1986). Generating applause: a study of rhetoric and response at party political conferences. *American Journal of Sociology*, 92, 110–57.

Hester, S. and Eglin, P. (1997). *Culture in Action: Studies in Membership Categorization Analysis*. Lanham: University Press of America.

Hirst, W. and Gluck, D. (1999). Revisiting Dean's Memory. In E. Winograd, R. Fivush and W. Hirst (eds), *Ecological Approaches to Cognition: Essays in Honour of Ulric Neisser* (pp. 253–81). Mahwah: Lawrence Erlbaum.

Hirst, W. and Manier, D. (1996). Social influences on remembering. In D. Rubin (ed.), *Remembering Our Past* (pp. 271–90). New York: Cambridge University Press.

Hoffman, E. and J. McCoy (1981). *Concrete Mama: Prison Profiles From Walla Walla*. Columbia: University of Missouri Press.

Hopper, R. (1988). Speech, for instance. *Journal of Language and Social Interaction*, 7, 47–63.

Hopper, R. (1989). Conversation analysis and social psychology as descriptions of interpersonal communication. In D. Roger and P. Bull (eds), *Conversation* (pp. 48–66). Avon: Multilingual Matters.

Hopper, R. (ed.). (1990/91). Ethnography and conversation analysis after Talking Culture. Special section in *Research on Language and Social Interaction*, 25.

Hopper, R. (1992). *Telephone conversation*. Bloomington: Indiana University Press.

Horwitz, H. (1988). 'I can't remember': skepticism, synthetic histories, critical action. *The South Atlantic Quarterly*, 87, 787–820.

Houtkoop-Steenstra, H. (2000). *Interaction and the Standardized Survey Interview: The Living Questionnaire*. Cambridge: Cambridge University Press.

Houtkoop-Steenstra, H. (1994). Meeting both ends: between standardization and recipient design in telephone survey interviews. In P. Ten Have and G. Psathas (eds), *Situated Order* (pp. 1–16). Lanham: University Press of America.

Hubel, D. H. and Wiesel, T. N. (1977). Ferrier lecture: functional architecture of macaque monkey visual cortex. *Proceedings of the Royal Society of London B*, 198, 1–59.

Hufford, D. (1982). *The Terror That Comes in the Night: An Experience-Centred Study of Supernatural Assault Traditions*. Philadelphia: University of Pennsylvania Press.

Hunter, J. F. M. (1971). 'Forms of life' in Wittgenstein's philosophical investigations. In E. D. Klemke (ed.), *Essays on Wittgenstein*. Urbana: University of Illinois Press.

Hutchby, I. and Wooffitt, R. (1998). *Conversation Analysis: Principles, Practices and Applications*. Cambridge: Polity.

Hutchins, E. (1995). *Cognition in the Wild*. Cambridge, MA: MIT Press.

Hutchins, E. and Klausen, T. (1996). Distributed cognition in an airline cockpit. In Y. Engeström and D. Middleton (eds), *Cognition and Communication at Work* (pp. 15–34). Cambridge: Cambridge University Press.

Hyman. I. E. (1999). Creating false autobiographical memories: why people believe their memory errors. In E. Winograd, R. Fivush and W. Hirst (eds), *Ecological Approaches to Cognition: Essays in Honour of Ulric Neisser* (pp. 229–52). Mahwah: Lawrence Erlbaum.

Jacobs, S. (1988). Evidence and inference in conversation analysis. In J. A. Anderson (ed.). *Communication Yearbook 11* (pp. 433–43). Beverly Hills, CA: Sage.

Jefferson, G. (1979). A technique for inviting laughter and its subsequent acceptance /declination. In G. Psathas (ed.), *Everyday Language: Studies in Ethnomethodology* (pp. 79–96). New York: Irvington Publishers.

Jefferson, G. (1984). 'At first I thought': a normalizing device for extraordinary events. (presented at the Katholieke Hogeschool Tilburg). Unpublished manuscript.

Jefferson, G. (1986). On the interactional unpackaging of a 'gloss'. *Language in Society*, 14, 435–66.

Jefferson, G. (1985). An exercise in the transcription and analysis of laughter. In T. van Dijk (ed.), *Handbook of Discourse Analysis, Vol. III*. London: Academic Press.

Jefferson, G. (1988). Remarks on 'non-correction' in conversation. (presented at the Department of Finnish Language, University of Helsinki). Unpublished manuscript.

Jefferson, G. (1989). Preliminary notes on a possible metric which provides for a 'standard maximum' silence of approximately one second in conversation.

In D. Roger and P. Bull (eds), *Conversation: An Interdisciplinary Perspective* (pp. 166–96). Clevedon: Multilingual Matters.

Jefferson, G. (1990). List construction as a task and resource. In G. Psathas (ed.), *Interaction Competence* (pp. 63–93). Lanham: University Press of American.

Jefferson, G. (1996). On the poetics of ordinary talk. *Text and Performance Quarterly*, 16, 1–61.

Jefferson, G. (1997). A note on laughter in 'male-female' interaction. Unpublished manuscript.

Jefferson, G. and Lee, J. (1992). The rejection of advice: managing the problematic convergence of a 'troubles-telling' and a 'service encounter'. In P. Drew and J. Heritage (eds), *Talk at Work* (pp. 521–48). Cambridge: Cambridge University Press.

Keenan, J. M., MacWhinney, B. and Mayhew, D. (1982). Pragmatics in memory: a study of natural conversation. In U. Neisser (ed.), *Memory Observed: Remembering in Natural Contexts* (pp. 315–24). San Francisco: Freeman.

Kenny, A. (1967). Descartes on idea. In W. Doney (ed.), *Descartes: A Collection of Critical Essays*. New York: Doubleday.

Kinnell, A. M. K. and Maynard, D. W. (1996). The delivery and receipt of safer sex advice in pretest counseling sessions for HIV and AIDS. *Journal of Contemporary Ethnography*, 24, 405–37.

Lakoff, G. (1987). *Women, Fire and Dangerous Things: What Categories Reveal about the Mind*. Chicago: University of Chicago Press.

Lamerichs, J. and te Molder, H. F. M. (2003). Computer mediated communication: from a cognitive to a discursive model. *New Media and Society*, 5, 452–73.

Langer, E. J. (1989). *Mindfulness*. Reading, MA: Addison-Wesley.

Lave, J. (1988). *Cognition in Practice: Mind, Mathematics and Culture in Everyday Life*. New York: Cambridge University Press.

Lavin, D. and Maynard, D. W. (2001). Standardization vs. rapport: how interviewers handle the laughter of respondents during telephone surveys. *American Sociological Review*, 66, 453–79.

Lettvin J. Y, Maturana, H. R, W. S. McCulloch and W. H. Pitts (1959). What the frog's eye tells the frog's brain. *Proceedings of the IRE*, 47, 1940–1959.

Levine, J. M., Resnick, L. B. and Higgins, E. T. (1993). Social foundations of cognition. *Annual Review of Psychology*, 44, 585–612.

Levinson, S. C. (1995). Interactional biases in human thinking. In E. Goody (ed.), *Social Intelligence and Human Interaction* (pp. 221–60). Cambridge: Cambridge University Press.

Locke, A., and Edwards, D. (2003). Bill and Monica: memory, emotion and normativity in Clinton's Grand Jury testimony. *British Journal of Social Psychology*, 42, 239–56.

Loftus, E. (1979). *Eyewitness Testimony*. Cambridge, MA: Harvard University Press.

Lutfey, K. and Maynard, D. W. (1998). Bad news in oncology: how physician and patient talk about death and dying without using those words. *Social Psychology Quarterly*, 61, 321–41.

Lynch, M. (1985). *Art and Artifact in Laboratory Science*. London: Routledge and Kegan Paul.

Lynch, M. and Bogen, D. (1996). *The Spectacle of History: Speech, Text, and Memory at the Iran-Contra Hearings*. Durham: Duke University Press.

Mandelbaum, J. and Pomerantz, A. (1990). What drives social action? In K. Tracy (ed.), *Understanding Face-to-Face Interaction: Issues Linking Goals and Discourse* (pp. 151–66). Hillsdale: Lawrence Erlbaum.

Mandelbaum, J. and Pomerantz, A. (1991). What drives social action? In K. Tracy and N. Coupland (eds), *Multiple Goals in Discourse* (pp. 151–66). Clevedon: Multilingual Matters.

Marr, D. (1982). *Vision: A Computational Investigation of the Human Representation and Processing of Visual Information*. San Francisco: Freeman.

Maynard, D. W. (2003). *Bad News, Good News: Conversational Order in Everyday Talk and Clinical Settings*. Chicago: University of Chicago Press.

Maynard, D. W. and Clayman, S. E. (1991). The Diversity of Ethnomethodology, *Annual Review of Sociology*, 17, 385–418.

Maynard, D. W., Houtkoop-Steenstra, H., Schaeffer, N. C. and Zouwen, J. van der (2002). *Standardization and Tacit Knowledge: Interaction and Practice in the Survey Interview*. New York: Wiley.

Maynard, D. W. and Marlaire, C. L. (1992). Good reasons for bad testing performance: the interactional substrate of educational exams. *Qualitative Sociology*, 15, 177–202.

Maynard, D. W. and Schaeffer, N. C. (1997). Keeping the gate: declinations of the request to participate in a telephone survey interview. *Sociological Methods and Research*, 26, 34–79.

Maynard, D. W. and Schaeffer, N. C. (2000). Toward a sociology of social scientific knowledge: survey research and ethnomethodology's asymmetric alternates. *Social Studies of Science*, 30, 323–70.

Maynard, D. W. and Schaeffer, N. C. (2002a). Closing the gate: routes to call termination when recipients decline a telephone survey interview. In D. W. Maynard, H. Houtkoop-Steenstra, J. van der Zouwen and N. C. Schaeffer (eds), *Standardization and Tacit Knowledge: Interaction and Practice in the Survey Interview*. New York: Wiley.

Maynard, D. W. and Schaeffer, N. C. (2002b). Standardization and its discontents: standardization, interaction, and the survey interview. In D. W. Maynard, H. Houtkoop-Steenstra, J. van der Zouwen and N. C. Schaeffer (eds), *Standardization and Tacit Knowledge: Interaction and Practice in the Survey Interview*. New York: Wiley.

Malcolm, N. (1991). The relation of language to instinctive behavior. In J. Hyman (ed.), *Investigating Psychology: Sciences of the Mind After Wittgenstein*. New York: Routledge.

Marlaire, C. L. and Maynard, D. W. (1990). Standardized testing as an interactional phenomenon. *Sociology of Education*, 63, 83–101.

McCloskey, M., Wible, C. G. and Cohen, N. J. (1988). Is there a special flashbulb memory mechanism? *Journal of Experimental Psychology: General*, 117, 171–81.

McHoul, A. W. (1987). Why there are no guarantees for interrogators. *Journal of Pragmatics*, 11, 455–71.

Mehan, H. (1979). *Learning Lessons: Social Organization in the Classroom*. Cambridge, MA: Harvard University Press.

Melden, A. I. (1961). *Free Action*. London: Routledge and Kegan Paul.

Miller, G. A. (1956). The magical number seven, plus or minus two: some limits on our capacity for processing information, *Psychological Review*, 63, 81–97.

Miller, G. A., Galanter, E. and Pribram, K. H. (1960). *Plans and the Structure of Behavior*. New York: Holt, Rinehart and Winston.

Mishler, E. G. (1986). *Research Interviewing: Context and Narrative*, Cambridge, MA: Harvard University Press.

Moerman, M. (1988). *Talking Culture: Ethnography and Conversation Analysis*. Cambridge University Press.

Molotch, H. and Boden, D. (1985). Talking social structure: discourse, domination and the Watergate hearings. *American Sociological Review*, 50: 273–88.

Neisser, U. (1967). *Cognitive Psychology*. New York: Appleton-Century-Crofts.

Neisser, U. (1976). *Cognition and Reality*. San Francisco: Freeman.

Neisser, U. (1981). John Dean's memory: a case study. *Cognition*, 9: 1–22.

Neisser, U. (1982a). Memory: what are the important questions? In U. Neisser (ed.), *Memory Observed: Remembering in Natural Contexts* (pp. 3–19). San Francisco: Freeman.

Neisser, U. (1982b). Snapshots or benchmarks? In U. Neisser (ed.), *Memory Observed: Remembering in Natural Contexts* (pp. 43–8). San Francisco: Freeman.

Neisser, U. (1988). 'Five kinds of self knowledge', *Philosophical Psychology*, 1, 35–59.

Neisser, U., Bergman, E., Schreiber, C. A., Palmer, S. E. and Weldon, M. S. (1996). Remembering the earthquake. *Memory*, 4, 337–57.

Neisser, U and Fivush, R. (eds) (1994). *The Remembering Self*. Cambridge: Cambridge University Press.

Neisser, U. and Harsch, N. (1992). Phantom flashbulbs: false recollections of hearing the news about the challenger. In E. Winograd and U. Neisser (eds), *Affect and Accuracy in Recall: Studies of 'Flashbulb Memories'* (pp. 9–31). Cambridge: Cambridge University Press.

Neisser, U. and Winograd, E. (eds) (1988). *Remembering Reconsidered: Ecological and Traditional Approaches to the Study of Memory*. Cambridge and New York: Cambridge University Press.

Nelson, K. (ed.) (1986). *Event Knowledge: Structure and Function in Development*. Hillsdale: Erlbaum.

Nelson, K. and Gruendel, J. (1981). Generalised event representations: basic building blocks of cognitive development. In M. Lamb and A. Brown (eds), *Advances in Development Psychology*, vol. I (pp. 16–42). Hillsdale: Erlbaum.

North, O. (1987). Testimony before the select committee of the House and Senate, transcript published in *Taking the Stand*. New York: Times Books.

Ochs, E., Schegloff, E. A. and Thompson, S. A. (ed.). (1996). *Interaction and Grammar*. Cambridge University Press.

O'Keefe, B. J. and Lambert, B. L. (1995). Managing the flow of ideas: a local management approach to message design. In B. R. Burleson (ed.). *Communication Yearbook 18* (pp. 54–82). Thousand Oaks: Sage.

Oksenberg, L., Cannell, C. F. and Kalton, G. (1991). New strategies for pretesting survey questions, *Journal of Official Statistics*, 7, 349–65.

Oxford English Dictionary: Second Edition on Compact Disc. Oxford: Oxford University Press, 2002.

Parker, I. and Burman, E. (1993). Against discursive imperialism, empiricism, and constructionism: thirty-two problems with discourse analysis. In E. Burman and I. Parker (eds), *Discourse Analytic Research: Repertoires and Readings of Texts in Action* (pp. 155–72). London: Routledge.

Philipsen, G. (1977). Linearity of research design in ethnographic studies of speaking. *Communication Quarterly*, 25, 42–50.

Pike, K. L. (1954). *Language in Relation to a Unified Theory of Human Behavior.* The Hague: Mouton.

Pillemer, D. B. (1984). Flashbulb memories of the assassination attempt on President Reagan. *Cognition*, 16, 63–80.

Pillemer, D. B. (1992). Remembering personal circumstances: a functional analysis. In E. Winograd and U. Neiser (eds), *Affect and Accuracy in Recall: Studies of 'Flashbulb Memories'* (pp. 236–64). Cambridge: Cambridge University Press.

Pillemer, D. B, Koff, E., Rhinehart, E. D. and Rierdan, J. (1987). Flashbulb memories of menarche and adult menstrual distress. *Journal of Adolescence* 10, 187–99.

Pinch, T. J. and Clark, C. (1986) The hard sell: 'patter merchanting' and the strategic (re)production and local management of economic reasoning in the sales routines of market pitchers. *Sociology*, 20, 169–91.

Pollner, M. (1987). *Mundane Reason: Reality in Everyday and Sociological Discourse.* Cambridge: Cambridge University Press.

Pomerantz, A. (1978). Compliment responses: notes on the co-operation of multiple constraints. In J. N. Schenkein (ed.). *Studies in the Organization of Conversational Interaction* (pp. 79–112). New York: Acdemic Press.

Pomerantz, A. (1980). Telling my side: 'Limited access' as a fishing device. *Sociological Inquiry*, 50, 186–98.

Pomerantz, A. (1984a). Agreeing and disagreeing with assessments: some features of preferred/dispreferred turn shapes. In J. M. Atkinson and J. Heritage (eds), *Structures of Social Action: Studies in Conversation Analysis* (pp. 57–101). Cambridge: Cambridge University Press.

Pomerantz, A. (1984b). Giving a source or basis: the practice in conversation of telling 'What I know'. *Journal of Pragmatics*, 8, 607–25.

Pomerantz, A. (1986). Extreme case formulations: a way of legitimizing claims. *Human Studies*, 9, 219–29.

Pomerantz, A. (1990). Conversation analytic claims. *Communication Monographs*, 57, 231–5.

Pomerantz, A. (1990/91). Mental concepts in the analysis of social action, *Research on Language and Social Interaction*, 24, 299–310.

Pomerantz, A. (1995). How important is context in teaching interviewing. *Journal of General Internal Medicine*, 10, 411.

Pomerantz, A., Fehr, B. J. and Ende, J. (1997). When supervising physicians see patients: strategies used in difficult situations. *Human Communication Research*, 23, 589–615.

Potter, J. (1996). *Representing Reality: Discourse, Rhetoric, and Social Construction.* London: Sage.

Potter, J. (1998a). Discursive social psychology: from attitudes to evaluations, *European Review of Social Psychology*, 9, 233–66.

Potter, J. (1998b). Cognition as context (whose cognition?), *Research on Language and Social Interaction*, 31, (1, Special Issue, *Analyzing Context*, K. Tracy, ed.), 29–44.

Potter, J. and Edwards, D. (2001). Discursive social psychology. In W. P. Robinson and H. Giles. (eds), *The New Handbook of Language and Social Psychology* (pp. 103–18). London: John Wiley and Sons Ltd.

Potter, J. and Edwards, D. (2003). Rethinking cognition: on Coulter, discourse and mind. *Human Studies*, 26, 165–81.

Potter, J. and Hepburn, A. (2003). I'm a bit concerned – early actions and psychological constructions in a child protection helpline. *Research on Language and Social Interaction*, 36, 197–240.

Potter, J. and Wetherell, M. (1987). *Discourse and Social Psychology: Beyond Attitudes and Behaviour*. London: Sage.

Psathas, G. and Anderson, T. (1990). The 'practices' of transcription in conversation analysis. *Semiotica*, 78, 75–99.

Puchta, C. and Potter, J. (2002). Manufacturing individual opinions: market research focus groups and the discursive psychology of attitudes. *British Journal of Social Psychology*, 41, 345–63.

Presser, S., Rothgeb, J. M., Coupee, M. P., Lessler, J. T., Martin, J. and Singer, E. (eds) (2004). *Methods for Testing and Evaluating Survey Questionnaires*. Hoboken, NJ: Wiley.

Raymond, G. (2003). Grammar and social organization: yes/no interrogatives and the structure of responding. *American Sociological Review*, 68, 939–67.

Raymond, G. and Heritage J. (2004). The epistemics of social relations: owning grandchildren. Unpublished Ms, Dep. of Sociology, University of California, Santa Barbara.

Resnick, L. B., Levine, J. M. and Teasley, S. D. (1991). *Perspectives on Socially Shared Cognition*, Washington, DC: American Psychological Association.

Rogoff, B. and Lave, J. (1984). *Everyday Cognition: its Development in Social Context*. Cambridge, MA: Harvard University Press.

Rorty, R. (1979). *Philosophy and the Mirror of Nature*. Princeton NJ: Princeton University Press.

Rosaldo, M. (1982). The things we do with words: Ilongot speech acts and speech act theory in philosophy. *Language in Society*, 11, 203–37.

Rumelhart, D. E. Hinton, G. E. and McClelland J. L. (1986). A general framework for parallel distributed processing. In D. E. Rumelhart, J. L. McClelland and the PDP Research Group (eds), *Parallel Distributed Processing: Explorations in the Microstructure of Cognition. Vol. I: Foundations*. Cambridge, MA: MIT Press.

Ryle, G. (1963). *The Concept of Mind*. Harmondsworth; Penguin.

Sacks, H. (1984). On doing 'being ordinary'. In J. M. Atkinson and J. Heritage (eds), *Structures of Social Action: Studies in Conversation Analysis* (pp. 413–29). Cambridge: Cambridge University Press.

Sacks, H. (1987). On the preferences for agreement and contiguity in sequences in conversation. In G. Button and J. R. E. Lee (eds), *Talk and Social Organization* (pp. 54–69). Clevedon: Multilingual Matters Ltd.

Sacks, H. (1992a). *Lectures on Conversation* (vol. I, edited by G. Jefferson). Oxford: Blackwell.

Sacks, H. (1992b). *Lectures on Conversation* (vol. II, edited by G. Jefferson). Oxford: Blackwell.

Sacks, H., Schegloff, E. A. and Jefferson, G. (1974). A simplest systematics for the organization of turn-taking for conversation. *Language*, 50, 696–735.

Sanders, R. E. (1987). *Cognitive Foundations of Calculated Speech: Controlling Understandings in Conversation and Persuasion*. Albany: SUNY Press.

Sanders, R. E. (1989). Message effects via induced changes in the social meaning of a response. In J. J. Bradac (ed.), *Message Effects in Communication Science* (pp. 165–94). Newbury Park: Sage.

Sanders, R. E. (1997). The production of symbolic objects as components of larger wholes. In J. O. Greene (ed.), *Message Production: Advances in Communication Theory* (pp. 245–77). Mahwah: Lawrence Erlbaum.

Sanders, R. E. and Freeman, K. E. (1997). Children's neo-rhetorical participation in peer interactions. In I. Hutchby and J. Moran-Ellis (eds), *Children and Social Competence: Arenas of Action* (pp. 87–114). London: Falmer.

Saussure, F. de (1986/1915). *Course in General Linguistics* (translated by R. Harris). LaSalle: Open Coure Publishers.

Savage-Rumbaugh, S. and Lewin R. (1994). *Kanzi: An Ape at the Brink of Human Mind*. New York: Wiley.

Savage-Rumbaugh, S., Shanker, S. G. and Taylor, T. J. (1998). *Apes, Language and the Human Mind*. New York: Oxford University Press.

Schaeffer, N. C. (1991). Conversation with a Purpose – Or Conversation? Interaction in the Standardized Interview. In P. P. Biemer, R. M. Groves, L. E. Lyberg, N. A. Mathiowetz and S. Sudman (eds), *Measurement Errors in Surveys* (pp. 367–92). New York: Wiley.

Schaeffer, N. C. and Maynard, D. W. (2002a). Occasions for intervention: interactional resources for comprehension in standardized survey interviews. In D. W. Maynard, H. Houtkoop-Steenstra, J. van der Zouwen and N. C. Schaeffer (eds), *Standardization and Tacit Knowledge: Interaction and Practice in the Survey Interview* (pp. 261–80). New York: Wiley.

Schaeffer, N. C. and Maynard, D. W. (2002b). Standardization and interaction in the survey interview. In J. Holstein and J. Gubrium (eds), *Handbook of Interviewing*, London: Sage.

Schaeffer, N. C., Maynard, D. W. and Cradock, R. (1993). *Negotiating Certainty: Uncertainty Proposals and Their Disposal in Standardized Survey Interviews*. University of Wisconsin, Madison, Center for Demography and Ecology Working Paper, 93-25.

Schank, R. C. and Abelson, R. (1977). *Scripts, Plans, Goals and Understanding*. Hillsdale: Erlbaum.

Schegloff, E. A. (1972). Notes on a conversational practice: formulating place. In D. Sudnow (ed.), *Studies in Social Interaction* (pp. 75–119). Glencoe: Free Press.

Schegloff, E. A. (1980). Preliminaries to preliminaries: "Can I ask you a question?", *Sociological Inquiry*, 50, 104–52.

Schegloff, E. A. (1987). Some sources of misunderstanding in talk-in-interaction. *Linguistics*, 25: 201–18.

Schegloff, E. A. (1990). Comment on 'Interactional troubles in face-to-face survey interviews'. *Journal of the American Statistical Association*, 85, 248–50.

Schegloff, E. A. (1991a). Conversation analysis and socially shared cognition. In L. Resnick, J. Levine and S. Teasley (eds), *Perspectives on Socially Shared Cognition* (pp. 150–71). Washington DC: American Psychological Association.

Schegloff, E. A. (1991b). *With Half a Mind: Interaction with Commissurotomies.* Paper presented at the First Rector's Colloquium, Tel Aviv University.

Schegloff, E. A. (1992a). To Searle on conversation: a note in return. In J. R. Searle et al. (eds), *(On) Searle on Conversation* (pp. 113–28). Amsterdam and Philadelphia: John Benjamins.

Schegloff, E. A. (1992b). 'Repair after next turn: The last structurally provided defense of intersubjectivity in conversation', *American Journal of Sociology*, 98:1295–345.

Schegloff, E. A. (1992c). Introduction. In G. Jefferson (ed.), *Harvey Sacks, Lectures on Conversation, vol. I.* Oxford: Blackwell.

Schegloff, E. A. (1996). Confirming allusions: toward an empirical account of action. *American Journal of Sociology*, 104, 161–216.

Schegloff, E. A. (1999). Discourse, pragmatics, conversation analysis. *Discourse Studies*, 1, 405–36.

Schegloff, E. A. (forthcoming). *A Primer of Conversation Analysis: Sequence Organization.* Cambridge: Cambridge University Press.

Schegloff, E. A. and Sacks, H. (1973). Opening up closings. *Semiotica*, 8, 289–327.

Schegloff, E. A., Jefferson, G. and Sacks, H. (1977). The preference for self-correction in the organization of repair in conversation. *Language*, 53, 361–82.

Schutz, A. (1967). *The Phenomenology of the Social World.* Evanston: Northwestern University Press.

Schwartz, R. M. and Garamoni, G. L. (1986). Cognitive assessment: a multibehavior-multimethod-multiperspective approach. *Journal of Psychopathology and Behavioral Assessment*, 8, 185–97.

Schwarz, N. (1994). Judgment in social context: biases, shortcomings, and the logic of conversation. *Advances in Experimental Social Psychology*, 26, 123–62.

Schwarz, N. and Sudman, S. (1996). *Answering Questions: Methodology for Determining Cognitive and Communicative Processes in Survey Research.* San Francisco: Jossey-Bass.

Searle, J. R. (1969). *Speech Acts: An Essay in the Philosophy of Language.* London: Cambridge University Press.

Searle, J. R. (1976). A classification of illocutionary acts. *Language in Society*, 5, 1–23.

Searle, J. R. (1980). Minds, brains, and programs. *Behavioral and Brain Sciences*, 1, 417–24.

Searle, J. R. (1983). *Intentionality: An Essay in the Philosophy of Mind.* Cambridge: Cambridge University Press.

Searle, J. R. (1998). *Mind, Language and Society: Philosophy in the Real World.* New York: Basic Books.

Shannon, C. (1948). A mathematical theory of communication. *The Bell System Technical Journal,* 379–423.

Shotter, J. (1993). *Conversational Realities: Constructing Life Through Language.* London: Sage.

Sillars, A., Roberts, L. J., Leonard, K. E. and Dun, T. (2000). Cognition during marital conflict: the relationship of thought and talk. *Journal of Social and Personal Relationships,* 17, 479–502.

Skinner, B. F. (1957). *Verbal Behaviour.* Englewood Cliffs: Prentice Hall.

Still, A. and Costall, A. (1991). *Against Cognitivism: Alternative Foundations for Cognitive Psychology.* Hemel Hempstead: Harvester.

Stivers, T. (2002). 'Symptoms only' and 'candidate diagnoses': presenting the problem in pediatric encounters. *Health Communication,* 14, 299–338.

Stivers, T., R. Mangione-Smith, M. Elliott, McDonald, L. and Heritage, J. (2003). 'Why do physicians think parents expect antibiotics? What parents report vs. what physicians receive. *Journal of Family Practice,* 29, 140–8.

Smith, D. E. (1978). '"K is mentally ill": the anatomy of a factual account', *Sociology,* 12, 23–53.

Stokoe, E. H. and Smithson, J. (2001). Making gender relevant: conversation analysis and gender categories in interaction. *Discourse and Society,* 12, 217–44.

Suchman, L. (1987). *Plans and Situated Actions: The Problem of Human-machine Interaction.* Cambridge: Cambridge University Press.

Suchman, L. (1988). Representing practice in cognitive science. *Human Studies,* 11, 305–25. Reprinted in M. Lynch and S. Woolgar (eds) (1990). *Representation in Scientific Practice* (pp. 301–21). Cambridge, MA: MIT Press.

Suchman, L. (2000). Making a case: "Knowledge" and "Routine" work in document production. In P. Luff, J. Hindmarsh and C. Heath (eds), *Workplace Studies: Recovering Work Practice and Informing Systems Design* (pp. 29–45). Cambridge: Cambridge University Press.

Suchman, L. and Jordan, B. (1990). Interactional troubles in face-to-face survey interviews. *Journal of the American Statistical Association,* 85, 232–41.

Sudman, S., Bradburn, N. M. and Schwarz, N. (1996). *Thinking About Answers: The Application of Cognitive Processes to Survey Methodology.* San Francisco: Jossey-Bass Publishers.

Swinney, D. and Prather, P. (1989). On the comprehension of lexical ambiguity by young children: investigations into the development of mental modularity. In D. Gorfein (ed.), *Resolving semantic ambiguity* (pp. 225–38). New York: Springer-Verlag.

ten Have, P. (1999). *Doing Conversation Analysis.* London: Sage.

te Molder, H. F. M. (1999). Discourse of dilemmas: an analysis of communication planners' accounts. *British Journal of Social Psychology,* 38, 245–63.

Tenney, Y. J. (1989). Predicting conversational reports of a personal event. *Cognitive Science,* 13, 213–33.

Terasaki, A. (1976/forthcoming). Pre-announcement sequences in conversation. Social sciences Working Paper No. 99, UC Irvine. Also in G. Lerner (ed.), *Conversation Analysis: Studies From the First Generation*. Washington, DC: University Press of America.

Thagard, P. (2002). Cognitive science. In E. N. Zalta (ed.), *The Stanford Encyclopedia of Philosophy* (Winter 2002 edition). URL = <http://plato.stanford.edu/archives/win2002/entries/cognitive-science/>.

Tourangeau, R., Rips, L. J. and Rasinski, K. (2000). *The Psychology of Survey Response*. Cambridge: Cambridge University Press.

Turing, A. M. (1950). Computing machinery and intelligence, *Mind*, 49, 433–60.

Waldron, V. R. and Cegala, D. J. (1992). Assessing conversational cognition: levels of cognitive theory and associated methodological requirements. *Human Communication Research*, 18(4), 599–622.

Walsh, L. (1994). *Final Report of the Independent Counsel for Iran/Contra Matters – United States Court of Appeals for the District of Columbia Circuit*. Washington, DC: Government Printing Office.

Wetherell, M. and Potter, J. (1992). *Mapping the Language of Racism*. Hemel Hempstead: Harvester.

Whalen, M. and D. Zimmerman (1990). Describing trouble: practical epistemology in citizen calls to the police. *Language in Society*, 19, 465–92.

Whalen, J. and D. Zimmerman (1998). Observations on the display and management of emotions in naturally occurring activities: the case of 'hysteria' in calls to 9-1-1. *Social Psychology Quarterly*, 61, 141–59.

Widdicombe, S. and Wooffitt, R. (1995). *The Language of Youth Subcultures: Social Identity in Action*. Hemel Hempstead: Harvester.

Wieder, D. L. (1988). From resource to topic: some aims of conversation analysis. In J. A. Anderson (ed.). *Communication Yearbook 11* (pp. 444–54). Beverly Hills: Sage.

Wiggins, S. (2002). Talking with your mouth full: gustatory 'mmm's and the embodiment of pleasure. *Research on Language and Social Interaction*, 35, 311–36.

Wiggins, S. and Potter, J. (2003). Attitudes and evaluative practices: Category vs. item and subjective vs. objective constructions in everyday food assessments, *British Journal of Social Psychology*, 42, 513–31.

Williams, M. (1999). *Wittgenstein, Mind and Meaning: Toward a Social Conception of Mind*. New York: Routledge.

Wilson, G. (1994). Take a number, *The New Yorker*, July 18, 49.

Winch, P. (1983). Im Anfang war die tat. In I. Block (ed.), *Perspectives on the Philosophy of Wittgenstein*. Cambridge, MA: MIT Press.

Wittgenstein, L. (1958). *Philosophical Investigations*. (2nd Edition) Edited by G. E. M. Anscombe and R. Rhees. Translated by G. E. M. Anscombe. Oxford: Blackwell.

Wittgenstein, L. (1967). *Zettel*. Edited by G. E. M. Anscombe and G. H. von Wright. Translated by G. E. M. Anscombe. Oxford: Blackwell.

Wittgenstein, L. (1969). *On Certainty*. Edited by G. E. M. Anscombe and G. H. von Wright. Translated by D. Paul and G. E. M. Anscombe. Oxford: Blackwell.

Wittgenstein, L. (1976). Cause and effect: intuitive awareness. *Philosophia, vol. VI, nos. 3–4.*

Wooffitt, R. C. (1991). 'I was just doing X . . . when Y': some inferential properties of a device in accounts of paranormal experiences. *Text, 11,* 267–88.

Wooffitt, R. C. (1992). *Telling Tales of the Unexpected: The Organization of Factual Discourse.* London: Harvester.

Woolgar, S. (1980). Discovery, logic and sequence in a text. In K. D. Knorr, R. Krohn and R. Whitley (eds). *The Social Process of Scientific Investigation* (pp. 239–68). Dordrecht: Reidel.

Wootton, A. J. (1997). *Interaction and the Development of Mind.* New York: Cambridge University Press.

Zimmerman, D. H. (1988). On conversation: the conversation analytic perspective. In J. A. Anderson (ed.). *Communication Yearbook 11* (pp. 406–32). Beverly Hills: Sage.

Zimmerman, D. H. (1992). The interactional organization of calls for emergency assistance. In P. Drew and J. Heritage (eds), *Talk at Work: Interaction in Institutional Settings* (pp. 418–69). Cambridge: Cambridge University Press.

Index